Zionism and the Fin de Siècle

THE S. MARK TAPER FOUNDATION

IMPRINT IN JEWISH STUDIES

BY THIS ENDOWMENT

THE S. MARK TAPER FOUNDATION SUPPORTS

THE APPRECIATION AND UNDERSTANDING

OF THE RICHNESS AND DIVERSITY OF

JEWISH LIFE AND CULTURE

Zionism and the Fin de Siècle

Cosmopolitanism and Nationalism from Nordau to Jabotinsky

Michael Stanislawski

UNIVERSITY OF CALIFORNIA PRESS
Berkeley · Los Angeles · London

*The publisher gratefully acknowledges the gener-
ous contribution to this book provided by the
S. Mark Taper Foundation.*

University of California Press
Berkeley and Los Angeles, California

University of California Press, Ltd.
London, England

© 2001 by the Regents of the University of
California

A version of chapter 5 appeared in German with
the title "Von Jugendstil zum 'Judenstil': Univer-
salismus und Nationalismus in Werk Ephraim
Moses Liliens," in *Zionistische Utopie-israelitische
Realität*, ed. Michael Brenner and Yfaat Weiss
(Munich: Beck, 1999), 68–101.

Library of Congress Cataloging-in-Publication Data

Stanislawski, Michael, 1952–.
  Zionism and the fin de siècle : cosmopolitanism
and nationalism from Nordau to Jabotinsky /
Michael Stanislawski.
      p.   cm.
  Includes bibliographical references (p.) and
index.
  ISBN 0-520-22396-9 (cloth : alk. paper) —
ISBN 0-520-22788-3 (pbk. : alk. paper)
    1. Zionists—Biography.   2. Zionism—History—
20th century.   3. Nordau, Max Simon, 1849–
1923.   4. Jabotinsky, Vladimir, 1880–1940.
5. Lilien, Ephraim Mose, 1874–1925.   6. Politics
and culture.   7. Nationalism.   I. Title.

DS151.A2 S73   2001
320.54'095694—dc21   00-055161
                                                CIP

Manufactured in the United States of America
10 09 08 07 06 05 04 03 02 01

10 9 8 7 6 5 4 3 2 1

The paper used in this publication is both acid-free
and totally chlorine-free (TCF).

To Ethan, Aaron, and Emma

Contents

Illustrations

Figures follow page 100

Acknowledgments

This book has taken far longer than expected, and hence my debt to colleagues, institutions, friends, and family is far more extensive than I can reconstruct here. First, I am grateful to the Jabotinsky Institute in Tel Aviv and the Kenneth Spencer Library at Kansas University, both of which opened up their archival holdings to me with the greatest hospitality and professional courtesy. Viktor E. Kel'ner of St. Petersburg worked long and hard to provide me with microfilms of rare Russian newspapers and archival holdings; this book could not have been written without his help. Crucial in this regard, too, were Benjamin Nathans of the University of Pennsylvania, Shaul Stampfer of the Hebrew University of Jerusalem, Mattityahu Minc of Tel Aviv University, and John Klier of University College, London. Olga Litvak of Princeton University served as an indispensable research assistant on this project while she was my doctoral student at Columbia. The staff of the Slavic division of Columbia University Library contributed crucial technical and fiscal support in dealing with dozens of rolls of microfilms dating from before the Second World War that often had to be reformatted in standard gauge before they could be deciphered. I wish to express my sincere gratitude for the generous support of my research by the John Simon Guggenheim Memorial Foundation, the Lucius N. Littauer Foundation, and the National Endowment for the Humanities.

Over the past several years I have lectured about Jabotinsky, Nordau, and Lilien to a large number of academic audiences throughout the

United States, Canada, Great Britain, Germany, and Israel, and the suggestions and questions that emerged in these deliberations were crucial to the final result. I particularly wish to thank the members of the University Seminar on Israel and Jewish Studies at Columbia, who heard early versions of several chapters of this book and helped me work out its arguments; and the participants in the two NEH Faculty Summer Seminars that I taught at Columbia, one on Zionism and the other on the Russian Empire and the Soviet Union as multinational states. The latter seminar was co-directed by my friend and colleague Mark von Hagen, with whom I have had an ongoing conversation about the issues of nationalism and cosmopolitanism for many years. I should also like to thank Marc Raeff, John Munder Ross, Yosef Yerushalmi, Arthur Goren, and David Weiss-Halivni of Columbia, Michael Brenner of the University of Munich, Elliot Wolfson of New York University, Elisheva Carlebach of Queens College, Aron Rodrigue of Stanford University, Abraham Ascher of the Graduate Center of the City University of New York, David Biale of the University of California at Davis, Derek Penslar of the University of Toronto, Ada Rappoport-Albert of University College, London, and Michael Silber and Ezra Mendelsohn of the Hebrew University of Jerusalem for their insights and support.

Stan Holwitz of the University of California Press has been the most gracious and supportive editor one could hope for, and his staff have been exemplary in their efficiency and professionalism.

My wife, Marjorie Kaplan, would not be comfortable were I publicly to chronicle the myriad ways in which she has contributed to this book. In dedicating this volume to Ethan, Aaron, and Emma, who have provided us with so much love and joy, I express not only my, but also their mother's, undying delight in them.

Introduction

This book has had a long and somewhat convoluted history. It began life as an intellectual biography of the young Vladimir Jabotinsky, a study of the road to Jewish nationalism taken by this most controversial Zionist leader of our century—indeed, possibly the most controversial Jewish figure of our century. What attracted me to Jabotinsky was the paradox that his ideological and intellectual journey was both idiosyncratic and emblematic: the figure who would be identified with the most extreme form of Jewish nationalism, often decried as chauvinism, was at the same time the most cosmopolitan, Europeanized, Russified, Gentile-like leader that either the Zionist movement or East European Jewry as a whole would ever produce. Even after becoming the enfant terrible of the Zionist movement in the 1920s and 1930s, alienating both colleagues and foes by his attacks on Chaim Weizmann, socialism, the British Mandate, and the Arabs as well as by his calls for the immediate evacuation of Polish Jewry and the establishment of an armed Jewish state on both banks of the River Jordan, Vladimir Jabotinsky would, in the privacy of his study or railroad car, continue to pen delicate short stories in Russian that recall those of Thomas Mann or divert himself by translating Verlaine or Rimbaud into any one of his many languages. Even today, sixty years after his death, his astonishing and unsurpassed renditions into Hebrew of "The Raven" and "Annabelle Lee" by Edgar Allan Poe can still be recited, when pressed, by Israelis of a certain age, who nonetheless despise Jabotinsky's political legacy.

As a historian who had spent many years chronicling the rise and then demise of the Russian-Jewish Enlightenment and hence Russian-Jewish liberalism, I fixed on Jabotinsky as the most fascinating figure in the story of the collapse of Enlightenment liberalism and its cultural politics in East European Jewry. And although the literature on Jabotinsky was vast, including thick biographies written by two of his most talented acolytes,[1] it was abundantly clear to me that there was much hard work still to do, since both the scholarly and popular studies of Jabotinsky were compromised by the ideological commitments of their authors, who were variously either firm adherents or virulent opponents of Jabotinsky's Revisionist Zionism. What was particularly lacking was a critical analysis of Jabotinsky's background, his intellectual and ideological development, and his relationship to the triple contexts in which he lived and worked: East European Jewish life and thought, Russian literary and political culture, and West European intellectual and ideological history.

While I could hardly pretend to pure objectivity in regard to Jabotinsky, I believed that I could summon sufficient detachment, as a professional student of the cultural and intellectual history of the Jews, to avoid the trap of hyper-politicization and to provide a crucial unwritten chapter in modern Jewish history: the turn to an ever-more militant Zionism on the part of so Russified and Europeanized a modern Jew. Moreover, the timing for such a venture was perfect. The fall of the Soviet Union and the consequent opening up of Russian archives and libraries previously closed to students of Jewish history and Zionism gave me access to troves of material on and by Jabotinsky. What now became available for the first time were literally hundreds of feuilletons, theater and opera reviews, and newspaper articles written by him in Russian before the Revolution and also a good deal of archival material on Jabotinsky's cultural and political activities before his departure from his motherland. All this material was made available to me, with great generosity, by diligent librarians and archivists in St. Petersburg and Moscow, aided by a large number of couriers, colleagues, and students.

But a funny thing happened on the way to this destination. The more I read Jabotinsky's voluminous early writings and the more I pondered his previously unexamined feuilletons, poetry, plays, translations, and short stories, the less I became interested in writing a standard intellectual biography of the man, even of his early years. This was not because these early and diverse materials were uninteresting, but the contrary: Jabotinsky's early writings were so intriguing that they led me ever more deeply and unexpectedly into the cultural, political, psychological, and literary maelstroms of the fin de siècle, both in Russia and in western Europe, which I had only known fleetingly and at second hand. Keeping one eye on Jabotinsky, my other eye began to wander, searching out the fascinating literature on the artistic, literary, political, and philosophical movements of the late nineteenth and early twentieth centuries, now especially abundant given our collective awareness of the malaise of our own fin de siècle. I became especially interested in other cosmopolitan European and Russian intellectuals who in this same period, and for similar reasons, turned to nationalism; and then in other Zionist leaders who took the same path.

Best known of the latter was, of course, Theodor Herzl, about whom there has been a biographical explosion in the past decades, but whose own road to Zionism, I felt, had not been sufficiently explained in the context of Jewish reactions to the European fin de siècle.[2] Without in the least claiming to have resolved the mystery of Herzl's inner life, I hope my small opening chapter on him sets the stage for the main characters in the drama I am studying and, equally important, clarifies the methodology I shall be using to analyze those figures. My attention turned next to a figure close to Herzl and identified with him, Max Nordau, the cultural critic, physician, novelist, and playwright who was Herzl's first and most famous convert to Zionism. Hardly a household name anywhere today—even in Israel, where his name is best known, it connotes a series of important streets and avenues rather than a real person—Nordau was an extraordinarily famous writer in fin-de-siècle Europe and the United States. His most often cited but rarely read book, *Degeneration,* which was an attack on cultural modernism as symptomatic of psychological and moral degeneracy, engendered a huge controversy. In the past few years there has been a mini-renaissance of interest in Nordau on the part of a small coterie of scholars, primarily students of German cultural history and the German-Jewish intersection, as well as others concerned with the history of biological and racialist theories of the late nineteenth century, the origins of racism and sexism, and the history of the body, gender, and sex. A flurry of articles on various aspects of Nordau's oeuvre has appeared, an international conference on him was held at the Maison des Sciences de L'Homme in Paris, and, most recently, the first full-scale scholarly biography of Nordau has been published.[3] But, again, as I immersed myself more and more in his life and prose, I came to the conclusion that the scholarship on him was challenging and innovative but had failed to resolve the abiding paradox of the relationship between his Zionism and the rest of his thought. While trying to solve this puzzle I discovered quite by chance a treasure trove of unknown letters by Nordau in Lawrence, Kansas, and the mystery began to unravel. Moreover, as I delved more deeply into Nordau's writings, I began to sense a similarity to the Jabotinsky story I had been immersed in for years, even beyond the parallel transition to Zionism that had attracted me to Nordau in the first place: a similarity in the versions of Zionism they created, in its values, rhetoric, and substance, all deeply imbued with and defined by the values, rhetoric, taste, feel, and touch of the European fin de siècle.

Finally, I came across the figure of Ephraim Moses Lilien, the first Zionist artist, a Galician Jew who made his way from his hometown of Drohobycz to the art academies of Lwów, Kraków, and Vienna and thence to the frontlines of art nouveau and Jugendstil in Munich and Berlin. Like Herzl and Nordau before him and Jabotinsky only slightly later, Lilien first entered headlong into the dizzying and intoxicating world of European cosmopolitan culture in the fin de siècle before wending his way to Zionism. In the process, he created a Zionist iconography of lasting import and influence, a fascinating mélange of decadence and Jewish nationalism that at once seethed with the passions and peculiarities of the European fin de siècle and had a jarring and revealing similarity with the ideologies and verbal representations of Zionism of Max Nordau and Vladimir Jabotinsky.

In this way, a new and rather different book was slowly materializing—a study of Zionism and the fin de siècle focused on the interplay between cosmopolitanism and nationalism in the lives and work of Nordau, Lilien, and Jabotinsky. Uniting the emerging chapters was yet another theme—a dissatisfaction with the entire literature on the birth and early years of the Zionist movement, and consequently on the life stories of the early Zionist leaders. Put simply, the works I encountered assumed the naturalness, if not the inevitability, of the emergence of Zionism, whether in the life story of a single person or en masse. Even while acknowledging and chronicling the massive opposition to Zionism both within and outside the Jewish community and the enormous difficulties and struggles of the movement before the establishment of the State of Israel, the existing works assumed that there was something ineluctable about the process, a trajectory leading clearly and irrevocably to the end result, however jagged the journey.

There are, it seems to me, two reasons for this approach, one internal, one external. First, there is the astonishing success story of Zionism itself. While at the beginning of the twentieth century only a small minority of Jews defined themselves as Zionists, by the end of the century the vast majority of Jews, both traditionalist and modernist, accepted the Zionist stance and supported the Zionist movement and its political, cultural, and philanthropic goals. This success was undeniably affected by historical events specific to the Jews, most especially the Holocaust, and by the dramatic struggle for existence on the part of the State of Israel both before and after its founding. Yet it is obvious at the same time that the spread of Zionism has been only one of the manifestations of the worldwide popularity of nationalism in this century, an unexpected phenomenon still not thoroughly understood by historians and social theorists, despite the vast literature on the subject. Every nationalist movement—like all revolutionary movements and possibly all political or religious movements of any persuasion—has had to invent appropriate histories of its origins and growth and appropriate biographies of its leaders and heroes. These "foundation myths" assert the inevitability and antiquity of their self-evident truths and do not admit too much complexity and contradiction in their narratives, especially in regard to the purity of their founders' ideological faith. Whether about George Washington, V. I. Lenin, Theodor Herzl, or Indira Gandhi, such hagiographies aver that their heroes either believed in their particular cause from birth or were irrevocably converted to it by a decisive demonstration of its eternal veracity. In either case, once converted, the hero can never sway from the proper course until his or her (usually premature) dying day.

About such "inventions of tradition" and "invented communities" there is now a formidable literature—indeed, a veritable new historiographical orthodoxy, from which I have learned much but also dissent from in important ways. First, although it is important to understand that nationalist movements—all nationalist movements—are creations of a specific moment in European and world history, share a consistent pattern of development and growth, and reconstruct (or distort) the history of their group as ineffably and inevitably leading to the emergence and success of their nationalist enterprise, it does not follow, as the regnant theory holds, that "nationalisms create nations, not vice versa." To be sure, the meanings of the terms "nation" and "people"— or, in the languages I shall be concerned with here, *Volk, narod, narodnost', 'am, leom*—have changed radically over the course of the past two centuries, precisely as the result of the rise and influence of nationalist movements. But as theorists of "ethno-nationalism" such as Anthony Smith have argued, contra the prevailing notion, this does not mean that terms such as "nation" and "Volk" had no ethnic valence in previous centuries, meanings in some ways similar to and connected with their later nationalist meanings, albeit in complex and nonlinear ways.[4] And beyond the terminological morass there lie sociological and ideational realities that are vastly undervalued by the school of thought whose Bible is Benedict Anderson's *Imagined Communities* and whose warring high priests have been Ernest Gellner and Eric Hobsbawm.[5] Indeed, although the case of the Jews has not yet received the sophisticated theoretical treatment it merits in this regard, suffice it here to say that long before 1789, Jewishness was conceived of by Jews and others as both what we now call an ethnic identity, or a "people," and as a religion—a theoretical dichotomy introduced, or at least popularized, by the Enlightenment's ontological distinction between the realms of the private and the public, the church and the state, the appropriate purviews of Caesar and of God. Hence, pre-eighteenth-century notions of Jewish peoplehood were very different in their essence and implications from later retrojections, whether nationalist or antinationalist. Symptomatically and symbolically, when modern Jewish nationalism was invented in the late nineteenth century, a new term had to be coined in Hebrew to convey the notions of nationalism and nationality—*leumiyut*—from one of the biblical synonyms for "nation" (*leom*) as opposed to the far more common *'am* (the perennial "people" of Israel). In modern Hebrew, there is a clear if largely unconscious distinction between the adjectives *leumi*, meaning "national," and *'amami,* meaning "popular"; Israeli passports and other legal documents distinguish between Jews and non-Jews on the basis of their *leom*, not their *'am*. But equally significantly, both *leom* and *'am* are ancient words, used continuously through the millennia to convey something akin to, if different from, their post-1789 meanings. Modern Jewish nationalism, one might conclude, did not invent the Jewish nation, nor did the pre-nationalist notion of nationhood coincide with its later meaning.

What all of this translates into in regard to the genre of biography, is that the first generation of biographies of the founders and leaders of the Zionist movement were penned by intimates, followers, and admirers of their subjects—whether Herzl, Ahad Ha'am, Jabotinsky, Weizmann, or pre-Zionists such as Leon Pinsker. In all of these gripping and at times superbly narrated accounts, all roads led irrevocably to Zion and to Truth, however difficult the life story. In none of these cases do we get a sense of the tortuous, often self-contradictory, stances of the protagonists—not even in the case of so obviously tortured a soul as Theodor Herzl, who was retroactively recast as Binyamin Zeev, Prophet and Progenitor of the Jewish State. While this type of biography is still alive and kicking—witness Shmuel Katz's recent two-volume hagiography of Jabotinsky—in the past decade or so, the anticipated revisionist approach has prevailed. Professional historians, particularly in our post-ideological age, make their living and sometimes their fame by pointing out the flaws and limitations of nationalist histories and popular hagiographies and delight precisely in the complexities and contradictions of the human condition and the historical record. That these revisionist renderings often overstate their case, and even more often have no effect on the public perception of reality, has yet to stem the tide of the historiographical zeal for correction and complexity. Several frankly negative biographies of Herzl, written by popular as well as academic authors, are imbued with overt anti-Zionism or at least opposition to Herzlian Zionism. More nuanced and more impressive biographies of such figures as Ahad Ha'am, Chaim Weizmann, and Berl Katznelson, all written by talented and erudite scholars with impeccable academic credentials, take a self-consciously critical, if usually still largely admiring, stance toward their subjects.[6] Thanks to these works, we now know far more about the lives and thought of these Zionist thinkers and leaders, including their hesitations, missteps, failures, and personal travails and regrets as well as their accomplishments, successes, and influence.

But perhaps appropriately, given the nature of the enterprise and the anticipated readership, these newer scholarly biographies, like their hagiographic predecessors, view their subjects from the vantage point of internal Jewish history, the history of the Zionist movement, and the Yishuv, the Jewish community of pre-1948 Palestine. In the best of these works, an attempt is made to situate these Zionist figures within the context of their Jewish communities of origin. But their connections to the outside world—to European, Habsburg, or Russian intellectual and cultural developments—are either left largely unresolved or vouchsafed to writers less scrupulous about crossing the boundaries of academic fields and more indulgent with comparisons and generalizations, unfortunately including irresponsible, ill-informed, and hyperbolic generalizations. In this book I deliberately cross and re-cross the boundaries not only between the histories of various Jewish communities, but also between Jewish history and European history. For too long, Jewish historians have spoken of a divide between the history of the Jews and something called "general history," on the usually unconscious assumption that the latter exists (somehow melding Japanese, Tunisian, and American history into one general stew) and can be differentiated from the historical experience of the Jews. Although this proposition has impeccable scriptural credentials, most contemporary professional Jewish historians would reject it if they gave it any sustained thought.

This book also aims to redress the "essentialist fallacy" of much of the historiography on early Zionism: the notion that in order to understand an individual's intellectual and ideological development, one can read backward from the end of the story to its beginning, seeking the roots of a figure's later ideological positions in his or her earlier writings. To do so, I believe, is to engage in a profoundly misleading, antihistoricist tautology, a teleological retrojection that effaces the complexity of human thought and development. As the literary scholar Benjamin Harshav has written in another context:

> To be sure, individuals often embrace ideologies or various beliefs, and some of them hold to them for a long time. Yet, in principle, it would be more appropriate to see the individual as an open semantic field through which various tendencies crisscross: some of them are involuntary and some he himself embraced and helped formulate, some become dominant and others merely hover in the field of consciousness. We are dealing here with sensibilities and attitudes, which are often fuzzy and ambivalent and not as systematic and consistent as ideologies would like to be. Individuals, even highly articulate ones, are often undecided on various matters, inconsistent, compromising between opposite ideas, changing their position with time.[7]

None of the subjects of this book had any inkling at the beginning of his adult life what he would believe at the end of his life; and, unless one believes in a rather vulgar version of either predestination or historical determinism, each could have gone in many different ways. This is what makes each of their ultimate journeys (and our own) so fascinating.

This volume, then, is an experiment in squaring three concentric circles. First, it is an analysis of the turn to Zionism on the part of Theodor Herzl, Max Nordau, Ephraim Moses Lilien, and Vladimir Jabotinsky, without either assuming the naturalness or inevitability of that turn or decrying it as reactionary or narrow-minded. Second, it is an attempt at situating their parallel conversions to Zionism in both their European and their Jewish contexts. And finally, it is an exploration of the similarities and intersections of the versions of Zionism created by Herzl, and especially by Nordau, Lilien, and Jabotinsky, against the backdrop of the European fin de siècle.

The chapters that follow do not pretend to exhaust their subject, nor do they tell the entire story of "Zionism and the fin de siècle"; many central figures and even entire literary and ideological trends will not be treated in these pages. But I hope the reader will come away from this study with a better sense of how Zionism emerged in the late nineteenth and early twentieth centuries, and how these fascinating and intriguing men were crucial figures in this story. For in the end, how Theodor Herzl, Max Nordau, Ephraim Moses Lilien, and Vladimir Jabotinsky made the tortuous shift from cosmopolitanism to nationalism is critical not only to an understanding of their vitally important lives, but also to the overarching revolution of modern Jewish life that ensued. And not only Jewish life—as in so many other realms, here too the case of the Jews can serve as an extraordinarily sensitive barometer to one of the central, shared, and as yet mysterious ideological shifts of our times, the abandonment of universalism for parochialism.

CHAPTER ONE

Cosmopolitanism, Zionism, and Assimilation

The Case of Theodor Herzl

In 1890, roughly half a decade before he became a Zionist, Theodor Herzl wrote a short story entitled "Der Sohn" (The son).[1] This rather flimsy tale of a trial opens in the "dying afternoon light of a marbled courtroom," in which the bored audience of unemployed lawyers, jaded court reporters, and drowsy stenographer and judges nods its collective head, barely keeping awake in the dark and overheated gloom of the fading winter day. Only the accused and the prosecutor stay awake, as the most intimate details of the former's life are revealed and rehashed in all their prosaic ignominy: in order to live beyond his means, he swindled money from unsuspecting creditors, defrauded widows and orphans, lived the high life of a gentleman while in truth he was a dishonest and disreputable scoundrel, as uncouth as he was unctuous. He must be punished with the most stringent penalties available, argues the prosecutor, in order to protect the public from such crafty and zealous predators.

After a short break, the accused rises to mount his own defense. Slowly and grandiloquently, he presents his case: his son sitting here in this room, all innocent and pure—he is the guilty party! He is responsible for everything the father is accused of! But, the accused implores, don't misunderstand me: my son is as pure as the driven snow, courageous, honest, brave:

> From his first day he has brought me only joy, and only once—I will soon tell you of it—did he bring me any pain. He is the reason for my sitting here

today. When he was born, my life was fulfilled. . . . While still in the cradle
he cured me of all my sarcasm and flippancy. Children are our best teachers.
He taught me true love of life! . . . From his first day on I was totally in love
with him, painfully, foolishly in love with him. I suffered, so to speak, from
monomania regarding my son.[2]

He could not bear to tear himself away from his son, continued the
accused: he was his first and most steadfast playmate, he accompanied
him through every stage of childhood, fulfilling his every wish, though
he was always, as now, a pure and unselfish soul. But the father was so
besotted with him that he let his business ventures sink into disrepair.
Soon he had to do everything the prosecutor charged him with: borrow
in order to stay afloat, then borrow more against the loans, shifting from
one creditor to the next until the bubble burst and he was bankrupt. No
one would lend him another penny; his credit was sacrificed on the altar
of his besotted love for his son! For days on end he wandered the streets,
trying to find a solution to his plight, to no avail. Finally, he decided
there was no way out, no solution but to bid farewell to life, to try to
shield his family from the horror and disaster of his own making. On
the appointed evening, he kissed his wife and daughter good night, as
usual, and then stopped in his son's room, where he stood staring at him
for a long time, then finally gave him a long, long kiss—"Now I know
that that kiss was my traitor!"

> I went into my room. I wanted to wait until they were all asleep. The revolver
> was ready. Then, my door opened suddenly: Hans! With one glance he took
> in the situation. I tried to grab the gun—he was quicker. He pushed me back,
> until I fell. Then he stood over me, with the gun in his hand:
> "Give it to me!" I screamed.
> "No! You're going to kill yourself!"
> "Give it to me! Yes, if you must know, I have to; I have no other choice."
> And I tried to get closer to him.
> "Not one inch closer Father!" And then he put the muzzle at his own
> temple. "One move and I'll fire!"
> At this horrendous moment, we began to bargain: he demanded my word
> that I would not hurt myself, or else he would shoot himself immediately.
> He didn't want to lose his father.
> And so, Your Honors, could I condemn to death my son, my only son?
> So I gave in to him once again, gave him my word that I would go on living.
> I'm alive. I'm sitting here. Declare me guilty![3]

This slight tale, later published as one of Herzl's *Philosophische Erzählungen,* is by no means of great literary or biographical import, but

it can serve here to raise all the complex methodological issues that attend a serious scholarly analysis of Theodor Herzl before he became a Zionist and, as well, of the other figures in this study. First, there is the problem of biographical reductionism: how much one can relate any work of art (however slim the artistry) to its author's life and real views? In this specific context, moreover, what can one say responsibly and not anachronistically about how such a story illuminates its author's attitude to Jewishness at the time it was written? Can we learn anything from works such as this courtroom drama about Herzl's Jewish identity before he became a Zionist, without projecting backward our knowledge that he would soon become one?

The only citation of "Der Sohn" that I have been able to locate is in one of the earliest, and still in many ways the most insightful, biographies of Herzl, Alex Bein's *Theodor Herzl*, first published in German in Vienna in 1934 and then translated into many languages, including frequent reprints in English and Hebrew. Bein cites the passage about the effect on the father of the birth and childhood of his son and provides the following analysis of the connection between this story and Herzl's life:

> His feuilletons became increasingly earnest and philosophic in the best sense. How much love and insight there is in that ripe product of his pen, "The Son," written in 1890. . . . The words were put in the mouth of a third person, but it needs no special insight to tell us what had happened: Herzl had become a father. On March 29, 1890, his daughter Pauline was born, and on June 10, 1891, there came a son. The effect of fatherhood is given us in the quoted feuilleton. But there was an outpouring in letters, too. He was no longer a mere spectator in the world. He was tied to tasks and to futurity. His life was to be changed by these facts; his outlook was to take on new clarity and depth.[4]

Before I pick apart this paragraph from Bein, it is crucial to understand its genre and context: Alex Bein was a talented and prolific historian who was employed at the Prussian State Archives in Potsdam until 1933, whereupon he moved to Palestine and held several positions at the Central Zionist Archives, becoming State Archivist of Israel from 1956 to 1971.[5] His biography of Herzl, penned soon after his arrival in Palestine in the shadow of Nazism, understandably presented one particular version of the relationship between fact and fiction in Herzl's oeuvre. The problem for us is not only that this version was highly skewed to present a positive picture of its subject; more interestingly, it was based on an obvious misreading of the plot of the story itself and—as Bein himself well knew—on a willful misrepresentation of essential aspects of Herzl's life.

In the story "Der Sohn," before the defendant rises to deliver his own defense, he pauses, and we are allowed to read his mind:

> There must be complete silence, lest even one of his precious words be lost. For the opening he has prepared an especially delicate first course, stirring appetizers for the epicure, saving the heavy stuff for the ending, thus assuring their proper effect: first, the sentimental slop, then the high-flown judicial prose; first, jerk their tears, then a quick jab of the dagger. An advertisement like this trial doesn't come too often.[6]

Rather than a paean to fatherly love, then, the protagonist's speech must be read as precisely the opposite, a cynical manipulation of paternal emotions and the audience's tears in order to extricate a dishonest and guilty man from his just punishment. The evocation of undying—indeed, obsessive—love for his son on the part of the father, we are told by the narrator, is but a coy and deliberately maudlin and melodramatic deceit, meant not only to shift attention away from the accused's crimes but to advance his career as well. While it may well be that the story is woven of autobiographical threads, to disentangle these from their avowedly fictional context requires, at the very least, fidelity to that life as we can reconstruct it. It is clear that "Der Sohn" was written either immediately before or soon after the birth of Herzl's daughter Pauline or during his wife's next pregnancy, which resulted in the birth of their only son, named, rather chillingly, Hans, as is the manipulated son in this story. Why would an author choose the same name for his real-life son after writing such a story? Herzl's letters and diaries (many of which were edited for publication by Alex Bein) do not answer that question, but they do reveal quite a different picture than Bein's description of blissful paternity resulting in a new clarity of purpose. Instead, we find Herzl expressing in his letters and diaries a tortured, totally self-absorbed ambivalence over his state of fatherhood within a terribly unhappy marriage. At the very same time that he wrote this story, Herzl seriously considered and repeatedly threatened to divorce his (probably pregnant) wife and abandon his newborn daughter. The couple decided nevertheless to remain married, however reluctantly, and their mutual antipathy remained intense long after Hans's birth and that of yet another child. Herzl's subsequent neglect of his children as well as his hatred of his wife were open secrets in the Zionist movement, to the extent that even the loyal Bein laconically quipped in another part of the biography that "the Jewish people owed a great debt of gratitude to Herzl's unhappy marriage."[7]

Moreover, Bein knew all too well the ultimate, extraordinarily horrific biographical resonance of this story (which, to be sure, Herzl would not have been aware of): forty years later, in 1930, Hans Herzl committed suicide by shooting himself in the temple with a revolver, unable to cope with his father's legacy and with his guilt over the recent death of his sister Pauline. As we shall see, Herzl's art was frequently imitated in real life, but the conundrum of his "prescience" is not susceptible to linear explication, or to any rational analysis.

Still, it does seem safe to conclude that at the time "Der Sohn" was written, Herzl undoubtedly had the implications of fatherhood on his mind. But, rather than demonstrating his delighted embrace of parenthood, this story must in some measure have reflected and refracted his profound ambivalence over the nature and meaning of fatherhood. Whatever Herzl's intentions, moreover, "Der Sohn" can be seen as an interesting literary meditation on the complex relationship between a father's love for his son and the deeply repressed resentment fathers feel toward their children (and particularly their sons)—what one psychoanalyst has termed the "Laius Complex."[8]

But there is more to be learned about Theodor Herzl in 1890 from "Der Sohn." This story is an excellent example of Herzl's cultural stance in the late 1880s and early 1890s, in that it is imbued with what Carl Schorske aptly characterized as "the personal frustration and aesthetic despair of the typical fin-de-siècle intellectual." Using Herzl as the prime example of the feuilletonist—the author of the classic fin-de-siècle genre, a composition style frequently employed by the writers studied here—Schorske portrayed such a writer as an intellectual who

> turned his appropriated aesthetic culture inward to the cultivation of the self, of his personal uniqueness. This tendency led to preoccupation with one's own psychic life. . . . The subjective response of the reporter or critic to an experience, his feeling-tone, acquired clear primacy over the matter of his discourse. . . . his characteristics were narcissism and introversion, passive receptivity toward outer reality, and above all, sensitivity to psychic states. This bourgeois culture of feeling conditioned the mentality of its intellectuals and artists, refined their sensibilities, and created their problems.[9]

In this regard, then, "Der Sohn" is a remarkably pointed expression of its author's narcissism, a rather disturbing manipulation of fatherly "feeling-tones" in the service of self-absorbed subjectivity. Theodor Herzl was not simply a fin-de-siècle Austrian-Jewish fop and writer of light-hearted parlor romances, as he has often been lampooned. His sartorial and aesthetic dandyism merely externalized a deep-seated psychological complexity not truly susceptible to responsible retroactive analysis, however enthusiastic the analyst. For, beyond the problems of psychohistory, most of Herzl's most personal and intimate letters were deliberately destroyed, and both his diaries and his surviving correspondence have been heavily censored by editors. To some extent, Herzl's literary remains help to explicate his complex psyche, but they must be read without the tendentious and retrojected assumptions they have heretofore been subjected to.

What is far easier to deduce from Herzl's oeuvre, and is often misunderstood, is his antibourgeois aesthetic, which he shared—not so paradoxically—with other sons of the fin-de-siècle bourgeoisie. In the Habsburg Empire as well as in Germany and France, this antibourgeois and often faux-aristocratic stance was often maintained alongside a generally liberal political posture, without any clear recognition or resolution of the profound antagonism between these positions. In Russia, as we shall see, the typical fin-de-siècle intellectual would harbor a more radical political posture, one equally at odds with his or her aesthetic stance. Moreover, given socioeconomic realities, in Vienna or Budapest (or Odessa or Drohobycz), the antibourgeois but yet decidedly bourgeois liberal or radical aesthete was more likely than not to be Jewish, though deeply and unavoidably confused and uneasy, if not deeply resentful, about his relationship to Judaism and the Jewish community. (And such conflicted individuals were usually male—the fate of the antibourgeois, bourgeois Jewish woman took different routes and resulted in different psychic tolls.)

Indeed, although the protagonist of "Der Sohn" is nowhere identified by name or by community of origin, there hovers over this story a discernible waft of Viennese Jewish middle-class society, which Herzl repeatedly deplored and satirized in his writings both before and, equally notable, after he became a Zionist. The protagonist's financial misdeeds are those of the stereotypically Jewish parvenu, as is his sloppily sentimental speech about a father's love for a child—rather like "Sunrise, Sunset" *avant la lettre*. There will develop a complex Zionist discourse that attempts to appropriate and thus to subvert previous condemnations of Jewish rapaciousness or sentimentality through a peculiar nationalist dialectic.

Here we come to the crucial problem of the overused and imprecise concept of Jewish "assimilation." In a deliberately provocative essay entitled "The Blessing of Assimilation in Jewish History," the great Jewish historian and former chancellor of the Jewish Theological Seminary of America Gerson D. Cohen pointed out decades ago that in its most common usage—the acceptance on the part of Jews of non-Jewish cultures, languages, and ways of life—assimilation was a largely beneficial leitmotif of Jewish history from antiquity to the present, in many ways the major source of Jewish survival and adaptability through the ages; to conceive of an eternal Jewish essence unperturbed by foreign admixtures was precisely to misunderstand and profoundly to caricature Jewish life and culture, whether in ancient Palestine or in the Diaspora. If, for example, the rhetorical principles that undergird and define talmudic hermeneutics were "assimilated" from the Greeks, what more need be said about the relationship between Jewish culture and that of the nations with whom they came into contact?[10] Cohen's point was that the slipshod (and largely derogatory) way in which the term "assimilation" has been used in modern Jewish internal polemics ought to be decoded and reconceived; though often cited by historians, Cohen's plea had little effect either within or, especially, outside of the academy. As a result, we do not yet have a history of the term as applied to the Jews nor in particular of its politicization as a term of opprobrium: it seems to have entered into discourse about Jews in the midst of the internal Jewish battle over Zionism in the last decades of the nineteenth century and the first decades of the twentieth century, with each side accusing the other of being assimilated Jews or promoting assimilation. Thus, Zionists routinely denounced deeply committed but non-Zionist Orthodox, Conservative, and Reform Jews as assimilated or assimilationist, and the latter returned the insult, decrying the largely secularist Zionist leaders as promoting Jewish assimilation. Thus, both "assimilation" and "assimilated Jew" became terms of opprobrium rather than of precise meaning; an "assimilated Jew" came to mean any Jew whose version of Jewishness one did not like.

In his autobiography, *Trial and Error,* Chaim Weizmann recounted his first trip to Germany, at the age of nineteen, to teach Hebrew and Russian at the prestigious Orthodox Jewish boarding school in Pfungstadt, near Darmstadt. Weizmann grew to hate this school for many reasons, but primarily because, as he explains,

> Pfungstadt was my introduction to one of the queerest chapters in Jewish history: the assimilated Jews of Germany, then in the high summer of their illusory security and mightily proud of it. . . . The head of this school was a Dr. Barness, a man who in his own way was even more bewildering to me

than the German gentiles. He was pious in the extreme, that is to say, he practiced the rigid, formal piety of Frankfort Jewish Orthodoxy. The school was *kosher;* it had in constant attendance a *Mashgiach,* or overseer of the ritual purity of the food. There were no classes on the Sabbath; no writing was done on that day; prayers were said three times daily, morning, afternoon and evening, . . . Dr. Barness was completely assimilated, and described himself as "a German of the Mosaic persuasion." He took his Judaism to mean that in all respects save that of religious ritual he was as German, in culture, background and personality, as any descendant of the Cerusci.[11]

Under no plausible reading could one assert that Weizmann was bemoaning the adoption of non-Jewish culture or language by Dr. Barness or the other Orthodox Jews of Germany, that is, their linguistic or cultural Germanization. By no means could Weizmann ever condemn such linguistic or cultural change—he himself was, after all, a graduate of the Pinsk gymnasium, spoke Russian fluently, and was preparing himself to become a chemist. Even more obvious, he could not have conceived that these strictly pious and observant Jews were dedicated to the self-obliteration of the Jews as a group. Rather, to Weizmann, the term "assimilation" was clearly a political epithet; it meant holding non-Zionist (or anti-Zionist) beliefs, in this case defining the Jews as members of a religious faith rather than of a nationalistically defined nation.

Recognizing this confusion, Jewish social historians in recent decades have adopted the terminology of an American sociologist, Milton Gordon, who distinguished between "assimilation," "acculturation," and "integration" to denote the different conditions of intergroup relations.[12] While to some extent useful in describing the nature of social change in Jewish society and the degree of receptivity to Jews by non-Jewish societies, this taxonomy is conceptually problematic because it projects an ostensibly linear progression from acculturation to "structural" assimilation, a teleology vastly overgeneralized from a stereotypical reading of American society in the 1950s and early 1960s. To describe subtle ideational and ideological phenomena—how, in this case, individual Jews in Vienna, Budapest, Paris, Berlin, or Odessa conceived of themselves and the Jews as a group and their relations to non-Jewish society and culture—Gordon's taxonomy is all but useless. Hence it is not surprising that one often finds the very same authors citing Gordon's sociological differentiations and yet retaining the vague, slippery, and polemically charged term "assimilation," ostensibly to denote cultural or intellectual stances.

"Assimilationism" is a less problematic term, though it too is often used in a slipshod way, as synonymous with "assimilation." Used precisely, the term denotes the belief in the desirability of the disappearance of a group, either by intermarriage, conversion, revolutionary reconstruction of society, or the like. Most Jews described (or decried) as assimilated or as believing in Jewish assimilation by no means advocated Jewish self-obliteration. As a result, the most careful students of modern Jewish politics have recently taken to using the more precise and neutral term "integrationist" to denote Jews who were committed to the future of Jewish life and faith in the Diaspora but who rejected or dissented from the Zionist movement.[13]

But neither Herzl nor the other figures studied here were truly "integrationists" before they became Zionists, for the most part because they had no clear, conscious, or sustained ideological position on the Jews or the so-called Jewish problem. As with thousands of other fin-de-siècle Jewish intellectuals and semi-intellectuals throughout Europe, their "identity" as Jews (to use an anachronistic term) was a complex and often semi-conscious web of action and inaction, beliefs and feelings, embarrassment and pride, always conditioned and complicated by familial, political, and social realities that varied from one individual to the next and from one society to the other. Rigorously to untangle this web requires not only a subtle understanding of both individual and collective lives, but also a refusal to confuse the prescriptive and the descriptive—a crucial distinction often ignored by even the most sophisticated scholars.

In the first place, then, figures such as Theodor Herzl and Max Nordau and the young Vladimir Jabotinsky acted as if their Jewishness had no bearing on their lives, their careers, their worldviews, their Kultur. They neither disavowed their Judaism nor proclaimed it publicly, believing (or pretending to believe) that it was essentially irrelevant to their lives. Moreover, in Germany or the Habsburg realm, it was possible formally to disavow one's Jewishness even without conversion to Christianity (legally to register as "konfessionslos," that is, without any religion). But Herzl and hundreds of thousands of other so-called assimilated Jews did not take this step, despite their distance from the Jewish community and from Judaism as a religious system. One of the most sophisticated analysts of this phenomenon, Carl Schorske, was aware of the paradox but both undervalued and overstated its content: "Their Judaism," he wrote, "amounted to little more than what Theodor Gomperz, the assimilated Jewish classicist, liked to call 'un pieux souvenir de famille.'"[14] Beyond its rather shocking dismissal of the effect of family ties on individuals' ideational and psychic worlds, Schorske's comment crucially confuses the descriptive and the prescriptive even in the life story of Gomperz himself, who therefore merits a short digression here, as a "control," as it were, to Herzl's relationship with the Jewish community and with Judaism.

Born to a prominent and wealthy Jewish family with ties to both the Mendelssohns and the Rothschilds, Theodor Gomperz (1832–1912) underwent a dramatic transformation in his own relationship to Judaism during his long and productive life. A renowned professor of classical antiquity in Vienna—an academic ranking fully possible in the Habsburg Empire without baptism, despite the frequent but incorrect generalization from Sigmund Freud's case—Gomperz was also an active and influential public figure and politician, a member of the Herrenhaus, the upper chamber of the Imperial parliament. As a lifelong Liberal and translator and friend of John Stuart Mill, Gomperz personified the unmitigated optimism and dedication to Enlightenment values of the generation of the fathers of Theodor Herzl, Max Nordau, and Vladimir Jabotinsky. Despite his thoroughgoing religious skepticism, through his forties Gomperz regularly attended the Seitenstettengasse temple presided over by the famous preacher Adolf Jellinek; moreover, he privately regretted his lack of advanced training in Hebrew and Talmud, pledging that in his older years he would devote himself to renewing his knowledge of the language and literature of *unseres Volkes* (the German phrase has a far stronger resonance of Jewish peoplehood than its English equivalent, particularly in the mouth of a Viennese professor of Greek in 1878).[15] To his wife he wrote that it was his wish that his sons, "with God's help, and despite whatever views they might have about religion, ritual, etc., go to temple wherever it be . . . every year on the anniversary of my death to say Kaddish, although this seems to go against the grain of my high-minded, areligious, republican Enlightenment."[16]

It was only in the 1880s, especially after the rise and success of antisemitic movements in Austria, Germany, and France threatened to undermine everything he held dear, that Gomperz increasingly began to believe that his profound faith in the possibility of a Jewish future in western European society was chimerical. Thus, in his will written in early 1887, he expressed his "emphatic desire that my children convert to Christianity, so that they bypass the transitional stage of Konfessionslosigkeit experienced by their parents."[17] He then went on at length about the problem of formal baptism in a faith one does not truly believe in and suggested (but did not demand) that his children choose Lutheranism over Catholicism, given the Jesuit domination of the Church in

Austria, despite his own personal love for Italy and aesthetic preference for the Roman dispensation. Indeed, he continued to worry about and to correspond with relatives about which denomination of Christianity his children should adopt and in his last years seems to have been all but obsessed by the unanticipated developments of the Judenfrage. Not surprisingly, he was a frequent opponent of Zionism in the pages of Herzl's newspaper, *Die Neue Freie Presse,* and was especially troubled by the Dreyfus Affair, following its every twist and turn with exceedingly careful scrutiny—in May 1902 he met personally with Alfred Dreyfus and his wife, confiding that "they both have very pronounced Jewish looks, I suppose his ultimate misfortune."[18] In the end, moreover, even this avowed proponent of the dissolution of Judaism did not—or as he put it, could not—disavow his erstwhile faith and was buried with full religious ritual in the Jewish cemetery in Vienna. Though Gomperz may well have wished his Judaism to be but a marginal and irrelevant "pious memory of family," it was in fact a complex and ever changing defining aspect of his life and worldview, if ultimately in paradoxical and painful ways.

Gomperz, then, can be regarded as a typical exponent of "assimilationism" rather than "assimilation." And the comparison to Herzl is interesting, since in the late 1880s and early 1890s, Herzl too flirted with the notion of Jewish self-obliteration, either through socialism or, more provocatively, through a mass baptism to be held at St. Stephen's Cathedral in Vienna. More to the point, perhaps, Herzl deliberately did not have his son, Hans, circumcised at birth in 1891, as a visceral token of his own unease about Judaism. (Hans would be circumcised as a teenager, at the behest of Zionist leaders after Herzl's death.)[19] But as several of his biographers have demonstrated, before he came to Zionism Herzl had already abandoned any hope in assimilationism as well, convinced that the rise of racialist antisemitism in Germany, Austria, and France would not permit such a solution to the "Jewish problem," quite independent of the question of its desirability. Like Gomperz, Herzl brooded about the unanticipated nature of this antisemitism, convinced that it betokened a radical new phenomenon in the relationship between Jews and Europe.

Most western and central European Jews did not agree with either Herzl or Gomperz. They believed that the antisemitism they were witnessing was not new, but merely a recurrence of traditional Jew-hatred in a new guise, a retrograde obscurantism deliberately cultivated by scurrilous politicians supported by the reactionary forces of society,

[marginalia, handwritten:] Herzl ø hope in assimilation

particularly the Church. They thus committed themselves to re-emphasizing their fealty to the Enlightenment values of universal truth and the unstoppable march of progress: the good guys, they genuinely believed, would inevitably and eventually defeat the bad guys. Contrary to Herzl's and Gomperz's conviction in the eternity and unstoppability of Jew-hatred, even in the homeland of Enlightenment and Emancipation, and thus their search for a radical solution to the Judenfrage, the most common reaction of central and western European Jews to the Dreyfus Affair was a belief that, in the end, French justice would triumph. After the Affair, they knew they had been right all along—the good guys did vanquish the bad guys; the true France of *égalité, fraternité,* and *liberté* beat out the forces of reaction and hatred. This, most were convinced, was the verdict of History.

But in the aftermath of Vichy and worse, such a stance seemed to many to be tragically naive and even self-destructive. The American Jewish writer Cynthia Ozick expressed the resultant widespread wisdom by deriding the optimistic Enlightenment beliefs of such Jews and quipping that "universalism is the ultimate Jewish parochialism."[20] Historically this is true only if one regards Christianity as the ultimate expression of Jewish parochialism, a position maintained most famously by both Voltaire and Nietzsche. But Ozick was on the mark in recognizing that most central and western European Jews in the nineteenth century did indeed believe in a universalist faith and that such a belief lay at the core of their rejection of the Zionist ideology. What Ozick and others do not sufficiently take into account, however, was that that faith was called Judaism—for decades, central and western European Jews had been taught by their rabbis and lay leaders (whether Orthodox, Liberal, or Reform) that Judaism as a creed was fully compatible not only with Emancipation and equal rights but also with Enlightenment conceptions of human equality and brotherhood. Their commitment to this worldview and hence their rejection of Zionism was not based on their assimilation or assimilationism but on their fundamental, dual self-conception as equal (or eventually equal) citizens of the states in which they lived and as Jews, adherents of a faith fully in accord with Enlightenment notions of the true and the just.

This was not the case for intellectuals such as Herzl or Nordau or later for Jabotinsky, on both spiritual and civil counts. Herzl and Nordau had long deliberately forgotten or rejected their rabbis' teachings, and Jabotinsky had never had any to forget or reject. Long before they became Zionists, they had equally rejected the conventional patriotism of bourgeois society, which they despised, in favor of an ostensibly avant-garde cosmopolitanism, which regarded itself as pan-European in culture and not delimited by any national or communitarian ties. They defined themselves as intellectuals more than as Austrians, Germans, Frenchmen, Russians—as cultured citizens of the world rather than of one particular nation, state, or community of faith. They believed, moreover, that such a transnational, humanistic culture and politics transcended and rendered essentially superfluous class, national, ethnic, and religious boundaries. This particular version of cosmopolitanism (like Marxism and most other offspring of the Enlightenment) assumed the superiority of European civilization over that of the rest of the world, primarily the "Orient" and the so-called primitive races. Hence, it expected and worked to foment a "Westernization" or "modernization" of other cultures and civilizations in the image of the West. To expect otherwise from most nineteenth-century Europeans is to engage in ahistorical, wishful thinking. The profound challenge to such a European cosmopolitanism came not from a presumptively egalitarian multiculturalism but from the enemies and opponents of the Enlightenment itself, from those forces of tradition and reaction that sought to restore the Old Regime and its supposedly divinely ordained values and institutions. Fed by versions of Romanticism that privileged the "primitive" over the ostensibly hyper-rational "modern," integral nationalists and their fellow travelers insisted on an exclusivist and increasingly biological definition of nationhood, rejecting the earlier inclusive and territorial definitions that had, not incidentally, rendered possible the Emancipation of the Jews. It was thus no coincidence that the new nationalist movements, as if by definition, tended to be antisemitic as well (at least outside of Italy).

In the face of the seeming dissolution of the cosmopolitan dream, Herzl began to obsess over the future of the Jews. Typically, of course, he is said to have come to Zionism as a result of the Dreyfus Affair, a claim he himself made repeatedly in later years. But in an important 1993 study, the historian Jacques Kornberg carefully analyzed Herzl's reportage on the Dreyfus Affair from the beginning of the case to its end and demonstrated that Herzl's reactions to the first stages of the Affair, well into 1897, were entirely typical of those of other writers in *Die Neue Freie Presse* or other liberal (and often Jewish-owned) newspapers, and indeed of most Jews in France and elsewhere.[21] It was only after Herzl was a convinced Zionist, and the case itself was transformed in the late 1890s into a cause célèbre, that he began to interpret it through

Zionist lenses. Nordau also went through exactly the same stages of Dreyfusardism, to the extent that he, too, would later counterfactually insist that it was the Dreyfus Affair that made him a Zionist.

Instead, as documented by Kornberg and others, Herzl came slowly and gradually to his idea of Zionism. In late 1894 and early 1895 he began to articulate a new and still largely inchoate "solution to the Jewish problem": a conviction in the invincibility of antisemitism even in the face of Emancipation and Enlightenment, and consequently in the necessity of the Jews returning in some way to their ancient political autonomy. There is no reason to doubt that until this point Herzl was unaware that other thinkers had come to the same conclusions; no evidence has emerged to challenge his repeated assertion, for instance, that he had never heard of or read Leon Pinsker's "Autoemancipation," written in German in 1882, or known of the Love of Zion movement that had begun in the Russian Empire and Romania under Pinsker's and others' influence. Herzl seems indeed to have come to his views independently, on the basis of his own cogitation—a rare and remarkable instance of spontaneous intellectual generation.

Indeed, like Pinsker before him, Herzl at first did not care where the "Judenstaat" would be—Argentina, Palestine, Africa, wherever—as long as it both removed the Jews from Europe and enabled them to establish their own home on the basis of his conception of modern civilization. Only after he was convinced that Zionism without Zion would not be supported by the Jewish masses, particularly in eastern Europe, did he become what was then known as a "Palestinophile." But Herzl's conversion to Zionism did not necessitate a rejection of his cosmopolitanism; on the contrary, Zionism for him seemed to be the perfect solution to the crisis of European cosmopolitanism, for the world at large as much as for the Jews. Here we come to one of the most difficult nodes of Herzl's thought, and that of many subsequent Zionist thinkers as well: his conviction that modern antisemitism was not an irrational residue of medieval obscurantism but, as he put it in a letter to the London *Jewish Chronicle* in January 1896, "a highly complex movement. I consider it from a Jewish standpoint, yet without fear or hatred. I believe that I can see what elements there are in it of vulgar sport, of common trade, of jealousy, of inherited prejudice, of religious intolerance and also of legitimate self-defense."[22]

It was this last phrase—antisemitism as "legitimate self-defense" on the part of Gentiles—that would put Herzl, Nordau, and later and most controversially, Jabotinsky, on a collision course with conventional Jewish thought and politics, for Zionism seemed to be not only accepting the claims of antisemites about the impossibility of Jewish life in Europe and their criticisms of Jewish society and behavior in European society, but feeding and advancing these claims and criticisms as well. By the late 1930s, Jabotinsky's call for the evacuation to Palestine of Polish Jewry seemed to be playing into the hands of vicious antisemites who persecuted the Jews and called for their exclusion from Polish society— the motto "Zydzi do Palestiny" (Jews to Palestine) could have multiple resonances.

For Herzl, to be sure, such future complications were both unforeseeable and beside the point. He was convinced that the only future for the Jews was their removal from European society and transplantation in a new soil where they could thrive and build a society that combined the best of their millennial culture and modern European civilization. Such a surgery would in turn serve to cure the ills of Europe as a whole: on the one hand, an indigestible element—whose very indigestibility was often used as an excuse for reactionary opposition—would be removed from its midst; on the other, Europe would benefit immeasurably from the establishment in Palestine of a model European society. It was so simple.

In Herzl's time the term "assimilation" came to be used as a polemical sword in the arsenal of inter-Jewish verbal warfare, and so, in *Judenstaat*, Herzl tried to argue that Zionism would cure Jewish assimilation as well, both in the sense of advancing Jewish integration into European mores and culture and allowing those Jews who wished to cease being Jews to do so without hindrance, given the disappearance of antisemitism. And so the debate about Herzl's putative "assimilation" and "assimilationism" was put in motion, resulting in the semiotic promiscuity described above.

But as we shall see throughout the rest of this book, it is precisely on this question of the relationship between fin-de-siècle cosmopolitanism and Zionism that so many of the central debates and divides of the Zionist movement were (and to some extent still are) based. It was one thing for Herzl, Nordau, Lilien, and Jabotinsky to abandon their hopes in the future of the Jews in European society; it is quite another thing to expect them to have altered their personal cosmopolitanism or their fundamental belief in the superiority and transnational applicability of the cultural and intellectual norms and values of late nineteenth-century European civilization.

Nowhere, of course, was Herzl's merger of Zionism and cosmopolitanism more clearly articulated than in his Utopian novel *Altneuland,* written in 1902.[23] As scores of commentators have noted from the time of its composition to today, Herzl's vision of the Old-New Land was unabashedly premised on fin-de-siècle European culture and ideals: religion would be relegated entirely to the private realm, with no distinction whatsoever between Jew, Muslim, or Christian in any aspect of life, law, or social intercourse; there would be absolutely no Arab opposition to Zionism, since the Arab inhabitants of Palestine would only benefit from the technological advance of their society and hence would unilaterally welcome massive Jewish immigration; the return of the Jews to their ancient land would thus solve the "Jewish problem" everywhere else—antisemitism would disappear from the world, and the Old-New Land would be a beacon of peace, prosperity, and progress for the rest of the world. To symbolize this cosmopolitan dream, a beautiful Peace Palace with Terence's famous line "Humani nihil a me alienum puto" carved above its portals would stand next to the rebuilt Temple of Jerusalem. The Temple itself would somehow have been restored without destroying the Mosque of Omar and would resemble in its aesthetic and ritual a central European Reform temple—with no mention, to be sure, of animal sacrifices. So transnational would be Jewish Palestine that no revival of the Hebrew language would be necessary—each person would speak whatever language came naturally, and there would be no need for the development of a secular Jewish culture based on the Hebrew tongue. In Herzl's vision, the Jewish elite would behave like English ladies and gentlemen, playing cricket and dressing for dinner in formal evening attire, retiring afterward to their salons for port and cigars for the men and gossip for the women, while the farmers would speak Yiddish and follow traditional Judaism under the tutelage of pious, though thoroughly Zionist, rabbinic authority. Moreover, Herzl insisted throughout the novel that the Old-New Land would rid itself of what he considered the worst invention of the nineteenth century, the fetish of nation-statehood: Zionism would not be realized through the establishment of a state but through the creation of a commonwealth, which Herzl defined as "a large co-operative association composed of affiliated co-operatives" with no true executive, a minimal legislature, no formal judiciary, no trappings whatsoever of a modern nation-state.

Herzl's vision of Zionism was most famously attacked by Ahad Ha'am, the Russian Jewish ideologue of cultural or spiritual Zionism, who penned a furious review of *Altneuland,* deriding with uninhibited sarcasm its author's scandalous ignorance of and disregard for the very fundamentals of Jewish history and faith, the Hebrew language, and the Jewish *Volksgeist*. Ahad Ha'am's ad hominem attack on Herzl was answered with even more furiously personalized venom by Nordau, who ridiculed Ahad Ha'am as an untutored ghetto Jew, oblivious of even the basics of modern European literature and culture, hopelessly mired in the obscurantist muck of the Pale of Settlement, despite his ostensible claims to modernity.[24] Though his Hebrew was allegedly elegant (a judgment, Nordau confessed, he could not make firsthand since he could not understand it), Ahad Ha'am's writings, when translated into German, revealed the fundamental emptiness and confusion of their author's uneducated Asiatic mind, according to Nordau. The characters in *Altneuland* speak German because the novel was written in German, Nordau explained, just as Shakespeare did not have Hamlet and Julius Caesar speak Danish or Latin; if Ahad Ha'am has never heard of Shakespeare, he can turn to his beloved Bible, where he will note that the Egyptians speak Hebrew, not Egyptian! In sum, Nordau concluded, Ahad Ha'am was not a Zionist but an enemy of Zionism, masquerading as a friend: he was a secular "Protestrabbiner"—the term Herzl invented to deride those German rabbis, Orthodox, Liberal, and Reform, who joined together to oppose the Zionist movement at its very origin. Ahad Ha'am's attack on Herzl from the standpoint of "secular Jewish culture" and "Hebraism" was merely a cover for his fundamentalist, if free-thinking, opposition to the very essence of the Zionist creed:

> *Altneuland* is too European. There are newspapers, theater, opera-houses for which one dons white gloves. Everywhere Europeans, European mores, European inventions. Nowhere any specific Jewish traces.
>
> Indeed! *Altneuland* is a piece of Europe in Asia. Here Herzl pointed precisely to what we want, what we are striving for. We want the reunified liberated Jewish Nation to be a modern cultured nation (*ein Kulturvolk*)—to remain as modern and cultured as we already are and as much as we can possibly become. In this we are not aping anyone, we are merely using and developing our own property: we have contributed more than our share to European culture, which is thus ours to the same degree it belongs to the Germans, French or English. We hold that there is no contradiction between what is Jewish—what is ours as Jews—and what is European. Ahad Ha'am might see European culture as foreign—we will make it accessible to him. But we will never concede that the return of the Jews to the land of their fathers is a return to barbarism, as our enemies slanderously claim. The Jewish people will develop its own culture alongside and within general Western culture, just like any other civilized nation, not from the outside in an uncultured Asiatic society, as Ahad Ha'am seems to desire.[25]

Though misleading (perhaps deliberately) about Ahad Ha'am's beliefs, Nordau's emphatic diatribe was by far the clearest précis of the synthesis between fin-de-siècle cosmopolitanism and Zionism that lay at the heart of the Zionist movement as Herzl and his closest colleagues conceived it. But Max Nordau was hardly a run-of-the-mill exponent of late nineteenth-century European culture and civilization; paradoxically, he was fin-de-siècle cosmopolitanism's most ardent and controversial critic. To flesh out this paradox, we turn in chapter 2 to an investigation of this most curious Zionist leader, Dr. Max Nordau.

CHAPTER TWO

Max Nordau,
the Improbable Bourgeois

In the summer of 1901, *Freiheit*, the London anarchist Yiddish press, published a series of brochures by Max Nordau, then the world's second most famous Zionist. This was hardly a signal of a softening of the intramural hatreds of Jewish political life on the cusp of a new century. On the contrary, although the stridently anti-Zionist Yiddish anarchists undoubtedly relished Nordau's words for their own sake, the fact that their author might be deeply embarrassed by their appearance at this moment could well have added a tinge of schadenfreude to *Freiheit*'s decision to reprint Nordau's missives. For the first of these brochures, entitled in Yiddish *Der lign fun religyon* (The lie of religion), contained the following description of the Hebrew Bible:

> Historical investigations have revealed to us the origin and growth of the Bible; we know that by this name we designate a collection of writings as radically unlike in origin, character and contents as if Wagner's Nibelungen Lied, Mirabeau's speeches, Heine's love poems, and a manual of zoology, had been printed and mixed up promiscuously and then bound into one volume. We find collected in this book the superstitious beliefs of the ancient inhabitants of Palestine, with indistinct echoes of Indian and Persian fables, mistaken imitations of Egyptian theories and customs, historical chronicles as dry as they are unreliable, and miscellaneous poems, amatory, human and Jewish national, which are rarely distinguished by beauties of the highest order but frequently by superfluity of expression, coarseness, bad taste, and genuine Oriental sensuality. As a literary monument the Bible is of much later origin than the Vedas; as a work of literary value it is surpassed by

everything written in the last 2000 years by authors even of second rank; and to compare it seriously with the productions of Homer, Sophocles, Dante, Shakespeare or Goethe would require a fanatized mind that had entirely lost its power of judgment. Its conception of the universe is childish and its morality revolting, as revealed in the malicious vengeance attributed to God in the Old Testament. . . . And yet men, cultivated and capable of forming a just estimate, pretend to reverence this ancient work, they refuse to allow it to be discussed and criticized like any other production of the human intellect . . . and they pretend to be edified and inspired when they read it.[1]

This was a rendering into Yiddish of one of the chapters of Nordau's second most important work, *Die conventionellen Lügen der Kulturmenschheit,* first published in German in 1883 and imprecisely translated into English as *The Conventional Lies of Our Civilization.*[2] Today largely forgotten, this was an extremely popular and influential work in the fin de siècle, quickly translated into Italian, Dutch, Swedish, Danish, Spanish, Rumanian, Czech, Hungarian, Hebrew, Russian, Japanese, Greek, Chinese, and Turkish, in addition to English and French. Banned not only by the Austrian and Russian governments but by the Vatican as well, *Conventional Lies* presaged Nordau's later and even more influential and controversial *Degeneration* by attacking contemporary European society as sick and rotten to its core, dominated not only by the lie of religion but also by the equally pernicious lies of monarchy, aristocracy, parliamentary democracy, free trade, capitalism, socialism, and, not least of all, marriage.

How to reconcile this worldview with Nordau's later Zionism has befuddled historians for the past several decades. Without entering into the details of the long-lived debate on this issue, it is only a slight oversimplification to claim that opinion has essentially been divided between those who see Nordau's Zionism as completely contradictory to his previous views and those who see his pre-Zionist views as seamlessly connected to his Zionism.[3] Both categories can be subdivided into two sets: those authors who admire or abhor his stance before he became a Zionist, and those who admire or abhor his stance after he became a Zionist. Intellectual detachment, to say the least, is not the hallmark of the scholarship on Zionism as a whole, or on Nordau in particular.

What all these permutations and combinations share is a basic agreement about the nature of Nordau's politics and thought before he became a Zionist: that he was a liberal and indeed the quintessential liberal of the middle and late nineteenth century. Thus, one student of Nordau, Peter Baldwin, writes:

Liberalism was for Nordau, the prodigal Jew, his personal salvation, and it became, in his version and opinion, that of all people. Nordau's liberal world-view was formulated in extreme terms of a broad scope, without nuance. . . . Chauvinistic nationalism he rejected as conservative and illiberal. More importantly, however, he also shied away from any notion of nationalism which could not be reconciled with his cosmopolitan attitude. [Thus] although many of his contemporaries had no trouble combining nationalism and liberalism into an integrated scheme of thought, Nordau found the task ultimately impossible. He led a dual life, torn between a nationalist ideology that appealed to the basic features of his conception of the world and a commitment to liberalism which his rarely flagging rationalism never allowed him to repudiate.[4]

In perhaps the most often quoted study on the matter, George Mosse reached a totally opposite conclusion, starting from the same premise:

Nordau was a Liberal . . . a champion of individual rights and liberties. While . . . his liberalism and Zionism seem in conflict, in reality his ideal of the new Jew, as well as his Jewish nationalism, were adapted to liberal ends. There is no need to go into Nordau's liberal credentials. . . . [He] had to balance his commitment to the regeneration and survival of the Jewish people with his concern for the rights of the individual. Thus in his novel *The Right to Love,* which appeared in the same year as *Degeneration,* the rights of individuals are suspended only when the survival of the species is at stake. A husband and wife must live in an empty marriage rather than endanger the adaptability of their children. He wrote this novel to refute Henrik Ibsen's *Doll House* with its portrayal of the free run of passions and man's selfishness. Indeed his view of women was traditional, characteristic of his concept of sexual morality.[5]

Mosse was on the right track, though he had not read his sources very carefully: *The Right to Love* is not a novel but a play, as its title page announces—and even a cursory reading of this drama reveals that it by no means preaches what Mosse says it does.[6] On the contrary, and fully in accord with Nordau's views on matrimony in *Conventional Lies,* his play is a satiric attack both on contemporary bourgeois conceptions of marriage and on the fashionable avant-garde alternatives to bourgeois marriage. I shall return to *The Right to Love* and Nordau's views on matrimony and sex below. But first, what is crucial to the overall proposition here is that to scholars on all sides of the Nordau-Zionism debate, Nordau was a prototypical liberal before he became a Zionist, a defender of bourgeois mores and politics who therefore either abandoned his liberalism when he became a nationalist or succeeded in synthesizing his liberalism with his nationalism.

But what is wrong with this conventional analysis is that Max Nordau was not a liberal, in any rational and historically apt sense of that term, before he became a Zionist. Rather, in both his pre-Zionist works and those written after he became a Zionist, he presented a cultural and political theory that was neither liberal nor conservative, neither radical nor reactionary, though it contained elements of all of these sensibilities. But neither was it especially idiosyncratic: Nordau's view of the world can only be understood through an examination of one of the most difficult thickets of fin-de-siècle European intellectual history, not to speak of fin-de-siècle Jewish intellectual history, Social Darwinism.

As Richard Hofstadter noted in 1944 when writing *Social Darwinism in American Thought,* although it is reflexive in our political culture to divide the world according to the architectural layout of the French National Assembly, the categories of Right, Left, and Center—or radical, liberal, and conservative—are totally unhelpful in describing the ideas of the mid- to late nineteenth-century heirs of positivism, the so-called Social Darwinists. Hofstadter, struggling with his own ideological contortions and with the implications of Social Darwinism on American society and politics, understood that Herbert Spencer and his devotees could perhaps be best understood not as liberals but as conservatives. However, Hofstadter questions the fit of this label:

> we may wonder whether, in the entire history of thought, there was ever a conservatism so utterly progressive as this. . . . A conservatism that appealed more to the secularist than the pious mentality, it was a conservatism almost without religion. A body of belief whose chief conclusion was that the positive functions of the state should be kept to the barest minimum, it was almost anarchical, and it was devoid of that center of reverence and authority which the state provides in many conservative systems.[7]

Even more cogently, a recent British study of Spencer explains that his thought and that of the other Individualists and Social Darwinists cannot usefully be labeled liberal, even though they had their genesis in the fin-de-siècle crisis of liberalism caused by a society experiencing profound social, economic, and political dislocation. Differing sharply both from contemporary liberals, conservatives, and radicals, such thinkers found in evolutionary science a new, post-Comtian positivism that claimed that proposals for social reform proceeded in ignorance of the fundamental laws of the development of society: political institutions cannot be effectively modified faster than the characters of citizens are modified. While Auguste Comte had preached "Savoir pour prévoir,

prévoir pour pouvoir," the outlook of Spencer and his colleagues was more adequately expressed as "Prévoir pour rien faire."[8]

Nordau's variation on this theme was, simply put, to extend this analysis from sociology and political science to cultural criticism; to apply the slogan "ontology recapitulates phylogeny" to the aesthetic and ideological innovations of his time. He believed that from paleontology we can easily deduce that there were reptilian phases for cultures as well as for individuals and for species, and that these evolved through the fish to the mammalian and then to the human stage. In devolution, meanwhile, an individual, society, or species may propel itself, or be propelled, in just the opposite direction.

Here lie the keys to Nordau's thought, expressed in *Conventional Lies* as well as many other works both before and after *Degeneration,* and both before and after he became a Zionist—plays, short stories, novels, philosophical works, scientific (or as we would now say, pseudoscientific) tracts, and reams of cultural criticism. Beyond the problem of controlling and analyzing the sheer mass of these materials, it would be extraordinarily difficult to order their mélange of crude determinism and anarchism, anti-aestheticism and reductionist pre-Freudian conceptions of the ego into a coherent ideology. As Peter Gay has put it, "nothing would be harder than to reduce . . . Social Darwinism to a consistent line of thinking, the confusions inherent in that doctrine as a cultural rationalization are beyond repair."[9]

But on most issues, Nordau was indeed both coherent and consistent from his first published works in the late 1870s to his death in 1923. Thus, for example, from *Conventional Lies* to his last major work, *The Interpretation of History,* Nordau hewed to the same evolutionary-psychological view of religion. After he became a leading Zionist ideologue, out of deference to some sensibilities he at times refrained from publicly condemning Judaism as pathetic and infantile and even claimed to regret his choice of words in the above-cited passage on the Hebrew Bible from *Conventional Lies.* In his highly inventive autobiographical writings, he even attempted to present himself as an admirer of the Scriptures and Talmud from the time he learned them at his father's knee. But this was purely a sop to his Zionist readers: many times after he became a Zionist Nordau authorized the reprinting of his attack on the Hebrew Bible in numerous editions and countless languages, and in his other books, stories, and tracts, and indeed in his personal life, he retained a thoroughgoing rejection of and disdain for all religious beliefs and practices—Jewish, Christian, pagan—a disdain that proceeded from his basic conception of the universe and the place of human beings in the evolutionary chain.

Outdarwinizing Darwin, in *Conventional Lies* Nordau fervently and clearly explained that his view of the world

> is from the standpoint of natural science. We look upon the universe as a vast aggregation of matter, possessing the attribute of motion which reveals itself to us in various physical laws, some of which we have discovered, defined, and proved, while we are as yet on the track of the rest. . . . If we descend from the universe to our race, to man, we see in him, as a necessary consequence of our conception of material nature, merely a living being, fitting perfectly into its allotted place in the ranks of living organisms, and governed *in all things* by the common laws of the organic world. We can discover no proofs of any special favors or privileges granted to man more than those enjoyed by every other living animal or vegetable organism. We believe that the development of the human as well as all other races, was perhaps first made possible by sexual selection, and certainly promoted by it; and that the struggle for existence, using the term in its most comprehensive sense, shapes the destinies of nations as well as of the most obscure individual and is the foundation for all forms of political and social life. . . . [A]ll individuals without exception are created, live out their lives and die in accordance with the same organic laws . . . every occurrence in this world is the result of certain irresistible and immutable physical laws. . . . We acknowledge the struggle for existence as the inevitable foundation for all law and morality.[10]

In line with this overarching theory, Nordau viewed all religions as a "functional weakness," the "physical relic of the childhood of the human race." Writing four years before the publication of Nietzsche's *Genealogy of Morals* and twenty-four years before Freud's *Totem and Taboo* but fully in line with Social Darwinist premises, Nordau explained that out of unresisting servitude to primitive conceptions of causality, in the course of their evolution human beings projected onto nature and thence onto a supernatural deity their own sense of actions emanating from will. They then collated the resulting fantasy of a superhuman will with their fear—infantile but understandable—of evil and death. Out of this cauldron of illogic and fear, what we call religion was born. Necessarily, this belief in a divine will, dispensing both life and death, good and evil, controlling nature and setting human beings at the zenith of the natural world, was rendered in anthropomorphic images by the Divinity's all too human inventors. Reflecting and seeking to overcome their own feelings of fallibility, fragility, and ignorance, men invented an omniscient, omnipotent, and perfect deity whom they could worship and in whom they could find hope and salvation.

Nordau could not quite decide if such a belief in God preceded or followed the belief in the immortality of the soul. In either case, the very concept of a soul was the consequence of the combination of fear and illogic that lay at the heart of religion: human intellect's inability to conceive of absolute nonexistence, and especially of its own nonexistence. Hence, the human intellect defined itself as an everliving I, an eternal Ego, an immortal thinking and feeling essence of itself separate and separable from its physical body, and subordinate to the will of an all-powerful, all-knowing, eternally living Creator. On this primitive base, Nordau continued, human cultures throughout time elaborated vast permutations of rites, rituals, theologies, and systems of power and oppression masked as theologies of grace and liberation. These filled the basic human need for community, our innate passion for solidarity, and a natural longing for emotional and aesthetic satisfaction. Thus the church, synagogue, mosque, or ashram became not only the main but often the only vehicle and venue of art, poetry, song, and intellectual accomplishment in their societies. At the heart of the "lie of religion," Nordau thus firmly believed, lay basic human drives and desires that could now, once correctly identified and analyzed by science, be channeled away from the primitive forms of religion to modern and socially useful expressions of culture and social organization.

This evolution from primitivity to modernity and from superstition to reason was inevitable and not dependent on human consciousness or agency. In due course, according to Nordau, secular poetry will inevitably replace sermons, and the theater and concert hall will do away with churches, synagogues, and mosques. To some extent, Nordau believed, this was already happening in his time, especially in countries with advanced, western European political forms, for to him political, cultural, economic, and social advance were not only connected, they were immutably intertwined in the evolutionary chain:

> A time is coming and is perhaps near at hand, when we will see a civilization in which men will satisfy not transcendentally but rationally, their need for rest and recreation, for elevation of the mind, for emotional release; when a solidarity of the human race will be the worship of a progressive and enlightened age.[11]

The circle is then squared—a collectivist aesthetic and corporatist politics will emerge out of the superseded shards of religion and superstition:

Such is my idea of the civilization of the future. I am convinced that the day will come when even the humblest man will find his individual life merged into the fuller life of the community, and his isolated, circumscribed horizon broadened by means of festivals of poetry, music, art, thought and humanity, until it coincides with the horizon of the entire human race, thus leading him on to nobler standards of development and setting before him the grand ideal of a perfected humanity. Until this picture of the future becomes reality, however, the masses will continue to seek the ideal exaltation which they find nowhere else, in Religion.[12]

Nordau then follows this line of argument with the vitriolic denunciation of the Jewish Bible cited above, along with a denunciation of the New Testament and an all-out attack on the Papacy as the most deleterious force in human affairs. No wonder that *Conventional Lies* was placed on the Index! Not only did Nordau detest both the Old and New Testaments as childish and revolting; he saw no reason to differentiate between Judaism and Christianity, or for that matter between Judaism and Christianity and either non-European or ancient religions, except that the continued popularity of Christianity and Judaism in nineteenth-century Europe was even more of a scandal and a lie than the more understandable retention of belief in "primitive" religions in less developed parts of the world or eras of human history:

Every separate act of a religious ceremony becomes a fraud and a criminal satire when performed by a cultivated man of this Nineteenth Century. . . . The continued existence and growth of these ancient, partly prehistoric forms of worship in the midst of our modern civilization is a monstrous fact, and the position accorded to the clergyman, the European equivalent of an Indian medicine-man or African almamy, is such an insolent triumph of cowardice, hypocrisy and mental indolence over truth and courage of opinion, as would be sufficient, taken alone, to characterize our civilization as a complete fraud, and our political and social order as necessarily temporary.[13]

This was hardly the attitude of a prototypical bourgeois liberal in the 1880s! Contrary to both pro- and anti-Zionist readings of Nordau, then, it is crucial to understand that when this diatribe was first published, in 1883, Nordau did not think of himself as a Jew in any meaningful sense of the term: he was a cosmopolitan intellectual, a German writer living in Paris, who neither denied nor acknowledged his Jewish origins. In the changed atmosphere of the late 1880s and early 1890s, when he was first identified in public as a Jew, Nordau exploded in furious indignation. As a cosmopolitan intellectual, he objected to all such attempts to categorize human beings by their origins, and thus he despised all the new nationalist movements he saw developing around him. Their "false patriotism" was yet another outrageous lie of contemporary European civilization, a pernicious—indeed, degenerate—retreat from scientifically determined progress. It would be nearly a decade after the publication of *Conventional Lies* before Nordau would acknowledge his Jewishness even in private correspondence. And even after he became a Zionist he refused to entertain any link between his Zionism and Judaism as a religious faith. It was after he became not only a Zionist but a renowned leader of the Zionist movement that he married his Christian wife and allowed her to baptize their daughter, insisting that there was absolutely no reason to expect his wife or daughter to believe in a religion which he rejected.

Thus, those who attempt to read Nordau's (or Jabotinsky's) pre-Zionist writing as expressions of an unconscious though ineffable Jewish "discourse"—either from a traditional Zionist or supposedly postmodernist and critical perspective—are not only flawed historians but bad storytellers as well.

But back to Nordau in 1883: at this time, contrary to what George Mosse claimed, Nordau frontally attacked bourgeois conceptions of marriage and sexuality. His chapter on the lie of matrimony opened with the following lines:

> Man has two powerful instincts which govern his life and determine all of his actions: the instinct for self-preservation and the sexual instinct. The former is expressed in hunger and the need to eat; the latter as love. The forces which produce the phenomena of nourishment and propagation are still obscure to us, but we can watch their operation clearly. . . . Paleontology gives us sufficient data to enable us without hesitation to announce as fact the parallelism of the laws governing the life and development of the individual and the species. . . . The act of sexual union between male and female, that most sublime function of the organism and with which are connected the most powerful sensations of the nervous system, cannot take place until it has reached its full maturity. . . . In our civilization as well as in its state of primitive development, the impulse for procreation must summon society to be a witness to its gratification and place itself under its protection. . . . Marriage is the only kind of union between man and woman countenanced by our society. But what have the lies of our corrupt civilization done to marriage? It has been diminished to a business agreement that gives as much place to love as the contract between two capitalists who form a commercial partnership. The pretext for marriage is still, as ever, the preservation of the species, but this is a pathetic lie, for contemporary marriage has nothing to do with the mutual biological attraction of two sexual beings but with common material interests. . . . When a wedding is planned, everything is considered—the living-room and the kitchen, the caterers and the honeymoon; only one thing is forgotten—the bedroom, in which the future of the family,

the nation, the human race is created. . . . Any nation that develops under these circumstances must inevitably face doom.[14]

In other words, Nordau took a stridently Darwinian position on the development of sexuality in human beings, arguing not only that sexual desire is as basic in humans as the desire for food and the fear of death, but that human society and history are essentially propelled by sexual selection. Sexual selection and thus sexual desire are as fundamental to women as to men—indeed, as a physician Nordau had long been interested in the problematics of women's sexuality; his thesis for his medical degree, awarded in Paris in 1882, was on female sterilization, a practice he deplored.[15] In "primitive" societies or among the lower classes of "civilized" societies, he believed, both men and women are not especially concerned or discerning about their sexual partners' personalities, since these societies are by their nature less evolved, less differentiated than modern industrial societies. In more advanced contexts, however, the greater differentiation among humans leads irrevocably to a more evolved concept of sexual desire, which we call love:

> Love is the instinctive recognition of the fact that one being, that it must be united with a certain other being of the opposite sex, so that its good qualities may be increased, its bad neutralized and its offspring prove at least no deterioration of its type, and if possible an improvement on it.[16]

This, Nordau continued, is primarily a chemical process, comparable to the affinity of the elements—a scientifically observable and determinable proposition, though at the same time, impervious to rational explication:

> These are elementary properties inherent in matter, which we do not attempt to explain. Why does oxygen unite with potassium? Why will not nitrogen unite with platinum? Who can tell us? And why does a man love this woman and not this other? Why does a woman want this man and spurn all others? Evidently because this attraction and indifference are founded on the innermost chemical properties of the beings in question and proceed from the same sources as the organic processes of life itself.[17]

However, Nordau lamented, contemporary European society paid only lip service, at best, to the idea of love and by no means organized its fundamental social forms—marriage and family—on the basis of this scientifically based phenomenon. Contemporary marriage has nothing to do with the mutual biological attraction of two sexual beings but with common material or class interests. In the upper classes, this leads to dissolute behavior and hence to "degeneracy"—it is in large measure the cause of the decay of aristocracy everywhere in Europe. But in the middle classes, the far more common result is loveless marriage, consummated for financial rather than sexual profit: the bourgeoisie has made marriage "a business agreement that gives as much place to love as the contract between two capitalists who form a commercial partnership." The disastrous consequences of this arrangement are manifold. First, it leads to mass unhappiness, which is manifestly unhealthy, psychological unhealth being as bad to society as physical illness. Second, it leads to avoidance of marriage on the part of large numbers of men who refuse to enter into a loveless marriage, much to the detriment of the species, since they and their genes are removed from the pool of potential propagators. While bachelors are in some way admired and even treated with kindness, unmarried women, on the other hand, are scorned and forbidden from pursuing even such nonsexual pleasures vouchsafed to unmarried men as travel and dining out. Third, it leads to an unhealthy and unnatural condemnation of sexuality per se, a preposterous Puritanism masquerading as morality. The most notorious promulgator of such a stance is at once the most influential—Christianity—and the most pernicious result of Christian antisexuality is the inhumane and immoral doctrine of celibacy.

But the most common victims of all of these sexual and social prohibitions are women: since humans are not naturally monogamous, society accedes to nature by institutionalizing duplicity among men, largely closing its eyes to the infidelity of both married and unmarried men while condemning women in loveless marriages to sexual dissatisfaction, and women outside of marriage to celibacy. The movement for the emancipation of women is not a solution to this problem, since it preaches the unscientific proposition of the equality of the sexes and would thus set men and women on an ostensibly equal plane, which inevitably would turn into a perpetual battlefield in which women would necessarily lose, given their biologically based physical inferiority. Moreover, as long as society is organized according to the "lie of matrimony," urging young women not to marry is to condemn them to a life not only of unhappiness but of poverty as well.

The solution, according to Nordau, is three-fold. First, recognize the scientifically necessary and natural universality of sexual desire in both men and women. Second, recognize that men are the natural breadwinners and women the natural preservers and defenders of future generations. Third, on this basis provide all women with free public education and guarantee them lifetime economic support, either in their parents' home or their own: "Society should look upon it as a disgrace if any woman, young or old, beautiful or ugly, should feel the pangs of want in any civilized community."[18] This plan would in one stroke eliminate the need for loveless marriages and for prostitution, proclaimed Nordau! The ideal, he concluded, is "[w]hen material considerations enter no longer into the contracting of a marriage, when woman is free to choose and is not compelled to sell herself, when man is obliged to compete for woman's favor with his personality and not with his social position and property; then the institution of matrimony will become a truth instead of the lie it now is."[19]

However preposterous or admirable, misogynistic or enlightened Nordau's view, it can hardly be considered a "traditional" nineteenth-century bourgeois or liberal stance on sex, women, and marriage. But Nordau hewed to this stance for decades, including in his play *The Right to Love*, published first in 1893, the same year as the publication of his most famous work, *Degeneration*. It is in some ways unfortunate that Nordau did not write more plays, since, unlike his favorite genres, the feuilleton and the novel, the drama was of a perfect length and nature for so didactic and yet imaginative a writer to manipulate successfully: in the shorter literary forms, Nordau was often either too cute or too pedantic, more committed to *épater les bourgeois* than to creating works of art. His novels, like most of his long philosophical and critical treatises, are horribly cumbersome, repetitive, and fundamentally unreadable today. But in his plays, Nordau was able to shine through as a gifted conversationalist and hence a rather good stylist. While his plots are either obvious or preposterous, and the dramatic development weak and labored, his characters come alive even on the written page. It is thus not surprising that, unlike Herzl, Nordau had some success with several of his plays on the German and Austrian stage, and in translation elsewhere in Europe and the United States.

There is no methodological danger in positing clear ideological stances from Nordau's plays. His views of the theater, often expressed, were both romantic and highly critical of contemporary fashion. He wanted theater once more to become, as it was in ancient Greece, the place of communal meeting and worship. But he thundered as early as 1883 that theater in his time was outrageous, with "its indecent plots, its street-song melodies, its idiotic laughter and its semi-nudity."[20] For Nordau, as for other synthesizers of radical and reactionary thought—one thinks invariably of Lenin—anti-aestheticism is masked as scientifically based progressivism, and art is conceived as a spectacle subordinate to the collectivity. In Nordau's ideal theater,

> we will see in beautiful corporate forms the passions struggling with the will, and personal greed conquered by the capability for self-denial, and where, with every word and action, like a grand accompaniment, we will hear a continual reference to the collective existence and development of the human race.[21]

The Right to Love followed this prescription—or so at least it appeared to its author. George Mosse is correct that this play was self-consciously Nordau's response to Ibsen's *Doll House*. For Nordau, the widespread admiration of Nora's abandonment of her husband and children in the name of love was regressive, not progressive, an act of selfishness rather than liberation. Nora was indeed unjustly condemned to a loveless marriage on the basis of hypocritical bourgeois norms, Nordau explained, but her solution was just as bad as the disease: egotistical satisfaction of one's desires is no way to combat hypocrisy. Moreover, Nordau insisted repeatedly and vocally, Ibsen's promotion of egocentrism was based not on a rejection of repressive Victorian mores, but unconsciously on his acceptance of Christianity, particularly the doctrines of original sin and the saving act of Christ, and thus on the most pernicious and antisensual forms of Christian mysticism. Hence, Ibsen—like Nietzsche, Wagner, Zola, Tolstoy, Whitman, Verlaine, and most other modernist authors of the fin de siècle—was diagnosed and decried as a "degenerate" by Nordau, at once victim and purveyor of the illness of psychological and moral degeneracy that was destroying European society.

This is not the place to analyze further Nordau's vulgar attack on fin-de-siècle culture, its crude Lombrosian psychology intermingled with equally reductionist positivist and Social Darwinist cultural criticism. Here it is only crucial to understand (*contra* Mosse et al.) that Nordau's attack on Ibsen and Nora was premised on his antipathy to what he termed the "egocentrism" of contemporary bourgeois society, that is, the selfish individualism of men or women putting their own needs and desires above those of society at large. Thus, the true villain of *The Right to Love* was not the haute-bourgeois wife, Bertha, who attempted to abandon her boring husband, the merchant Joseph Wahrmund, but rather her seducer, the philandering bachelor Otto Bardenholm. Otto was an amoral bureaucrat who lived off the largesse of his prey, the

unsatisfied wives of the upper middle class; he was thus the personification of all the vices of modernity. Poor Bertha thought that after she
left her husband, her lover Otto would embrace her in gleeful rapture,
marry her, and adopt her children. In the event, of course, he was hor-
rified at the prospect of her being free and had no interest in marrying
her or anyone else for that matter, not to speak of raising somebody
else's children. Obviously encouraging the audience to ponder what really would happen to Nora *after* she slammed that famous door, Nordau
led Bertha and also Joseph to their ultimate tragic denouement: a life
together without either love or sex, a farcical pantomime of a happily
married couple. Only they would know that at the core of their life
henceforth there would be only misery and betrayal, hate and disgust.
As for so many bourgeois couples who married for convenience and
comfort rather than out of physical attraction and true love, there was
no other way this drama could enfold.

Such a loveless bourgeois marriage, such a conventional bourgeois
life was not for Max Nordau—not in theory and not in practice. To
understand his transition from cosmopolitan antibourgeois Social Darwinist to Zionist, in chapter 3 we delve into a fascinating and previously
unstudied chapter of Nordau's life, his romance with an antisemitic Russian noblewoman at the very same time that he was becoming a Zionist.
But before doing so, it is crucial to skip ahead a quarter of a century
from the publication of *Conventional Lies* to 1909, when Nordau's last
major book, *Der Sinn der Geschichte,* was first published in Berlin. (The
first English edition, titled *The Interpretation of History,* appeared in
New York in 1910.)[22] Although Nordau was at this time a very influential Zionist leader and ideologue, Zionism is not mentioned even once
in *The Interpretation of History,* and it would be impossible for any
reader who did not know of its author's Zionism even to guess that
Nordau could be sympathetic to that movement. On most fronts, Nordau merely repeated the same basic views he had enunciated in the *Conventional Lies:* human vanity apart, the human species is no more unique
or imbued with innate purpose or morality than flies or mosses. The law
of history is not teleology, but causality—a highly complex causality
that brings to bear upon every man, at every moment of his life, the
whole past and present of the human species. Central to this past, and
to the future, is the struggle for existence. Human history is thus merely
the record of humans' historic attempts to master nature by means of
the struggle for existence; to speak of a purpose of human life or a goal
in the universe is to engage in errant, irrational nonsense. The only prog-

ress that has been achieved or that can be achieved is technological progress, that is, scientific mastery over the natural environment. Terms and
concepts such as "moral progress" and innate "good and evil" are just
twaddle, whether uttered by Plato or Schegel. Religion is but a primitive
"epiphenomenon," an unscientific self-delusion used to mask men's fear
of death and their consequent unfortunate need to subordinate themselves before their sense of powerlessness by means of "parasitism."

What is new in Nordau's *Interpretation of History* is not this crude
Social Darwinism, but an extended attack on the idea of nationalism,
from its origins in the thought of Herder to its latest exponents, the
theorists of *Völkerpsychologie* (the psychology of nations). The latter
were often cited by contemporary Zionists, including Vladimir Jabotinsky, but Nordau unilaterally rejects their claims as unscientific and hence
fallacious:

> the notion of a special national individuality and physiognomy is entirely in
> the air, one of the facile generalizations that lie at the root of so many errors
> and prejudices. . . . The idea of a "collective organism is a mystical delu-
> sion"—there is no such thing as an "organic nation" or an "organic state"—
> the real thing is the psychology of the individual. . . . Man is born with cer-
> tain simple impulses, and grows completely into the external conditions
> around him. He therefore appears to display national characteristics so long
> as he bears the single impress of a certain set of conditions—so long, that is,
> as he remains at a stage of culture removed from the influence of active
> intercourse. . . . When complete intercommunication is established through-
> out all countries and races, and differences removed and universal similarity
> effected by the mutual interpenetration of civilizing forces, the conceptions
> of "nation," "race" and their psychology will cease to have semblance of
> significance.[23]

Nor is language the source of innate national divides, as the nationalists claim. Slavic languages are spoken "natively" by non-Slavs, Germanic languages by those without roots in Germanic tribes. Language,
then, is not essentially conditioned by the peculiar spirit of the group
that created it, and hence "language is no proof of the existence of
national character." The differences between what we call nations is
thus merely superficial and "can be fully accounted for by the undeniable
characteristics of individual psychology," claims Nordau.

> Some peoples write from left to right, others from above downwards, others,
> again, from right to left; some burn their dead, others bury them, the position,
> again, varying between lying and squatting. . . . some house under one roof
> with their animals, others apart from them; some dwell in straggling villages,
> others build in a circle. The reason is that they have always done so, and not

otherwise, and see no reason for troubling to change their habits and discover new ones.[24]

States, too, are not "organic" developments of national wills, either in the sense used by Herderians or Hegelians of any stripe, or as a result of Rousseauian or Socialist social contract theories: "The foundation of the State was neither a contract nor a recognition of the value of rational cooperation: it was organized parasitism, the exploitation of the weak many by a ruler."[25] This is not to say, as anarchists do, that the state is an immoral form of political organization, for what is called morality is itself a mystification of power relations based on the struggle for existence between the strong and the weak, continues Nordau.

> The famous saying "My country, right or wrong" recognizes this with cynical frankness. . . . the supreme control may commit all the enormities in the shape of massacres, robbery, fraud that mark every invasion. . . . yet, because all of this is done in the soul-stirring name of country, it is held to be the duty of every subject, even by the abuse of the honorable idea of "sacred duty," to acclaim these base actions, to support that power that performs them through thick and thin, even to be proud of it. Such is the morality of the "organic moral personality" which the State is supposed to represent.[26]

Thus, the old taxonomy of states and constitutions, from Plato and Aristotle to the present, is sheer nonsense: "The difference between the despot of the East and the Western community, with its constitutions, codes of law, legal procedure and questions of appurtenances, is only a difference of form." The despot takes what he wants from his subject by means of naked force, the "legal State" by something called "law," which is the same thing. When Louis XIV said "L'état c'est moi," he expressed the truth with brutal brevity, as did Friedrich Engels in his definition of the state as "exclusively the State of the governing class, the machine whose essential purpose is to keep down the oppressed and the exploited."[27] Where Engels was wrong was in his condemnation of this fact of life and the struggle for existence, on the basis of his own mystical delusions about human nature and the future of humanity. In the end, only knowledge gleaned from a truly scientific study of life and nature will triumph over poverty, sickness, and the self-obliterating and parasitical delusions of religion, asserts Nordau.

> Knowledge, as it widens and deepens, will reduce almost to a vanishing point the evils that men impose on one another—evils which form the most horrible of their sufferings. The noble pleasure of art and science will become more general and more intense as the intellect and the nervous system become capable of more subtle enjoyment. Acute joy will be provided by the organic

impulses and kinestheses of youth, joy, love, health and the sense of vigor, which must certainly be richer and more robust when man is free from care, and lives in the lap of luxury, than when he was always restless and often starving. The beauty of the future will be different from that of the present—more natural, more lofty, more harmonious; and it certainly will not feel privation in the want of the Sadic alloy of poverty and sorrow, sin and cruelty.[28]

In the present, however, Nordau counsels each individual and each group of individuals not to succumb to mystifications, either about the nation or the state or the downtrodden masses or the supernatural, but instead to strive to understand the brutal realities of human life and to act on the basis of a rational calculus of one's own place in the chain of the cosmic struggle for self-preservation.

As we shall now see, this restatement of individualistic Social Darwinism was neither the cause nor the effect of Nordau's turn to Zionism between the writing of *Conventional Lies* and *The Interpretation of History*. Even as a Zionist, Nordau could not fully accept the regnant theories of nationalism—his Jewish nationalism, one must conclude, was tactical rather than ontological, a concession to the unfortunate realities of life rather than a rejection of universalism in favor of an "organic" conception of national divides. Thus, the link between his Zionism and his general weltanschauung was neither "organic" nor "logical," neither internally contradictory nor inevitable, but the result of a series of events and circumstances that we can trace most clearly in a previously unknown and untapped source—Nordau's correspondence with a bizarre and fascinating woman, the antisemitic and reactionary Russian Olga Novikova.

CHAPTER THREE

Nordau and Novikova

*Romance with an Antisemite
and the Road to Zionism*

In 1895, two years after the first appearance of Nordau's play *The Right to Love* in German, an English translation was published in New York.[1] Few readers of this translation noted that it was dedicated to "Her Excellency Madam Olga Von Novikoff, Born Von Kireeff," and that this dedication was followed by an elaborate paean to Madame von Novikoff. Indeed, so unknown was the dedicatee to Nordau's American publisher that no one at the New York publishing house marked a glaring typographical error on the first page of the book: "In Place of a Preface—to Her Excellency Madam von Nordau of Moscow." There was at this time no "Madame von Nordau" anywhere in the world, much less in the realm of the tsars. But there was indeed a "Madame von Novikoff"—an obscure but colorful and fascinating figure who played a minor but well-documented role in British and Russian politics in the fin de siècle, and a major, but as yet undisclosed, role in the life and thought of Max Nordau.

Olga Alexeevna Novikova, née Kireeva, was born in 1840 to a Russian noble family of high rank and political influence.[2] Her father, Alexei Kireev, was a Russian military commander who played an important role in the suppression of the Polish Uprising of 1830 and later was intimate with many leaders of the Slavophile movement. One of her brothers, Nicholas, carried the family tradition into battle by joining the Serbian rebel forces in 1876, was killed in action, and became a celebrated martyr to the Pan-Slavic cause. Another brother, Alexander, followed his father into the army, rose to the rank of general, and then became rather well known for his writing espousing Slavophilism, Pan-Slavism, and the Old Catholic movement.[3]

In 1860, Olga Kireeva married Ivan Novikov, the scion of an even more prominent aristocratic family—his mother was Princess Dolgo-rukii, and his brother served as Russian ambassador to Vienna and Con-stantinople. In addition to his own career as a general in the Russian army, Ivan Novikov was an amateur classicist, and after retiring from military service pursued his academic interests, in time becoming curator of St. Petersburg University. He and Olga Alexeevna had one child, Alexander, born in 1861.

In the mid-1860s, Olga Novikova became an intimate of one of the most famous salons of St. Petersburg, the reactionary circle surrounding Grand Duchess Elena, widow of the youngest brother of Tsar Nicholas I. In this salon, Novikova drew close to Count Keyserling, the noted rector of Dorpat University, and to Constantine Pobedonostev, the tutor to Crown Prince Alexander and later Ober-Procurator of the Russian Holy Synod. But her closest ideological and personal ties were with her father's friends, leaders of the Slavophile movement such as Iurii Sa-marin and Alexei Khomiakov. To promote their ideas—the idealization of pre-Petrine Russia, the Slavic soul, Russian Orthodoxy, as well as their rather peculiar Anglophilia and hence interest in the Old Catholic movement—in 1868 Novikova established her own salon, held not in St. Petersburg or Moscow, but in London—usually at Claridge's Hotel, where Olga Novikova repaired for several months each autumn after a tour of Continental spas and resorts. For more than thirty years, she gathered around herself at Claridge's and other posh hotels a motley crew of mostly elderly British politicians, clergymen, and publicists, ranging from Prime Minister William Gladstone to less famous but still well-known British figures such as Alexander Kinglake, J. A. Froude, and W. T. Stead. Particularly after the death of her brother Nicholas in 1876, the bulk of Novikova's activity was dedicated to the ideals of Pan-Slavism, to the ancillary cause of the promotion of the union of the non-Roman churches under the guise of the Old Catholic movement, and most especially to the attempt at forging an Anglo-Russian alliance to oppose the Ottoman and Austrian domination of the Balkans.

To promote these goals, Novikova began to publish books and news-paper articles, establishing her reputation as an active and prominent propagandist for the Russian autocracy.[4] Her alliance with Gladstone was the greatest, and most controversial, accomplishment of her career,

giving rise to her semi-affectionate sobriquet, "the M.P. for Russia."
Particularly irksome to her antagonists was her tendency to impute opposition to her (and Gladstone's) views to the religious and racial origins
of the opposing camp; thus, the Habsburg Empire's Balkan policies were
condemned as extensions of the desires of the heretic Papist Holy See,
and Tory support for the Turks was explained by Benjamin Disraeli's
"Semitic" origins.

Such views were not, to be sure, unique to Novikova, but it is nonetheless clear and noteworthy that antisemitism (as well as anti-
Catholicism) was an essential part of her worldview. From the start of
her public career in England, she frequently and forthrightly broadcast
her anti-Jewish opinions, hoping to dissuade the British reading public
from its sympathy for the downtrodden Jews of Russia. The Jews, she
often explained, were hateful "locusts" who were commanded by their
religion to detest Christians and thus took every opportunity to attack
Christianity and Christian interests around the world. Novikova argued
that the alleged sufferings of the Jews in Russia were caused by their
own religious intolerance, by their consequent economic exploitation of
the Slavic peasantry, and by their prominence in the revolutionary movement, which was an embodiment of the anti-Christ.

Blatant antisemitism was of course typical of Novikova's class and
background and did not prevent her from establishing cordial (and even
intimate) social relations with a handful of prominent Jews such as the
novelist Berthold Auerbach. But from the late 1870s on, the sharpness
of her anti-Jewish invective increased, at times reaching quite surprising
proportions. Her first book, *Is Russia Wrong?*, published in 1877, included a preface by her admirer James Anthony Froude that vouched
for and cited three of the best-known antisemites of the age, Wilhelm
Marr, Adolf Stoecker, and Heinreich von Treitschke. Froude quoted
with approval the claim in Treitschke's *A Word About Our Jewry* that
"up into the very highest circles of culture, amongst men who are as far
removed as possible from every thought of ecclesiastical intolerance or
national pride, one hears it said with unparalleled unanimity, 'The Jews
are our misfortune. There has always been a gulf between the Western
and the Semitic character.' "[5]

After the ascension to the throne of Alexander III in 1881 and the
eruption of pogroms against the Jews of Russia, Novikova became an
ever more combative presence in the British press. Her articles defended
the Russian government against charges of mistreatment of the Jews,
and she translated into English and promulgated the antisemitic senti-

ments of reactionary defenders of the Russian autocracy, including those of her mentor Pobedonostev, with whom she kept in touch.

Due in part to her publications but even more to her continued lobbying on behalf of an Anglo-Russian entente, through the mid- and late 1880s and early 1890s Novikova was often publicly attacked as an agent of the Russian regime and possibly even a spy, though in fact she often came into conflict with the official, St. Petersburg–based Russian diplomatic corps, who both resented her intrusions and differed with her aggressively Muscovite, Pan-Slavic politics. But her connections with Gladstone and other prominent figures of British and Russian public life protected her, at least until the mid-1890s, when Gladstone broke with her over Russia's treatment of the Armenians, which she had defended wholeheartedly. Even without the prime minister's patronage, she continued her salon and her influence-peddling until the outbreak of the Russo-Japanese War in 1904. By 1915 she seems to have settled permanently in London, where she remained after the Russian Revolution, penniless and without influence. She died alone and in obscurity in London in 1925.

Sometime in the summer of 1886, during the height of her influence and fame, Olga Novikova wrote an admiring letter to Max Nordau, then well known for his *Conventional Lies of Our Civilization*. Though this letter has not been preserved, Nordau's response can be found in Novikova's archives, now housed at the Kenneth Spencer Library at Kansas University—along with an additional 301 letters written in French by Nordau to Novikova and dating from August 1886 to February 1902.[6] These remarkably frank letters have never before been read by any scholar; indeed, their existence has not been known to any chronicler of Nordau's life and work nor, it seems, to the keepers of his own archives.

Yet the letters are crucial to an understanding of Nordau's thought, since they detail in a graphic and candid manner not only the nature and extent of the Nordau-Novikova relationship, but, far more important, Nordau's intellectual, ideological, and emotional development in this period, including his conversion to Zionism and the meaning of his newfound Jewish nationalism.

Nordau's first letter to Novikova, penned on August 22, 1886, begins with his delight at receiving her epistle: "Rarely has a letter given me as much satisfaction as yours. It is truly encouraging to find oneself in accord with one of the most distinguished spirits of the age, and this is consoling in the face of persecution, calumnies, and infamy."[7] He tells

Novikova that he has long known of her and admired her, particularly for her marvelous coup in making "that old idiot Gladstone into your slave." But what has truly impressed him is her independence of spirit, and the "wild and savage energy" with which she defends her political convictions against hostile opponents—"the vigor of your hatred of the forms of a civilization that nonetheless has made you a patrician and given you such enviable privileges. You are an impulsive and original spirit, in no sense a copy. Isn't this, not to be banal, the highest degree of development to which an individual can aspire?"[8]

Nordau found admirable not only her spunk and defiance of bourgeois propriety but her ideas as well, especially her attacks on the growing power of the mass press to sway governmental policy, which she decried as "government by the press." But, Nordau advised her,

> You must be consistent. Whoever says: government by the press is saying: government by the masses, themselves governed by men who speculate on their worst instincts and prejudices. But then, one must not stop with the press; the same vices apply to parliamentarism and especially to universal suffrage.[9]

It does not seem that Nordau, the ardent antimonarchist whose *Conventional Lies* was banned in Austria and Russia due to its "radical" views, found any irony in preaching against parliamentarism and the universal suffrage to a self-declared admirer of the Russian autocracy. The problem of government by public opinion, Nordau continued, as well as the attendant issue of the tyranny of the majority, has long occupied him, and if Madame Novikova reads German, she ought to read his recently published book, *Paradoxes*, which treats these issues extensively. Meanwhile, he would love to meet her if she passes through France, since he rarely gets to London due to the ties that keep him at home.

From the start of their relationship, then, we see Nordau attracted to Novikova by her combination of personal charm, aristocratic hauteur, and antibourgeois politics. Though not endorsing her frankly reactionary views, neither was he troubled by them, seeing in her a potential disciple and ally in the cause of opposing all that was vile and ugly in contemporary society. No mention was yet made of her well-known views on Russia or religion, not to speak of the Jews. These were totally incidental, if not irrelevant, to Nordau's ideological concerns and quasi-philosophical interests.

In addition, it is obvious from the start that Nordau's interest in Novikova was more than ideational: wafting discernibly over his florid French prose is the scent of the flirt, the words of a "ladies' man" prospecting a fresh conquest. This approach has become far more overt in his next letter, written a fortnight later, after Novikova has sent him both a portrait of herself and news of an accident in which she was not hurt, but which delayed her response to his first letter. "You caused me great anxiety," he confesses; this is what happens when one enlarges the circle of "pensioners of the heart." But the only way to avoid such suffering and pain and to achieve pure tranquillity and happiness is not to love anyone; this lesson he has known for a long time, but cannot put into practice.[10]

Her portrait, he continues, has given him great pleasure. It shows a face of great character, rare in a woman, a scornful mouth evident of a silent, hidden melancholy, and eyes that droop slightly in the corners, revealing a strong and impassioned, indeed passionate, woman who has known suffering and pain, but who is most of all a "thinking woman." And although it is in the worst taste to criticize a woman's toilette, he cannot refrain from complaining about her appearance in the photograph: "How can you, a Russian patrician woman, put on your elite head that horrible hat, criminal in its banality . . . considered the height of fashion by all the daughters of tradesmen—Oh Madame!"[11] On his own copy of her portrait he has corrected this offense by pasting a piece of black taffeta over the hat, so as not to disturb his admiring gaze. He is sending her a likeness of himself and hopes that she will not be disturbed by his white hair and beard, which are a function not of his age but of his heredity, as he turned totally gray at the age of eighteen.

He thanks her, as well, for the delightful article she wrote on the Bulgarian crisis, but he will not hide from her that he disagrees with her point of view, her belief that Russia's goal in support of Bulgaria is the latter's independence, as opposed to Russia's desire to swallow up Bulgaria and all the other Slavic lands. But the contents of the article and their political disagreements are beside the point; "the verve and the brutality" of her style charmed him, as did the fact that it will jolt the English. Most important, he concludes, "you are an exceptional woman, and I congratulate myself on having the right to address you."[12]

Novikova was clearly not offended by her new admirer's criticism of her attire, nor by his cynical views on Russian foreign policy. On the contrary, she seems to have reveled in her new conquest and been delighted by his attention. She mockingly reproached him for his impertinence and sent him a different photo along with a copy of a new piece calling for an Anglo-Russian alliance that she had just written for the *Pall-Mall Gazette.*

Nordau responded with an even more frontal and flirtatious letter. He has been inspired by her new article, but once more by its verve and spirit rather than its content: "Your argument is full of zest, lacking in logic, all offense, no defense. In a word: a woman, from the first letter to the last."[13] Her idea of an Anglo-Russian alliance is pleasant, the marriage of a whale and an elephant, but unworkable; the English, despite their cold exteriors, will never ally themselves with an emperor whom the "penny dreadfuls" constantly denounce as a despot and tyrant. But yet again, what is important is not these issues of haute-politique but the spirit and vivacity of her prose: "Vive la femme qui sait bien haïr. Elle sait bien aimer aussi."[14]

Novikova apparently responded in kind to this line of attack and conquest, and as 1886 ended and 1887 began, their exchanges became more and more frequent and intimate, his letters following her from London to St. Petersburg to Marienbad and back. Each scolded the other for a delay of more than a few days in responding. He continued to flatter her fiery pen and her fiery disposition while disagreeing with and discounting her political views. How can a woman of her taste, charm, and intelligence admire the scoundrels she does, such as Mikhail Skobeleff, about whom she has written an entire book? But her errors in judgment are caused by her two essential attributes that he most admires, her passionate feminine nature and her blind devotion to her homeland:

> You are cruel, cruel, not wanting me to see you to avoid seeing your faults. Come on—that is pure and simple coquetry. I do not know if you have any faults, but hope that you do, there's nothing more annoying and more unbearable than perfection. All you risk in letting me come to know your faults is that I shall be inspired even more by you than I already am.
>
> How I love your ardent patriotism, since, Madame, this is my greatest prejudice and my most dangerous fault: I love it when one is true to one's country, that is, to one's nation, and in this realm I admit to having the same fanaticism.[15]

What he meant by this he amplified in a letter written on May 18, 1887, in which he responded to her inquiry about his origins: "You ask me in one of your last letters what nationality I am. If I say I am sentimental, you will understand that I am a German. In truth, I was born to German parents in Budapest, Hungary."[16] Though this was not quite "the truth," he still saw no need to enter into the precise details of his birth and nationality, even as he continued to admit Novikova into his private life. He explains that his long delay in responding to her letter was caused by a profound family crisis: he has always lived with and supported his mother and younger sister, but the latter has long suffered from a nervous disorder that finally required moving her out of their home. This was so painful an ordeal that for weeks he could not pick up a pen. He hesitates to write about this, knowing how vulgar it is to confide such personal matters to anyone but an intimate friend, but now he feels that they are indeed intimates, and it is senseless to continue a purely formal epistolary relationship. They must begin to share their joys and pain, their satisfactions and disappointments, their lives. She made a grave error not stopping in Paris, or somewhere close by like Brussels on her return to Russia, since they must meet in person, and soon: "We must see one another, we must speak to one another. We will either prove disillusioned and everything will be over, cleanly, finally, if not without regret, or we will quickly become the best of friends. . . . Will you meet me on the way back from St. Petersburg?"[17]

Novikova, however, was not quite ready to do this, instead dispatching from St. Petersburg a letter that Nordau described as "almost branding me in disgrace." She shifted the subject to an impersonal discussion of the meaning of life and of human nature. She had written that "every human being forms a world apart" but, Nordau responded, this was errant nonsense, reeking of theology and of "la philosophie idéalistique-lunatique," rather than science. Certainly there are differences among individuals, but these are negligible compared to their similarities. Hence individualism is a dream, "a beautiful, proud dream, but not a reality":

> The same laws of thought and of sentiment rule all of humanity, including every living being. That which we believe to be purely personal and original is deplorably banal; we believe ourselves to feel and to act as a result of our internal wills but in reality we are but puppets, manipulated by the same general mechanism that we cannot see, but which controls everyone in the same way in our poor part of the universe. We say "I" with pride. We are wrong. Let us be more humble. We ought to say "we," that is, we ought to recognize that we are all fundamentally identical, distinguished from each other by minor particularities, purely external, unessential, completely negligible. The theory of individualism, this monstrous error, has led to tragic consequences for the world, justifying all sorts of injustice, all sorts of egoism. Its demolition will be the first step toward a more just and more moral order of things.[18]

This was, in fact, a rather insouciant précis of Nordau's current credo as articulated in his many writings of the mid- and late 1880s. To

Novikova he emphasized not his antimonarchism and atheism, but his opposition to bourgeois individualism coupled with an admiration for the pride and honor of the aristocracy; thus, he recommended to her a novel written by his friend Robert Halt, *Les infortunes d'un gentil-homme,* which documented the horrible history of France since the Revolution, the displacement of the aristocracy by the forces of "the monopolizing bourgeoisie."[19]

At the same time, Nordau recognized, at least in part, the pretentiousness, if not the absurdity, of his position, and perhaps even the danger of finding himself in the camp of the reactionary opponents of bourgeois society and politics. Novikova had recently expended much time and energy in helping the ailing Slavophile Mikhail Katkov and then mourning his death. Nordau praised her actions as the wonderful outpouring of deep friendship, though Katkov's death, he commented rather harshly, was "no loss to humanity."[20] He thanked her for her delightful recommendation that he make the acquaintance of Queen Olga: "I would undoubtedly have the greatest pleasure in knowing this excellent majesty, but since she doesn't frequent my *brasserie,* I'm afraid that we'll have trouble meeting."[21]

For her part, Novikova engaged in the same sort of flirtatious banter in her ever more frequent notes and cards to him. She wrote to him from Marienbad in late July 1887: "Why did I read your terrible Paradoxes? It does not please me, in my capacity as a woman. . . . No, it's even more horrible than the novels of Zola, which I detest platonically, not having ever read them."[22]

The platonic nature of their relationship continued to bother Nordau, who continued to express his profound desire for a personal meeting. There was a chance they could meet in the late summer, when he was on vacation in Ostende and she was on her way back to London for the fall season. But he was diverted to Brussels to tend to a patient and then was consumed all fall with a trial he had initiated in Leipzig over the pirating of his books in Germany—a constant source of frustration and legal maneuvering that would occupy him for several years to come, ultimately ending in failure and in great financial loss. Throughout the next several months, while Novikova was back in London for the autumn season, he wrote her letter after letter bemoaning his dual frustrations: his inability to obtain justice in Germany, due to the "tartufferie" that masquerades as a legal system, and his consequent inability to leave the Continent to come face to face with her, so close but yet so unattainable. It is impossible to describe all his feelings in a letter, he confided: there are things that can only be expressed "face to face, eyes in eyes, hands in hand. . . . When shall we meet? *A quand, á quand?*"[23]

Even after the Leipzig trial ended, Nordau tried to get to London to see her. First, he hoped to be there for Christmas but then was unable to leave Paris due to his many obligations and responsibilities. Indicating his frustration, he amended the salutation "à vos pieds" that he had used from the start of the correspondence; now he signed off "still at your feet, but alas! only in theory."[24] On Christmas Day 1887 he finally exploded in frustration at her refusal to come to see him in Paris, rather than vice versa: what are the "chains that bind you," he demanded to know, what do her "semi-transparent" allusions to her private life refer to, "you must tell me about your life!"[25] For the next several months, he implored her not to leave for St. Petersburg without first coming to Paris, since he simply could not get away. This is absurd, he lamented, "is Europe so large that we can never meet?"[26] But by the spring of 1888 Novikova had returned to Russia, as was her custom every year, without stopping in Paris on the way home.

Still, they kept in close touch, writing constantly and with great candor. After she described to him her latest appearance at the tsar's court, he could barely contain himself: "How you must laugh when you find yourself in the midst of all these coiffed dogs and bejeweled monkeys! I'd give up several days of my poor sterile life to see you carrying out the rules of court etiquette!"[27] When she came down with a case of laryngitis, he dispatched a prescription on his medical stationery, followed it up with detailed instructions to her on how to use the treatment, and fantasized that he'd take the train to St. Petersburg, have himself announced at her door, hand over the prescription, talk briefly, and then leave.[28] On her part, she appears to have become incensed by a parenthetical reference in one of his letters to another woman. "Don't worry," Nordau calmed her down, "she is but a friend—do you think I'd be so vulgar as to mention by name a woman who is more than just a friend?"

After she returned to Marienbad en route to London, the tension mounted—indeed, one of his letters to her seems to have been so forthright that later she (or someone else) took a scissors to its most sensitive passages. But the die was cast. To meet in Marienbad would require too much deception on her part, so a rendezvous was arranged for August:

> What pleasure—you will arrive in Boulogne the 18th or 19th of August. I'll meet you at the train. . . . You'll come to the spot where I will have established my summer residence, either at Portel or Ornival, your room will be

ready . . . where I'll be able to squeeze your hands, after having kissed them respectfully.

I will stay with you for as long as it takes for a very, very thorough consultation, and then I'll leave. . . .

My entire day will be at your disposal, and the night as well, until I fall to my feet with exhaustion and am forced to ask your permission to retire.[29]

He arrived at the Grand Hotel at Ornival in early August; she joined him there on August 18.

By the beginning of September, he had returned to Paris, and she to London, but his life had changed. On September 3 he sent her a quick letter, surprising in its coldness and matter-of-factness. The next day, he explained:

My great, dear friend,

This time, I am alone, completely alone, and I must begin by explaining yesterday's truly humiliating contretemps. It was seven o'clock when I came back home to my mother, who was waiting at the door for me, and cried with joy while embracing me. I found a mountain of business letters, news-papers, cards. After I read everything, dined quickly, and answered dozens of my mother's questions, it was 10 p.m. I told myself that if I were to write to you immediately, the letter would not really be worth anything, so I decided to wait for the next day, and went to sleep thinking of you. I finally fell asleep, and slept for the first time in four weeks [that is, since arranging her visit].

Yesterday morning, I was another man. If only you were there to confirm it! I then ran around, shopped, took care of everything I had neglected for four weeks.

At 4 o'clock, I went home. This time, in order to write to you. The letter was addressed, just as the doorbell rang. Enter the Jacobsens. Who stayed until the very moment that I had to leave for the Gard du Nord to wait for my sister, who was arriving from London. My dilemma: to write to you as I promised, under the gaze of another's indiscreet curiosity, with the envelope already addressed . . . how could I write to you what others should not read? Bravely (the epithet will make you smile, *méchante*) I decided to write to you what I did, trying to put in as many nuances as possible, incomprehensible to a coarse and narrow spirit, but understandable to that delicate intellect that I call Olga.[30]

He then poured out his heart:

You have enriched my life in an unforgettable, rich, tender, unique way. I now know you a bit, guess at the rest, love you very much. I want not to recall that you are a woman, but as a woman, you stir me. I remember every word, every conversation without cease, your charming Muscovite accent with the piquant archaisms of your Molière-like French. Your mouth, the corners of your eyes—I can't sort the reality from the dream, I wonder whether I still possess my thoughts, my intonations. Madame Jacobsen asked me yesterday whether I've ever met so interesting a woman as you. Well—certainly not! I've long searched for and compared, and now know that I've never met another woman like you. You are absolutely incomparable, incomparable, and will remain so. From now on, I repeat, I'll be wise and measured. Pardon me today. I kiss your expressive hand a thousand times. To you, my dear friend, now and forever, from the one you have never called anything but Nordau.[31]

Throughout the months that followed, Nordau continued to write such love letters to Novikova, repeating in language frank and candid (though, at her request, rarely sexually explicit by late twentieth-century standards) his undying love and passion for her, the jealousy that raged through him when he thought of her other men—especially men who bed women without any emotional entanglement, only to satisfy their carnal desires. In Nordau's mind, their relationship was of a different order precisely because it combined sexual, emotional, and intellectual intimacy and thus rose above the pathetic and immoral sham either of bourgeois monogamy or of upper-class promiscuity. Thus, Nordau could at one and the same time pledge his love for Novikova with all his soul and might, yearn to be reunited with her, and describe in graphic detail a complicated mess he got himself into with another married woman, who fell in love with him and wanted to leave her husband and children to be with him—an outcome he rejected, since he really did not love her as she could not compare to his beloved Olga. "Do not compare yourself to . . . that poor woman," he wrote to Novikova; "you are of an elite nature, you are a radiant creature who gives the man chosen by you the right to think himself grand."[32]

Quite obviously, this was the real-life story behind the fictional plot of *The Right to Love* itself—hence complicating in a fascinating manner Nordau's reason for dedicating this play to Novikova in the first place.

By this time, then, Nordau and Novikova had established a clearly defined pattern to their romance: regular letter-writing punctuated by an occasional encounter either in Paris or at a summer resort. But what is most fascinating and important to the student of Nordau about this relationship is that it reveals hitherto unknown, and crucial, evidence about the deepest emotional—and later ideological—aspects of Nordau's life.

Nordau's love for Novikova clearly was intense, and it provided a crucial emotional tonic for an otherwise rather desolate and lonely man. On October 5, 1888, he wrote to Novikova:

> What details would you like me to give you about myself? If I interest myself so little, how can I imagine others to be interested in me? Everything is gray, banal, inexpressive about me. A cold or a case of indigestion to cure over here; stupid correspondence for a newspaper, over there. Is this worth the pain, worth living for? And most of all, is this worth talking about? I read, I think, I observe, I accumulate impressions, and then I frequently interrupt this totally interior work with the question: *à qui bon?*[33]

Two weeks later, on the second anniversary of his sister's removal from their home, he confessed that after that event he was so depressed he considered suicide and only stopped himself out of consideration for his mother. But since then, he has seen no purpose in life, no goal: "Until two years ago, I knew why I lived and worked. Now, I no longer know. I have no goal, no plan of attack. I navigate by chance, I let myself be moved and pushed by all passing winds and currents, since truly I know not where to go."[34]

This emotional state would continue even after the appearance of *Degeneration* and the consequent public storm over Nordau's rather extreme antimodernist views. Indeed, it is obvious that there is an intimate connection, though it is difficult to reconstruct, between Nordau's personal and his ideological despair: without resorting to any reductionist reading, we see here a man decrying the slow ebbing away of the world he cherished—the world of cosmopolitan European culture and intellectual life of the 1860s and 1870s, in which belief ran high that progress would be inexorable, based on scientific advance, and expressed through both political and aesthetic progress. By the late 1880s, Nordau's undying belief in that worldview appeared to be wildly anachronistic, superseded on virtually all fronts—artistic, political, scientific—by movements and attitudes he decried as irrational, unscientific, immoral, and evil: modernism, socialism, monarchism, bourgeois politics, Nietzscheanism, Tolstoyanism, and so on.

And, of course, among the central evils asserting themselves at precisely this time was a new racial antisemitism that insisted precisely on the Jews' unassimilability, their biological differentness, their alleged conspiratorial longings to overtake and ultimately to destroy European civilization and Christianity as a whole. It was this new sort of antisemitism that Nordau would soon be forced to face, ever so reluctantly and painfully, amidst his overarching ideological and personal despair. For central to his cosmopolitan worldview was his deepest conviction that he had superseded his Jewish origins and become a consummate European, a proud citizen of the world and bearer of the German language and German culture. Until the early 1890s, he truly, passionately, and profoundly believed that his Jewishness was an accident of birth that he had overcome and hence was totally irrelevant to his life, work, and future. He would soon be forced to reassess this primal self-understanding.

[handwritten margin note: Nordau thinks, "Overcome Jewishness"]

Not surprisingly, the first time we find Nordau seriously grappling with this issue is in his correspondence with Olga Novikova. Until late 1889, he had been able to ignore her antisemitic writings, to treat them as simply another aspect of her naive if charming political idiosyncrasy. But on December 18, 1889, he exploded in rage in response to one of her new articles on the subject:

> My opinions "without restriction" on your article. . . . But when, *ma grande amie,* did I get you used to opinions "with restrictions"?
>
> What I think is the following: you have fallen, I believe, into the fault that you ascribe so wittily to the English: that is, to judge facts that you do not know. You do not know the subject that you treat, forgive the brutality of my assertion. I do not know whether the Russian Jews have any Russian patriotism. If they do, they are either angels or abject slaves, but certainly not human beings. Whose fault is it if their condition is so miserable? Who other than Holy Russia? They are forbidden from living in most provinces of the country, and certainly the intellectual centers; they are forbidden entry into the high schools and universities (above 5 percent of the registered students); they are forbidden all careers, and you reproach them for being uneducated, for "exploiting" the people, of not loving Russia? Really, is this you, the open heart, the great spirit, the noble and sympathetic creature, who talks this way?
>
> It is a trite banality, but true: each country has the Jews it deserves. Give the Jews the freedom to be educated, to become men, to become Russians, and you will see, in ten years, in no time at all, the results of this freedom!
>
> And moreover, even were the Russian Jews everything you say, that would not justify massacring them, burning them, maiming them, raping their wives and daughters, chasing them along with the sick, suckling infants, in the midst of the Russian winter, as was done to thousands of them five or six years ago. One does not treat rabbits or scabrous dogs—excuse me, if you can—the way these human beings have been treated.
>
> But these are things that you do not know, since no one has told them to you. . . . At your feet, my dear and charming friend.[35]

Novikova was clearly incensed at this attack, and a bit confused as well: from her vantage point, she had written nothing new on this subject, and she could not quite comprehend why Nordau was reacting like this to points she had made dozens of times before, both long before and many times since the onset of their friendship. She demanded an apology—and received one immediately from him:

My great and dear friend,

I most humbly ask your forgiveness—humility being admissible vis-à-vis a woman—for causing you even a moment of pain. I ought to have foreseen the effect of my letter and controlled myself, even if I was right, or more, because I am right. But I am like you: everything for the truth. In the service of that divinity, so ungrateful and cold before all else, I got carried away beyond all justifiable limits of prudence, and my egoism took hold.

Yet still, Madame and great friend, you are a bit unjust both to yourself and to me by saying that I mocked you, that I ridiculed you. Ridicule you! Mock you! And you write this seriously? And believe this? Is this the true opinion you have of my friendship, of my devotion for you? You punish me severely for some sharp expressions committed not against you, but against a current of opinion, a way of seeing, that you certainly do not share in your heart, so great and generous.

Forgive me and allow me, penitent and punished, to return to your good graces. I lay down all my weapons at your feet.[36]

Apparently, this apology was not quite sufficient, for several weeks later he felt it necessary to insist that he was still totally enthralled by her "charming fault that renders you adorable: your blind and intolerant idolatry for Russia and everything Russian, including the faults, especially the faults."[37]

And so their correspondence continued along its former path, following her back to Russia in the spring and once more to Marienbad in the summer, raising the possibility of a rendezvous in London in the fall. Then, out of the blue, her husband died in St. Petersburg, and she was forced to return home to assume the role of a grieving widow. At first, Nordau felt uncomfortable maintaining the tone of their previous correspondence, but Novikova led him back to the proper track, especially after she signaled the end of her period of formal mourning by accepting a position as honorary inspector of the Russian prison system (in other words, official apologist abroad for the tsarist Gulag).[38] Quickly, the tone of Nordau's letters returned to normal—a witty and flirtatious combination of international gossip, discussion of the latest books and political fashions, and, most of all, his admiration of her charm and spirit, with no attention paid to her views on the Jews or his attack on her of the previous fall.

At the end of 1890, the Jewish question asserted itself again in their correspondence, when Olga Novikova became embroiled even more directly than before in the mêlée surrounding the Russian government's current policies on the Jews. Earlier that year, the tsarist regime had begun to introduce a variety of new restrictive measures against the Jews, beyond the recently introduced educational quota to which Nordau had alluded: new orders expelling Jews from villages, rural settlements, and border territories; new restrictions on Jews in Kiev, Moscow, and St. Petersburg; and an exclusion of Jews from the newly reorganized organs of municipal government, the zemstva. In protest against these actions, a group of famous Russian writers, including Vladimir Solovev, Vladimir Korolenko, and Leo Tolstoy, issued a public proclamation against the government's Jewish policy, branding it with the newly coined word "anti-Semitism" and proclaiming that "the movement against the Jews, spread and fostered by the Russian Press, after the fashion of Germany, represents an unprecedented violation of the most fundamental principles of justice and humanity. . . . We must emphatically condemn the anti-Semitic movement not only as immoral in itself but also as extremely dangerous for the future of Russia."[39] In the West, both the English and the American Jewish communities began to organize public protests against tsarist treatment of the Jews, summoning to their cause high governmental, ecclesiastical, and cultural figures. In London, a protest meeting was announced for December 10, 1890, in the Guildhall, with the Lord Mayor of London and the Archbishop of Canterbury as main speakers.

A fortnight before that meeting, Olga Novikova sent to the editor of *The Times* a letter opposing the Guildhall protest as absurd and outrageous:

What a comedy is life!—a comedy degenerating sometimes into the lowest farce! And so it is not about your submerged millions at home, or the atrocities of your own officers abroad that you are to have this meeting at Guildhall. I should have thought—if I may venture the observation without offense—that your Lord Mayor might have found something more worthy of his attention nearer home. A public meeting might be less useless if those who attended it were imbued with a little sense of responsibility, a little elementary knowledge of the facts, a little experience of the difficulties of the case with which they propose to deal. I am far from pretending that we have solved the Jewish difficulty. Far from it. We are painfully aware of that fact. . . . The Jewish question in England is quite different from the Jewish question in Russia; and an army of 60,000 men is less dangerous than an army of four millions and a half! . . . But while your meeting will have no effect whatever upon Russians, it will have a great effect among the Jews of Russia. It will proclaim aloud, in the hearing of these millions, that England and its great Lord Mayor, with all the wealth of London at their back, have undertaken the cause of the Russian Jews. And these poor people will believe it. And thousands, and tens of thousands, will sell all they have and come over to experience the first fruits of the generosity which promises them a new land of Canaan—in the City of London.

I adjourn the further discussion of the Jewish question until you have had, let us say, 10 per cent. of the immigration which these meetings will invite.[40]

This letter elicited a furious response from many quarters, with one of Novikova's opponents denouncing her on the pages of *The Times* as "one whom the whole Jewish race recognize as their bitterest enemy in the form of a woman."[41] She replied in another letter in which she affected compassion and concern, pleading that the writer who defamed her was clever but perfectly wrong; in reality, she increased the venom of her attack:

I am a Greek Orthodox; our Church is not only opposed to lex talionis, but commands us to love our enemy. Personally I have several friends of Jewish origin, but they are no staunch Talmudists. The latter, to be consistent with their creed, have to be hostile to the Christians.

I do not suppose that even Lord Beaconsfield [Benjamin Disraeli], with all his cleverness and talents, so charmingly described by Mr. Froude, could ever have been Prime Minister had he not embraced Christianity. If a man of his judgment gave up the faith in which he was born, he surely must have had reasons for doing so.

In fact, it is because I feel for our poor Talmudist Jews that I deeply regret the harm which will be the only result of the meeting organized by the Lord Mayor and his party. . . . It is simply madness to imagine that the Russian government needs advice or guidance from the Guildhall. When Lord Beaconsfield returned to his former religious sympathies, and seemed determined to declare war against a great Christian people, Mr. Gladstone and his party organized splendid meetings all over Great Britain, to save England from unnecessary loss of money and lives. But these meetings were held by Englishmen for the enlightenment of their own countrymen. The weapons they used were English weapons, the interests they appealed to were English interests. . . .

The less hostile feelings are excited amongst human beings obliged to live together, the better. There are certain measures which might improve the Hebrew-Russian entente cordiale, but here again the Russian government can alone effect this—viz., if there were a law prohibiting our Jews from lending money to Russians, and especially to boys under age, it would wipe out at once the greatest cause of the present indignation and protest in Russia.[42]

This letter, to be sure, only increased the ire of Novikova's opponents, and it was answered on the pages of *The Times* by such diverse figures as the Chief Rabbi of the British Empire, Hermann Adler, and by Victor Alexander, the Duke of Westminster, who denounced Novikova's views as stemming from her "antecedents and known sympathies with the most odious form of persecution." But Novikova once more added fuel to the fire, as the Guildhall meeting approached: she insisted that her "known sympathies" were simply and purely those of the Christian faith, that she had organized protests against Disraeli only because he was an "anti-Christian," and that she was glad that her opponents agreed that British actions would only lead to renewed Jewish immigration to England, though she was less sanguine than others about the quality, nature, and effect on English life of those immigrants, since "nobody can deny that a Jewish worker is cheaper and less exacting than an English workman." Perhaps some Englishmen want these sorts of Jews, but they ought to know that "as moneylenders they are simply fatal; and there is another peculiarity in Russian Talmudists, which to a military country like Russia, is to the last degree antipathetic—viz., their dread of military service. Incredible numbers either desert or mutilate themselves to avoid enlistment."[43]

But the main point, she repeated, is the interconnection between the Jews' noxious religious faith, its commandment of cruelty and immorality, the Jews' consequent immorality, including their retention of polygamy, and their control of the press:

> I do not know the Jewish daily Prayer Book, which the Duke of Westminster had before him whilst writing his reply to me. The lex talionis is no invention of mine. It permeates all the Old Testament:—"Eye for eye, tooth for tooth, hand for hand, foot for foot. Burning for burning, wound for wound, strife for strife." (Exodus, xxi, 24, 25.) Then again, "And thine eye shall not pity, but life shall go for life, eye for eye, tooth for tooth, hand for hand, foot for foot." (Deuteronomy, xix, 21, &c.) A doctrine like this needed the coming of Jesus Christ himself in order to be reversed, as it is by Christianity.
>
> I know still less about the uniformity of Jewish rituals. According to Al-lioli's "Handbuch der Biblischen Altenthumskunde," "It is only among European Jews that Rabbi Gerschon ben Tehuda [Gershon ben Yehudah] had introduced monogamy. In the East polygamy is frequent among their race even now." Thus it seems there must be a very important dissemblance, indeed, amongst the 12 tribes. The law does not abolish polygamy even now.
>
> The Duke of Westminster says that Lord Beaconsfield was never brought up in the faith in which he was born. But I referred less to his actual baptism than to his professed sympathies, which obviously inclined towards the

Christian Church, without which he could not at that time have obtained success in English political life. Whether England may soon be governed by a Talmudist Prime Minister, or how far that might be desirable, is a question of which the English people are the only judges, and upon which I venture no opinion.

Referring to the Guildhall meeting, I must say again that it cannot bring the results expected from it by the Lord Mayor and his party. The agitation of the Jewish Press, with all its unscrupulous legends and calumnies, had made Russia very indifferent to oratorical displays. I repeat that a great military Power, having at her disposal an army of two millions of well-disciplined and drilled soldiers, whom no European country dares to attack single-handed, can face calmly, and even good-humouredly, both the wild attacks of unscrupulous publicists and mistaken protests of philanthropic meetings, though these be imposing and brilliant as the Lord Mayor's Show itself.[44]

The controversy over Novikova's views did not cease after the Guild-hall meeting was held on December 10. The next day, *The Times* in its editorial column hailed the great success of the meeting and directly assailed Novikova: "That the meeting was not what it has been represented by a notorious semi-official agent and apologist of Russia is plain from the names attached to the memorial."[45] But this did not end the mutual attacks and recriminations by Novikova and her foes, which continued on the pages of *The Times* and other papers for many months; Novikova was apparently so proud of her epistles on this subject that she reprinted them in a shilling pamphlet entitled *The Philo-Jewish Meeting at the Guildhall—Some Letters by Olga Novikoff (O.K).*

Nordau's reaction to this controversy is one of the most intriguing and astonishing matters to emerge from the trove of his correspondence with Novikova. On December 16, 1890, he thanked her for the copy of her November 22 letter to *The Times* on the subject:

This is simply a masterpiece of sharply-whetted polemic, one of the most adorable things I've ever read signed by the name of a woman. What cheek! What verve! What malice! What male pride! What feminine perfidy! What spirit! What good sense! You are truly a redoubtable adversary and I pity the dull-witted Englishman, be he an eloquent Duke, who is forced to cross swords with you. . . .

It is true that there are certain imbeciles—I am one of them, alas!—who believe nonetheless in human solidarity and feel justified in pleading the cause of all the unfortunates they find. . . . One can well laugh at the impotence of some of the twaddlers speaking at the Guildhall, but still one feels that the public opinion of Europe, in the midst of the twaddle in Guildhall and the vain declarations of newspapers, is a force with which even a country of 100 million inhabitants is obliged to deal.

This is in regard to your article in general. In particular, it would be difficult for you to demonstrate how preventing the Jews from attending universities and freely becoming municipal councillors or forbidding them to lend money to Russian minors . . . [ellipsis in original]

But enough of the Russian Jews, for otherwise you may suppose that I too take you to be "the bitterest enemy of the Semitic race" and truly this stupidity has never entered into my brain. I know you to be generous, I believe you are just, and you have infinitely more spirit than to fall into convenient generalizations, always false. You individualize. What more can one ask?[46]

Two weeks later, he responded to her December 3 letter to *The Times* with a fascinating allusion to his views on the Bible expressed in *Conventional Lies,* but put here to a new, and unanticipated, effect:

I've read with great interest your new letter to *The Times.* You are beautiful and proud when you speak of your "antecedents and well-known sympathies" and when you proclaim with hauteur that the truth is on Russia's side. I find you less strong—forgive my sincerity—when you engage in argument. But I do not have the time to show you that it is unfair to reproach contemporary Jews for the polygamy or lex talionis of a book dated 900 years before Christ. The Gauls were cannibals 700 years after the redaction of the Bible. Does this prove anything about the English and French of today?[47]

Clearly, Nordau was attempting the virtually impossible: to maintain excellent and indeed intimate relations with a woman he admired and even loved, but whose views on this particular subject—so close to home, but yet so complicated—he could no longer abide. In early February 1891, he tried to be at once more forthright and more appeasing, saying that he admires heroism, and Novikova is indeed heroic in this battle to take on not only British, but European public opinion as a whole on this issue about which she is so ardent, but misguided:

This is a child's lost fight that you are pursuing with such beautiful valor and such joyful fearlessness. . . .

You want contemporary Jews expressly to repudiate polygamy? Oh really, my dear friend, do you take me for a little Duke of Westminster? Really this is not serious—Do you see even one contemporary Jew in a civilized country declaring polygamy legal? And where do you find among the English and the French contemporary descendants of the ancient Celts, who by a written law or declaration of principle abandon in theory and expressly the practice of feasts of human flesh? Please don't give me this as an argument. That the English meetings "do no good for the Jews of Russia," I do not doubt. That "the Jews of Russia" are bad, I do not know at all, but it is possible. "And then, I do not like the Jews, they are unlikable"—*à la bonne heure.* And there's the truth that frees you of any unsustainable argument. At your feet, *chère amie*. P.S. What you say about the farceur Tolstoy literally brought me solace.[48]

It is thus clear that Nordau, though increasingly disturbed by Novikova's blatant anti-Jewish views, refused to regard her as a true antisemite and did not think her position on this matter important enough to affect their friendship and intimate connection. Quite to the contrary, the postscript to the last letter speaks volumes about Nordau's feelings at this time: Tolstoy, as one of the preeminent exponents of what Nordau would define as "degeneracy," was the enemy, not Novikova; the fact that the former attacked the Russian government's treatment of the Jews and the latter defended it was a curious and largely irrelevant side issue to Max Nordau even in 1891.

Throughout the next several months, their correspondence continued apace, with Nordau complimenting Novikova on several new pieces that she wrote and describing to her his two new works, *Comedy of Sentiment* and *Degeneration*. From April to December 1891, for reasons that are not clear but do not seem to be related to any ideological or personal disagreement, their correspondence lapsed—the longest break since the onset of their relationship. But then the letter-writing resumed, with no change of tone or content. Indeed, in February 1892, Novikova apparently asked Nordau to dedicate a book to her; he replied that his next book—*Degeneration*—was too violent a polemic against sexual immorality, religion, politics, Tolstoy, the French elite, and so on and would doubtless unleash a furious attack against him; thus, it would not be possible to dedicate that book to her: "One does not precede oneself in a battle with a being whom one loves, and who one wants to spare from danger, attacks, horrors."[49] He would therefore dedicate the next book after this one to her, probably a novel.

At this very time, we find Nordau raising a new issue very fleetingly: fury at being labeled a Jew in public. In an obvious rage he wrote to Novikova:

> If you want to know the true sentiments of your friend M. de Vogüé, see his article in your dear Revue des Deux Mondes! This gentleman of the Academy, wanting to express a certain esteem for the tendencies of my books, calls me "a Hungarian Jew." Thus it seems that even being French, it is enough to be married to a Russian to become an antisemite! For my part, I don't care a whit. But it's characteristic for the gentleman in question.[50]

This fascinating outburst reveals just how deeply Nordau still felt about his transcendence of his Jewish origins: anyone who was so coarse, so uncouth, so rude as to call him a Jew in public must be an antisemite! This does not mean that Nordau was at this point obsessed with antisemitism or his putative Jewishness. On the contrary, it is self-evident from this correspondence that these issues were marginal, dedicated as Nordau was with writing *Degeneration,* responding to the attacks against him, and with mounting his new play, *The Right to Love,* on the stage in Berlin. If there was any tension between him and Novikova now it was over entirely other issues—such as the causes of the 1870 war, which elicited a nasty exchange of letters between them but did not affect their romance; in October 1892 they again had a rendez-vous in Paris, after Nordau arranged a discreet hotel room for her there.[51]

But nonetheless, without overstating its centrality in Nordau's life and mind at this point, it is clear that Nordau was indeed forced by the rise of antisemitism and by his own notoriety to confront and address the issue of his national and religious origins. Soon after their most recent encounter, on December 4, 1892, Nordau wrote a letter to Novikova that both detailed his views on nationalism and chauvinism and zeroed in on his own upbringing and identity:

> It seems to me that nothing is more false than confusing patriotism and chauvinism. The first is a rational though tender attachment to a group of traditions, beliefs, sentiments, and impressions that comprise the idea or the concept of a homeland; the latter is an egotistical *fatuité* and a stupid mania for false greatness, a moral obtuseness and brutal fanaticism. The patriot loves his country, his people, his language, but he renders justice to the rest of the world, and does not feel obliged to hate anyone. The chauvinist loves his homeland less than he despises and hates other peoples. In a word: patriotism is above all love, chauvinism, hatred.
>
> Why do you think I was born in the Baltic provinces? That's an error. I was born in Pest—which does not make me too proud—of a Prussian father and a Baltic mother, and I was raised by my father in purely German traditions, so that I've always considered myself to be a German and have remained entirely foreign to the country in which I was born entirely by chance.[52]

This was rather a peculiar way to describe his parents. His father, Gabriel Südfeld, was indeed technically born in Prussia—in Krotoschin, a town in the Posen province of Poland annexed to Prussia in 1793. From Nordau's later post-Zionist memoirs we learn that Gabriel Südfeld was an itinerant rabbi and Hebrew teacher who served as a tutor to the household of some of the most famous and pious rabbis of the age. While remaining a devoutly observant Jew, he composed a few

grammatical and literary treatises in Hebrew, dabbled in German poetry, and may even have written a play in German. In other words,
Nordau's father seems to have been a typical figure of the minor intelligentsia of Posen Jewry in the first half of the nineteenth century—a
maskil, a representative of the Jewish Enlightenment movement, though
of its religiously more conservative bent. Though deprived of Prussian
citizenship and even (until the 1830s) the opportunity to become "nat-
uralized" Prussian subjects, such Jews did indeed become passionately
devoted to German culture and may even have begun to define themselves as Prussians while retaining their firm grounding in and commitment to their primary Jewish identity. Thus, it is difficult to imagine
Nordau's father raising him "in purely German traditions"; later, after
becoming a Zionist, Nordau would boast that, on the contrary, his father gave him a thoroughgoing traditional, talmudic education—undoubtedly, also a creative exaggeration.[53]

Nordau's mother, Rosalia Sarah Nelkin, was born in Riga and raised
in Vilna, before marrying her husband and moving to Budapest and
then, with her son and daughter, to Paris. We know much less about
her than about her husband—Nordau described her as a pious Jewish
woman of the old school, who retained her kosher kitchen and devotion
to Jewish ritual even after she followed her impious son to Paris, where
she lived with him (and later, his non-Jewish wife and children) until
her death. Thus, although technically a "Baltic" in the literal sense of
the term, such a description of the aged Mrs. Südfeld to Olga Novikova
was hardly meant by Nordau to convey a precise identification of his
mother.

Six months after he wrote that description of his parents, Nordau
elaborated on his origins and sentiments to Novikova in another fascinating letter:

> You do not understand how I, Max Nordau, could insist that Mr. Novikov
> pay me a visit before inviting me to dinner. The explanation is quite simple.
> In the past, I have always laughed at all formalities. Unfortunately, though,
> circumstances have forced me to be ridiculously touchy. I have never known
> or felt that I am a Jew. But I am forced to know that now, since if I continue
> to ignore that fact, others will take it upon themselves to remind me of it.
> Mr. Novikov is a Russian, therefore suspected of being an antisemite, until
> proven otherwise. The most injurious form of this sentiment is not hatred,
> but scorn. I will therefore not permit a Russian, whom I do not know per-
> sonally, to mock me, since unfortunately I am obliged to interpret every lack
> of form as a manifestation of disdain on the part of a Russian noble for a

"Jew" for whom one does not have to go to the trouble of abiding by the "puerile and honest" rules of civility. It is sad to have come to this. But whose fault is it?[54]

This letter was written by Nordau on May 7, 1893; four months later, he was obliged to confront antisemitism, and thus his Jewishness, in a much more personal, malicious, and devastating manner. Late in the summer of 1893, he agreed to spend a vacation at the North Sea resort of Borkum with the editor-in-chief of one of the German newspapers he wrote for. At first, the rest was soothing, though it was disturbed from the beginning by the mounting attacks on *Degeneration* and by a not unconnected personal scandal: Nordau had recently published a novel entitled *The Comedy of Sentiment,* which detailed the unsavory relationship between a Parisian-German litterateur and a "woman of loose morals." Now, some of Nordau's attackers were dredging up the presumed autobiographical basis for this novel, an affair Nordau had had with a woman who not only closely resembled the depraved heroine of his tale but also publicly identified herself as that woman. Apparently, the point of this scandal was to demonstrate that the author who attacked everyone from Ibsen to Nietzsche and Tolstoy as morally and sexually "degenerate" was hardly a paragon of sexual and moral probity.

Nordau felt beleaguered by this attack but accepted this as the price of fame: "when one reaches a certain degree of notoriety," he wrote to Novikova, "one has to realize that one is the natural butt of the malice and idiocy of blackguards, bandits, and imbeciles, and one cannot complain of being the object of lies, calumnies, and abominable rumors. This is as inevitable as sickness or death."[55]

But soon, a new and radically different attack was launched against him at Borkum, as he explained to Novikova:

When I accepted the invitation of [his editor] to join him at Borkum, I did not have the slightest hint of the fact that I now know, but too late, though it is known to all Northern Germans: that Borkum has been erected as a Counter-Jerusalem by the German antisemites. I had a personal experience of this fact. For the first few days, everything went well. I was not known. The only thing that I noted was the lack of character of the scenery of Borkum and the incommensurable ludicrousness of its visitors. But within four days, the situation changed. My name appeared in the list of visitors, "I was found out" [in English in the original]. And then there began a dastardly and ignoble persecution which evoked more disgust in me than sadness or anger. The mail brought me letters, naturally anonymous, full of base insults; at the dinner table, under plate, I found other missives, equally anonymous and equally full of filthy *immodices* in words and drawings. Moreover, I received by post an entire collection of writings against the Jews.

What would you have liked me to do? Try to find out the author of these insults? There was no question of that, especially since I hardly intended to use my vacation, so parsimoniously short, to engage in a work of punishment or at making myself a martyr of Judaism. I therefore took the only practical course: I left the island and abandoned the antisemites to their hatreds and their worries.

Today, I can only smile disdainfully about this adventure. But at the time, I did not laugh, I was profoundly distressed. I had to ascertain for the first time in my life that a German author, aware of having contributed not without a certain fame to the renown of German letters, could not without being ignobly injured, remain on a piece of German soil, in the midst of a public comprised exclusively of pastors, judges, bureaucrats, professors, officers, that is, the intellectual elite of the nation.

To regain my equilibrium, I wandered a bit in Holland and Belgium, and came here [to Barcelona] among comrades who show me affection. And that is why I cannot send you photographs from Borkum.[56]

It is undeniable that this incident had profound implications for Nordau, convincing him of the potency of antisemitism and thus scarring and affronting him profoundly and permanently. At the same time, it would be simplistic and misleading—as Nordau himself later claimed, and in his wake, several commentators also claimed—to link the Borkum incident directly to his conversion to Zionism, which did not take place for another three years. Rather, the Borkum incident combined with a series of personal defeats and tragedies to challenge Nordau to rethink his basic commitment to the possibilities of the cosmopolitan, pluralistic future he had held dear and believed inevitable for so long.

The first and foremost discouragement was the extent of the criticism of *Degeneration,* as well as the personal nature of the attacks, which he had not anticipated. From Russia to the United States, critics savagely attacked Nordau for his calumnies against some of the most popular authors, artists, and cultural heroes of the day and began to probe deeply into Nordau's personal life, dredging up most especially and gleefully his many love affairs and sexual escapades, in order to cast doubt upon his own morality. Indeed, his relationship with Novikova became the subject of scandal-mongering in the popular London press.

At the same time, two of Nordau's closest friends died: Wilhelm Loewenthal, professor of hygiene at Lausanne and Berlin; and Richard Kaufmann, a noted Danish author living in Paris. Nordau noted both their passings to Novikova, expressing his profound grief and stating that these friends—the men who understood him best—could never be replaced. Particularly worrisome was the fate of Kaufmann's widow, Anna, left to tend alone to her four young children; several years later this problem would be solved when Nordau married Anna Kaufmann and took on the responsibility of her children.

Meanwhile, however, his relationship with Novikova continued apace, including another rendezvous in Paris in September 1893; soon thereafter Nordau reported with pride that "her play," *The Right to Love,* was produced with great success in several cities, from Milan to Kraków to Milwaukee. They continued to disagree profoundly about many subjects—the Russian Jews, the Armenians, an Anglo-Russian alliance—but the disagreements were always amicable and glossed over with much humor and affection. To her basic defense of Russian autocracy—that it was the deepest tradition of the Russian people, who were not to be judged by Western mores—Nordau responded with a typical riposte:

> If I had to answer you, I'd amuse myself by writing a letter by a Dahomian who says to the English: "Mme de Novikoff is completely right. Each people has its constitution, appropriate to its nature, and pays no regard to that of others. Our constitution consists of serving ourselves up to be slaughtered by our king. This constitution is natural to us. We like it. We are used to being slaughtered. That pleases us. Why then, do you meddle into our affairs? What would you say if we proposed to you to be slaughtered by your queen? You wouldn't like that. Then please leave us alone with our constitution." That's your mode of reasoning. But everything you say against parliamentarism is true.[57]

Though the general tenor of their relationship remained the same, beginning in late 1893 there is discernible between the lines of their correspondence a slight shift in sensibility on Nordau's part, undoubtedly caused by two seemingly unconnected, if not contradictory, changes occurring simultaneously in his life: his new consciousness of his Jewishness and consequent drift to Zionism; and his increasing commitment to Anna Kaufmann, the widow of his best friend.

At first, only the first issue surfaced in the correspondence with Novikova; indeed, these letters are crucial to an understanding both of the timing of this conversion and Nordau's innermost feelings about the subject. For Nordau's letters to Olga Novikova chronicle in an intimate, reliable, and detailed fashion Nordau's at first hesitant and then more and more enthusiastic reception of Theodor Herzl's new ideas.

Nordau and Herzl had known each other for several years through their many common interests and professional activities. Both, after all, were Germanized Budapest Jews working as foreign correspondents for German liberal newspapers in Paris, composing feuilletons and writing light plays on similar subjects for similar audiences. Nordau was by far the more accomplished and successful: *The Conventional Lies of Our Civilization* and *Paradoxes* had made him famous throughout Europe, and his novels, short stories, and plays were well received both in the German-reading world and beyond; moreover, his medical practice and general standing in the Parisian literary world secured him a social and intellectual position far beyond that which Herzl would ever command. Throughout the early 1890s, Herzl attempted to get Nordau to contribute pieces to *Die Neue Freie Presse,* a paper Nordau intensely disliked as far too bourgeois and conventional and, equally important, one that paid its authors very little. Only after Herzl returned to Vienna to serve as feuilleton editor of the paper did Nordau agree to write for him, as a personal favor.

In the midst of these journalistic deliberations, Herzl began to reveal to Nordau his own newfound ideas about the Jews. Thus, Herzl noted in his diary on July 5, 1895: "Last night with Nordau over a glass of beer. Naturally, a conversation about the Jewish Question. I have never agreed with Nordau so much about anything. We spoke exactly the same words; I've never felt so strongly how close we are to each other."[58] Four months later, on November 17, he noted a longer discussion with Nordau about the Jewish Question and concluded, "I believe that Nordau will follow me though fire and water. I conquered him easily, and perhaps this is the most important of my conquests."[59] Only several weeks later, however, after Herzl had made an unsuccessful trip to London, he confessed to his diary that "Nordau is much more cautious now than before."[60]

How Nordau actually felt about all this at the time has not been clear, and scholars have been forced to extrapolate his position either from Herzl's diary entries or from Nordau's later account of the events, obviously colored by his later feelings and polemical needs. But in the letters to Novikova, we see expressed Nordau's growing involvement in matters Jewish and his reaction to Herzl's new views.

Thus, in late July 1895 (roughly a fortnight after the discussion over beer reported by Herzl), Nordau wrote to Novikova, reacting to an interview that erroneously quoted his mother: "My mother could not have said that I was born in Vilna. I love Russia and the Russians very much, but I shudder at the thought that I could have been a Russian Jew, that is, the most miserable thing in the world."[61]

Three months later, his increasing Jewish consciousness surfaced in another digression:

> Why do I not admire the Gospels? This book is one of the most beautiful productions of the Jewish Spirit, and as a Jew I am as proud of this work by my fellow Jew as of Spinoza's Ethics or Heine's Buch der Lieder. There is to be sure a goodly amount of mysticism and dogmatism in the Gospels, but this does not spoil the Sermon on the Mount, the stories of the Good Samaritan and the adulterous woman Madelaine the sinner, etc.[62]

Soon thereafter, rumors that Nordau was becoming involved in some new "society" reached Novikova through the newspapers—though at this point she thought that this had something to do with his medical practice: she asked whether he was involved in founding a society to spread hypnotism. He responded on November 4, 1895: "I have founded no society. What a nonsensical idea! Me, the most individualistic of men, the most jealous of my independence, founding a society. It is true, though, that I do use hypnotism a lot as a therapeutic device."[63]

By the end of the year, though, the connection to Herzl and to a new movement still lacking a name surfaced in the correspondence. On December 30 Nordau wrote a long letter to Novikova with greetings for the New Year, and by-the-by raised the subject of Herzl: first, he detailed their journalistic connections and his reluctant decision to succumb to Herzl's pleas and write for Die Neue Freie Presse. He then continued:

> I have no idea at all what you mean by a "conference in London" at which I must "decide" something; I know nothing either about an emigration that I'm supposed to be proposing, whose aim is to be Palestine. Who could have invented this new and not exactly uplifting pleasantry? For my part, I'm staying in Paris, and I would not know what to do in Jerusalem.[64]

It is difficult to discern whether Nordau at this stage was hiding some of his new commitments from Novikova, or whether he was accurately conveying his struggles with the ideas and possibilities he had gleaned from Herzl. Clearly, Herzl was widely trumpeting Nordau's support of his ideas—Nordau was, as Herzl himself noted, his most famous name to drop. Only a few weeks after his December 30 letter to Novikova, Nordau wrote to Herzl about the latter's recently completed Judenstaat:

> I have read your Judenstaat twice. Today I unfortunately do not have enough time for a detailed analysis—therefore, only my impressions, in short strokes:

from the objective point of view it is possible to judge your pamphlet from various positions; from a subjective point of view, it is simply a great accomplishment. If you had never written another line, or will never write anything else—this pamphlet assures you a permanent heroic place forever. For an artist who delights in style, your avoidance of every verbal acuity, the succinctness and modesty of your exposition is an act of courage. But your indescribable act of courage is to burn all the bridges behind you—you now cease to be a "German writer," an Austrian patriot. In the future you will be able to influence a reader solely by your evocation of the deepest humanitarian emotions; the cheaper emotions, those evoked by love of homeland, "Landsmanschaft" and the like, will now be closed to you. And the most courageous act of all is your bravest assertion, strong as death?, of the feelings held by all Jews but buried deeply within their souls. Uriel Acosta did less, Martin Luther did no more. I am not thinking especially of the influence that you intend, nor on the project that you are planning, but of the subjective aspect of all this, of you. You alone can understand my feelings. For I do not know what will come out of this pamphlet, but I do know that you have revealed yourself in it.[65]

Although this letter has been understood by scholars as an enthusiastic endorsement of Herzl's position, it is clear from the Novikova correspondence that Nordau was still tentative, drawn powerfully to Herzl's bold ideas but uncertain of their "objective" truth or practicability; this was still a positivist, after all, who believed that social problems were scientifically soluble, if only the correct formula could be deduced from the objective evidence. A few weeks after the letter to Herzl, Nordau wrote to Olga Novikova suggesting that she read Herzl's booklet. She apparently did so while in Moscow for the festivities surrounding the formal coronation of Tsar Nicholas II. Upon her return, on June 15, 1896, Nordau chided her for not informing him that she was going to the coronation events, since she could then have met with many of his friends there; he then proceeded to reveal to her his growing commitment to the nascent Zionist movement:

This time the gossip is not as baseless as last: my friend Herzl is due to arrive in Paris at the end of the month, and from here to go to London, to attempt to organize the first committee of the "Society of Jews." He wrote to me from Vienna that he is counting absolutely on me, that I must accompany him to England, that I must join the committee, etc. I've avoided answering most of his demands and have promised nothing about the others. I have no intention of leaving Paris in July—perhaps M. Herzl has taken his desires to be facts and has written thus to London. As regards the rest, an agitation in favor of a Jewish emigration to Jerusalem—there is not yet a question of that. That is very far off, very hypothetical. For the present, it consists in discussions of the preliminary question: "Do there exist Jewish elements with whom one can attempt a serious colonization, and if so, how could this be accomplished and they transplanted? Since M. Herzl has occupied himself with this matter (and involved me as well, alas!) I have learned many things that I totally was unaware of before and are surprising. Before, I did not even suspect the existence of a so-called "Zionist" movement, but it exists, there is no doubt about it.[66]

For the next sixteen months, there is no mention of Zionism or the Jews in Nordau's many letters to Novikova: she clearly was far more interested in other aspects of his life—how he could suddenly go off to London at Herzl's behest, when he never came there to see her; his correspondence with Pobedonostev on literary matters, in which he used her name without permission; his being called "the most important philosopher of the century" by the Italian psychiatrist Cesare Lombroso and his trip to Turin to help the society "Scuola e famiglia" founded by Lombroso's wife and daughter.

But on September 13, 1897, upon his return to Paris from Basel, where the First Zionist Congress was held in late August, Nordau wrote a detailed letter to Novikova with crucial information on his conversion to the new movement:

> I do not know what you mean by my "successes." At Basle, I did not intend to speak beauty and my speech was not an aria by a strong tenor, sung in order to evoke applause. This speech will soon appear as a brochure, and the first copy—naturally—will be for you. You will read it, I trust, and you will see if in the presence of a scene so tragic, so sincere, so elemental, there can be any question of something so frivolous, so despicable, as a "success."
>
> At the beginning, I smiled at "Zionism." My friendship for Herzl—I am always the victim of my affections—led me to come to his aid, without conviction, but he had the cleverness to put me out in front and in public view, while I wanted to work for him discreetly, behind the scenes.
>
> How I would be happy to see you and to talk to you. You could become the benefactress of the unhappy Jews of Russia, of whom I saw, for the first time in my life, the most surprising specimens in Basle. I know no one among the governing classes in Russia, and there are so many things to tell them about the Jewish Question, matters that I would not in the least ever consider writing in books or in the newspapers.[67]

Three weeks later, Novikova came to Paris for what would be their last rendezvous. Several months after her return to London, he wrote to her:

> I would love to have the time to tell you who Herzl really is, he who is already being crucified by calumny before being able to be the savior of his people. Unfortunately, I am too burdened by demands and this will have to wait for

calmer times. Meanwhile, one request: suspend your judgment about Herzl—those who malign him are the Jewish slaves who delight in their yoke. I do not know whether Herzl will go to Jerusalem, but I do know that he will do so if this seems useful to the cause to which he has dedicated his life.[68]

At this point, there is an extraordinary break in the Nordau-Novikova correspondence—a nine-month lapse between January and September 1898, by far the longest such lapse in the correspondence since its onset more than a decade earlier. This obviously was the result of the second, and contemporaneous, revolution in Nordau's life, alongside his conversion to Zionism: his marriage to Anna Kaufmann—a Danish Protestant—in the summer of 1898.

The fact that this marriage took place after Nordau joined the Zionist movement (in precise Zionist chronology, between the First and Second Zionist Congresses) is striking, since it speaks volumes about the nature of Nordau's Zionism and understanding of his Jewishness at this time. (In these very same months Nordau would write his play *Doktor Kohn*, analyzed in chapter 4, on the subject of a Jewish nationalist marrying a non-Jew without effacing his national pride.) In the biography of Nordau written by his wife and daughter, this sensitive subject is handled thus:

> It should be emphasized that his love only served to deepen his Zionist adherence and Jewish loyalty, although his future wife was a Danish Protestant, the descendant of a long line of gentlemen farmers and army officers, and had known no Jews except through the medium of the Bible. The first time she had ever heard of anti-semitism was when Bjoenstjerne Bjoernson had brought up the subject in the studio of the Finnish painter, Albert Edelfeldt. The notion revolted her and she proposed to Nordau that she become a Jewish proselyte. His reply was that such an action would not provide her with Jewish ancestors. She was indeed worthy of being a Jewess. But fate had not desired it so. . . .
>
> His marriage was certainly not received well in all circles. He had the consolation that his aged mother took his wife sincerely to her heart and that the racial and religious differences faded in the face of a beautiful mutual understanding. The family of Madame Nordau welcomed her remarriage and her happiness without reservation. . . .
>
> When he announced his marriage to Herzl, the latter replied: "I congratulate you with all my heart. The noble woman whom I know only slightly, and whose highmindedness was described to me by Feldman, will give you peace at home which will fit you better for the battle outside the home."
>
> Herzl reasoned against Nordau's fears of the probable reaction to his marriage outside of his own faith. His chief point in allaying these fears Herzl formed thus:
>
> "What are we today? We are citizens of that ideal Jewish state whose

realization on earth is the fairest hope of our life. If our work were accomplished, a Jewish citizen of that Jewish state would certainly not be restrained from marrying a foreigner. Politically the woman would become a Jewess, quite aside from any question of religion. If you should have children, they will be Jews, which in our immediate situation counts only as far as sons are concerned. Moreover, you can cite some very striking instances. If I am not mistaken, Moses married a Midianite.

And then—do you believe for a moment that I nurse any illusions concerning some future change in the opinion of the people? If we succeed in carrying out our enterprise no one will be more attacked than you and I. There's a fine and profound German proverb: 'God breaks the tools which he had used.' "

In this intimate note between man and man shone the scope and character of Herzl's political views, also shared by Nordau.[69]

To Novikova, who was troubled by the question of this mixed marriage from a different perspective, Nordau was more forthright. At one point, he jested that he had converted his wife to Judaism, and

I must guard myself, lest she convert me to Judaism after she's embraced it. In any event, she would be the only believing Jew in the household. But enough of such jokes. The base souls who attack me so viciously do not understand that I am not a Jew by religion but by race, by historical sentiment, a Jew in response to the calumnies that afflict us, a Jew because of the tortures inflicted on those of my race. If the Jews were happy, I'd have very little to do with them, alas![70]

The nature of Nordau's new Jewish consciousness is no better revealed than in a related matter—his and Anna's decision to raise in the Protestant faith their daughter Maxa, born a year after their marriage and named after her doting father. To Novikova's incessant questioning about the faith of the child, Nordau answered clearly and, it seems, without any hesitation or doubt: "Little Maxa was baptized according to Protestant rites. She will have a Protestant education and will not be allowed to read her father's books until the age of twenty-one. She has learned to join her hands together so cutely, pretending that she's 'saying her prayers.' "[71]

Seemingly unself-conscious of the anomalies of a Zionist leader raising his children as Christians, he continued to keep Novikova apprised of the Christian rites of passage celebrated by his family—the plans for the first communion of his stepdaughter Lily was a matter that was "preoccupying the whole household."[72]

What is so important and fascinating about these intimate glimpses into the Nordau household is that they bring to life in an exceedingly

vivid manner the precise nature of Nordau's sense of Jewishness even as
he entered into the forefront of the Zionist movement. In the correspondence with Novikova, obviously not intended for outsiders' eyes,
Nordau interlaced details about his daughter's baptism and his stepdaughter's communion with furious asides about the refusal of the mainstream Jewish leaders to acknowledge the truth of the Zionist cause.
Thus, in the letter about Maxa's baptism were comments on quite different subjects:

> I've just returned from a crazy trip to Vienna, Berlin, and Cologne, where I
> had to speak to thousands of hostile Jews who wanted nothing more than
> to massacre me. I am almost dead of overwork. . . . It's so hard to want to
> regenerate a downtrodden and battered people. It's a superhuman effort, and
> those who attempt it will surely succumb. But does one have the right to
> recoil from this effort when it affects one's entire race, all of whose members
> are united by the hatred of enemies? . . .
>
> The point of my trip was to have meetings in Vienna, Berlin, and Cologne,
> to brand with a red fire the rich Jews and their obsequious servants the salon-
> rabbis, because they make fun of or attack the Zionist movement, and vilify,
> calumnize, basely attack its protagonists in so cowardly and ignorantly a
> fashion. I do not know if I gained any adherents to the Zionist cause in those
> three cities, but I intended to howl at those who condemn it, and that ap-
> peared to me a great success. . . .
>
> My role? That of a Jew exasperated by base antisemitism who decided to
> lift up his race, to render them, by the grandeur of their moral and physical
> regeneration, worthy of respect and sympathy, and thus to confound their
> enemies.[73]

Herzlian

To Novikova he kept repeating his frustration at not being able to
explain his Zionism adequately in these letters—an hour of face-to-face
conversation, he explained to her, would suffice for him to explain his
beliefs and to convince her of them. He seems truly to have believed not
only that he could make Novikova into a supporter of Zionism, but also
that there was a possibility of enlisting her as a personal plenipotentiary
to the Russian government on the part of the Zionist movement. For
wouldn't Zionism be advantageous to the Russian regime, he kept repeating to her: if you don't want to allow the Jews to be educated, to
live anywhere in the Empire, to take up all professions, then let them
leave for Palestine, where they absolutely want to go. He counsels her
not to forget that if they go there with the powerful support of Russia,
they will establish in the Holy Land a Russian colony, without inciting
a world war, and the Jews, "not suffering any longer, will have for
Russia that eternal and passionate gratitude, for which my race is well
known." For its part,

Russia must understand that it has as much interest as we do of getting rid of the Jewish Question by getting rid of its Jews, that is, by facilitating by its diplomatic influence on the Sultan their settlement in Palestine. Does the Russian government have this much wisdom and this much generosity? Doesn't it wish to annex Palestine in this way? That is the formidable point on the horizon.[74]

In line with these ideas, Nordau appended to his Christmas greetings of 1899 news of an extraordinary letter that he had written to Novikova's friend Pobedonostev "to explain to him the Jewish question and Zionism and to request of him that the Russian government support our project of mass emigration, in exchange for which we ask official and direct aid and protection before the Sultan."[75] For Nordau to propose such a deal between the Zionist movement and the most noted and infamous antisemite in the Russian government was indicative of the extent to which he was essentially oblivious not only of political and diplomatic realities, but also the sensibilities of the rank and file of the Zionist movement, who would soon vociferously object to a similar, though far less frontal, appeal on the part of Herzl to the Russian government. It also is a fascinating augury of the equally controversial approaches, decades later, to the Ukrainian and Polish governments by none other than Vladimir Jabotinsky, berated for his readiness to "deal with the devil" to save the Jews.

Pobedonostev, to be sure, never answered Nordau's letter, which the latter took to be not a response to an unrealistic, if not mad, suggestion, but simply a personal affront. But never mind, he wrote to Novikova, that is Pobedonostev's loss and, moreover, "a humiliation suffered in the cause of the unhappy shames he who inflicts it, not he who suffers it."[76] At the same time, any notion on Nordau's part of using Novikova to effect such a rapprochement with the tsarist regime was dispelled by her reaction to the concurrent event that would come to obsess Nordau and to cause an irreparable rupture in their relationship: the second trial of Alfred Dreyfus, held in Rennes in late 1899.

Nordau attended the Rennes trial as a foreign correspondent and wrote much about the experience. But in this regard, Nordau's memoirs are, once more, only half true: although he often claimed that he became a Zionist as a result of the Dreyfus Affair, it is abundantly clear that he, like Herzl, barely took notice of the first Dreyfus trial and interpreted the second trial through already convinced Zionist eyes.[77] Nonetheless, the experience in Rennes was riveting—and Novikova's reaction deeply offensive and incomprehensible.

Even before the trial began, Nordau saw it as the supreme test of the relations between Jews and Christians in Europe and predicted the worst outcome: "I predicted massacres when everyone else laughed at me and took me for a grotesque visionary. I'm waiting for them now, too. But what do you want me to do? I am a soldier and I will die at my post if that's necessary. I am here in a lion's den, and know who my enemies are. I must take whatever is destined to come."[78]

As the trial proceeded, he wrote detailed descriptions to Novikova of the outrages of the anti-Dreyfusards, pointing out to her especially the vile and cynical behavior of the monarchist and Catholic parties and condemning the support expressed to the reactionary forces by her fellow Slavophiles and Pan-Slavs in Russia. "Do you still persist," he wrote to her from Rennes, "in preferring the assimilation of the Jews to their separation? But we have tried that, all of us honestly, many of us passionately. But it failed so miserably, and God knows, not through our fault!"[79]

Slowly but surely her letters in response caused him great pain: they sound like they are right off the pages of *La Libre Parole* or other antisemitic papers, he complained; she simply was misinformed and refused to see that her informants were imbeciles and vile creatures. Particularly offensive was her repeating the rumor that behind the pro-Dreyfus forces stood an international Jewish conspiracy headed by Russian Jews—that, somehow, large sums of money were collected in Berdichev and other towns in the Pale of Settlement and funneled to France by the international Jewish network of high finance. Although this charge flowed quite naturally from Novikova's previously and often expressed views of Jews, Nordau now could not abide this kind of talk:

> I defy you to show me one Russian Jew who paid one kopeck to any cause having to do with Dreyfus. This is simply a grotesque lie invented by the Jesuits who apply to the Jews their own habits and tricks. . . . The charge of a "syndicat" is only propagated by criminal antisemites and is only believed by the cretins of the *Revue des deux mondes* who also believe in ritual murder.[80]

Nordau was clearly incensed, and almost beyond control, causing him to go on in this letter to accost Novikova at the core of her beliefs:

> You are gracious for pardoning me for not believing in Jesus Christ. An excellent Christian, Aryan by blood, a great and noble thinker, named Dr. Fr. Strauss, affirms with scientific proofs, that Jesus Christ was a beautiful

mythological figure who never existed, any more than Jupiter or Brahma. Sort it out with Strauss.

Now, I swear this to you: if you can prove to me the existence and divinity of Jesus Christ, as clearly as the innocence of Dreyfus has been proven, I will believe in Jesus Christ as ardently as is possible, and will conform to his moral doctrine, which is the quintessence of Jewish morality, certainly more so than that of nine-tenths of those who claim to be Christians. And since this doctrine was first Jewish, then generally human, I claim to be a better Christian of the Sermon of the Mount than those who go to mass.[81]

Quite predictably, Novikova was incensed by this attack, by this accusation of being an antisemite, by his comparisons between Dreyfus and Christ. She wrote back an angry and hurtful letter, to which he replied unapologetically and angrily:

I never said that you read *La Libre Parole*, only that your letter sounds like that kind of trash. How can you write of "my belief in Dreyfus's innocence"—it's not "belief" but certain knowledge based on a profound study of all the facts. I never said that Dreyfus was better than Jesus Christ or that Christ never existed, only reported what others have said. The idea of a Russian-Jewish plot behind Dreyfus is a stupid invention of the antisemites, the only true "International" is the antisemitic conspiracy. And do not try to back up the claims of international Jewish financial support for Dreyfus by citing the Baron Hirsch and all the other Jewish financiers who claim to help their people but are merely great carnivores who harm the Jews in incomparable ways.[82]

But Novikova would not relent: she continued to bombard him with questions about his wife's and daughter's religion, as well as the lex talionis and why he had ceased writing to her often enough and had seemingly grown so cold. To all of these questions, he now responded with no humor, and with palpable irritation:

I don't know whether I'll forgive the question of whether I desire the conversion of my wife to Judaism. If someone told you that I was accused of stealing handkerchiefs, would you ask me if that was true? As for me, I have no religion, and thus would be difficult to require any sort of religious conversion, and especially on the part of a soul so strong, very satisfied with her own religion, and very conscientious of her responsibilities towards five children.[83]

A few days later, in response to yet another series of offensive queries on her part, he wrote:

Maxa was baptized because she is a Protestant! . . .

The "law of talion" is no more the law of Moses than of Jesus. But I don't have to defend the law of Moses or attack that of Jesus, all this makes no difference because you no more observe the law of Jesus than the Jews observe the law of Moses.[84]

Finally, the tension between them led to a rupture. For the first time in fifteen years, he failed to send her Christmas and New Year's greetings marking the onset of 1902. She wrote him yet another letter, expressing her hurt, and sent him a new book chronicling her relationship with another one of her famous admirers, Alexander Kinglake. Nordau replied with a fascinating letter that marks the end of their preserved correspondence:

> I haven't forgotten you—don't think I'm different.
>
> I just received the book about Kinglake; I hadn't realized the degree of intimacy that existed between you two. I'm flattered that I was your friend while he still was too. How poorly we know one another, in the end! One can have a sympathetic relationship from a distance, but intimacy?
>
> Maxa is delightful.
>
> You poorly remember *The Conventional Lies,* no offense meant. I never denied the charms of family life, I only fought against family life based solely on material interest.
>
> *Toujours à vos pieds,* M. Nordau.[85]

Clearly, Nordau and Novikova could no longer sustain even an epistolary relationship, for he was no longer the insouciant, cosmopolitan bon vivant to whom she wrote that first fan letter of 1886, who eloquently and passionately thundered against bourgeois marriage, bourgeois nationalism, and bourgeois culture and thus delighted in Novikova's cool hauteur and aristocratic prejudices. Although Novikova's recollection of his views on marriage in *Conventional Lies* was, in fact, more accurate than Nordau would admit, and although between the lines of his last letter there still lingered a somewhat proprietary indignation that he was not her only, or most important, lover, all that was secondary to him now, for he was a happily married man, a loyal and devoted husband, a doting father and stepfather to five children—quite a contrast from the ladies' man and scandalous flirt of the not-so-distant past.

And equally important to Nordau, and more to us, he was now an ardent Jew, a Zionist activist who understood the world through Zionist eyes, utterly alive to the vitality and dangers of antisemitism. Whereas in the past he had taken no especial notice of her antisemitic utterances and activities, now he could no longer abide them and felt constrained to end the relationship between them.

Yet as the correspondence between Nordau and Novikova helps to illuminate with such clarity, Max Nordau's road to Zionism was hardly a conventional one, and neither was it a repudiation nor a logical outgrowth and affirmation of his previous worldview, as has variously been claimed. Rather, just as the personal and family life that he created was a strange mixture of the conventional and the idiosyncratic—a proper middle-class Christian family utterly devoted to the Zionist cause of the paterfamilias—the version of Zionism which he came to espouse and to preach was highly personal and idiosyncratic, imbued through and through with the values, mores, and cultural axioms of the cosmopolitan weltanschauung he had long both promulgated and personified. It is to this fascinating blend of the personal and the political, the Zionist and the fin-de-siècle European cosmopolitan, that we now turn.

CHAPTER FOUR

Nordau's Zionism

From Heine to Bar Kochba

As we have seen, long after he became a Zionist, Max Nordau continued to write books, novels, plays, short stories, and essays that continued the themes of his *Conventional Lies* and *Degeneration* and rarely had any connection, overt or covert, with the "Jewish problem." Thus, it is profoundly misleading either to bifurcate his life into pre-Zionist and Zionist periods, as has often been done, or to seek Zionist messages in his general writings either before or after he became a Zionist. As I understand it (and as I think his correspondence with Olga Novikova demonstrates), Nordau's intellectual and ideological history was neither seamless nor radically disruptive; his gradual conviction about the necessity and truth of Zionism evolved in tandem both with his personal experience of antisemitism and with the huge fracas over *Degeneration,* which demonstrated all too publicly the success of the very forces he opposed. The broad-based and vituperative rejection of his cultural and ideological critique coincided both temporally and substantively with his fundamental rethinking of his own Jewishness and of the fate of the Jews as a group. He became convinced that the forces of degeneracy—which he variously labeled Nietzscheanism, Ibsenism, Tolstoyanism, and so on—had taken control of European culture so thoroughly that the voices of sanity and science were all but overwhelmed. He understood the rise of racial antisemitism to be yet another facet of this all-embracing degeneracy—not, as most Jews believed, a reactionary response to modernism but, rather, an inherent part of the regnant modernist fallacy. The battle could not be given up, as the fate of human civilization as a whole depended on it. Nordau therefore dedicated the rest of his life to this fight on two fronts: the defense of Science, Truth, and Art in the name of civilization as a whole, and the defense of the Jews via a militant and transformative Zionism. The irony, of course, was that like all such "restorative" ideologies, Nordau's attack on the "malaise of the fin de siècle"—a term he did much to make famous— was thoroughly conditioned and defined by the culture he so detested and sought to dislodge. His personal life, his aesthetic theories, his scientific certainties, his psychological analyses, and his Zionism were all deeply embedded in the intellectual and cultural maelstrom of the European fin de siècle.

For this reason, to isolate his Zionism from the rest of his thought and practice is to run the risk of misrepresenting its content and contours. What is needed is an organizing principle, an analysis of his Zionism that at once foregrounds its specificity and relates it reliably to his general principles. For that reason, rather than attempt a chronological narrative of the evolution of his Zionist thought, in much of this chapter I focus on a hitherto unnoticed theme that runs through Nordau's Zionism from start to finish and relates it continually back to his overarching cultural views: his reworking of the legacy of Heinrich Heine, as poet, as thinker, and as Jew. Without claiming that Nordau's use and abuse of Heine is the crucial "key" to his Zionism or the most important node of his Zionist thought, I propose to examine Nordau's Zionism by focusing first on his relationship to Heine, as a means of gauging the mixture of the Jewish and the universal, the Zionist and the cosmopolitanism, in Nordau's Zionist thought.

Let us begin with a speech he gave on November 24, 1901, at the dedication of a monument to Heinrich Heine at the dead poet's gravesite in the Montmartre Cemetery in Paris. Publicly identifying himself only as one of the "freethinking German-Austrians" who had financed the memorial, Nordau praised Heine as the most immortal symbol of true Germanness, the personification, along with Goethe, of the best that German culture and the German language have contributed to humankind. Unmistakingly making reference to the poet's warning, at the end of his "Germany: A Winter's Tale" that poetry will survive even its most powerful opponents, Nordau warned his audience that Heine's enemies were even more powerful now than they were in his day:

A half-century after his death there still rages, and ever more furiously with time, a battle around Heine and the battle for which he fought fiercely while alive, and in whose name he delivered such powerful blows. I know of no more flattering a form of afterlife. Heine can say today about himself: "I am insulted and abused, therefore I am"—Increpor, vituperor, ergo sum.[1]

In the end, however, Nordau declared, Heine would triumph over his enemies since he represents the highest aspirations of not only *Deutschtum* but also the human race as a whole:

> We stand here at the zenith of humanity [*Wir stehen hier auf Menschheitshöhen*]. This poet's grave is a mountaintop. Over the valleys there hover clouds, the dead of night lingers over the plains, and out of the darkness wild noises are heard. But here we stand in the bright light of the sun, whose rays are visible just beneath the horizon. They will rise again and shine forth once more, until the great noon day is reached. And then Light will glisten again over the lowlands.[2]

At first glance this would seem to be a strange homily in the mouth of a man who was at this point the second most important Zionist in the world and by far the most widely known celebrity in the fledgling movement. For decades Nordau had been broadcasting his message of despair about the fate of European culture as a whole, and for the past two years he had been preaching far and wide his newfound conviction in the pathology of Jewish "assimilation" and hence the necessity for Jews to abjure any hopes in the future of European society. How then could that message be squared with admiration for Heine, perhaps the most famous Jewish "assimilationist" of them all, the man who had voluntarily sold his patrimony for his "ticket of admission into European society"?

The answer to this question strikes at the very heart of Nordau's highly idiosyncratic version of Zionism, a synthesis between militant Jewish statism and an equally steadfast belief in the cultural and political ideology he had articulated in the early 1890s. To be sure, by any rational criteria Heine was as far from either Social Darwinism or Zionism as one could be, even *avant la lettre*. But the evocation of Heine as the consummate expression of both European cosmopolitanism and the paradoxical role of Jews in that culture was hardly irrational or indeed idiosyncratic to Nordau, as Mark Gelber has demonstrated in his evocative study of the Jewish "reception" of Heine throughout the nineteenth century. Moreover, the circumstantial parallels between Heinrich Heine and Max Nordau were rather obvious: both were German-language authors who had exiled themselves to Paris to fight against the "lies" of their respective generations; both had vociferously rejected the bourgeois lives for which they were groomed, denouncing the moral and political "philistinism" of middle-class society; both had cut their ties with their erstwhile Jewish faith in the name of a belief in the unity of the human race; both came to realize, however, that despite their own actions and intent, they were still regarded as Jews.

The ineluctability of this shared and innate Jewishness was nowhere more overtly proclaimed by Nordau than in a poem published in 1909 in his *Zionistische Schriften,* entitled "Nachtrag zu Heinrich Heine's 'Deutschland, Ein Mintermärchen'" (Supplement to Heinrich Heine's "Germany, A Winter's Tale").[3] Written in the same faux-folkloristic meter and rhyme scheme as the original, Nordau's supplement presents itself as "caput 28," an afterword to Heine's great work that chronicled the poet's love-hate relationship with Germany, his detestation of its chauvinism and militaristic venom, and yet his profound desire to influence its destiny and to create beauty in its language. In its last chapter, "caput 27," Heine admonished kings not to malign poets, since poetry will outlive all monarchs and consign them to eternal damnation.

Nordau's supplement begins by announcing that Heine's prophecy about poetry was not fulfilled. Instead, the dead poet is imagined rising from his marble tomb and "with the staff of a Wandering Jew / Sets out for the German lands." There, however, he is rejected by seven cities, who claim in unison that they have no need for Jews, that their Fatherland has no room any longer for Heine or for his all too Jewish sort of wit. Astonished and wounded, he wanders away until he reaches the island of Corfu, where he is taken in by a kind old woman who has built a pantheon for the true heroes of this world, poets, artists, singers of the songs of love and humanity. But history overtakes this noble dream. The old woman is killed, and in her place and into her palace there arrives a brutal king, who with a harsh Prussian "Jawohl!" trashes her beloved pantheon and throws the wandering poet out:

> This palace was but a land of lies
> Its hopes a senseless dream
> There is no room for Heine
> Under the Kaiser's banner.
> And with a harsh fist in his face
> He is thrown out of the temple
> Thus, his old Jew's fate
> Caught up with him even in the Achillion.[4]

To decode this poem, one must first know its factual basis, the story of the Achillion palace and Heine's role therein. In the late 1880s,

Empress Elisabeth of Austria-Hungary, universally known as Sisi, built an elaborate home on the island of Corfu that reflected her idiosyncratic passions for Greece, for Achilles, and for Heinrich Heine. She named the palace after the Greek hero whom she worshiped, not as a military figure but as the embodiment of tragic grief and the hatred of "kings and traditions"—a somewhat ironic position on the part of the empress of a vast dominion, famously estranged from the emperor and his minions. On the grounds of her Achillion palace she consecrated a memorial to Heinrich Heine, whom she considered her personal Master and poetic muse; she wrote poetry after his style, believed that he appeared to her in dreams, surrounded herself with busts and portraits of the poet, collected editions of his works, called on his aged sister Charlotte von Embden in Hamburg, and visited his grave in Paris. Her Heine temple, strategically located on a rise in the Achillion's gardens, held a new statue of the poet specially ordered by the empress, showing him in his ailing last years, dressed only in simple shirt, contemplating his poetry. The radically nonheroic iconography of this statue shocked many of the empress's staff, but this was her emphatic response to the controversy she had inadvertently gotten herself involved in several years earlier, when she donated a fortune to have a different statue of Heine erected in Düsseldorf. That plan was scuttled when German nationalists and antisemites objected to memorializing Heine in any manner and denounced the empress as "a slave to the Jews." As one antisemitic newspaper put it: "Let Jews and those who are enslaved by the Jews rave about this shameless Jew; we Germans turn from him with loathing and call out to all our racial comrades: Here you see how the Jew thinks, how all of Jewry takes his part, how they beat the drums for him and how, sadly, some Germans also march to the beat of this Jewish drum."[5]

This theme was repeated in the reactionary press of Austria and France as well, and eventually the statue was rejected by several other German cities, until it ended up in New York City. In the event, however, Empress Sisi did not long enjoy her shrines to Achilles and Heine: she was assassinated in 1898 by an Italian anarchist, and her heirs left the palace empty for several years, until they sold it in 1907 at a bargain rate to Wilhelm II, emperor of Germany. When the Kaiser renovated the palace to fit his very different Prussian-style cult of ancient Greece—replacing Elisabeth's statue of a grief-ridden, sensitive Achilles with one of the Greek god as virile military hero—he immediately had the statue of Heine removed and sold off, replacing it with a monument to the late empress herself. Though Wilhelm II was hardly a philosemite, he undoubtedly objected even more to Heine's strident antimonarchism, hatred of Prussian chauvinism, pro-French sympathies, and radical political views than to the poet's complicated and famously lapsed Jewishness.[6]

To Nordau, however, it was obvious that Heine's Jewishness was the reason for his eviction from the Achillion, and therein lay the Zionist lesson of the poem. But unlike others who have read Nordau's supplement as appropriating Heine as a Nationaljude or as evidence of Nordau's ostensibly philo-Hellenistic version of Zionism, I see it rather as a highly revealing, pained eulogy to the worldview espoused and personified by Empress Sisi as much as by her beloved Heine. Sisi wrote of Heine in words that could have come right out of the pages of Nordau's *Conventional Lies:*

> Heine hoped to see the day when people would object to being mere puppets with their monarchs pulling the strings; when the rulers themselves would cast aside their glittering rags to impress their subjects. . . . Heine hoped the time would come when monarchs would liberate themselves, be free as other people, yet retain their privilege to enforce justice; do good and make their fellow humans happier, and permit their own hearts and minds to speak frankly. . . . And the others? The motley crowd of gapers, unable to form their own opinion, lacking the courage to denounce these fakirs' tricks? They are neither good nor bad, they are just stupid. . . . It is this category of living beings against whom Heine raged. A noble wrath lent the biting darts of satire to his tongue. He did not write with a pen, but with the scalpel of a surgeon. Attempting to cure humanity, he lanced its festering boils.[7]

Even more Nordau-like was Sisi's evaluation of Heine's religious commitments. In her diary she wrote:

> Absorbed by Heine's writings, I ponder long over his confession of faith. He was born a Jew and yet he was a Christian . . . to be sure, only as I interpret the word "Christian" and not in the meaning of that world-wide multifarious sect bearing the name. Heine has taught me to look upon these disliked and persecuted people in a new light. This Jew Heine had the true conception of Christ. He loved Christ not because he was a legitimate God . . . but because he [was] democratically minded, disliking the pomp and ceremony with which, in the course of time, human tradition had endowed him. . . . What is wrong with the Christians of today? They completely lack Christianity. . . . Those clever ones who call themselves Christians are aware that humanity is still far from finding a moral god through enlightenment, self-discipline, and will power. Therefore, they try ever so hard to convert their neighbours to *their* Christianity. Thus they have a certain hold on a religion which, if the truth be told, they do not practise themselves because it is too taxing; moreover it does not pay enough. Although infidels [are] converted and

baptized day after day, all this outpouring of holy water does not help much.
. . . Monopoly of a state church is just as inimical to religion as is any other
monopoly to industry and commerce.[8]

Although Nordau the Zionist would still emphatically endorse these
views, it had become brutally apparent to him that the enemies of Sisi
and Heine, the combined forces of "degeneration" and of antisemitism,
were in control in the world at large. The shrine to Heine erected by
such a Habsburg empress would inexorably be destroyed by the forces
of evil and Jew-hatred, shouting a Prussian "Jawohl!" as they evict
Heine from their own pantheon to insanity and unreason. But Nordau
firmly and passionately believed that Heine's legacy could still be res-
cued, by continuing to battle for Heine's goals (or, more precisely, Nordau's restatement of Heine's goals) and by a recognition of the necessity
of Jews achieving these goals through Zionism.

Thus, Nordau envisioned a new form of Jewishness, informed at its
very root by the truths of science and culture that reached their apogee in
nineteenth-century Europe; his vision was parallel to Herzl's attempt to
synthesize Zionism and cosmopolitanism but was both more radical and
more militant. At the same time, Nordau (unlike Herzl) sought to link this
new Jewishness with the innate structures of the Jewish past, now recon-
sidered through Zionist lenses. Nordau could not have premised his own
Zionism on a call for a return to the Bible, a work which he continued to
denounce as intellectually childish, morally revolting, and of no sustained
literary value. A "secularization" of biblical Judaism à la Ahad Ha'am
or other Zionist thinkers was preposterous and self-contradictory, he
believed, redolent only of an irrational nostalgia and unhealthy unconscious projection of infantile desires. But there were other models in Jewish history that could be retrieved and restored to their prominence in a
new, but historically evolved, Zionist Jewish identity. Some of these figures, to be sure, articulated religious motivations or believed themselves
to be inspired by God; this was but a time-bound delusion that could
safely be stripped away in the age of science and reason.

Thus, at the Seventh Zionist Congress, held in Basel in 1905, Nordau
eulogized the recently deceased Theodor Herzl by conjuring up a pantheon of Jewish heroes supposedly admired by the late leader: Judah the
Maccabbee, Bar Kochba, Yehuda Ha-Levi, Spinoza, Heine.[9] This was a
highly revealing list, which would have set the teeth of most contemporary believing Jews on edge: Jewish military heroes of antiquity were
preferred over their rabbinic contemporaries and implicitly stripped of
their religious faith; Yehuda Ha-Levi was refashioned as the most prom-

inent proto-Zionist in Jewish history, his songs of Zion obliterating memory of his antirationalist philosophy or his profoundly spiritual liturgical poetry; Spinoza, the excommunicated heretic of Amsterdam, was claimed as the spiritual mentor of Zionism (a reclamation soon shared by adherents of virtually every other secular Jewish ideological movement in the twentieth century; previously, Maimonides had served the same role in the nineteenth century for the Jewish Enlightenment and the new denominations of Orthodox, Reform, and Positive-Historical Judaism); and finally Heine the apostate was retroactively restored to his rejected Jewishness and raised to the pinnacle of Zionist heroism.

This lionization of Heine made an obvious point: since religion was irrelevant to Jewishness, conversion to any other faith was pointless or even counterproductive, since Christianity, like Judaism, was but a fossilized residue of infantile projections of human beings' fear of death and the dissolution of their egos. All religions will continue to be discarded as rational criteria for human collective self-fashioning, as the species continues its ascent up the evolutionary ladder. Thus, the antisemites who condemned Heine as a Jew despite his baptism (and contrary to Christian dogma) were in a sense correct, if both morally reprehensible and scientifically wrongheaded. Baptism could not obliterate Jewishness, which was a national rather than a religious phenomenon.

Here one must be very precise: although Max Nordau often used the term "race" in general and "Jewish race" in particular, he by no means can be categorized as a racist thinker like Joseph Arthur Gobineau, Houston Stewart Chamberlain, or Karl Eugen Duehring—or for that matter, Jewish scientists who shared their racial taxonomy. Rather, in a way often misunderstood in the current literature on the history of racism, like many other fin-de-siècle figures, Nordau used "race" loosely and metaphorically to refer to what in German was called "Stamm"—"stock" or family or "tribal" origin. In his earlier writings Nordau believed that nationality was based on and synonymous with language (thus he often described himself as a German). After becoming a Zionist he changed his mind about the basis of national identity, adopting not a purely biological definition but rather a definition with biological roots that nonetheless could be shared by those sympathetic to the Zionist cause. He believed that his wife and daughter could be good Zionists, whatever their "biological" origin or religious views, as could anyone else who elected to join the Jewish people via Zionism. In theory, of course, the corollary to this thesis was that individual Jews could also elect to join other national collectives, if those were defined correctly and nonbiologically. Nordau did hint that this could be possible in the absence of antisemitism, as in the cases (he thought) of contemporary Britain or the United States, but he did not pursue this line of thought very far, unlike some later Zionists such as Lewis Namier or the young Arthur Koestler, who maintained that after the establishment of a Zionist homeland, all Jews who desired to remain Jewish would have to move there, and the rest would have to cease being Jewish, there being no possibility of Jewish life of any kind in the Diaspora.

But Nordau's Zionism was centered on other themes, refracted in continuing ways through the image of Heinrich Heine. In a very curious way Heine even lay behind one of Nordau's earliest and most interesting Zionist works, his play *Doktor Kohn*, which has often been analyzed in the scholarly literature but not, to my knowledge with any realization of its important Heine connection.[10] Many times in his writings Heine referred to the play *The Force of Circumstances* (*Die Macht der Verhältnisse*), written by his friend Ludwig Robert, a minor early nineteenth-century Romantic German playwright who was also the brother of Rahel Varnhagen.[11] In Robert's play, a Jewish writer named August Weiss falls in love with Sophie, the daughter of Count von der Falkenau, the minister of justice, but their love cannot lead to marriage since a bourgeois and a Jew cannot marry the daughter of a nobleman. At the same time, Sophie's brother Count Gustav boasts to his fellow army officers of his love for August's sister Emilie Weiss. August hears of this and protests against the affront to his sister's honor. An argument ensues, in which August is struck by Gustav, who then rebuffs August's challenge to a duel, since a German nobleman cannot get "satisfaction" from a man who is both a bourgeois and a Jew, and thus of doubly lower status. August then tricks Gustav into a fight, in which the Jew is stabbed and wounded but then kills the nobleman with a gunshot. August's prosecution for murder, however, is complicated by the revelation that he is the illegitimate son of none other than the father of both Gustav and Sophie, Count von der Falkenau. Guilt stricken that he has killed his own half-brother, August requests and receives a vial of poison from the count, which he then drinks. As he lies dying, he is pardoned by the prince of the realm, but to no avail. Sophie gets the last word: "False, unnatural conceptions of justice and honor and prejudices inherited over a thousand years" are to blame for this tragic denouement.[12] As others have noted, the moral of this story (at least as interpreted by

Heine) was not a critique of the German code of chivalry or of the duel as the ultimate emblem of that code, but that a Jew is indeed *Satisfaktionfähig*—that he does indeed have the "nobility of spirit" that his Christian adversaries deny him. This reading of *The Force of Circumstances* was often made by Heine, especially in his correspondence with his friend and banker, Moses Moser, another convert from Judaism who was also a friend of the converts Ludwig Robert and Rahel Varnhagen.[13]

Nordau started *Doktor Kohn* in early 1897 and finished it in the late summer of that year, while vacationing in Calvados with Anna Kaufmann and her children before leaving for the First Zionist Congress in Basel. He subtitled the play "Bürgliches Trauerspiel aus der Gegenwart" (A present-day bourgeois tragedy), an evocation others have related to Herzl's *The New Ghetto,* also subtitled a "Bourgeois Tragedy." Although there are many similarities between Herzl's and Nordau's plays, the parallels and subtle evocations of *The Force of Circumstances* make *Doktor Kohn* seem like nothing more than a Zionist reworking of Robert's drama. Set in a provincial university town, the story revolves around the tragic love affair between Dr. Leo Kohn, a brilliant university lecturer of mathematics, and Christine Moser, the daughter of one of the most distinguished Lutheran families of the town. At the start of the play, we learn that despite his intellectual prowess and worldwide renown, Dr. Kohn has just been denied a professorship at the university, since he refuses to convert to Christianity. This refusal is not based on religious faith; Dr. Kohn proudly announces that he has no religion, as little faith in Judaism as in Christianity.[14] But our updated August Weiss is a Zionist, a proud and defiant Jew who rejects emancipation and assimilation as evil chimeras and insists upon the Jews returning to their own country, reclaiming their own language. Crucial to the play, however, is the fact that this steadfast Zionism in no way intrudes upon Leo's desire and intention to marry Christine. When his potential future father-in-law protests that he does not understand the logic of this apparent contradiction—"you hold firmly to your name, because you feel yourself a portion of your race. You are proud of your Jewishness yet you choose a Christian wife"[15]—Leo declares:

> My apparent contradictions are resolved by pure humanism. I love Fraulein Christine, my love is the most absolutely personal thing about me, a thing with which neither my forefathers nor my race have any connection. Here I am an individual, and nothing else, an individual who loves and is battling for the happiness of my life.[16]

What about the children, Christine's father asks.

> I shall strive to develop their souls by love and beauty, and to accustom their
> minds to distinguish things which are proved, and are capable of proof, from
> mere assertion. When they are mentally and morally mature, they will them-
> selves decide whether they desire to profess any religion, and which one.[17]

But matters are not so simple, Dr. Kohn quickly discovers. It turns
out that Christine's father, a privy councilor and captain of the Land-
wehr, is himself a baptized Jew, who became a Lutheran not only to
marry his wife, the daughter of an aristocratic home and sister of the
town's Lutheran bishop, but out of his desire, reached on the battlefield
at Sedan, to unite himself with the German Volk. Thus, Christine's father, the erstwhile Julius Moses, was transmogrified at the baptismal
font into Christian Moser. (Surely it was not coincidental that Nordau
named his counterpart to Robert's Count von der Falkenau "Geheimer
Kommerzienrath und Landwehrhauptmann Christian Moser"; but it is
unlikely that many readers could have decoded such a clouded private
joke regarding Heine's and Robert's banker friend Moses Moser, who
indeed became a Christian.) Although totally integrated into this hoch-
deutsch family and society and dedicated to the complete disappearance
of the Jews as a religious or national group, Christian Moser still retains
some primeval Jewish characteristics—as Nordau puts it in a stage direction, Moser "mit einer jüdischen Geberde" (with a Jewish gesture)—
the head bowed, raising both hands with the palms flat and turned out-
ward—cries out, "Herr Jesus."[18] Moreover, in a shocking display of all-
too-Jewish sentimentality (reminiscent of Herzl's "Der Sohn"), Moser
loves his daughter so much that, although he is shocked by Kohn's newfangled Jewish pride, he gives his approval to the couple's betrothal. Not
so Frau Moser, born von Quincke, or her two sons, the noble officers
Carl and Ernst, who vehemently reject Dr. Kohn's suitability as a match
for Christine. Soon Frau Moser's bishop brother is drawn into the fray,
and he reveals that he never approved of the marriage of his sister to a
Jew in the first place, since "mixed marriages are an evil and a crime.
Whenever a Jewish person forces an entrance to a Christian hearth, gross
materialism and moral obtuseness follow." Baptism, he concedes, may
make a Jew into a Christian, "but it never makes an Oriental into a
German." He then concludes that because of this stain on his family's
honor, he will not permit his own daughter, Maria, to marry her beloved
cousin Carl, Christine's brother—once more a parallel to the Gustav-
Emilie pair in Ludwig Robert's play. The bishop then storms out of the

Moser home, followed by his sister, never to return. Furious at this turn of events and the loss of his own bride, Christine's brother Carl confronts Leo Kohn, a verbal altercation ensues, and then Carl utters the crucial words: "A man of honor would not bring discord into a united family." These were fighting words, according to the well-honed German code of gentlemanly honor: a third-level insult, the gravest offense possible, requiring not only a duel, but one to be settled not with swords but only by pistols. Despite pleas by Christine and her father, Leo will not—cannot—ignore the insult and dodge the duel; as he explains,

> So far as I am personally concerned, I would shrug my shoulders at the insult. My self-respect does not depend upon an angry exclamation from an excited young man. But this matter will become well known, there is no doubt of it—and it will be discussed in the usual way. People will not condemn me, the individual, Leo Kohn, but the Jew—all Jews. The disgrace to which I submit will rest upon my whole race. This dictates my duty.[19]

To which Christine—quite naturally—replies: "So your race [*dein Stamm*] is dearer to you than I?" And Kohn responds, reflecting his creator's anti-Noraism:

> You are dearer to me than everything the world contains. But I can worship you without becoming a traitor to my race. Perhaps I am in the unhappy position solely because each individual Jew has not kept before his mind the fact that his enemy's hatred imposes upon him the honor of being the legitimate representative of his whole race. The forces that encountered each other in this room today were currents of thousands of years of history. So much the worse for the individual who has the misfortune to stand at the point of contact.[20]

Christine then cries out to her two beloved Jews: "Papa, help me! We cannot let this happen. Leo, I don't want this, I don't want this!" But to no avail. The duel proceeds, and Leo does the unthinkable: he fires into the air, a clear violation of the code of chivalry and the honor of Carl, who thereupon has no choice but to fire back at his opponent, and our brave Dr. Kohn is shot and soon dies. As the final curtain falls, Christine—her life destroyed—calls out to her father: "Oh Papa, why do human beings have to hurt one another so?"[21]

To the end, Nordau has kept intact the very structure of Robert's *The Force of Circumstances,* giving Sophie's last line a particularly keen fin-de-siècle twist in Christine's lament.

Perhaps the most famous—and furious—contemporary review of

Doktor Kohn came, not surprisingly, from Ahad Ha'am, who in his Hebrew essay "Ha-musar ha-leumi" (The national ethic), first published in the fall of 1899, found the play, and Nordau's entire view of Zionism, repulsive. What offended Ahad Ha'am profoundly and irredeemably was Nordau's very acceptance of the Gentile notion of honor and chivalry:

> I need not explain how thoroughly this deed is opposed to the very bases of *our* national ethics—i.e., not just to the commandments of our faith but to the very essence of the ethical spirit that lives in our hearts. The nations of Europe as a whole—apart from some singular intellectuals and authors—cannot to this day free themselves from the vulgar notion that insults inflicted upon one by others can only be responded to with bloodshed. But the true Jew, in whom the national ethic moves the very strings of his heart, knows and feels instinctively that his thousands-of-years-old culture raises him far far above such wild acts, the residue of the brutality and cruelty of primitive ages past, and his "sense of honor" is not affected a whit by the insults of some brute. He responds to these with a condescending glance and goes his own way. . . . What is Dr. Kohn then? A "political Zionist" to be sure, but is he also a national Jew (*yehudi leumi*)? Can a man be considered a nationalist when he is so far from the spirit of his people, that even when he wants sincerely to fulfill his ethical responsibility to his people he is motivated by the emotions of another nation, and *their* concept of morality, without even noticing that he is contravening the very essence of the nation he is allegedly speaking for?[22]

Interestingly, Ahad Ha'am's attack on Nordau's conception of Jewish Zionism was itself shot through with fin-de-siècle and Social Darwinist concepts of human evolution, of the *Volksgeist*, and indeed of Jewish ethics. Even on the linguistic level, for example, to express a notion of "culture" in his juxtaposition of Hebraic and European conceptions of honor, Ahad Ha'am tellingly used the calque "kultura" rather than the older Hebrew word "tarbut," undoubtedly since the latter seemed to lack the ethical component of the concept of civilization which resounds in the German "Kultur" or even more so in the Russian "kulturnost'." Even more redolent of Ahad Ha'am's own distance from whatever might be objectively definable as an internal Jewish ethics, he did not strongly object to the theme of intermarriage that defines Nordau's play. Ahad Ha'am explained that marriage to a Gentile does not constitute an overriding moral concern to the "Jewish national ethic" but merely a contingent tactical issue: in the current state of Jewish dispersal, nationalists have the obligation to defend the integrity of their people and to sacrifice for it their own personal happiness.[23] Nordau's response to this critique has not been preserved, but it is not difficult to imagine what his rueful reply would have been. Even more than the better-known dispute between the two over Herzl's *Altneuland,* this frontal clash of sensibilities and conceptions of "Jewish honor" highlights the fundamental cultural and ideological divides not only between Max Nordau and Ahad Ha'am, but also between the ideologies of political and cultural Zionism they would spawn. For cultural Zionists, and later socialist Zionists, Zionism was a road out of the despised ghetto, a deliberate rejection of the parochialism of traditional Jewish society they had been born to, in favor of an ostensibly universalist vision that did not, however, veer to any substantive extent away from an insular and insulated Jewish identity. For Nordau—and other political Zionists such as Herzl and, later, Vladimir Jabotinsky—Zionism was on the contrary a painstaking movement away from and visceral rejection of universalism, in favor of Jewishness, but a particular sort of Jewishness defined and fashioned in line with the regnant cosmopolitan values, rhetoric, taste, feel, and weltanschauung of the European fin de siècle. Indeed, *Doktor Kohn* is perhaps the clearest expression of this amalgam. By the time of its composition, Nordau had concluded that his previous worldview, which held his Jewishness to be an incidental accident of birth and irrelevant to his life and thought, was now scientifically unsound. What had changed was not science, nor his overall belief that "the struggle for existence, using the term in its most comprehensive sense, shapes the destinies of nations as well as of the most obscure individual and is the foundation for all forms of political and social life"—what had changed was the unanticipated spread of yet another conventional lie of "civilization"—antisemitism. As he put it in *Doktor Kohn:*

> The greatest hostility to civilization is to make a gifted people an object of loathing and mockery to themselves, and to discourage them from every attempt at development. Baptized or unbaptized, the Jew is the modern Helot (that is, serf). He must become himself again. That is his only deliverance. If the Aryan thrusts back the Semite, and shuts him out of the Aryan race of humanity, the Semite must seek to become a virile man as a Jew. And virile manhood requires a consciousness of nationality which the individual acknowledges to himself and to others. [24]

Before turning to this last sentence—"virile manhood requires a consciousness of nationality which the individual acknowledges to himself and to others"—it is crucial to note that *Doktor Kohn* includes yet another central and complex trope of Nordau's Zionism, which was also indebted in curious ways to Heinrich Heine. After Leo Kohn is shot, his parents are summoned to see him; they appear onstage clad in traditional Jewish garb, speaking Judeo-German, steadfastly maintaining the rituals of their faith. Though socially far inferior to the Mosers, not to speak of the von Quinckes, they are presented as exemplars of dignity and moral fortitude, untainted by the falseness and vanities of their supposed superiors. This positive portrayal of traditional Jews was far more famously articulated in the speech Nordau gave immediately after completing *Doktor Kohn,* his address to the First Zionist Congress in Basel in late August 1897. Undoubtedly his most often quoted self-presentation as a Zionist, this speech hammered home three main points with the zeal of a new convert's faith: that everywhere the Jews lived they were suffering from *Judennot* (Jewish distress), either physical or moral pain. In western Europe, they were financially comfortable but in psychological and moral agony, since Emancipation was proven to be a failure by the rise of racial antisemitism; in central and eastern Europe, they were politically persecuted and in socioeconomic crisis, but morally and ethically they were far more intact than their brethren to the West, the "ghetto" providing them both succor and self-confidence.[25]

Although much of this was already standard Zionist fare, Nordau's presentation was electrifying; Herzl is supposed to have responded to it with the words "Monumentum aere perennius" (a monument more enduring than bronze).[26] This was not only due to Nordau's remarkable rhetoric skill but because he was who he was: by far the most famous person at the congress, a psychiatrist and cultural critic who used his vast knowledge, both scientific and humanitarian, to diagnose the malady of the Jewish people and to prescribe the solution to its plight. Most striking was his psychological analysis of the contrast between West and East European Jews, a frontal inversion of the fundamental taxonomy of modern Jewish history at least from the time of Moses Mendelssohn, in which Jews in central and eastern Europe were held to be culturally, religiously, and, perhaps most important, morally inferior to those in western Europe, if reformable along western European lines. To the contrary, Nordau the famous psychiatrist declared:

> The word "Ghetto" is today associated with feelings of degradation and humiliation. But the psychologist of nations and the historian of morals knows that the Ghetto, whatever may have been the intentions of the people who created it, was for the Jew of the past not a prison, but a refuge. . . . What mattered it that outside the Ghetto was despised that which within it was praised? The opinion of the outside world had no influence, because it was the opinion of ignorant enemies. One tried to please one's brethren, and

their pleasure was the worthy contentment of one's life. So did the Ghetto Jew live, in a moral respect, a real full life. Their external situation was insecure, often seriously endangered, but internally they achieved a complete development of their individuality, with no fragmentation of the self. They were human beings in harmony, who were not in want of any elements of the normal existence of a member of a community. . . . Kaftan, sidelocks, fur caps and jargon (i.e., Yiddish) obviously have nothing to do with religion. But the Eastern Jews suspect anyone who dresses according to European style and speaks any language properly as beginning the process of apostasy, since he has cut the ties between himself and his community, and they consider such ties the only guarantee of belonging to the community, without which an individual cannot exist for any length of time morally, psychically, and even physically.[27]

This is very different from analyses by other Zionist thinkers of the distinctions between East and West European Jews: for example, Ahad Ha'am's well-known essay "Slavery in Freedom" focused on the self-delusion of emancipated Jewry but hardly lionized so-called ghetto Jews as models to emulate. Instead, Nordau's words are closest to Heinrich Heine's, who in 1823 published his account of his journey east a year earlier, entitled *On Poland* (Ueber Polen), where he first encountered traditional East European Jews in all their authenticity. Heine confessed:

A shudder runs down my spine when I remember my first experience (just beyond Meseritz it was) of a Polish village inhabited mainly by Jews. Not even the *Berlin Weekly* under Wadzeck's editorship, stewed, physically, into a porridge, could have nauseated me as utterly as the sight of those filthy and ragged apparitions. Not even the high-minded orations of a fifth-former enthused by the thoughts of gymnastic exercises and the fatherland could have hurt my ears as excruciatingly as the jargon spoken by Polish Jews.[28]

But, he continued,

compassion soon shouldered out disgust when I took a closer look at the way these people lived; when I saw the pigsty-like hovels which they inhabit and in which they jabber, pray and haggle, and are miserable. . . . At the very least, however, the Jews always pored over their Hebrew books of learning and religion, for the sake of which they had left their fatherland and their creature comforts behind. They failed, clearly, to keep pace with European civilization, and their spiritual world sank into a morass of unedifying superstition squeezed into a thousand grotesque shapes by a super-subtle scholasticism. And yet, and yet . . . Despite the barbarous fur cap that covers his head and the still more barbarous ideas that fill it, I value the Polish Jew much higher than many a German Jew who wears his hat in the latest Simón Bolívar fashion and has his head filled with quotations from Jean Paul. In rigid seclusion that Polish Jew's character became a homogeneous whole; when breathing a more tolerant air it took on the stamp of liberty. The inner man did not become a composite medley of heterogeneous emotions, nor did it atrophy through being constrained within the walls of the Frankfurt ghetto, ordinances decreed by the high, wise, and mighty city fathers, and disabilities charitably decreed by law. I for my part prefer the Polish Jew with his filthy fur, his populated beard, his smell of garlic, and his jabbering jargon, to many another who stands in the all the glory of his gilt-edged securities.[29]

What Nordau had done, then, was in many ways to accept Heine's highly ambivalent portraits of both "ghetto" and "modern" Jews, but to update them according to the canons both of Lombrosian psychology and of Herzlian Zionism. It is fascinating to note that in its most popular translations into both English and Hebrew, Nordau's speech to the First Zionist Congress has been stripped of much of its controversial fin-de-siècle language. Typical but hardly difficult German terms such as "Völkerpsychologe und Sittengeschichtsschreiber," "Normaldasein," and "seelisch" are either mistranslated or omitted entirely; his "scientific" certainty that traditional Jewish garb and Yiddish have nothing to do with religion is subtly effaced by rendering the German word "offenbar" (meaning "obviously") as "apparently" or by omitting this point entirely.[30] In this way, Nordau's words are severed from their time and context and, most important, from his undying certainty that moral, psychological, physical, and cultural phenomena are interrelated in a way that is completely susceptible to rigorous Darwinian analysis. Morality and religion, the relationship between "normal" and "healthy" individual psyches and the collective, can be plotted along universally applicable axes of evolution and devolution entirely parallel to the evidence of geological strata or fossil remains. The author of *Conventional Lies* and *Degeneration* has not disappeared or given up his former faith upon his conversion to Zionism. It is only that he has become convinced that the only strategy for survival for the Jews is to uproot themselves from the ecologically unhealthy and inhospitable soil of Europe for their "native land" of Palestine, where they can lead normal and healthy lives.

But Nordau's Heine-like construct of a Jewish "noble savage" was—like its Rousseauian predecessor—not only historically inaccurate but profoundly disingenuous. Based primarily on an aversion to its presumptive mirror image, that of "civilized man" in the former case and "emancipated bourgeois Jews" in the latter, this rhetorical celebration of a fictionalized state of grace was deeply ambiguous from the start, marked by a pandering cultural condescension and a deeply embedded and only partially acknowledged aesthetic and physical revulsion to the objects of its supposed veneration. Soon, these contradictions would come to the fore as this countercultural juxtaposition of East and West European Jewry would become a central theme in German-Jewish thought, both Zionist and non-Zionist, and in the ideology of that most western European–like East European Zionist, Vladimir Jabotinsky. Of course, the most influential figure in this regard was Martin Buber, whose groundbreaking interpretations of Hasidism began to be published to great acclaim at this time—in yet another manifestation of fin-de-siècle culture, the cult of the "primitive" and the irrational. But these lionizations of traditional East European Jewish life and culture were viscerally and indeed instinctively rejected by the vast majority of East European Jews, including East European Zionists, whose very lifeblood was hatred of the traditional Jewish society out of which they sprung. Consequently, they dedicated themselves to extirpating from their midst and from Jewish culture as a whole the Yiddish language, vestiges of Hasidism and other forms of traditional Jewish piety, and what they derided as either the "ghetto" or "*galut* mentality" of East European Jewry, which for them was defined by cowardice, obsequiousness, and physical and moral weakness. For decades to come the Kulturkampf within the Zionist world itself would be fought along these counterintuitive cultural divides, for example with German-born Zionists (and to some extent disciples of Jabotinsky) frequently praising and even advocating the spread of Yiddish culture, while the majority of native Yiddish–speaking Zionists, whether socialist or liberal, opposed these moves with ferocious intensity.

But long before that, the internal contradictions in Nordau's own view of East European or unemancipated Jews as a whole came to the fore. As we have seen in *Doktor Kohn*, dying in a duel for one's honor and the honor of one's nation, so abhorrent to Ahad Ha'am, was both a duty and a metaphor of the new Jew that Nordau was dedicated to creating as a Zionist and via Zionism. For Nordau, a central goal of Zionism was transforming both the "ghetto" and the bourgeois Jew—both alleged to be effeminate, weak, cut off from nature, cowardly, sickly, desexualized—into a physically robust, healthy, and sexually potent man, in the process rebuilding himself, his land, and his people. Nowhere, of course, was this image so famously and yet so strangely articulated than in Nordau's call for the creation of a "Muskeljudentum," a Jewry of muscle, most clearly explained in a speech he delivered in June 1903 to a Zionist gymnastic club. Given the centrality of this address both to Nordau's view of Zionism and to those of Ephraim Moses Lilien and especially Vladimir Jabotinsky, it is important to reproduce it here in its entirety, without the ellipses and mistranslations so common in its presentations elsewhere:

> Two years ago, during a committee meeting at the Congress in Basel, I said: "We must think again of creating a Jewry of muscle."
>
> Again! For history is our witness, that such once existed, but for long, all too long, we have engaged in the mortification of our flesh. I am expressing myself imprecisely. It was others who practiced mortification on our flesh, and with the greatest success, evidenced by the hundreds of thousands of Jewish corpses in the ghettoes, church squares, and highways of medieval Europe. We ourselves would happily have renounced this "virtue." We would rather have cared for our bodies than allowed them to be destroyed—figuratively and literally. We know how to make rational use of our life and we appreciate its value. Unlike most others, we do not consider [our bodies] our greatest good, but they are valued and we look after them with care. But for centuries we could not do so. All the elements of Aristotelian physics were meted out to us in a miserly fashion: light and air, water and earth. In the narrow Jewish street, our poor limbs forgot how to move joyfully; in the gloom of sunless houses our eyes became accustomed to nervous blinking; out of fear of constant persecution the timbre of our voices was extinguished to an anxious whisper, which only rose to a strong shout when our martyrs on their stakes cried out their last prayers in the face of their executioners. But now, force no longer constrains us, we are given space for our bodies to live again. Let us take up our oldest traditions; let us once more become deep-chested, tightly muscled, courageous men.
>
> This desire to take hold of a proud past finds a powerful expression in the very name chosen by the Jewish gymnastic society [Turnverein] in Berlin. Bar Kochba was a hero who refused to suffer any defeat. When victory was denied him, he knew how to die. Bar Kochba was the last embodiment in world history of a battle-hardened and bellicose Jewry. To evoke Bar Kochba's name is an ambitious undertaking. But ambition is well suited to gymnasts, who strive for perfection.
>
> Gymnastics has so critical an educational mission for no other nation as much as for us Jews. It will straighten us in body and in character. It will give us self-confidence. Our enemies claim that we already have too much of that. But we know best how false that assumption is; we lack it entirely when it comes to an assured trust in our physical strength.
>
> Our new muscle-Jews [Muskeljuden] have not yet matched the heroism of our forefathers, who in large numbers streamed into the gymnasia to take part in competitions, and pitted themselves against the well-trained Hellenistic athletes and the powerful Nordic barbarians. But morally the new muscle-Jews surpass the ancient Jewish circus-fighters, who were ashamed of their Jewishness, and tried surgically to conceal the sign of their covenants with a surgical operation, as we learn from the outraged rabbis of the times,

while the members of the Bar Kochba society loudly and freely profess their nationality.

May the Jewish Gymnastic Society flourish and thrive and become ardent models for Jewish life everywhere.[31]

Much has recently been written about fin-de-siècle views of gymnastics and masculinity, and about the connections between these conceptions and nationalism, including Zionism. The foremost scholar of this interconnection was George Mosse, who wrote many volumes on these subjects in both the German and Jewish contexts. Mosse's intuition was impeccable, and his erudition vast, but as we saw in his frequently reprinted misrepresentation of Nordau's *The Right to Love,* Mosse's work on Zionism was often derailed both by a sloppiness in regard to detail and by his passionate ideological opposition to political Zionism, a tendency shared by many of his less talented students.[32] His analysis of masculinity and Zionism suffers from the same erroneous evaluation of the Zionist movement as a whole—as typically and essentially liberal and bourgeois—without appreciating the cardinal role of its antibourgeois essence. Thus, for Nordau and Herzl, following Heine, at least as insidious as the ghetto Jew was the bourgeois Jew, represented as a fat (and effeminate) cigar-smoking capitalist with a carefully coifed wife (or mistress) on his arm or as a deracinated German- or Austrian-Jewish student, intellectual, lawyer, or journalist at home in the coffee house and lecture hall but cut off entirely from nature, from military life, from "real" manhood.

In one crucial respect that has recently all but dominated the discussion of fin-de-siècle conceptions of masculinity, Mosse was absolutely on target, breaching a taboo that had been universal in any discussion of European nationalism and, all the more so, of Zionism: Mosse argued that as the late nineteenth-century idea of masculinity, including its borrowed Greek standards of male beauty, was drafted by European nationalisms into service as national symbols or stereotypes, its obvious homoeroticism was sublimated into the national ideal itself. This largely unconscious homoeroticism must be distinguished, he astutely insisted, from homosexuality, as the originators and leaders of the English, German, Czech, and other nationalist youth and scouting movements were for the most part heterosexuals, good husbands and family men, just like Max Nordau (and Ephraim Moses Lilien and Vladimir Jabotinsky, as well).[33] Indeed, Mosse could have used Nordau's call for a "muscular Jewry" as a prime text in this regard, since Nordau overtly and unashamedly ended his speech with the blatant and evocative image of the publicly displayed circumcised Jewish phallus as ultimate symbol of Jewish national pride as well as newfound Jewish masculinity. His call for deep-chested, tightly muscled, battle-ready Jews was shot through with homoerotic resonances, even though Nordau himself notoriously and repeatedly denounced homosexuality as a prime example of "degeneracy" and mental illness.

But beyond this important indebtedness to fin-de-siècle conceptions of manhood, Nordau's conception of Jewish masculinity and, hence, the new, Zionist, Jew, was profoundly informed and defined by an innovative reappraisal that would become vastly influential both in the Zionist movement and beyond it, in the century to come. Nordau's earlier diagnosis of the psychic intactness of pre-modern Jews and their contemporary unemancipated brethren was here crucially, if paradoxically, complemented by a devastating critique of their physical weakness and its inevitable psychological consequences, as "Aristotelian" light, air, water, and earth are juxtaposed with Jewish gloom, darkness, immobility, anxiety, and depression. Many commentators have noted, usually with acute discomfort, the obvious acceptance here by Nordau of antisemitic stereotypes of Jews. An astute analyst of the Zionist "resort to force," the Israeli historian Anita Shapira wrote about Nordau's concept of "Muskeljudentum" without the typical apologetics of the genre:

> In [Nordau's] case, acceptance of the antisemitic diagnosis did not entail concomitant acceptance of the racist deterministic prognosis preached by antisemitic ideologues . . . that analysis did not contain any self-hatred, along the lines of Otto Weininger and others; rather, it harbored a wish for self-improvement. Enhancement of the sense of Jewish solidarity, awareness of Jewish ethnicity, bolstering of self-pride—all these were to be the necessary preliminary stages preceding the truly momentous task that lay before the Jews as a people.[34]

Shapira also drew attention to the parallels between Nordau's evocation of Bar Kochba and other Zionists' frequent appropriation of the Maccabees as Jewish military heroes of antiquity, commenting: "In particular those with a spotty knowledge of their people's past were often the ones who cited the Maccabees as an example of Jewish bravery and prowess"—a phenomenon later replaced in Israeli popular culture with the cult of Masada. But a closer reading of Nordau's text reveals that his analysis of the Jewish past and his appropriation of Bar Kochba were far more complex than that. "Mortification of the flesh," the translation I and others have offered, is but the closest approximation in literary English for the original German "Fleischabtötung" (literally, "flesh-

killing"), a term more precisely rendered (if without its crucially evocative Christian resonances) by Nordau's Hebrew translator as "hamatat-
basar."[35] Nordau's apology for ostensible imprecision at the very
beginning of his address—"for long, all too long, we have engaged in
Fleischabtötung. I am expressing myself imprecisely. It was others who
practiced *Fleischabtötung* on us"—was a brilliantly subtle rhetorical device that revealed the double-edged sword of his condemnation of Jewish
physical self-abnegation: the Jews were indeed complicit in their own
all but fatal disembodiment, he believed, alongside and in collaboration
with their persecutors. Indeed, his rendering of the post–Bar Kochba
Jewish past as an endless chronicle of persecution and pain was a highly
idiosyncratic but crucial step in the Zionist recasting of Diaspora Jewish
history as merely a "Leidensgeschichte" (history of suffering) as opposed
to the "Leidens-und-Gelehrntengeschichte" (history of suffering and
scholarship) of the regnant liberal or Breslau school of Jewish historiography. In Nordau's version, only when they were persecuted did Jews
truly become men, the nervous twitter of their all but extinguished voices
turning into powerful, full-throated, manly shouts on the stake. Here
again, one must return to the original to appreciate the full force of the
point: the German word he used to depict the cries of Jews at death's
door was "Jauchzen," typically meaning "joyful or exuberant shouting," as in the jubilant cheering of a crowd. Similarly, Bar Kochba was
not just a brave military hero or a politician who grasped the importance
of fighting for the land of Israel against the Roman occupiers; he was a
Jewish soldier who, when victory was denied him, "knew how to die."

Without entering here into the minefield of the relationship between
Romanticism and fin-de-siècle thought, suffice it to say that Nordau's
evocation of Bar Kochba's knowing how to die was a fascinating projection into the historical account of the fin-de-siècle cult of death and
dying, epitomized in the Symbolist poets' and painters' obsession with
the details of the death process and with contemporary psychologists'
debates over "a will to death," ultimately leading to Freud's stark and
highly controversial dualism of Eros and Thanatos. Moreover, Nordau's
lionization of Bar Kochba's death as a model to be emulated was inventive on his part, parallel to his peculiar attribution of masculine prowess
to Jewish martyrs on the stake. Heinrich Graetz, the most widely read
Jewish historian in the late nineteenth century and most likely the source
of Nordau's knowledge about Bar Kochba, celebrated him as a "much
reviled and misunderstood personage," "the perfect incarnation of the
nation's will and the nation's hate," and one who had "[s]o energetic a

mind, combined with great military talent, even though it failed to secure
a favorable result [that he] should have received juster recognition from
posterity, and certainly does not deserve the prejudice which it met with
from interested contemporaries."[36] But Graetz asserted, "the end of the
mighty Bar-Kochba is not known," skeptically challenging the historic-
ity of the only known account of his demise, the famous talmudic legend
in which Bar Kochba slays Rabbi Elazar of Modiin, one of the most
important sages of the day, on suspicion of active collaboration with
the Roman enemies. As a result, a heavenly voice (*bat-kol*) comes forth
saying:

> "Woe to the worthless shepherd who abandons the flock: the sword shall be
> upon his arm and upon his right eye, his arm shall be wholly withered and
> his right eye blinded" (Zechariah 11:17). You slew Rabbi Elazar of Modiin,
> the arm of Israel and their right eye. Therefore your own arm shall be wholly
> withered and your right eye utterly blinded.
>
> Immediately, sins brought it to pass and Betar was captured and Bar
> Kochba was killed. They came carrying his head to Hadrian. He asked them,
> "Who killed this man?" A certain Cuthean replied, "I killed him." Hadrian
> said to him: "Show me his corpse." He showed his corpse to him, and there
> was a snake coiled around it. He said, "If God had not killed him, who would
> have been able to do so?" And he applied to him the verse, "Not unless their
> rock had given them over, and the Lord had handed them over" (Deuter-
> onomy 32:30).[37]

In other words, although in the traditional sources Bar Kochba is
depicted as a "gibbor," a glorious warrior, fierce in battle, he is also
said to have been killed by God in punishment for his egregious sin, his
murder of a rabbinic sage who, like most of his colleagues, preached
cooperation with the Romans in order to preserve Judaism as a faith
and the Jewish people as a holy nation.[38] Nordau's creative evocation
of his brave and noble death was a remarkably potent and pregnant
symbol of his own overarching subversion of traditional Jewish categories and conceptions in the name of a new form of Jewishness totally
defined by the values and aesthetic of the European fin de siècle. The
new Jew—the Zionist—would be an embodiment of late nineteenth-
century conceptions of tight-muscled, broad-chested, masculine men, in
sharp contradistinction to the effeminate and weak and cowardly, if
psychically intact, ghetto Jew. And the new Jew would also betoken a
return to noble Jewish heroes of antiquity, defined not by their faith in
their God but as the personification of a "kriegsharten waffenfrohen
Judentums" (rendered as "a battle-hardened and bellicose Jewry" in the
translation above of Nordau's "Muskeljudentum" speech). But the term

"waffenfrohen" literally means "weapons-happy," a Jew who experiences true manly jubilation not on the martyr's pyre but by wielding his weapons proudly and in defense of Jewish "honor," now redefined in a way that would shock not only the rabbis of yore or those of Breslau, but their weak-kneed, shrill-voiced, and effeminate disciples, the so-called cultural or spiritual Zionists as well.

Bar Kochba, of course, died in defense of the town of Betar, and it was with total self-consciousness and symbolic intent that Vladimir Jabotinsky, Max Nordau's most important disciple, would choose that town's resonant name for the youth movement he founded to propel his version of Zionism. But before we turn to Jabotinsky's own journey from cosmopolitanism to Zionism, a Russian variation on the road traversed by both Herzl and Nordau, we pause en route from Paris to Odessa to examine the most fascinating graphic representation of the debt of early Zionism to the culture and aesthetic of the fin de siècle, the drawings of Ephraim Moses Lilien, the first Zionist artist.

CHAPTER FIVE

From Jugendstil to "Judenstil"

*Cosmopolitanism and Nationalism in
the Work of Ephraim Moses Lilien*

In 1900, a book of profoundly philosemitic poems entitled *Juda* was published in Berlin,[1] written by Freiherr Börries von Münchhausen, a descendant of the eighteenth-century "Lügenbaron," famous for his delightful tales of wildly improbable adventures at home and abroad. As the author of several collections of neo-Romantic German ballads, the new Baron von Münchhausen had achieved minor fame for his attempt to revive, in a disingenuously naive voice, the lost tradition of German chivalric verse. His book *Juda* was a retelling in simple German verse of some of the most seductive stories of the Hebrew Bible—Rahab, the harlot of Jericho, the witch of Endor, Samson and Delilah, and the like. For many German Jews of the generation that came to maturity in the fin de siècle, this beautifully published volume became a cherished work, for here was a well-known German noble poet singing praise to the aristocratic traditions of the ancient Hebrews and their Book of Books. Soon after its appearance *Juda* was lavishly acclaimed and fulsomely reviewed across the ideological spectrum of German-speaking Jewry, from *Die Neue Freie Presse* to *Die Welt*. Even Stefan Zweig—hardly a sentimental type—gushed in exuberance: "In this book, the first and best of the modern German ballad-poets takes on a new and fascinating face, strong and forceful; in his verses the images glisten like rubies, illuminated by the suggestive pathos of the Psalms and Biblical poems, the monumental rock-like strength of the Old Testament and the dark ecstatic rhythms of its songs ... are rejuvenated in these sonorous verses."[2]

Zweig was, at this stage, rather well disposed toward the fledgling Jewish national movement, but in retrospect it is difficult to imagine how the vast majority of German Jews, non-Zionist or anti-Zionist, could have welcomed this book with any zeal, for the overt message of *Juda* was a call for the Jews to return forthwith to their ancient homeland, in order there to revive their erstwhile aristocratic patrimony. *Juda*'s initial poem, entitled "Euch" (To you), summed up the entire volume in its third and last stanzas (which do not lose much more than the rhyme-scheme in translation):

Respected nation, I point out to you the bridge
Away from hate and scorn and back to your youthful joy
Lost tribe, I show you the way
Your road is marked "back home."

... Leave your shops and scales behind
Be what you are, ancient Israel,
Your God still lives, and his columns march forth
Hear O Israel![3]

Collaborating with Börries von Münchhausen on *Juda* was the young Galician Jew Ephraim Moses Lilien, who provided extensive illustrations and ornamentation in an astonishing new artistic style—a nationalist Jewish version of Jugendstil. Indeed, this highly embellished and artfully designed volume served as Lilien's debut as an artist specializing in Jewish themes with an overt Zionist message and self-consciously Zionist style. This was a substantial departure from Lilien's previous work—before *Juda,* Lilien had been known only as a minor member of the Jugendstil circles in Munich and Berlin and a contributor to a variety of socialist, modernist, and avant-garde journalistic and artistic ventures. Within a few years he would become perhaps the most innovative and famous Zionist artist of his time, until his untimely death in 1925 at the age of fifty-one.

Lilien has now been largely forgotten, except by students of Jewish, Zionist, and Israeli art; a parallel group of experts in the history of German graphic art and book design; and a tiny number of historians of Zionism interested in its visual and symbolic representation.[4] The small literature on Lilien is informative, and our knowledge of his life and work was immeasurably advanced a decade ago with the publication by the Leo Baeck Institute of his charming *Letters to His Wife,* edited by his son.[5] Unfortunately, however, the bulk of the existing scholarship on Lilien is remarkably uncritical and unschooled in the intellectual, ideological, and political contexts, roots, and resonances of his work. Particularly missing is any sustained appreciation either of Lilien's transformation from a poor Galician heder-boy to, first, a decadent Vienna/Munich/Berlin cosmopolitan artist and then to a Jewish nationalist or of his application to the Zionist cause of an artistic style and worldview that was avowedly sensualist, erotic, aestheticist, individualist, antibourgeois, antirationalist, and, at least originally, aggressively antinationalist.

Nowhere is Lilien's extraordinary mélange of decadence and Jewishness—the admixture of Jugendstil and *Judentum* that I have here somewhat playfully termed "Judenstil"—more obvious than in his own early ex libris plate, roughly contemporaneous with his drawings for *Juda* (figure 1). Here we see a jarring juxtaposition of Lilien's Hebrew signature and a typical art nouveau, Beardsley-like figure of a nude woman whose flowing tresses cover her genitals, with her face buried in and obscured by a book and a motto, in rather stilted Hebrew, "la-tehorim kol tahor" (to the pure, everything is pure). Seemingly a scriptural prooftext but avowing a decidedly un-Hebraic sentiment, this motto is, in fact, a rendering into Hebrew of Paul's famous anti-Jewish dictum in the *Epistle to Titus,* warning the Cretans against Jewish "vain talkers and deceivers . . . who teach things which they ought not, for filthy lucre's sake" and exhorting them "not to give heed to Jewish fables and commandments, of men who turn away from the truth. To the pure all things are pure, but to them that are defiled and unbelieving, nothing is pure."[6]

Why was a self-consciously Zionist, avant-garde artist borrowing such a New Testament homily in the service of a new nationalist Jewish art? Can we hear in this motto reverberations of Münchhausen's call for the Jews to abandon their degrading shops and scales, their undignified search for lucre, for the purity of their ancient bearing? In contrast to most of the literature on Lilien, I argue here that Lilien, deliberately and self-consciously, was attempting to create a nationalist Jewish art that would at once decry the sterility and unnaturalness of bourgeois Jewish society, celebrate sexuality and physicality as well as the life of the workingman, and promote the rejuvenation and potential freedom of the Jewish people—a rejuvenation, as it were, of the Jewish body as well as the Jewish body politic. In line with the overall Secession creed, Lilien

Left: Figure 1. *Ex Libris E. M. Lilien,* from E. M. Lilien, *Sein Werk, mit einer Einleitung von Stefan Zweig* (Berlin and Leipzig, 1903).

Figure 2. "The Wheel of Time" (*Das Rad der Zeit*), from Lothar Brieger, *E. M. Lilien, eine künstlerische Entwicklung um die Jahrhundertwende* (Berlin and Vienna, 1922), 39.

Figure 3. *Right:* End page from Johann von Wildenradt, *Der Zöllner von Klausen* (Berlin, 1892), reproduced in E. M. Lilien, *Sein Werk, mit einer Einleitung von Stefan Zweig* (Berlin and Leipzig, 1903).

Figure 4. "Genius Before the Bar of Prudery" (*Genius vor dem Richterstuhle der Prüderie*), from E. M. Lilien, *Sein Werk, mit einer Einleitung von Stefan Zweig* (Berlin and Leipzig, 1903).

Figure 5. *Left:* "The Silent Song" (*Das stille Lied*), from Börries von Münchhausen, *Juda* (Goslar, 1900).

Figure 6. "Passover" (*Passah*), from Börries von Münchhausen, *Juda* (Goslar, 1900).

Figure 7. *Above:* "From Ghetto to Zion" (*Von Ghetto nach Zion*), from E. M. Lilien, *Sein Werk, mit einer Einleitung von Stefan Zweig* (Berlin and Leipzig, 1903).

Figure 8. *Opposite, top:* "At the Sewing Machine" (*An der Nähmaschine*), from Berthold Feiwel, *Lieder des Ghetto* (Berlin, 1903).

Figure 9. *Opposite:* "The Jewish May" (*Der jüdische Mai*), from Berthold Feiwel, *Lieder des Ghetto* (Berlin, 1903).

Figure 10. "The Creation of Man" (*Die Erschaffung des Menschen*), from Berthold Feiwel, *Lieder des Ghetto* (Berlin, 1903).

116

Denn ich kröne ihn zum Herrscher.
Meiner Flammen schenk' ich her
Einen Teil. Er soll regieren
Über Erde, Luft und Meer.

Fallen soll das Tier der Lüfte
Seiner Macht. Wenn's ihm behagt,
Soll der Fisch im Wasser fallen
Und der Löwe auf der Jagd!"

Da erschraken Gottes Räte:
„Dieses Menschlein — Schaum und Rauch —
Wenn es soll die Luft beherrschen,
Kommt's noch in den Himmel auch."

Und sie sprachen also: „Mach' ihn,
Herr, nach unserm Angesicht.
Gib ihm Geist und gib ihm Stärke,
Aber Flügel gib ihm nicht.

Nein, er darf nicht Flügel haben,
(Fliegen wird er mit dem Schwert)
Nicht betreten soll den Himmel,
Wer da herrschet auf der Erd'!"

Und Gott sprach: „So soll's geschehen.
Euer Rat ist klug und fein.
Doch nicht alle Menschenkinder
Sollen ungeflügelt sein.

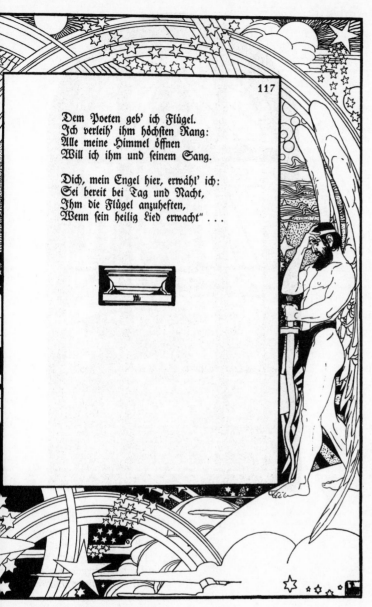

Dem Poeten geb' ich Flügel.
Ich verleih' ihm höchsten Rang:
Alle meine Himmel öffnen
Will ich ihm und seinem Sang.

Dich, mein Engel hier, erwähl' ich:
Sei bereit bei Tag und Nacht,
Ihm die Flügel anzuheften,
Wenn sein heilig Lied erwacht" . . .

Figure 11. "The Creation
of Man" (*Die Erschaffung
des Menschen*), from
Berthold Feiwel, *Lieder des
Ghetto* (Berlin, 1903).

Figure 12. "Moses" (*Mose*), stained-glass window in B'nai B'rith Lodge in Hamburg, reproduced in Lothar Brieger, *E. M. Lilien, eine künstlerische Entwicklung um die Jahrhundertwende* (Berlin and Vienna, 1922), 81.

Figure 13. *Left:* "Moses Breaks the Tablets" (*Mose zebricht die Tafeln*), from E. M. Lilien, *Biblisches Lesebuch* (Braunschweig/Hamburg, 1914), reproduced in Lothar Brieger, *E. M. Lilien, eine künstlerische Entwicklung um die Jahrhundertwende* (Berlin and Vienna, 1922), 217.

Figure 14. Herzl overlooking the Rhine, photograph by E. M. Lilien (1897).

Figure 15. "Women at the
Wailing Wall" (*Frauen
an der Klagemauer*), from
Lothar Brieger, *E. M.
Lilien, eine künstlerische
Entwicklung um die
Jahrhundertwende* (Berlin
and Vienna, 1922), 197.

believed that to show modern man his true face required a frontal assault on bourgeois culture and morality, including bourgeois Jewish culture and morality; what was required was an excavation of the quasi-archeological instinctual and erotic life that had special ramifications for the Jews. Thus, there is a clear parallel between Lilien's artistic and ideological quest and the work and thought of his far more famous contemporary Gustav Klimt, in whose "constantly shifting representations of space and substance" (as Carl Schorske so beautifully put it) "from the naturalistically solid through the impressionistically fluid to the abstract and geometrically static—we can see the groping for orientation in a world without secure coordinates."[7]

Closer to home, there is a parallel between Lilien's glide from Galician poverty to socialism, cosmopolitanism, decadence, and then to Jewish nationalism and the ideological and personal trajectories of other famous Zionists who followed similar paths—most notably Theodor Herzl and Max Nordau, and, as well, Vladimir Jabotinsky.

The following analysis of Lilien's role in the creation of a Zionist iconography is based on no new documentary discoveries, but solely on my own—I hope, fresh—reading of his art, his extant writings, and those of his contemporary admirers and detractors. What especially intrigues me is not solely the parallelism of the directions of the personal and ideological journeys of figures such as Lilien, Nordau, and Jabotinsky, but more interestingly the haunting similarities in the versions of Zionism they created, deeply imbued with and defined by the values, rhetoric, taste, feel, and look of the European fin de siècle.

It was rather a long road that Ephraim Moses Lilien took to his final destination. He was born on May 23, 1874, in Drohobycz, an important Eastern Galician town in the Lemberg district that was also the birthplace of Maurycy Gottlieb, perhaps the first and most talented East European Jewish painter of note. At the time of Lilien's birth, Drohobycz was a bustling center of the petroleum trade with a population of nearly 20,000, not quite the "poverty-stricken little village" portrayed in much of the literature on Lilien, which is remarkably—though perhaps not surprisingly—ill informed about the social, cultural, and political history of Galician Jewry in its early post-Emancipation days. By the time of Ephraim's adolescence, the Drohobycz Jewish community was not the homogeneous and traditional East European shtetl as stereotypically portrayed. Rather, it had experienced all of the social, economic, ideological, political, and religious turmoil attendant upon the modernization of Galician Jewry, including the development of a substantial modern Jewish culture. In 1883, for example, the Drohobycz Hebrew printing press had issued a translation of Schiller's German reworking of *Macbeth;* soon, a noteworthy Zionist newspaper would appear, written in German in Hebrew characters. At the same time, the social structure of Drohobycz Jewry underwent dramatic shifts, with the development of a thriving Jewish bourgeoisie, at first Germanized and then more and more Polonized. From this social complex there later would emerge the extraordinary writer Bruno Schultz.

Significantly, Lilien's family was not part of either the intellectual or the socioeconomic elite of the town, though it was related to the latter. His father was a poor wood-turner who could not afford to allow his talented son more than a few years of study in the local gymnasium, thereafter apprenticing him to a sign-maker in appreciation of his artistic gift. Some of the extended Lilien family, however, who were well-heeled members of the Lemberg Jewish bourgeoisie, objected to this undignified trade for young Ephra; they subsidized his attendance first at Lemberg's *Realschule,* and then at the Cracow Art Academy, where he studied under the famous Polish realist painter Jan Matejko. When his funds ran out, he was forced to return home to Drohobycz, where he apparently spent the two years between his eighteenth and twentieth birthdays supporting himself with signmaking and portrait painting.[8]

In 1894, he won first prize in a competition to design a diploma conferring the freedom of the city of Drohobycz on the famous Polish poet Ujejski; the cash prize he received allowed him once more to leave home, this time heading—like most Galician Jews seeking success—for Vienna, where he hoped to study in the Academy of Arts. Lilien arrived in Vienna precisely at the time when the artistic and cultural world of the Habsburg capital was exploding in the first throes of its fin-de-siècle exhilaration or malaise, depending on the stance of the observer: the Jung-Wien movement was now gaining steam, challenging "the moralistic stance" of nineteenth-century literature, culture, and art "in favor of sociological truth and psychological—especially sexual—openness," as embodied in Arthur Schnitzler's novels and dramas of playboys and Hugo von Hoffmansthal's aesthetes.[9] Very soon, in the fateful year of 1897, Gustav Klimt would establish the Secession, the revolt in plastic arts by *die Jungen* against the classical realist tradition as well as the stolid politics and morality of the Viennese Establishment.

It is unclear whether Lilien abandoned his plan to study at the Viennese Academy out of pecuniary or artistic distress, or, most likely, a combination of both, but he soon quit Vienna for a brief stay once more in Drohobycz, followed by a fateful move to Munich, again supported by his rich relatives in Lemberg, who must have appreciated his still unrealized artistic talent, if not his increasingly avant-garde aesthetic strivings and socialistic political leanings.

Lilien's choice of Munich was, of course, hardly coincidental, for Munich was then the true capital of avant-garde art, politics, and culture in the German-speaking world, far more bohemian than Bavarian. The city served as the central site of the peculiar German variation on the pan-European fin-de-siècle combination of artistic experimentation, sexual liberation, lionization of the Arts and Crafts sensibility, and café-Left political plotting. The young Lilien was perfectly positioned to be swept up in this exciting maelstrom: unlike most of his comrades and colleagues, he was the son of a proletarian craftsman and had himself worked by the sweat of his brow before embarking on his true, artistic, calling. Lilien was also poor, barely surviving on an income that, as he later jokingly put it, was "zum Leben zu wenig, aber auch zum Verhungern zu viel" (not enough to live by, but not enough to starve, either).[10] While working on his own drawings—which at this point were indistinguishable from the Jugendstil mainstream—he bought a camera and became an accomplished photographer, winning second prize in a photographic competition that brought him to the attention of Minnie Hauck, the famous German actress. Hauck commissioned Lilien to come to Lucerne to photograph her—a curious intermezzo in his Munich years about which we know precious little, save the cryptic remark of his first biographer that "here he found peace and rest and like-minded people. . . . When he returned to Munich he was a different Lilien than the disappointed art student from Cracow and Vienna."[11]

Lilien now quickly became fully embroiled in the blossoming Jugendstil movement in Munich, publishing fourteen drawings in the pages of its primary journal, *Jugend,* as well as other sketches in various radical and avant-garde newspapers, especially Eduard Fuchs's important socialist paper *Süddeutsche Postillon.* His greatest success came in the publication by the Vorwärts press of his extensive illustrations to Johann von Wildenradt's novel *Der Zöllner von Klausen,* a rather mediocre protest against the exploitation of the peasantry in the Bauernkrieg. Lilien's India-ink drawings adapted the pseudo-folklorist and populist tone of the novel by mimicking the style of medieval German woodcuts but with an overtly socialist intent. Issued first serially in a weekly journal of novels and stories for the working class, the combination of Lilien's drawings and Wildenradt's prose was popular enough to warrant a second printing as a self-contained novel, again issued by the famous Vorwärts. Lilien's name was even more recognized following the publication by the Social Democratic Party of his May Day poster entitled "The World Is Mine."[12]

This recognition gave Lilien the wherewithal to make the move from the still provincial Munich to the city that attracted the most talented youth from all of central and eastern Europe—Berlin. He arrived there in 1899 and quickly became affiliated with perhaps the most prominent circle of progressive artists, poets, and writers in the German-speaking world, "Die Kommenden," a group that included such diverse figures as Else Lasker-Schüller, Stefan Zweig, Rudolph Steiner, and the wonderfully named masochistic poet Dolorosa (née Maria Eichhorn), whose collection of poems *Confirmo te Chrismate* is adorned with a Lilien cover page. In this circle, too, Lilien first met and befriended Börries von Münchhausen, a less bohemian and more socially secure type than the other members of Die Kommenden. Thus the strange collaboration between the Silesian noble poet and the Galician socialist Jewish artist began to take root. Meanwhile, Lilien's artistic career started to flourish: he had his first ex libris plates published in the newly founded *Zeitschrift für Bücherfreunde;* contributed "decorative frames" to Franz Servaes's *Literary Portrait of Theodor Fontane;* co-chaired the opening of the first German poster exhibition in Berlin in 1899; and, perhaps most significantly, had his first public showings as an up-and-coming new artist. His drawings in the journal *Jugend* were included in the collective exhibit of the Association of German Illustrators at the Great Berlin Art Exhibition of 1899, and then in 1900 he had his first one-man show, held in Leipzig.[13]

The progression of Lilien's work in these Munich-to-Berlin days can adequately be represented by three of his drawings, which require little commentary or explication. "The Wheel of Time" (figure 2), published in the Bavarian socialist newspaper *Süddeutsche Postillon,* is a stereotypical lionization of the workingman, struggling vainly against the march of time—though already here we see the beginning strokes of nonrealistic, lyrical, and Symbolist decorative devices so characteristic of Jugendstil art. This drawing foreshadows his far more important drawing for Morris Rosenfeld's *Lieder des Ghetto* (see discussion of figure 8, below), created after his switch to Jewish themes. By the time we get to the end page of *Der Zöllner von Klausen* (figure 3), the turn to the more rebellious, eroticized aspect of art nouveau is evident in the evocative pose of a nude woman, once more with flowing hair, crucified on a cross entitled "Freedom." Here, as in his own ex libris and countless other works, Lilien's use of women's hair both as a decorative and an ideational, symbolic device is striking, firmly placing him in the mainstream of fin-de-siècle art, in which, as one of its most astute critics has noted, "there is no more striking or more common feature . . . than the representation of women's hair, either as a sign of her benign aspect (symbol of man's aspirations) or of her malevolent aspect (symbol of all that prevents their realization)."[14] In Lilien's drawings, usually it is the benign reading that seems to be evoked by his women's flowing tresses, symbolic of potential human freedom, artistic, political, and sexual. Finally, we see the more elaborate "Genius Before the Bar of Prudery" (figure 4)—one of his most allegorical works, technically adept but suffering from an overabundance of ornamentation and obscure symbolism. Yet for all its possibly deliberate obscurity, "Genius Before the Bar of Prudery" is wonderfully representative of its time and place, and its creator's artistic thrust: a condemnation of deformed, hypocritical moralism masquerading as prudery, savagely attacking the angelic but enslaved genius, clearly associated with both artistic and sexual freedom. This intertwining of sexual, artistic, and political freedom would soon be the subject of the well-known *History of Erotic Art* (*Geschichte der erotischen Kunst*) by Eduard Fuchs, Lilien's first publisher. Fuchs's argument that sensuality was the highest and noblest purpose of art was twinned with a Marxist taxonomy of historical periods in which eras of peace, equality, and healthy eroticism were contrasted to periods marked by class strife, struggle, and "perverted" erotic representations.[15]

It is against this backdrop that we can approach Lilien's turn to Zionism and to a new Jewish nationalist art, which can be dated roughly from the onset of the new century. Unfortunately, Lilien left no verbal documentation of his initial (as opposed to his later) involvement with Zionism; instead, his early steps must be inferred from his graphic representations, beginning with the publication of *Juda* in 1900. It must be emphasized, in contradistinction once more to prevailing scholarship on him, that Lilien's "Judenstil" was not a break, departure, opposition, or nationalistically inspired "purification" of Jugendstil or art nouveau, but a seamless extension of genre, approach, and technique from the German and cosmopolitan to the specifically Jewish arena. Indeed, long after his turn to Zionism, Lilien continued to produce drawings and ex libris plates on non-Jewish themes and in a typical Jugendstil manner, and it is impossible to detect any difference, either stylistic or ideational,

between his "Jewish" and his "non-Jewish" art.[16] On the contrary, what
we see in his work beginning with *Juda* is a conscious attempt to apply
the Secession creed to Jewish subject matter, an attempt to create a Jewish art at once nationalist and modernist, didactic and decadent.

As Carl Schorske aptly reminds us, "Marx once observed that when
men are about to make revolution, they fortify themselves by acting as
though they are restoring a vanished past. . . . Where in Rome the elders
pledged their children to a divine mission to save society, in Vienna the
young pledged themselves to save culture from their elders."[17] So, too,
Lilien attempted to save Judaism from its elders by creating a usable
Jewish past, both substantive and symbolic. In this effort, he contributed
mightily to the popularization of symbols such as the menorah, the Star
of David, and the olive branch as inherently Jewish and Zionist, and to
the depiction of Jewish heroes, past and present, in mock-Oriental, ostensibly ancient Hebraic garb. Though it has not yet objectively been
analyzed in this context, Lilien's effort obviously shared in the widespread attraction of so-called primitive and Oriental cultures for European and American artists seeking refuge from the materialism of their
societies in ostensibly purer, more authentic, and less hypocritical parts
of the world or eras of human history. Frequently, this search led to a
passion for archaic symbols and archeological relics that would both
reveal the richness of vanished or unknown cultures and excavate the
primary instinctual aspects of life, including—as in the case of Freud's
passion for archeology and Egyptology—the erotic aspects of life. And
though originally and typically cosmopolitan in their orientation, such
searches for vanished pasts proved all too easily accessible to new nationalistic ideologies seeking to explore, and most often to invent, a
historical (or, rather, pseudo-historical) basis for their political aspirations.

This is a complicated phenomenon, which cultural historians are only
now beginning to decode. Thus, to cite only one example, Debora Silverman has recently argued in her *Art Nouveau in Fin-de-Siècle France*
that the domestic and organic natures of art nouveau were used to reinforce French solidarist sentiments in the late nineteenth century, while
the rococo revival was itself a stamp of French nationalism.[18] Similar
findings have been advanced with regard to the development of Polish,
Czech, Italian, and Russian nationalist art in the modernist vein.[19]

Ephraim Moses Lilien's creation of a "Judenstil" can only be understood, therefore, against this broad canvas, as well as against the background of the turn to Jewish nationalism on the part of many previously

cosmopolitan Jewish intellectuals who despaired of the promises and possibilities of a now apparently defunct universalist Liberalism but hardly abandoned the basic tenets and thrust of their erstwhile faiths after their conversion to Zionism. On the contrary, they imbued much of early Zionism itself with the basic values, cultural tenor, and ideological colorations of the European fin de siècle. This we see in Max Nordau's call for a "Muskeljudentum" and also in Vladimir Jabotinsky's creation of a militant Jewish nationalism, a version of Zionism that consciously attempted to destroy the effeminate stance of East European Jewry through a self-consciously hard, cold, dignified—indeed, virtually Aryan—masculinity.

Lilien's variation on this theme, once more, was visible for the first time in the drawings and decorations for *Juda*. Here we note only two crucial aspects of this work: any scene from the ancient Judean past was illustrated by Lilien in a highly ornamental and sensualist Orientalist fashion, stressing the physical beauty and sculpted bodies, both male and female, of these ancient Israelite figures. In typical Secession style, objects and clothing are dissolved in an ornamental flat surface, while faces and visible parts of the bodies of portrayed persons are painted three-dimensionally (see "The Silent Song," figure 5). In sharp contrast, Lilien chose to represent the Jew in Exile as an old, sad, tired, bearded, and bedraggled Orthodox Jew, usually surrounded by or enmeshed in thorns, which at times take on the aspect of barbed wire, visibly testifying to the enchainment and degradation of the Jew in *galut*. Thus in "Passover" (figure 6), we see a pathetic figure enslaved in Egypt (which is represented by that other stereotypical Jugendstil device, the sphinx); a slight tear falls from the captive's right eye as the rising sun of Zion beckons him from across an impassable abyss.

This iconographic counterpoising of Judean youthful sensuality and abysmal Exilic degradation would be continued and expanded as Lilien became more and more involved in the Zionist movement in the early years of the twentieth century. He is reported to have begun holding Zionist meetings in his atelier in Berlin in 1900, and he quickly became a central figure in the fledgling group of young Zionist artists dedicated to creating a plastic representation of Jewish national art, parallel to other attempts in the literary genres. At the Fifth Zionist Congress, held in Basel in late December 1901, Lilien organized the exhibition of Jewish artists in which twelve of his drawings were shown, alongside the radically different, stylistically far more traditional work of men such as Oscar Marmorek, Alfred Nossig, Lesser Ury, and Hermann Struck.[20]

This exhibition was both part of and emblematic of the central issue splitting the Fifth Congress: the sharp divide over the formation of a new, secular Jewish culture as a primary goal of the Zionist movement. As is well known, this issue pitted Herzl's and Nordau's political Zionism—and their desire to court Orthodox Jews, so steadfastly opposed to any secularizing tendencies within the movement—against the cultural Zionists led by Martin Buber and Chaim Weizmann, under the spiritual guidance of Ahad Ha'am. Thus, in a major speech to the Congress asserting the basic premises of cultural Zionism, Buber went on at length about the accomplishments of the new, modernized Jewish culture so integral to Zionism, describing the work of the various Zionist artists and singling out for special praise and commendation none other than Ephraim Moses Lilien:

> The best known of our artists is perhaps the youngest as well, Ephraim Moses Lilien. (Lively applause, rising to a warm spontaneous ovation for the artist, who was present.) He is deeply immersed in the wonder of our people, has recognized the meaning and worth of our ancient symbols, and made them his own. He personifies in himself the cause of Zionism, has absorbed it into the very fabric of his being. Especially since he belongs to the young generation [Buber was himself all of twenty-five years old at this time!] he is so important to us. But still, I await from him much more than he has yet delivered. He has drawn marvelous pictures, and has at his disposal a rich and ripe technique. But still his art is more promise than fulfillment, like the overall strivings of the new generation. Still, his book and Hebrew ex libris have won our love, and we imbue him with all our hope, which is worth more than the greatest praise. He is more to us than an admired master, he is our friend, our brother.[21]

In the subsequent deliberations of the Congress, Lilien played an interesting role. He first spoke out not as an artist but as a member of the opposition, the so-called Democratic Faction, objecting to the rather heavy-handed autocratic rulings of Herzl and Nordau, who repeatedly tried to limit debate on the controversial cultural issues. At all times, though (and in contradistinction to his more unruly and obstreperous Russian comrades), Lilien attempted to be polite, respectful, and mediating.[22] This was especially apparent in his major contribution to the debate, a response to the famous claim by Rabbi Yitzhak Reines, the leader of Orthodox Zionists, who said that "the cultural question is a disaster for us. [The demand for a secular] culture will destroy everything. Our audience is entirely Orthodox and will be lost by this demand for culture. Cultural matters ought not be included in the Basel Program. . . . We must be prepared to devote our lives to our nation, to our land,

and then God will help us."[23] At this point, Lilien took the podium and tried to strike a conciliatory note:

> When I hear discussions about culture and religion, it always reminds me of the following scene: two good friends meet in a dark alley, and begin to fight, not recognizing one another. They fight so long, until they gasp in pain, and then they recognize one another and go home together. The conservatives believe that we so-called Culturmenschen have something against religion, and the supporters of culture display great distrust of the conservatives, believing that the latter are opposed to culture. In reality it seems that the former misunderstand culture, the latter religion. . . . I understand very well the mistrust of our conservative friends regarding culture. I am not surprised by it, since the form of culture which Judaism encountered before the rise of Zionism was a foreign, not a Jewish culture. Then, when a Jew tasted of culture, it was a foreign substance he assimilated, and had nothing further to do with Judaism. Therefore, [the conservatives] think that those who are for culture, are no longer Jews. But today things are different. When we demand culture, it is a Jewish culture that we are calling for. (Applause) Culture will make us into complete Jews, and will enrich our Jewishness. Previously, when a Jew became a Culturmensch he belonged to another nation. Since the rise of Zionism, the Jew who makes a mark in science or art and is a Zionist, belongs to his own nation. He is contributing to the creation of a Jewish culture. Therefore, Judaism has nothing to fear from culture, quite the contrary. Culture will win large numbers of intellectuals [over to our cause].[24]

This rather naive, if not disingenuous, attempt at a conciliatory formulation of the demands of cultural Zionism and its lack of opposition to traditional Judaism had little effect on Rabbi Reines and the other proponents of Orthodox Zionism, but it undoubtedly lay behind the peculiarly muted iconography of one of Lilien's most famous drawings, "From Ghetto to Zion" (figure 7), widely distributed as the "Gedenkblatt" for the Fifth Congress and thereafter frequently reproduced, including as an Israeli postage stamp in 1977. Here again the Galut Jew is represented as an old, depressed, cowering figure imprisoned in thorns, watched over by a youthful angel pointing in the direction of Zion (in this case, the angel figure is apparently male but unusually desexualized). Zion is symbolized by the rising and beckoning sun, this time accompanying the physically rejuvenated figure of the traditional Jew at his proper work as a farmer setting off for his fields behind an ox and plow. Under this picture and entwined in the angel's wing is the poignant phrase from the Shemoneh Esreh prayer, recited thrice daily: "vetehezenah einenu be-shuvkha le-Zion be-rahamim" (our eyes will behold Your return to Zion in mercy). Though the more sophisticated viewer may well argue that there is implicit here a radically nontraditional reading of this prayer—who, after all, is returning to Zion?—it does not seem far-fetched to assert that, in order to appeal to the widest possible audience, Lilien deliberately and uncharacteristically depicted the revivified Palestinian Jewish farmer as a traditional and older Jew, rather than a more youthful, muscular, *haluz* type. Indeed, in subsequent years Lilien would be encouraged and at times pressured to change that figure to a more youthful and secular figure, but he steadfastly refused to do so, shocked at the idea of tampering with a piece of art.

Nonetheless, immediately after the completion of his drawing for the Fifth Congress, Lilien returned in his own work to the more aggressively modernist and sensualist thrust of his *Juda* drawings, twinned, at times, with touches of his older, more realist, style. This is most evident in his next major work, the illustrations to *Lieder des Ghetto*, Berthold Feiwel's translation into German of the Yiddish poetry of Morris Rosenfeld, one of the most popular of the so-called sweatshop poets of New York City's Lower East Side. Published in Berlin in 1903,[25] this is one of the most curious and fascinating works ever produced by German Zionism, a remarkable example of the little-studied other side of the infamous *Ostjudenfrage:* the lionization on the part of West European Zionists of East European Jewry and the Yiddish language, in radical opposition to the disdain for East European Jews and everything associated with Yiddish on the part of the mainstream of German Jewry and their strange bedfellows in this particular struggle, the vast bulk of the East European Zionists. *Lieder des Ghetto* merits a detailed analysis, which it has not received in the historical literature and cannot be provided here. Suffice it to say that from its first page to its last, Feiwel's translation of selected poems by Rosenfeld was intended to celebrate the ostensibly authentic Jewishness and naturalness of the Yiddish poet's life and verse, as opposed to the supposed assimilationism and stultification of German Jewry—to bring to the minds and eyes of de-Judaized German Jews the inherently simple and fetching voice of the politically oppressed but spiritually free *jüdische Juden,* expressed through the words of one of its native and naive bards. Inarguably, this representation of Rosenfeld was as much an ideologically driven distortion of the real Morris Rosenfeld and his poetry as was his contemporaneous apotheosis as revolutionary hero on the part of the anti-Zionist Jewish Left. But here we must focus not on the use and abuse of Rosenfeld's verse in the twentieth-century wars of the Jews, but on Lilien's illustrations to this volume, which included some of the most powerful drawings and images he would ever create.

Consider first "At the Sewing Machine" (figure 8), a rather jarring drawing that combined Lilien's realistic, Jewish, and Symbolic styles. While the figure of the tailor is merely a Judaization, with beard and yarmulke, of Lilien's "The Wheel of Time" from his Munich days, the sweatshop boss is astonishingly represented as a bejeweled hermaphrodite vampire, sucking the blood of the worker through what appears to be a narghile. Whether or not inspired by Beardsley's *Ali Baba,* as has been claimed,[26] this characterization of the clearly depraved, degraded, freakish, bloodsucking Jewish boss hearkens unmistakably back to Lilien's adoption as his personal motto a Hebraized form of Paul's attack on the defiled Jewish lust for lucre—"la-tehorim kol tahor." "The Jewish May" (figure 9) is yet another variation by Lilien on the theme and technique he employed in "Passover" and "From Ghetto to Zion," though now imbued with both more Jugendstil and more "Judenstil": the old bearded Jew, representative of the Exile, is still enmeshed in thorns but is a bit sprightlier. He is given a Zionist *kippah* to wear rather than the traditional *kappel* and is allowed to gaze with head upright straight across to Zion, which has now taken on the actual physical cast of Jerusalem, set against the now-classic rising sun. At the same time, a typical art nouveau touch adds a somewhat chilling note to the hopeful scene: three strange, erect, snake-like creatures snarl and snap at the old Jew's feet, growing ominously and unnaturally, though effortlessly, at the edge of the precipice of Exile.

Perhaps most interestingly, we see in *Lieder des Ghetto* the first instances of one of the most bizarre facets of Lilien's work, indeed a virtual trademark of his style from this point on: the use of the face and physical features of Theodor Herzl in strange and unexpected circumstances. This is evident first in "The Creation of Man" (figure 10), one of Lilien's most often reproduced works. The angel on the left is virtually a photographic likeness of Herzl, at least of Herzl's face—it is unlikely that his musculature was so finely sculpted. Although many commentators have noted the use of Herzl's features in this drawing, nowhere, to my knowledge, has this been seriously analyzed or adequately explained. Supposedly illustrating Rosenfeld's poem entitled (in the Yiddish) "Mayse breishis," Lilien's drawing of four male angels with glorious physiques greeting with lyre and horn the birth of the bewinged first human being in fact contradicts the clear moral of Rosenfeld's poem— as has been noted by the most perceptive analyst of this drawing, the noted Israeli poet and critic Natan Zach.[27] And lest we miss the Herzl allusion, Lilien framed Feiwel's translation of this poem with two matching angels bearing Herzl's features, though this time they are vouchsafed somewhat more modest genital coverings in the form of loincloths (figure 11).

After "The Creation of Man" (figure 10), Herzl would appear countless times in Lilien's work, either as a angel, usually bearing a clearly phallic sword, or as a heroic figure from the Bible. Most obviously, Lilien used Herzl to portray Moses, the liberator of the Jews from Exile, as in his well-known stained-glass window for the B'nai B'rith lodge in Hamburg (figure 12), and in illustrations to a very popular ecumenical edition of the Bible in German published in Braunschweig in the years before the outbreak of the First World War (figure 13). In addition to Moses breaking the tablets and Moses on Mt. Sinai, Herzl appears in this Bible as Moses before the burning bush, as the avenging angel expelling Adam and Eve from the Garden of Eden, as Jacob wrestling with the angel of the Lord, as Aaron the High Priest in full clerical garb, as King Solomon dispensing worldly wisdom, and even as Jonah caught in and finally expelled from the whale.[28]

Lilien's fascination with Herzl is apparent, too, in the many photographs that Lilien took of the Zionist leader, including possibly the most famous photo of Herzl of them all, capturing him gazing wistfully out over the Rhine from Basel, espying Germany but, we are urged to believe, in his mind's eye contemplating Zion (figure 14).

Indeed, one Israeli journalist has advanced a rather sensationalist theory connecting Lilien's famous photographs of Herzl, his documented tendency to base his drawings on photographs, and the profusion of nude Herzls in his art. In August 1902, Herzl wrote Lilien a letter with the following request: "The photograph which you sent me is too piquant—please destroy the negative and do not show it to anyone, because it would be possible to infer from it very unpleasant conclusions, which you in your artistic naivete cannot even imagine." According to this journalist, the photograph in question must have been one of Herzl posing for Lilien in the nude and so could be taken as evidence of a possibly physical relationship between the two that may have caused Herzl to reward Lilien with commissions for artistic work on the part of the Zionist movement.[29]

Though this theory lacks any real basis and was patently launched for extra-scholarly purposes, *pour épater les juifs,* it does touch on a very important matter, never mentioned in the scholarly literature—the undeniable and possibly even unconscious homoerotic undercurrent in Lilien's depiction of Herzl. Thus, to return for a moment to "The Creation of Man," the attention given to the broad chests and carefully crafted lower bodies of the angels is striking, and the entire tableau—the transmutation of the first man into a prepubescent boy with visible genitalia, attended to and admired by adult men—is at odds with both the biblical account of creation and the Rosenfeld poem and is paradigmatic of the depiction of the ideal of male love in much of fin-de-siècle art and literature.[30]

This does not mean that Lilien was consciously enamored of Herzl in an overtly sexual manner. Rather, throughout his entire oeuvre Lilien was fascinated with, if not obsessed by, the meaning of the new embodiment of Jewishness (or, at least, of male Jewishness) so central to the Zionist creed in its earliest years, which sought the transformation of the so-called ghetto Jew—allegedly effeminate, weak, cut off from nature, cowardly, sickly, desexualized—into a physically robust, healthy, earthy man, tilling the soil and in the process rebuilding himself, his land, and his people. As George Mosse has argued, the late nineteenth-century idea of masculinity, including its borrowed Greek standards of male beauty, was drafted into service as national symbols or stereotypes; in the process, the overt homoeroticism of this cult of the male body was sublimated into the national ideal itself. Therefore, for all the apparent homoeroticism of German and English nationalist youth movements, their originators and leaders were for the most part heterosexuals, good husbands, and family men[31]—just as was Ephraim Moses Lilien.

Be that as it may, Lilien rather idiosyncratically combined Nordau's fascination with the new "Jews of Muscle" with a related though distinct phenomenon, the widespread admiration of Theodor Herzl's allegedly Assyrian, ancient Semitic regal look. It has long been noted that Herzl's physical appearance and demeanor—the fact that he did look like a typical eastern or central European Jew—played an important role in his political success, and particularly in his adulation on the part of the Jewish masses as the putative "King of the Jews." In a fascinating manner, fully ensconced within the discourse of the fin de siècle, Lilien graphically transformed this adulation of the physical Herzl into an emblem of the idealized Jewish male, the ideal *Muskeljude,* who existed, as Nordau claimed so eloquently, both in the ancient Judean past and in the potential Palestinian future.

Perhaps ironically, this aspect of Lilien's Zionist iconography, along with most of the other typically fin-de-siècle attributes of his "Judenstil," gradually faded away as Lilien became more and more familiar with Palestine itself. In 1905 he spent five months in Jerusalem as one of the original members of the teaching staff of the Bezalel School, until he had a falling-out with its founder and guiding spirit, Boris Schatz. Later, Lilien would return three more times to the Land of Israel, first in 1910 on an extended tour with his wife, the daughter of a prestigious and highly assimilated German-Jewish family; then in the spring and summer of 1914 (though he had to flee Palestine, largely by foot, after the out-break of the world war); and finally in the waning years of the war, as a staff photographer for the Austrian Army in the Middle East.[32] In Palestine Lilien discovered a new style and a new obsession, the topog-raphy, flora, fauna, and human inhabitants of that ancient land—his drawings render the scenes with photographic accuracy and a heavy dose of sentimentalism and kitsch (figure 15).

The reasons for this radical switch in styles and subject matter, oc-curring within a complex context of personal, political, aesthetic, and ideological causes, can only be hinted at here. First and foremost, for reasons entirely unrelated to Lilien and his art, Jugendstil and art nou-veau were fading quickly from artistic fashion, dismissed as hopelessly retrograde and old-fashioned as avant-garde art headed off in entirely different directions. In response, many of Lilien's former colleagues and friends, in addition to far more famous Symbolists and Secessionists such as Aubrey Beardsley himself, took to religion, mysticism, or other pri-vate passions to lick their wounds. In Vienna, Gustav Klimt "gave up philosophical and allegorical painting almost entirely, [shrinking] back to the private sphere to become painter and decorator for Vienna's *haut monde*," largely portraying wealthy Jewish women.[33] At roughly the same time, Lilien, now burdened with family obligations and the de-mands of a new, haut-bourgeois German-Jewish life in the troubled days of the early Weimar Republic, abandoned working in pen and ink and began to use etching as his exclusive artistic medium, finding a ready market for his simple, sweet, and realistic renderings of the streets of Jerusalem, the Western Wall, the handsome and noble faces of Yemenite- and Bukharan-Jewish scholars, picturesque Bedouin chieftains, and Ga-lician market scenes, all of which he churned out in the thousands until his premature death.

Whether, in his last years, Lilien looked back with pride, regret, or astonishment at the liquid nymphets, androgynous angels, and be-muscled Hebraic heroes of his youth, we cannot know, just as we can only speculate about how he would have reacted to the ideological transformation of his beloved Börries von Münchhausen. During the Weimar period, with whose politics and literary culture he was obviously out of sync, Münchhausen largely retired from active literary life, self-consciously fashioning himself into a country squire in the English manner; he served as the literary editor of the conservative, but not Nazi, Munich journal *Volk und Rasse*. In 1933, he greeted the Nazi revolution with reserved enthusiasm, welcoming its pure German nationalism but deploring its excessive antisemitism. While Münchhausen believed that "Judaism was the terrible enemy of our German culture," he persisted in maintaining excellent contacts with many Jewish authors and organizations, who remembered in this time of troubles that it was Börries von Münchhausen who had published, some thirty-three years earlier, a famous book of profoundly philosemitic poems entitled *Juda*. On March 16, 1945, as the Red Army approached Berlin, Münchhausen committed suicide in order to avoid capture by the Soviets.

Obviously, in the fin de siècle, none of Münchhausen's Jewish admirers could have presaged that this sort of philosemitic Gentile Zionism could, in due course, all too easily be transmuted into anti-Jewish hatred; that the call for the Jews to return to their native land and Hebrew heritage could all too logically be turned on its head into a vengeful cry for the exclusion of Jews from German soil and German Kultur.

But such unanticipated vagaries of the transmutation of fin-de-siècle cosmopolitanism in its intersection with nationalism form a chilling backdrop, *mutatis mutandis,* to the subject of the following chapters, the road to Zionism of the young Vladimir Jabotinsky.

CHAPTER SIX

Vladimir Jabotinsky, from Odessa to Rome and Back

"Dichtung und Wahrheit"

On the twenty-sixth of April 1898, Vladimir Jabotinsky, a seventeen-year-old student at the Richelieu Gymnasium in Odessa, wrote a letter to Vladimir Korolenko, then one of the most famous and influential writers in Russia, seeking the master's literary blessings and imprimatur.[1] Jabotinsky recently had had his first attempt at journalism published in an Odessa newspaper and had begun to write short stories and to translate English and French poetry into Russian. Confident of his abundant literary talent, he had decided to abandon his formal studies at the gymnasium in order to travel and write in western Europe. Indeed, despite his young age, he convinced the editor of one of the Odessa daily newspapers to subsidize his travels in Switzerland and Italy as a roaming foreign correspondent. At the same time, he began to seek ways to get his literary works published at home. The letter to Korolenko, the first of a series to Russian literary figures, managed to be at once fawning and self-congratulatory and came with a copy of one of Jabotinsky's recent stories, which, he claimed, no one in provincial Odessa was capable of appreciating.

Jabotinsky's initial letter to Korolenko was recently discovered in the latter's archive in St. Petersburg and brought to the Jabotinsky Institute in Israel, where it has been included in the recent—and generally superb—edition of Jabotinsky's correspondence up to the First World War.[2] But the diligent editors of this correspondence did not seek to discover if there was an extant answer from Korolenko—a task easily enough done, for Korolenko's collected letters were published in Moscow in 1936.[3] The reason for this neglect, quite clearly, was that the editors of the correspondence assumed they knew who Jabotinsky was and what Jabotinsky's letter to Korolenko was all about: they were working, after all, for the Jabotinsky Institute, housed in the headquarters of the Likud Party, located in a building called "Mezudat Ze'ev" (the fortress of Ze'ev). Moreover, in his autobiography Jabotinsky had described this episode in the following terms: "I wrote a novel, whose name and content I cannot recall, and sent it to the Russian author Korolenko. He answered me politely, that is, he advised me 'to continue.'"[4]

But in fact Korolenko's reply to the aspiring young author was rather different. Two weeks after receiving Jabotinsky's letter, the older author responded:

> I have read your story . . . as well as the afterword to it. The story evoked a complicated reaction in me: it demonstrates clear signs of literary—or more precisely—artistic talent, but it is also clear that you have employed that talent poorly, and the aim to which you strive requires a completely different treatment. You have chosen the form of a fairy-tale, devoid of any concrete, ethnographic specificity, which makes your story read like a translation from the Greek or whatever. Moreover, the basic plot of the tale is inconceivable. The twelve-year-old heroine of your story already displays clear signs of erotomania in its worst form (with a tendency to sadism), but the author considers it necessary to characterize her dreams as "bashful but pure. . . ." In general, the story leaves one with an impression utterly contrary to that which you claim in your postscript—not edification, as you submit, but a decidedly unhealthy pornographic aftertaste. I am by no means an advocate of dry artistic didacticism, but your tone is false and possibly unhealthy.
>
> I am writing so candidly precisely because I see in you clear talent—but hardly anything can come of that talent unless you mend your ways. . . . Healthy realism requires a subtle harmony of colors, shades, and light, as in life; in you there is apparent a certain artificially exotic refinement . . .
>
> If you would like to send me something else to read, I would gladly do so, with the hope that the negative characteristics I have just pointed out are merely fortuitous aspects of this one particular short story. I wish you all the best. V. L. Korolenko.[5]

On Korolenko's own copy of this letter, the handwritten note appears: "Vl. Jabotinsky, admirer of Verlaine; very intelligent; very stupid afterword written in artificially decadent taste."[6]

This exchange beautifully foreshadows the main themes, both substantive and methodological, of the chapters that follow—which are an analysis of the intellectual, psychological, and ideological transformation of Vladimir Jabotinsky from a cosmopolitan Russian intellectual in the fin de siècle to an original and highly controversial Zionist ideologue in the years between the Kishinev pogrom of 1903 and the outbreak of the First World War. The portrait of Jabotinsky developed here is radically different from that found in the vast literature on him, which—as explained in the introduction—has been written almost exclusively by scholars and popular authors deeply enmeshed in intramural Zionist disputes, either firm devotees or sworn opponents of Jabotinsky's Revisionist movement. On one side of this bitter and still raging battlefront, admirers chronicle his majestic and unparalleled accomplishments, comparing him to Aristotle, Maimonides, and Da Vinci or, at the very least, to Lincoln, Clemenceau, Churchill, and Gandhi.[7] On the other side, detractors insist on the unmitigated evil of his demonic ways, preferring comparisons to other extreme nationalists of his day, usually Mussolini, and at times even Hitler.[8]

But on the essential development of Jabotinsky's life and views both friends and foes agree, since they all accept as accurate and reliable his own autobiographical writings. As we see in the Korolenko correspondence, Jabotinsky's various autobiographical writings are hardly accurate and reliable: like all autobiographies, they are a self-conscious and highly inventive literary creation that deliberately, if quite naturally, present a selective and factually distorted portrait of their author, often omitting the most salient and revealing truths. Therefore, before proceeding to a new reconstruction of Jabotinsky's intellectual and ideological development, a brief excursus on the problem of untangling truth from fiction in the received tradition of Jabotinsky's life story is necessary.

Jabotinsky's first autobiographical writing was his "Story of the Jewish Legion," which first appeared serially in Yiddish in 1926–1927 in the Warsaw Zionist daily *Haynt* and the New York *Morgen-Zhurnal*.[9] Soon thereafter, a book-length Russian version of this work was published in Paris, a Hebrew edition in Jerusalem, and a Yiddish edition in Warsaw. German, Italian, French, Polish, Spanish, and English translations followed in due course. At the same time, a short memoir of his imprisonment in the Acre prison was published, first in the Hebrew press of Palestine and then in the Russian-language Revisionist Zionist journal *Rassvet* in Paris.[10] Buoyed by the success of these memoirs, in late 1932 and early 1933 Jabotinsky published several autobiographical vignettes about his early years in Odessa, his father, and his gymnasium education. These appeared first in installments in the Yiddish-language Zionist press of Warsaw and New York and, several years later, were reworked and incorporated in a longer, self-standing autobiography, penned in Hebrew and entitled *Sippur yammai* (*The Story of My Life*). This was published first in Tel Aviv in 1936 in a volume of collected pieces entitled *Exile and Assimilation* and was later reprinted by his son Eri in the late 1950s in a volume of Jabotinsky's collected works entitled *Autobiography*.[11] This volume included "The Story of My Life," "The History of the Jewish Legion," and the Acre prison memoir.

What is crucial to underscore is that at the time he wrote these various pieces, and especially those concerning his youth and transformation into a Zionist, Jabotinsky was the embattled but brazen leader of the Revisionist Zionist movement and perhaps the most controversial figure in the Jewish life of his day. At the height of his polemical zeal, he was lionized by his supporters but denounced and hated by his opponents, both within and outside of the Zionist camp. In the midst of all this frenzy, it is only natural that Jabotinsky presented a portrayal of himself fit for public consumption and the ideological battle that defined his adult life. The result is a beautiful and frankly heuristic tale of an "assimilated" Odessan Jew who in his childhood and early years knew nothing about Judaism and cared nothing about the Jews but in his heart of hearts always knew that the solution to the Jewish plight was the establishment of a Jewish state in Palestine. Since his primary opponents were socialists—either socialist Zionists or socialist anti-Zionists—Jabotinsky presented himself in his youth as a callow lad who flirted with socialism during his student days in Italy but then saw the light and found his way back to the Jewish people through the examples of Garibaldi and Mazzini. Somehow, however, he was able to merge this integral nationalism with radical individualism. Since his most livid enemies denounced him as a fascist—and, indeed, called him the "Jewish Duce"—he insisted that he was, and always had been, a liberal in the classic nineteenth-century sense of the term, who was only pleading with his colleagues to return to the true, authentic Zionism espoused by Theodor Herzl and Max Nordau but negated and traduced by their successors due to a combination of abject cowardice and ineptitude.

It does not take much detective work to establish that this self-portrayal is not only entirely retroactive and polemically charged, but almost totally invented out of whole cloth. Jabotinsky's autobiographical writings are chock-full of factual errors—incorrect dates, years, names, and the like, on matters both trivial and substantive; we shall have occasion to note, for example, that the story Jabotinsky loved to tell of his one and only personal encounter with Theodor Herzl was a highly embellished fictionalized account, putting words into Herzl's mouth that the founder of political Zionism never spoke. Indeed, the sloppiness of Jabotinsky's factual account is so striking that his most honest, if worshipful, biographer was forced to concede that he had to correct his subject's version in many ways, excusing this as permissible since Jabotinsky himself admitted that he had no memory for names and dates. To protect himself against even more zealous readers, Joseph Schechtman went on to belittle these emendations by retelling the hoary tale of the professor of German literature who, upon reading Goethe's statement in his autobiography "Lotte I loved above all others" noted "Hier irrt Goethe" (here Goethe is mistaken).[12]

Of course, we have learned all too well in recent decades that the problem of discerning historical reality from autobiographical self-construction is far more complicated than that, and Jabotinsky's auto-biography is by no means unusual in the challenge it provides to objective historical reconstruction. Indeed, Jabotinsky himself hinted that beneath the sanitized version of his life presented in his memoirs there loomed another, more complex and more intriguing, story. Though obviously far removed from postmodern ponderings about the multiple valences of memory and identity, Jabotinsky's first autobiographical vignette, published in 1933, begins:

> Everyone writes memoirs; if someone doesn't write memoirs it begins to raise doubts—it almost creates the impression that he's trying to fool the public into thinking that he's still young. Secondly, this business of writing memoirs seems to bring some needed respite both to the writer and his readers, who are probably tired from the constant battles. So I, too, will try to do so; I won't, God forbid, write my memoirs in order, but will do so bit by bit, at times when my soul yearns for a little rest, for a cessation from battle. And so, another note: real memoirs require one to tell "the truth, the whole truth, and nothing but the truth." This I cannot promise: truth is hardly a typical commodity in the market-place, and too dear to expend even in personal memoirs. I'm convinced that memoirs are not in the realm of political commentary, where truth is of course essential; memoirs are literary works (I don't want to be attacked by other memoir-writers; I'm just talking about myself) and in them it's probably better to mix "Dichtung und Wahrheit" [Poetry and Truth] as Goethe put it.[13]

A few years later, in *The Story of My Life*, he cautioned his readers:

> Here I have told only half the story of my life: that of the author and politician, not that of the private man. These two sides of my life are separated by a very high fence; as much as possible, I have always avoided breaching

the boundary between the two. As a man, I have had and still have friends, ties, experiences, memories, traditions, that have never and will never affect my public activities; and even though in my real life, my inner life, the latter are far more important than anything else, and my personal story is deeper, filled with greater action and meaning than my public story—that you will not find in these pages.[14]

These words, then, provide an exciting challenge to any subtle student of Jabotinsky: not to succumb to the enticement of his own narrative, but to attempt to breach the boundaries between his public and private selves, to discern precisely how the one emerged from and intermeshed with the other. This I shall attempt to do by rewriting the story of the earliest strata of Jabotinsky's life on the basis of the hundreds of previously inaccessible works by the young Jabotinsky. In place of the usual pallid and cliché-ridden morality tale of yet another "assimilated" Jew who finds his way back to his people after confronting pogroms and persecution, we encounter a sensitive, hugely talented, and extraordinarily ambitious young Russian Jew reacting to and participating in the political, artistic, and intellectual maelstroms of the fin de siècle. We also examine the personal and historical crises that led to the formative event of his life: his abandonment of universalism, decadence, and a hoped-for career in Russian literature in favor of a new, and gradually more and more monistic, self-definition as a Jew, a Jewish nationalist, and a Zionist. In the process we see that while, in the end, the trajectory that his life took was utterly evocative and emblematic of his time and place, it bore no internal and ineffable logic, no preordained teleological sweep leading inexorably from the broad boulevards of Odessa through the winding alleyways of the Eternal City and finally to his ultimate resting place on Mount Herzl, in Jerusalem—an ending mired in the controversy and melodrama that pervaded much of his adult life and continues to this day.

We must begin on the northern littoral of the Black Sea, in Odessa, where Vladimir Jabotinsky was born on October 5, 1880. It is crucial to understand that his early life was not spent in the typical East European Jewish shtetl; indeed, it was very similar to the urban, middle-class upbringing of Herzl or Nordau. Like them, Jabotinsky was a second-generation bourgeois Jew. His father, Evgenny, was himself not a Yiddish-speaking, traditional East European Jew; rather, he was a secularized Russian-speaking son of the southern steppe, born in the tiny town of Nikopol, on the Dnieper, in the region known as "New Russia," which at the time of his birth numbered roughly three hundred Jews. Typical of the Jewish bourgeoisie that emerged in the heady years of the reign of Alexander II, Evgenny Jabotinsky rose to an influential position in the Russian Company of Navigation and Commerce, an important firm in the extraordinarily profitable grain trade on the Dnieper River. The woman he married, Eva Sack, hailed from a more traditional Jewish background, a well-heeled family in Berdichev (a city in which even the Gentile porters were reputed to speak Yiddish). But in tune with the gendered customs of the Jewish middle classes even in the mid-nineteenth-century Pale of Settlement, she was educated in the German language and the classics of German literature deemed appropriate for such young ladies—most especially the works of Friedrich von Schiller. Together the Jabotinskys settled in Odessa, the main seat (along with the largely inaccessible Kiev and St. Petersburg) of upwardly mobile, Russified Jews. Their three children were born in Odessa; Vladimir—Volodya—was the middle child and second son, followed by a daughter. The family's happiness was soon cut short by the death of their firstborn son, and then by the news that Evgenny himself was mortally ill. For several years the family lived in Germany, seeking treatment from one famous professor of medicine after another, depleting their substantial resources, all to no avail. Evgenny Jabotinsky died back home in Ukraine, at Alexandrovsk on the Dnieper, in December 1886, leaving his widow and two surviving children virtually penniless.

Returning to Odessa, Eva Jabotinsky attempted to continue to rear her daughter and son in the ways and mores of the Odessan Jewish middle class. She reputedly angrily broke off relations with rich relatives who dared to suggest that young Vladimir be apprenticed to an artisan to learn a craft, insisting that both her son and daughter attend private Russian-language elementary schools and then go on to gymnasium, whatever the sacrifice. Although for political purposes the mature Jabotinsky (like Nordau before him) made much of his mother's native piety and observance of Jewish dietary laws, the Jabotinsky home—typical of many middle-class Jewish families in fin-de-siècle Odessa—was largely devoid of Jewish knowledge, content, or ceremony. Most significantly, young Volodya never attended any Jewish school, neither a heder nor a modernist Enlightenment-style establishment, of which there were many in Odessa. In later years he could not even recall the minuscule introduction to Judaism he must have received in the religious instruction classes called *zakon bozhii* (literally, divine law), which were compulsory for all Jewish pupils in general Russian schools. Jabotinsky did recall, and boast of, being tutored in Hebrew by the well-known Hebrew writer Y. H. Ravnitsky, but this was simply in preparation for his bar mitzvah and had no lasting effect on his mind or psyche, as is abundantly clear from his painful first attempts at learning and writing Hebrew as an adult. Moreover, as a typical child of the Russified Jewish bourgeoisie, he knew virtually no Yiddish and in his adult years had to learn that tongue in order to communicate with his followers.

In this lack of Judaic background, Jabotinsky was typical, rather than idiosyncratic, for his class and milieu: although it goes against our received stereotypes about East European Jewry in the nineteenth century, it was possible, indeed not at all abnormal, for an upper middle-class Russian Jew to be born, be bred, and grow into adulthood largely ignorant of Yiddish, Hebrew, and Judaism. In his later years, Jabotinsky himself pondered the nature of his youthful lack of Jewish consciousness and devoted much time and energy to a depiction of what he then decried as the "assimilation" of Odessan Jewry during his youth. His fascinating if complexly tendentious novel *Piatero* (The five) is dedicated in its entirety to this subject. Given his later ideological turn, it is not surprising that he could never really sort out the subtleties and complex contradictions of Jewish acculturation and embourgeoisment in late nineteenth-century Russia. As discussed earlier, the linguistic muddle regarding "assimilation" and its quasi-synonyms is merely the tip of the iceberg of the conceptual morass that still pervades the understanding of Jewish cultural history in modern times. Thus, to cite just one example, Jabotinsky later seemed truly baffled that, on the one hand, as a child, teenager, and young adult, he had virtually no interest in anything Jewish, never read a book on a Jewish topic, never studied any ancient Jewish lore; and yet, on the other hand, in school the Jewish children sat together and played together, barely associating with the non-Jewish children.

But this experience was in fact neither idiosyncratic nor paradoxical: nowhere did the Jews' "acculturation" result in an effacement of their social or even cultural distinctiveness, as both proponents and opponents of Jewish modernization had anticipated. Indeed the extent to which even German Jews at the height of their Germanization were fully "assimilated" in any true sense of the word has been the subject of intense debate, with many believing that German Jews constituted a distinct subculture within German society despite their perception of complete integration and Germanization.[15] And Jabotinsky was, of course, a Russian Jew: in his day even the most Russified Jews understood (as they do today) that they were not Russians in the emerging nationalist sense of the term, nor could they ever become Russians, unless they converted to Russian Orthodoxy. They were Jews, however one defined that term. Even as they adopted Russian as their mother tongue, abandoned the traditional practices of the Jewish religion, replaced the Bible and the Talmud and Jewish folk culture with Pushkin and Turgenev and Gogol and the talk of the street, they could become bearers of Russian culture, creators of Russian culture, and even proud and loyal citizens of Russia, but not Russians, that is, not Russian by nationality.

This, it must be stressed, was not primarily the result either of antisemitism or of Jewish ethnic/national/religious pride, not to speak of an ineffable Jewish spirit or *Volksgeist,* as Jabotinsky would later believe, though both antisemitism and the Jewish will to survive were crucially involved. Of overriding importance was the fact that the Russian Empire was a multinational state, dominated demographically and politically by Russians, but an empire in which there was always a clear distinction between the Russian nation and its underlings: Jews, Poles, Georgians, Lithuanians, Uzbeks, and the like. All of these minorities could and did experience a substantial amount of Russification over the course of the eighteenth and nineteenth centuries, becoming bearers of the Russian language and Russian culture—but they never became Russians. Indeed, in the Russian language there is a crucial distinction between two adjectives that we translate into English as "Russian": *russkii* (Russian by nationality) and *rossisskii* (Russian by political or cultural affiliation). In sum, there was, and remains today, a distinction, clear and palpable if often difficult to articulate, between Russians and Jews that could not be effaced, even if and when the Jews were entirely Russified.

This was radically different from the situation that obtained not only in France, England, Germany, and the United States, but even in neighboring countries such as Hungary and Poland. In all these lands, Jews could and did believe themselves to be Frenchmen, Englishmen, Germans, Americans, Hungarians, or Poles of the Jewish religion, "Mosaic faith," or Jewish origin. Though much of Jewish cultural, ideological, and intellectual history in the modern period has revolved around debates over the saliency of these terms and their political correctness, no one would doubt that masses of Jews so conceived themselves and were conceived by others since the French Revolution. But Russia was different: Russians and Jews seemed to inhabit two distinct semantic spheres, no matter how much they interacted. Though one could conjure up appellations such as "Russians of the Jewish faith," this was understood by all to be an artificial construct, since it was clear that Russians were Russians and Jews were Jews, even if the content of both of those terms would radically change over the centuries.

At the same time, however, a small part of Russian Jewry did experience a social and economic transmutation parallel to its counterparts not only in the United States, England, France, Germany, and the Austro-Hungarian Empire, but also in Congress Poland, Romania, and parts of the Ottoman Empire. From the 1860s on, Jews from increasingly affluent and mobile families in Russia had rushed headlong into the liberal professions as well as cultural and commercial roles at which they were particularly adept, becoming lawyers, physicians, bankers, pharmacists, engineers, international traders, journalists, and publishers in numbers far out of proportion to the size of their community. In the process, many of their children, second-generation bourgeois Jews, lacked any intimate connection with or interest in Judaism and the Jewish culture of their grandparents. Foreign to them, as well, was the experience of their contemporaries in the small towns of the Pale of Settlement, struggling firsthand with the turmoil of the confrontation between Jewish tradition and modernity. To some extent, their Jewishness consisted in the social stigma attached to their origins, compounded and exacerbated by legal restrictions that made their educational and social advancement difficult (though not impossible). The fact that Vladimir Jabotinsky was neither a participant in nor substantially affected by the Haskalah, the Hebrew Enlightenment movement, was a crucial determinant of his later ideological development—indeed, the determinative difference between his attitude to the Jews and Judaism and the attitude of most eastern European Zionists.[16]

This estrangement from Judaism and Jewishness on the part of young Jews from Jabotinsky's milieu was particularly acute (however paradoxically) during the decade of the 1890s in which young Vladimir came into his teens and young adulthood. Although the historical literature on Russian Jewry gives one the impression that after the pogroms of 1881–1882, all Russian Jews became Zionists, socialists, or a combination of the above or left the country entirely, this was far from the case: the vast majority of Russian Jewry remained at home and many, if not most, remained committed to their traditional religious ways. Even the minority who abandoned that culture did not always rush en masse to the newfangled ideologies of nationalism or revolution. Indeed, the most powerful external stimulus to such radical views—the anti-Jewish violence of the early 1880s—had ceased during the 1890s. Though the newly introduced quotas on Jewish students in schools, gymnasia, and universities were bothersome, many bourgeois Jews could circumvent them either by bribes to relevant officials or by sending their children abroad to study in Switzerland, Germany, or France. While some sons and daughters of the Russian-Jewish middle classes went on to become active Jewish nationalists or revolutionaries, their numbers were outweighed by those who, like young Jabotinsky, found their solace and their identities not in politics or emigration but in Russian culture.

Young Jabotinsky, moreover, was growing up in Odessa, a unique port city located geographically in Ukraine but populated by a mix of inhabitants: Russian bureaucrats, Greek and Italian merchants, and tens of thousands of Jews fleeing both the economic constraints and the religious and cultural conservatism of the Pale of Settlement. Odessa in Jabotinsky's youth was still a frontier town, a place noted for its irreverence and heterodoxy, its strange mixture of cosmopolitanism and seediness, Russianness and Europeanism. Dominated by its raunchy port, it reminded some visitors of Marseilles, others of Istanbul, and others, such as Mark Twain, of a Mississippi River town. Only a short time earlier the street signs of Odessa were in Italian and the largest ethnic group was the Greeks.[17] By the time of Jabotinsky's youth, Odessa's Jews made up the largest group after the Russians and were far more Russified than those in any other part of the Russian Empire, save the tiny numbers allowed to live in St. Petersburg, Moscow, and Kiev. In their homes, schools, and theaters, and increasingly in the street, Russian was the language of choice and of culture.[18]

Far, far away was the Odessa of the ex-yeshiva students from the Pale who flocked to the city to escape their traditionalist parents, their teachers, and, very often, their first wives. The Odessa canonized in modern Jewish literary and intellectual history—the home of the Hebrew Renaissance of Ahad Ha'am and the young Hayyim Nahman Bialik, the home of Mendele Mokher Seforim's and Sholem Aleichem's fledgling attempt to build a modern Yiddish culture, or the attempts to found a Russian version of the Wissenschaft des Judentums movement—may have been happening only down the street but may as well have been on a different planet from young Vladimir Jabotinsky and his friends in the fancy Richelieu Gymnasium. Equally distant and unknown was the world of the Moldovanka, the neighborhood of the traditional, Yiddish-speaking Odessan Jewish lumpenproletariat. Though later on Jabotinsky would bemoan this gulf, the irony is that it would have taken the young gymnasium student but a short walk to espy these traditional Jews. But to a sensitive and intellectually curious child of the Jewish bourgeoisie, the traditional Jewish ghetto was culturally, emotionally, and psychologically further away than the setting of Verdi's latest work—or so it seemed at the time.

In this context Jabotinsky was born and raised and soon displayed precocious literary talents and even more precocious self-confidence and ambition. At the age of sixteen he began to translate Paul Verlaine, Edgar Allan Poe, and the Hungarian poet Sándor Pétofi into Russian, and to write his own Symbolist-inspired fiction, including the "decadent" short story or novella that so upset Korolenko (unfortunately, this particular piece of juvenilia has not been preserved). A month before his seventeenth birthday, one of the many offerings Jabotinsky submitted to countless newspapers and journals was actually published—a newspaper article entitled "A Pedagogical Note," printed under the heading "From the World of Children" in the newspaper *Iuzhnoe Obozrenie* (Southern Review).[19] Characteristically, in his autobiography Jabotinsky made a point of noting the precise date of the publication of this, his literary debut, except he got the date wrong![20] He did, however, accurately remember the content of the article—a schoolboy's attack on the system of grading in Russian schools and gymnasia, which was unfair, he claimed, because it introduced unnecessary competition among the students and stifled creativity, maturity, and individuality in the students. Though clearly the work of an adolescent, the article's tone was poised, the argument coherent and well presented, and the Russian crisp and idiomatic, bearing no trace of the author's ethnicity.

Soon after the appearance of this piece Jabotinsky abandoned his gymnasium, Odessa, and the Russian Empire for his first sojourn in the West, in search of literary fame. He headed first to Bern, chosen because his mother permitted him to leave home only if he would go to the Swiss capital, where the son of another Odessan Jewish middle-class family was studying. While en route, he described the long journey by train in great detail in many pieces submitted to the *Odesskii Listok*, the liberal Odessa Russian-language daily that agreed to print his wares. These picturesque travel reports belied their author's age and lack of worldly experience, amusing his readers with insightful and entertaining accounts of the fascinating and exotic Galicians, Croatians, Hungarians, and Italians he encountered on his westward journey. Not surprisingly, these reports made absolutely no mention of Jews: it would not have occurred to Jabotinsky or to the editors of the newspaper, also Russified

Jews serving a readership composed of primarily other Russified Jews
(and perhaps some ethnic Russians and Russified Ukrainians), to betray
their ostensible cosmopolitanism and sophistication by revealing such
clannish interests.

It was only much later, in his autobiography, that Jabotinsky recalled
that as the train from Odessa to Bern passed through the villages and
shtetlach of Galicia and Hungary, he was moved by the sight of Hasidim
crowding into the third-class coaches, by the naturalness and unself-
consciousness of their demeanor, at once uncouth—indeed, barbaric—
and yet mysteriously self-assured. We can only speculate to what extent
Jabotinsky's retrospection had its roots in any youthful inner reflection.
What is certain, however, is that at the time Jabotinsky made no mention
of Jews in any of his journalistic pieces, and indeed it would have been
impossible for anyone to discern that their author was a Jew.

Only in one very early Russian poem, published under a pseudonym
soon after his arrival in Bern, did Jabotinsky reflect on any Jewish concern. Entitled "Gorod mira" (City of peace), this poem appeared in the
Russian-Jewish journal *Voskhod* in November 1898, though it may well
have been written long before that.[21] This jejune verse obviously embarrassed the mature and far more sophisticated Jabotinsky, who confessed his shame that it was based on an elementary if common error—
the belief that the Hebrew name for Jerusalem, *Yerushalayim*, originally
meant "city of peace" (*ir shalom*). Undoubtedly as important to Jabotinsky, but left unstated, was the fact that this early poem was devoid
of any literary inventiveness or linguistic dexterity, a far cry from the
fascinating imitations of Symbolist and neo-Romantic verse that he
would soon write and publish.

Yet without overstating its importance, the poem "Gorod mira" can
serve as an interesting indication of the adolescent Jabotinsky's background and attitude to matters Jewish. The poem tells a simple story: a
visitor to Palestine, whose ethnicity or religion is never revealed, camps
outside the walls of Jerusalem with his Arab guide. He is frightened by
the eerie sound of a keening and wailing woman, clad in white, floating
over Zion to the accompaniment of an overstrained, sobbing harp. Be-
wildered by this image, which he takes to be a mirage, he awakens his
guide, joins him in his morning prayers to Allah, and then hears the
mystery of the spectre revealed:

Bless the Almighty
Who has shown us this wondrous sight

This spectre is the City of Peace
I have heard, that every year
This woman sings
A song of mourning over Zion.

I have heard among the Arabs
That He, Whom we all revere
Promised in the days of yore
This land to the Jews

There is no Sovereign but God
"La illaxhu il Allah"
The wrath of the strong is but clay
But the word of the Lord is a rock .

But centuries have passed
And in incessant sorrow
Sadly lived the Jews
Outside their Promised Land

They lived, deprived of home and honor,
By the will of Fate,
Only their Faith they preserved
From their majestic past

This wonder—the City of Peace—
Is the mother of this people
Every year she cries in sorrow
Over Zion from the heavens

And beckons from their dispersion
To the peaceful paradise of her fields
Her exhausted sons
Long punished by God.[22]

Quite obviously, the young Jabotinsky was confused about more than the etymology of the word "Jerusalem." The core of this poem is a rather bizarre transposition into the mouth of a devout Muslim of one of the most cherished motifs of traditional Jewish lore, the figure of the matriarch Rachel hovering over Ramah lamenting the loss of her children, refusing to be comforted. Even Jabotinsky knew better than to claim that this poem was revelatory of his innate Zionism—a claim made by some of his more zealous followers, who ignored the fact that *Voskhod*, the journal it was published in, was at this time steadfastly opposed to Zionism and so would hardly have published a poem perceived as supporting that movement. Exactly why this juvenile poem was in fact accepted for publication is difficult to discern, expect that one of the stated goals of the journal was to advance the creation of a Jewish culture in the Russian language, and the pickings that month must have been slim. But for our purposes it is sufficient to note that the poem was palpably the work of a teenager unschooled not only in the Hebrew language but in the internal metaphors, tropes, and clichés of Jewish culture and society. While not oblivious to the plight of the Jews or their religious faith, the creator of this verse sounds clearly like an observer from the outside who required a translator and guide to understand the internal rhythms and myths of Jewish culture. It would be many years—and not until he imbibed those rhythms and some of those myths—before Vladimir Jabotinsky would return in print to Jewish subject matter.

Meanwhile, however, he arrived in Bern and registered at the local university, formally to study law. But, as he later claimed with much pride, he barely attended classes at all and instead lost himself in the vagaries and freedom of the Swiss capital and its throbbing and hyperbolically overideologized colony of Russian and Russian-Jewish students. As Jabotinsky later recalled, in an oft-repeated story, he gave his first public talk here, which was also, of course, his first Zionist talk:

Twice a week there were meetings in the [Russian] "colony," usually debates between the camps of Lenin and Plekhanov or between the Social Democrats and the Socialist Revolutionaries. (My contemporaries understand the difference, which it doesn't pay to explain to others.) From time to time they held a "soiree," and sang Russian songs; but Zhitlovsky—I can't remember if he was a student at Bern University or only visited us for a while—sometimes insisted that they also sing in Yiddish. Once Nahum Syrkin visited the colony and preached the synthesis of Zionism and Socialism; he didn't find too many disciples, since there were then only a few Zionists in that circle. But I well remember that talk, since it was there that I gave the first public talk of my life, and a "Zionist" one at that. I spoke in Russian, and in this way: I don't know if I'm a Socialist, since I haven't yet studied that ideology; but I am a Zionist, without a doubt, since the Jews are a very terrible people, its neighbors justly hate them, their fate in Exile is bound to be a general "St. Bartholomew's Night" and their only salvation a mass migration to the Land of Israel. The chair of the meeting, the young Lichtenstein (later a respected businessman in Palestine, who died there a few years ago) translated my talk into German in a very brief summary: "The speaker is not a Socialist, since he doesn't know what Socialism is, but he is a total anti-Semite and advises us to hide in Palestine lest they slaughter us all." Apparently, my impressions of my trip through Galicia affected me so deeply! At the end of the meeting Charles Rapoport (now one of the leaders of French Communism) came up to me and said with a broad grin: "I didn't think that among Russian youths there are still such zoological types of anti-Semites!" "But I'm not a Russian!" I answered, but he didn't believe me.[23]

Although this recollection has been cited by many biographers and commentators to demonstrate the ostensible longevity and innateness of Jabotinsky's Zionism, there is no contemporary record of the event and none of those mentioned by Jabotinsky recall his speech in their own memoirs. It is thus impossible to know whether the actual event occurred, a problem only exacerbated by the fact that, to his later embarrassment, he had garbled the names of two very different Syrkins active in Zionist circles—Nahum and Nachman Syrkin.[24]

But the more interesting point about this anecdote is its startling underbelly: according to Jabotinsky himself, the audience of his virgin speech perceived him as a Russian antisemite rather than a Jewish Zionist. His supposedly innate Zionism was indistinguishable to anyone, including real Zionists, from antisemitism! Not surprisingly, then, when his biographer and supporter Joseph Schechtman retold this tale, he emended it in a crucial fashion. Jabotinsky recalled saying, "I am a Zionist, without a doubt, since the Jews are a very terrible people, its neighbors justly hate them." Because Schechtman could not easily repeat that, his version had Jabotinsky saying that he was a Zionist because "the enemies of the Jews were not completely wrong, since in dispersion the Jews are a painful abscess in the organisms of other nations."[25] Quite a difference.

As has already been hinted at, one of the thorniest and most controversial dilemmas in Jabotinsky's life would be his idiosyncratic readiness to negotiate with antisemites for the betterment of the Jews. More subtly, Jabotinsky's critique of East European Jewry—perhaps even more so than Nordau's—was astonishingly but unreflectively alive with criticisms and characterizations of the Jews in terms not dissimilar to those of antisemites. But that is putting the cart substantially before the horse: here it is crucial only to note that the only source for this alleged proto-Zionism on the part of Jabotinsky was Vladimir Jabotinsky himself, some thirty years after the fact, and that even he did not claim any substantive connection between this alleged and confounding early incident and his later conversion to Zionism.

In sum, before departing Bern for Italy, Jabotinsky appears to have been a typical member of the second-generation Russian-Jewish middle class: culturally Russified, not totally unaware of his Jewish origin but largely oblivious to and uninterested in its meaning and import. To call this stance that of an "assimilated" or even an "acculturated" Jew is vastly to understate and underrate the psychological, ideological, and social complexity of political and cultural identity for cosmopolitan Jews in the fin de siècle, a dilemma experienced by a very large number of modern Jews well beyond the borders of Russia.

From Bern Jabotinsky moved to Rome, where he lived for the next three years of his life. Almost four decades later, living out of his suitcase in Warsaw, London, or New York, enmeshed entirely in the turbulent inner wars of the Jews, he rapturously recalled his heady days in the Eternal City:

> If I have a spiritual homeland it is Italy more than Russia. In Rome there was no "Russian colony": from my first day there, I was absorbed in the milieu of Italian youth, and lived that life until the day I left. All my views on the problems of nation, state, and society were formed there under Italian influence; there I learned to love architecture, sculpture and painting, and also Latin music, which in those days was ridiculed by the Wagnerians just as today it is ridiculed by the disciples of Stravinsky and Debussy. At the university my teachers were Antonio Labriola and Enrico Ferri, and the faith in the justice of the socialist system which I learned from them I maintained as a "self-evident truth" until it was destroyed by the Bolshevik Revolution in Russia. The myth of Garibaldi, the works of Mazzini, the poetry of Giacomo Leopardo and Giuseppe Giusti added depth to my shallow Zionism, transforming it from an instinctive sentiment into a worldview.[26]

Taking this recollection as factual, scholars have proceeded to flesh out the importance of Italy, and specifically of Italian nationalism and socialism, on Jabotinsky's ideological development. They have delved with great care and erudition into the varying versions of socialism espoused by Labriola and Ferri and have tried subtly to reconcile these with the contested visions of Italian nationalism of Mazzini and Garibaldi. Given the inherent complexity (if not virtual contradiction) of such an ideological mixture, this is not an easy task, especially since barely ten pages later in the very same autobiography Jabotinsky asserts that after he left Italy he put aside the ideas of Labriola and Ferri:

> [I] emphasized only one idea: the idea of individualism . . . the idea that were I a philosopher, I would place at the base of my system: In the beginning, God created the individual, every individual is a king, equal to his friend, and his friend is a king as well; it is better for an individual to sin against the collective than for society to sin against the individual. Society was created for the individual, and not vice versa, and the future end of the days, the messianic era, will be a paradise for the individual, a glistening state of

anarchy . . . You might assert that there is a contradiction between this view
and my nationalistic pronouncements; one of my friends, who read this manuscript, said that he heard another theme from me—In the beginning, God
created the nation. But there is no contradiction between these two views. I
developed the second theme in opposition to those who assert that in the
beginning "humanity" was created. I believe with perfect faith that in a contest between these two views, the nation must take precedence; and similarly,
that the individual comes before the nation. And even he who subjects his
whole life to service to the nation, that is not a contradiction in my eyes—
he does so voluntarily, not by force.[27]

How to reconcile these confessions of faith has engendered a veritable
cottage industry in Jabotinsky scholarship—with different writers
choosing various sides: socialism versus nationalism; nationalism versus
individualism; socialism versus individualism. Parallels have been drawn
between Jabotinsky and Benito Mussolini or Jósef Piłsudski, or to other
integral nationalists who abandoned socialism on the road to nationalism, or vice versa.[28] However, no one seems to have been troubled—
as, I hope, readers of this book now are—by the fact that Jabotinsky's
testimony about his Italian years was written almost forty years after
the event, at the end of his ideological and personal journey, not at its
beginning. Just like his claim about an "instinctive Zionism," his paean
to the Italian nationalist influence on his thought was a figment of his
later autobiographical imagination. In fact, in none of his hundreds of
writings before he became a Zionist is there any evidence whatsoever
that he ever was truly a believing socialist, and his claim that he retained
such a belief until 1917 is belied by dozens of his writings in the decade
and a half before the Bolshevik Revolution, in which he attacked socialism with fierce and combative words.[29]

More tellingly, the evidence is ample that although he paid a great
deal of attention to Italian politics when he was in Rome and remained
enamored of Italy, Italian culture, and the Italian language for the rest
of his life, by no means was Jabotinsky an admirer of nationalism of
any sort, Italian or Russian or Japanese, while he lived in Italy or for
several years thereafter. It was only decades later, after he became a
Jewish nationalist—and then a famous ultranationalist to boot—that he
attempted to impose both coherence and unity on his thought, largely
effacing its torturous course.

If we look at his actual, datable writings from the years he spent in
Italy, we find a mass of articles, letters, poems, plays, and essays that
articulate a view of the world entirely at odds with his later nationalistic

worldview but also entirely in keeping with the avant-garde culture of the age. As we have seen in Nordau's and Lilien's works (and as emulated by many intellectuals throughout Europe), the new movements of Symbolism and Decadence and art nouveau and Jugendstil all exhibited, in their many permutations and combinations, the excitingly new cosmopolitan and international culture of the fin de siècle.

In Russia—which remained the most important context for Jabotinsky's thought, even while he was in Italy—this period was retrospectively defined as the Silver Age of Russian culture. Now, Pushkin and Turgenev—and even Tolstoy and Dostoyevsky—began to be overshadowed by Chekhov and Gorky and such radically different and vastly enticing Symbolists as Dmitrii Merezhkovskii, Zinaida Gippius, Aleksandr Blok, and Konstantin Bal'mont. And Sergey Diaghilev's Ballets Russes was perhaps the most famous export of avant-garde Russian culture.[30] The foreign literary heroes of the previous generation of Russian intellectuals—Goethe, Schiller, Heine—were now less important than Verlaine and Rimbaud, Ibsen and Maeterlinck, D'Annunzio and Poe. Though to the purist this seems like a confused jumbling together of disparate and contradictory artistic, aesthetic, and ideological trends, to the cohort of the 1890s and early 1900s, all of these authors were daring innovators who rejected the narrow-minded utilitarianism and social realism of previous generations while celebrating eroticism and sexuality in an unprecedented manner. Though already torn by serious differences over aesthetic theory and politics, the Russian cultural avant-garde rejected the monolithic worldview of the older Russian intelligentsia, which had "enjoined the individual to devote his or her life to serving the people. The value of the individual, the supremacy of aesthetic-spiritual over materialistic-utilitarian considerations, and the exaltation of cultural creativity over economic progress constituted the main tenets" of the new generation.[31]

In his years in Rome, Jabotinsky enunciated a worldview typical of his time and place, and shared by thousands of young Russians in the capitals as well as the provinces. Radically individualistic, antinationalistic, quasi-nihilistic and aestheticist, this stance nonetheless more often than not was combined with radical political sentiments—not the highly theoretical and utilitarian conceptions of Lenin or Martov or even Bakunin, but a generalized sympathy for the idea of a revolutionary transformation of Russian life, society, and, most especially, culture. What was unusual about Jabotinsky's view of the world at this stage was not its content but its context: here he was, a rather naive and provincial but utterly self-confident Jewish kid from Odessa, living in Rome, serving as the foreign correspondent of distinguished (if small-time) liberal Russian newspapers. Virtually every word he wrote was published back home, consumed with avid interest by thousands of like-minded but less fortunate readers, largely Russified Jews, desperate for a taste of Europe, of Kultur—or rather what the Russians call *kulturnost'*, more akin to the English word "cultivation."

Indeed, Jabotinsky's precocious *kulturnost'* was the centerpiece of the dozens of columns he sent back home to Odessa. They first appeared in the liberal Odessa newspaper *Odesskii Listok* and then in its rival the *Odesskie Novosti*, the newspaper he would work for intermittently through the First World War. In these years, his feuilletons from Rome were printed at least once and sometimes up to four times a week, and this pace continued upon his return in 1901 to Odessa, when he became the chief cultural critic for *Odesskie Novosti*. In addition to his column, he published theater and opera reviews, short stories, poems, transla-tions of foreign poetry, and soon his first dramas. In line with the custom of the age, he rarely used his own name in any of these pieces, signing them with a variety of pseudonyms until he settled on the nom de plume Altalena, meaning "swing" in Italian, though he later confessed he thought it meant "seesaw" when he adopted it.[32]

In his mature years, he was embarrassed by most of these early writ-ings and sought to dismiss their importance as meaningless juvenilia. Ironically, the greatest collaborator in keeping this massive oeuvre hid-den was the Soviet government, since most of these early pieces were available only in libraries and archives in the Soviet Union, not accessible to students of Jewish history or Zionism until the fall of that state. More-over, since most historians of Zionism, even experts on Jabotinsky, couldn't read these pieces in their original Russian (only a tiny number were written in Italian), they relied on the small and heavily edited se-lections translated into Hebrew by his supporters from the 1930s to the present. Even those few scholars who could read Russian cited only a few snippets, interpreted (or rather, I claim, misinterpreted) through the retrospective lenses of the mature Jabotinsky.

Now that all of Jabotinsky's works from this period are available to scholars, they must be read not through a retroactive and teleological eye that looks for the "roots" of his eventual worldview, but rather contextually, as revealing who he was and what he believed at the time of their composition. Given the enormous amount that he wrote during these years, I select just a few representative examples of his prose, drama, and poetry in order to sketch a portrait of Jabotinsky's political and cultural views while in Italy.

First, a very early political commentary (published in the *Odesskii Listok* on March 13, 1899), a paean to the recently deceased Italian politician and litterateur Felice Cavallotti. Cavallotti was a leading member of the Radical Party, a leftist party that broke ranks with the Socialists on many issues of theory and practice, much to Jabotinsky's reportorial delight. Most controversially, Cavallotti agreed to serve in the Italian parliament, which required taking an oath of allegiance to the king, thus confronting him with an ethical dilemma parallel to that of both Ultra-Orthodox and Arab members of the Israeli Knesset today. In parliament, Cavallotti served as the nemesis to the strongman of Italian politics, Franceso Crispi, who started his political life as a revolutionary republican but soon became the personification of Italian nationalism and imperialism. In earlier columns, Jabotinsky had often discussed his hatred of Crispi and everything he stood for. In the March 13, 1899, paean, he lauded Cavallotti as the best Italian politician of his generation, especially since he was at the same time the author of many avant-garde literary works, from a decidedly antirealist perspective. Especially attractive to Jabotinsky and other young intellectuals was Cavallotti's noble death—he died in a famous, if pointless, dual, rather like the fictional Dr. Kohn and the fictionalized Bar Kochba.

But most important and impressive to Jabotinsky in 1899 was Cavallotti's legacy of anti-imperialism, his crucial opposition to the renewal of Italian colonial aspirations, first under Crispi and then under his successors. Early in 1899, King Umberto I decided to send an expedition to China to establish an Italian naval base in the bay of San Mun. This move was applauded by Crispi and the Italian nationalists as further proof of "Italian virility" but led in due course to a farcical contretemps that seems straight out of a bad Italian opera. The Chinese government refused to allow Italy to establish a beachhead on its territory; the Italians took this as an offense to their honor and demanded an apology, threatening war. Four hours later a second telegram was sent countermanding the first, but this second cable arrived before the first one![33]

Jabotinsky, reporting on all of this from Rome to his Russian audience, applauded Cavallotti's opposition to this "cursed African dream" of Italian imperialism:

> The government has discovered some new "Italian interests" in China. How do you like this idea? After this, one can talk about Chinese interests in Italy. This is how the idea of the rapprochement of nations is progressing! If Russia,

England and France have to defend their interests in countries bordering on their colonies, what does Italy have to do with this? Italy has *d'autres chiens à fouetter:* people are not dying of hunger, that's true, but are still hungry; this is the cause of the incredible number of criminals, the incredible level of emigration, and the incredible dissatisfaction, which could sooner or later lead to rebellion. The government has long promised several economic *provvedimenti;* but instead of these has passed new politically repressive laws on the press, association, on recidivist criminals—all of which will only increase the *malcontento* in the country, and is enlarging the navy "in order not to lose prestige abroad." But you've got to be *ignorant comme un maître d'école* not to see that the prestige of Italy abroad has already suffered tremendously . . . The newspaper *Tribuna* blames Russia for the failure of the Italian venture in China. If this is true, one only hopes for further Russian successes in China and further losses for Italy. That wouldn't solve the problem, of course, but would at least add one more strike against Italy's significant, but not yet significant enough, sad experiences.[34]

This article can be taken as representative of the many political feuilletons written by Jabotinsky during his years in Italy. In addition to his irritating tendency to appear sophisticated by loading up his Russian with far too many Italian and French phrases, he trumpeted as heroes the antimonarchist, antipapist, anticolonial republicans and denounced with sarcastic contempt their enemies, especially on the Right but also on the Left. In another column written a year later, Jabotinsky hailed the choice of the centrist Giuseppe Zanardelli as prime minister of Italy, a move applauded by many liberals and radicals, especially after he issued a program calling for progressive taxation, legalization of divorce, and a more tolerant attitude to strikes.[35] In other words, contrary to the universal claim that Jabotinsky was influenced by Italian nationalism during his years in Italy, the extant evidence demonstrates the contrary.

Nowhere is the real Jabotinsky's emerging worldview and true "Italian influence" better articulated than in a previously unanalyzed major work that he wrote while in Italy, his first play. Entitled in Russian *Krov'* (Blood), it is a thinly veiled dramatization of the rise and fall of Francesco Crispi.[36] This play was, Jabotinsky himself later recalled, a reworking in verse with many emendations and additions of a prose play by an Italian friend of his, the otherwise unknown Roberto Lombardo. In his Hebrew memoirs, Jabotinsky explained:

In the fall of 1901, the [Odessa] Municipal Theater presented my first play— "Blood." Who would believe that in my youth I wrote a pacifist play, against wars in general and England in particular? I wrote it while still in Rome; the subject, connected with the Boer War, I took from the manuscript of one of my friends, but changed the plot, introduced new characters, etc.; three acts and in verse yet! The best "stars" of our city troupe, headed by Anna Pas- khalova, performed in the play; but the theater was empty—maybe 300 peo- ple, maybe fewer, half of them my friends or acquaintances, who applauded, of course and called for me to appear at the curtain call at the end: I went out to take my bow, in tails ordered especially for the event, and tripped on the curtain rope; had not Madame Paskhalova caught me, I would have fallen off the stage. I didn't sleep all night long; at daybreak I rose and ran off to buy the newspapers, all the newspapers, even the Police News, and devoured the reviews. The critics were gentle—even in the Police News, and didn't wreck my joy; but the play was only performed twice in the Odessa theater.[37]

And for good reason: this three-act play in rhymed verse is sixty-four printed pages long (no copies were available outside of Russian libraries until 1991). It has fourteen major characters, many minor parts, and no discernible action onstage. As Jabotinsky explained, in a still unpub- lished letter to one of the most famous actors of the Russian stage, this was deliberate, since "the theme of the play is blood, war; therefore, necessarily, all the action takes place behind the scene, and on stage there is expressed only the gravity of the hidden actions, setting a mood." Rhymed verse, he maintained, was absolutely essential to the "Symbolist nature of the play."[38]

The story, such as it is, is simple: Georg Gamm, the minister of the interior and foreign affairs of an undisclosed state, as well as president of the cabinet of ministers, is visited by his former teacher, a dignified foreigner, who demands that Gamm stop the bloody, unjust, and im- perialist war he is leading. Gamm is shocked by this assault and rebuffs his professor, explaining that he is no longer the idealistic youth he once was. Exit the professor and enter Gamm's lady friend, an elegant and noble woman, who pleads for the release from service of a poor soldier, the husband of a desperate young acquaintance of hers, the sole support of his wife, child, and aging father. Gamm tries to accede to his friend's pleas, but he is too late; the soldier's ship has already sailed, and, we soon learn, the young man has been killed in a bloody battle that ended in hopeless defeat.

The second act opens in the home of the soldier, where we meet his elderly father, his wife, and assorted friends and colleagues, including once more the brave old professor, who reports on the perfidy of his former pupil and the tragic immorality of the war. The soldier's father has been temporarily swept up in the patriotic fervor of the crowds chanting support for Gamm and his war, but he abandons this sup- port—and indeed loses his mind—upon hearing of his son's death.

The third and final act takes place at the seaside dacha of Gamm's wealthy paramour, where the bereaved widow and her now deranged father-in-law seek solace, and to which Gamm, too, soon repairs—for the war is going badly, and he has been disgraced and is now under criminal investigation. His old mentor, the honest professor, has died, decrying his student's actions to the end. Gamm, unable to come to terms with his own grief and that of the crazy old man whose son he himself sent to death, realizes the error of his ways and flings himself into the sea as the final curtain descends.

Despite the obviously limited dramatic and literary qualities of the work, as always with Jabotinsky, the Russian is supple, rich, and idiosyncratically alive. It is not surprising that Jabotinsky would later link this play to the Boer War, which began in 1899, when he was in Italy, and ended in mid-1902, when he was back in Odessa. At the time of the play's performance, the British seemed to be winning, much to the chagrin of radical and liberal public opinion throughout Europe, including in Russia and Italy.[39] But whether this play was based on Crispi's African adventures or the British is not really important here. What is fascinating is that *Krov'* attempted to be a Symbolist play with an overt and obvious political polemic at it heart. Its pacifism and anti-imperialism, however jejune, are conveyed in rather sharply worded monologues attributed to the aged professor. One brief snippet should suffice to convey the tone and point of view:

> . . . For years your legions have
> Pitilessly sent their sons—their best sons—
> To a far-off sandy hell devoid of rain
> Uninhabited from end to end
> And waited for every last one of them to die
> Not knowing why, for what, for whom. . . .
>
> Out of idle greed, for the benefit
> Of dishonorable leaders
> You have driven innocents to a deadly,
> Bloody battle with savage hordes . . .
> A holy war for the right to plunder.[40]

But Jabotinsky's *Krov'* was not simply a pacifist and anti-imperialist tirade: it was an anti-nationalist tirade, an attempt dramatically to express—albeit in a rather hapless and wooden manner—a condemnation of nationalism as imbued with an unconscious and immoral lust for power. Minister Gamm is not an unself-conscious lout. On the contrary, he is portrayed as a genuinely moral man, but one blinded by his

patriotism, sense of national duty, and attraction to power. In perhaps
the most authentically dramatic moment of the play, Act I ends with
Gamm frantically but compellingly rebutting the arguments of his erstwhile teacher about the immorality of the war:

> I decisively and directly recognize
> The utter horror of this war
> But I am ready for anything
> I send young men off in droves
> "To a far-off sandy hell, devoid of rain"
> In order later to cover it with gardens
> To settle millions of people.
> And if the honor of my homeland
> Which I—son and leader, am entrusted to serve
> With my trusted sword and all my might demands it—
> I will trample, if I must, on everything that is sacred
> Everything! Like others, I hold law and freedom dear
> And have done so all my days
> But let law and freedom not come at the expense of my nation!
> . . . If I must stand in a pool of blood
> Like an automat, like a wild beast, unrestrained
> That is my duty, and I have no regrets![41]

To the young Jabotinsky, such a stance was the height of immorality
and political incorrectness—though it is fascinating to note that he was
able to parse with deftness and subtlety its psychological and ideological
attractiveness.

But it was not only Italian politics that absorbed the young Jabotinsky
in the years he lived in Rome. Culture, especially the current literary and
operatic scenes in Italy, was of great interest to his readers back home
in Odessa, a town in love with Italian opera as with most things Italian.
What emerges from the dozens of cultural feuilletons is Jabotinsky's
dexterous touch, his light but convincing tone, striking the pose of a
somewhat jaded, sophisticated man of the world reporting back home
to the provinces on what was happening in the beau monde of Rome,
Florence, and Naples. This blasé sophisticate would indulge in contemporary political commentary but felt himself to be essentially above politics, which was much too vulgar an interest for the true aesthete.

Perhaps the clearest articulation of this aspect of Jabotinsky's Italian
period was a long feuilleton on Gabriele D'Annunzio written on March
2, 1901. Although later in his life Jabotinsky would, not surprisingly,
admire D'Annunzio both politically and aesthetically, translate some of
his poetry into Hebrew, and to some extent cultivate a D'Annunzio-like

cult of his own, in 1901 Jabotinsky attacked the author who had recently abandoned decadence and progressive causes in both his literary works and his life. D'Annunzio now was a rightist member of parliament whose recent poetry expressed imperialist, elitist, and racist Italian nationalism. To Jabotinsky "this talented deserter of decadence" and "former Nietzschean who didn't understand even one word of Nietzsche" was then at the height of his poetic talents but was largely a disappointment since he discarded the previous lofty subjects of his art and was now trying to write about quotidian matters for the common man. True, the Italian passion for Symbolism was very short-lived, Jabotinsky noted, and D'Annunzio shrewdly switched gears to suit public taste. But it was a terrible shame that this extraordinarily talented craftsman had never written anything of lasting aesthetic value. The problem, Jabotinsky concluded, was that D'Annunzio lacked both imagination and the power of observation, and hence his verse, dramas, and novels were at once superficial, affected, insincere, boring, and dry. Finally, Jabotinsky turned to D'Annunzio's recent verse, the first installment of what would later be published as *Elettra,* D'Annunzio's most stridently politicized collection of verse, in which his imperialism was combined with a pseudo-Nietzschean lionization of "the Italian race" and the "Latin Superman." Jabotinsky admitted that this work, especially its ode to Garibaldi, was much more successful than its predecessors, since hero worship does not require real imagination. Moreover, D'Annunzio's Italian was so beautiful, his linguistic dexterity so extraordinary, that it was impossible to resist his charm, and hard for foreigners to appreciate his attraction to the Italian public. Thus, although hope was not lost that D'Annunzio would at some point be able to create enduring art, expressing the innermost emotions of his soul and his people, the omens were not good for any imminent rescue of this all-too-popular and talented poet from the twin curses of his reactionary politics and his shallow notion of art.[42]

It is important to understand that Jabotinsky's cosmopolitan aesthetic did not reject the notion of an "Italian soul." On the contrary, he and his colleagues reveled in the variety of distinct artistic traditions—national, regional, rural, and religious. This was not a pallid universalism, as often described, but an antirealist and deeply Romantic aestheticism that highlighted and foregrounded human differentness and exotic civilizations but nonetheless rejected nationalism and the overt politicization of art. Hence, in a review of P. Mascani's new opera, *The Masks,* whose Roman premiere Jabotinsky covered for the *Odesskie Novosti* in

late December 1900, he could at one and the same time praise the "witty
Symbolism" of the opera, its ode to eternal Art, Truth, and Humanity,
and its pure Italianness, its refusal to succumb to artificial and unnatural
foreign influences.[43]

A similar concatenation was evident in Jabotinsky's second dramatic
piece, *Ladno* (All right), also written during his stay in Italy. Pinning
down the exact date of the writing of this play is impossible, since it was
never published; but a typescript was found in the theater archives of
St. Petersburg after the fall of the Soviet regime.[44] Until then, the only
information about *Ladno* was that supplied by Jabotinsky himself in a
small, self-deprecating paragraph in his memoirs:

> A year later, they performed my second play, also in verse, but in one act,
> again with Paskhalova; but this time the critics did not take pity on me, and
> wrote—every one of them, as if in a conspiracy—the same pun on the name
> I gave to the play: "*Ladno*"—i.e., All right; they called "*neladno*" "nesk-
> ladno"—not all right, incoherent. . . .[45]

And right they were—although, here again, behind an even weaker
dramatic façade there hovers the philosophy of life with which the young
playwright was struggling in life, on the stage, and in his other literary
works. *Ladno*—whose subtitle is "A Scene from the Life of Youth"—is
best described as a very brief one-act sketch, a sketch so flimsy in dramatic interest or poetic power that it is difficult to imagine it being
performed on a stage, even if only once. The scene opens with an extended though very laconic conversation between a schoolteacher
mother and her schoolteacher daughter over whether the younger
woman should marry a man she barely knows and does not love, but
who promises her a life of comfort and ease. The young woman seems
to decide to accede to this offer, if ever so reluctantly, but her musings
are interrupted by the appearance of some former students of her
mother, who have come to celebrate the award to one of them of a silver
medal in the gymnasium for a piece he wrote on the philosophical theme
of "Jura in se ipsum" (the right over oneself). There is much fuss over
this medal—especially by the proud mother-teacher—and much discussion of the appropriate drinks and pastries needed to celebrate this accomplishment, much laughter and foolish banter of youth, much bemoaning of the poverty and hunger of student life. Presently, we learn
that the recipient of the medal is, in fact, the true love of the daughter,
but she rebuffs his advances, and indeed his love, because his philosophical devotion to unbridled freedom of the self prevents him from

committing himself to the young woman in any honorably sustainable fashion.

Soon, we get to hear the prize-winning oration, declaimed in verse with the accompaniment of some comic relief, but meant with great earnestness by the student, and his alter-ego, the playwright:

> "No man can be a master of himself." So spake Rome, and long thereafter this view was held and confirmed as the core of ethics especially here [in Russia]. And so, in the last decades it has led to the denial of the right of a man over himself. Duty to one's nation is held to be the core of morality. . . . I reject such a morality:
>
> I recognize one and only one law for myself, one untrammeled and seamless law. No one is bound by any duty. There is no duty. A child does not come into the world voluntarily, and life is cruel and harsh, who can be blamed for dedicating himself solely to a struggle for happiness, for one's self.
>
> We, of the future, have a new Holy Writ: Pursue your own wishes, be happy, jealously guard your own desires . . . wherever they may lead, to love, to art, to knowledge, to idleness, or even to the ancient calling of service to your nation. But even if you follow such an ancient path, follow your own spirit, not out of duty, but out of your own desires. . . . For the world is sick, ugly, putrid; we will grant it a flood of magnificent power, much beauty, and much fresh blood; but with one and only one command: fight for happiness, ruthlessly fight anything that stands in your way![46]

This cri de coeur is followed and expanded in a mock-Nordic epic about a young hero, Vitmald Eagle, who resists the blandishments of the gods and the king to rescue a beautiful damsel in distress, actually the imprisoned princess of the realm. (This bizarre and ornately written piece was reprinted by Jabotinsky under the title "Noella" and can be found in his collected verse in Russian and in an adequate, if bowdlerized, Hebrew translation in his Hebrew collected works.)[47] To rescue the maiden from her horrible imprisonment, the hero must desecrate his own father's grave, which he does willingly:

> What do I care, my spring lily of the field—
> About the sacred spirit of my father, my fatherland, my nation?
> I want you—I want to be intoxicated again and again by the caresses of
>   your beloved eyes
> and press my lips again and again against your silken skin;
> To satisfy your soul, I will destroy temples of God, desecrate all that is
>   sacred.[48]

Then the hero rides off on his steed into the sunset with his beloved princess.

But *Ladno* itself does not end so happily—the boy does not get the girl, although she offers herself to him in lines so forthright that the Russian censor forbade their utterance on the stage in Odessa. The problem is that *Ladno*'s heroine feels duty-bound to her impoverished mother and brothers to accept the offer of the man she neither loves nor can ever grow to love; but she is torn, and leaves it to the hero/philosopher to decide her fate: duty or passion? To which he answers "*ladno*" (Okay, all right, whatever) and walks off the stage without looking back as the curtain falls.

Given the aesthetic quality of this sort of play, we need not ponder too long the classic dilemma of separating the speaker from the author or the dangers of a biographically reductionist reading of verse. That Jabotinsky was here revealing his own view of the world and indeed his own conception of self is obvious. Indeed, this combination of cocky self-confidence and naiveté, *kulturnost'* and overwrought writing, was evident not only in his reportage and drama, but also in the many original poems he wrote while in Italy. Thus, an ode to Rome and to Italian culture entitled "Piazza di Spagna" was a rakish love song to his new home, composed in lilting Russian rhyme:

> Everything I love: even the navy-blue gloom
> that hangs ceremoniously over Rome;
> and 'round the fountain of Master Bernini
> autumnal flowers bloom.
> All the little shops, alleys, piazzas,
> the hidden two-towered churches,
> the dragon-steps, where linger
> the motley village maidens come to Rome.
> But not for me these fresh but tasteless rustic girls
> Not for me their holy simplicity.
> I am besotted by the thrilling charms
> of another sort of beauty.
> I see them on the Corso: a proud, bold,
> swarm of female patricians
> kissed from time to time
> by a thick boa of cold white dust.
> Their foreheads enamel with a patina of frost
> shiny leather pressed against their satiny arms
> their clothes emitting slight hints of scent
> that linger when they're gone
> and the fabrics in which they are draped
> shamelessly and transparently reveal
> a naked heat, like the half-light haze

of the hour of love.
The virgins, priding themselves on invisible poisons,
glide by shedding tantalizing waves,
meeting their straightforward, haughty gaze.
I lower my eyes.
I know them: the morning-star crumples their freshness,
the light of day singes their sheen.
Perhaps, in their touchy bodies
burn the dreams of whores.
Their smiles are lies, their friendship poison
they've taken from thousands what they're due,
their necklaces sparkle with the tears of slaves.
All this I know—but care not a whit
I am a son of my times. I know its goodness and evil
its brilliance and its rot.
I am a son of my times—and love all its stains.
All its poison I love.[49]

Not a terrible "decadent" poem, circa 1900—especially not when one considers that its author was barely out of adolescence and had hardly wallowed himself in the "naked heat . . . the half-light haze of the hour of love." Although the story mentioned at the start of this chapter sent by Jabotinsky to Korolenko has not been preserved, the master's private comments on it could just as easily have been applied here: "Vl. Jabotinsky, admirer of Verlaine; very intelligent . . . artificially decadent taste."

The last poem we consider here, even more revealing of Jabotinsky at this point, is another early Roman poem, called "Shaflokh," after the mountain by the same name in the Bernese Oberland.[50] This was obviously a reworking into Russian of Heine's famous "Berg-Idylle"—one of the best known and most successful of his *Harzreise* cycle. Unlike Nordau's Heine-esque verse, Jabotinsky's recasting of the "Berg-Idylle" poem into Russian was terrible. Although it preserved the meter, rhyme scheme, and story line of the original, it effaced the essential timbre of Heine's voice, the idiosyncratic blending of a classic folk tale of seduction and lust with quasi–Saint Simonian utopianism, a good measure of cynicism, and, of course, poetic genius.

Nonetheless, Jabotinsky's "Shaflokh" was not entirely devoid of talent or indicative of poor poetic potential—as evinced by the favorable comments of Ivan Bunin, to whom Jabotinsky sent an early draft in 1899. What is discernible in this juvenile piece is its author's utter mastery of the Russian tongue and literary idiom, his deep-rootedness

in both Russian and European poetry, and a literary sensibility totally
defined by avant-garde culture. In Heine's "Berg-Idylle," written in the
early 1820s, the hero is a young urbane traveler who comes upon the
young and simple daughter of a miner, whom he wants to seduce. She
is intrigued but questions her suitor:

> That you've prayed too much, I doubt
> And I wonder, says my fair
> What has caused that sneering quiver
> Round your lips, I'm sure not prayer . . .
> And I also doubt that really
> You believe in thoughts that lead
> To a faith in God the Father
> Son and Holy Ghost—our creed.

To which the traveler responds that as a child he believed in God the
Father, when he grew older he believed in the Son, but that now he
believes in the Holy Ghost:

> He performed the greatest wonders
> Works still greater ones; he broke
> Tyrants' overawing strongholds
> And he burst the bondsmen's yoke. . . .
> He renews our ancient right;
> Men are all born free and equal
> Race of noble mind and might. . . .
> And the Holy Ghost selected
> Thousand knights to serve His will . . .
> You no doubt would like to see such
> Valiant champions, too, my girl.
> Look at me and kiss me darling
> Champion of the Holy Spirit
> I myself am such a knight.[51]

Such politics, as well as a superseded Christianity and veiled sexuality, were obviously fetching to the young Jabotinsky, but outdated and
naive. Thus, in his reworking, the maiden is now a class-conscious university student who grills the visitor not on his belief in the Trinity but
on his political stance:

> You're an odd one—said the girl
> I don't know your point of view
> One thing tell me, what's your twist
> Are you really a Marxist?

To which he replies:

My dear lady, I won't hide or lie
In my youth, dear Fräulein Zina
I rejected all that's old and true
Was an unruly boy and a great liberal

I loved Freedom then
With all the devotion of puppy love
Prayed to her, dear goddess:
Spread your wings of liberty over us, too!

But Liberalism was too pallid a weltanschauung for Jabotinsky's young hero, so he moved on not to Marxism but to Moralism (as opposed, of course, to bourgeois morality). In due course, however, he had to reject that stance as well, since he realized that only cowards and petty minds need gods, or political ideologies of any sort. Politics, creeds, ideological systems are unnecessary and beneath the dignity of the unfettered artiste, the man without labels or beliefs, for whom the world stretches out in all its grandeur, and, not incidentally, in unfettered erotic possibilities:

Do you want to see the world?
If you do, give me your hand!
For dear girl, beside you stands
a man without labels or tags.[52]

This last line—"a man without labels or tags"—is of crucial importance, since it almost uncannily places the young Jabotinsky in his precise cultural and ideational context. On August 4, 1888, Anton Chekhov wrote the following words to his friend the poet Alexei Pleshcheyev:

I'd be happy to read what Merezhkovsky had to say. Good-bye for now. Write me once you've read my story. You won't like it, but I'm not afraid of you and Anna Mikhailovna. The people I am afraid of are the ones who look for tendentiousness between the lines and are determined to see me as either liberal or conservative. I am neither liberal nor conservative, nor gradualist, nor monk, nor indifferentist. I would like to be a free artist and nothing else. . . . Pharisaism, dullwittedness and tyranny reign not only in merchants' homes and police stations. I see them in science, in literature, among the younger generation. That is why I cultivate no particular predilection for policemen, butchers, scientists, writers or the younger generation. *I look upon tags and labels as prejudices.* My holy of holies is the human body, health, intelligence, talent, inspiration, love and the most absolute freedom imaginable, freedom from violence and lies, no matter what form the latter two take. Such is the program I would adhere to if I were a major artist.[53]

The Russian words for "labels and tags" used by Chekhov in this credo—which Kornei Chukovsky called "a gauntlet flung in the face of

an entire age, a rebellion against everything it held sacred"—were *firma*
and *iarlyk*.[54] They are precisely the words used by Jabotinsky in his
"Shaflokh," written twelve years later, at the height of Chekhov's
greatest success, the year he wrote *Three Sisters* and saw *The Seagull*
transformed from an early failure to an international sensation. Indeed,
Jabotinsky's debt to Chekhov was expressed in the first serious piece the
young litterateur had published in Italian, an essay entitled "Anton Cekhof e Massimo Gorki: L'Impressionismo nella literatura russa," which
appeared in 1901.[55] Previous biographers have noted the appearance of
this article, in order to demonstrate Jabotinsky's wide-ranging cultural
interests, but have not attended to the crucial message it reveals about
Jabotinsky's worldview at the time of its composition. After introducing
Chekhov and Gorky to an Italian audience (to whom they were un-
knowns), and presenting them as representatives of a new trend of Russian literature, Jabotinsky tried to convey what was so new and revolutionary about their works, which he claimed rather pompously "were
absolutely original, not resembling anything in other literatures except
very vaguely." This school arose spontaneously in Russia, he claimed,
because of the crisis of the day, the crisis of faith of the intelligentsia in
the fin de siècle:

> The notion of an *idea* or *ideal* at the heart of literature was useful twenty
> years ago but is completely useless in our day. I'm speaking about Russia in
> particular: there, for the vast majority of the intelligentsia there are no more
> questions—i.e. the women's question, the poor, freedom of speech and of
> conscience, all these and more are no longer discussed, since everyone accepts
> them as guiding principles. I daresay that there is at present nothing new,
> nothing fundamentally new to believe in: thought has overtaken reality.
> There is still a long battle ahead to realize these goals, which the conscience
> of humanity has recognized as just. Only at the end of that battle will new
> ideas or new ideals become possible. For now, there are no new causes, no
> new horizons to conquer, and indeed we really do not have the desire, energy,
> or courage for the requisite battle. We are too Hamlet-like . . . a degenerate
> Hamletism (*amletismo*) is the bourgeois sickness of the age, described so
> simply and horrifyingly by Anton Chekhov, whereas Maxim Gorky still ex-
> presses our ardent desire to shake up our eternally fruitless self-reflection,
> our torpid inertia, our cheap skepticism. Is there any higher social goal than
> this?[56]

To be sure, this claim that no one in Russia was still being stirred by
the great political issues of the day was a vast overstatement, ignoring
the many dedicated activists in the various ideological movements of the
day. But it acutely portrayed the other side of the coin, which is often

ignored in treatments of political history—and totally missing in analyses of Jewish history on the assumption that everyone became a Zionist or socialist after 1881. In fact, for the vast numbers of young educated men and women at the turn of the century, the various nationalisms or socialisms held no particular allure. "I look upon tags and labels as prejudices," Chekhov had written, and many of the young intellectuals such as Vladimir Jabotinsky repeated that notion in their poetry, plays, and prose. All that remained was Art, Literature, Culture, the callow aestheticism of Jabotinsky's plays, poems, and feuilletons of his Roman days.

Forced by the exigencies of real life to return home to Odessa and to the provincial drabness so exquisitely described by Chekhov, Jabotinsky would soon find—like so many others of his generation and worldview—that the life of the litterateur, the cultural critic without a truly riveting cause, could not fill the aching void, the listless emptiness that would soon emerge at the very center of his being.

CHAPTER SEVEN

Jabotinsky's Road to Zionism

In early 1901, the twenty-one-year-old Vladimir Jabotinsky returned to Odessa from Rome. He was hired immediately as a daily feuilletonist for the *Odesskie Novosti* (Odessa News), charged especially with covering the cultural scene in Odessa, a thriving hotbed of Italian opera and Russian drama. This was a perfect job for the young and ambitious litterateur, giving him the opportunity to display his recently acquired European sophistication to a readership keenly aware of its own rather precarious *kulturnost'*. Though fully convinced of its cosmopolitanism, the largely Jewish Russian-speaking bourgeoisie of Odessa knew that they were looked down upon as provincials and parvenus by the cultural elites of Moscow and St. Petersburg, as well as by the somewhat déclassé but still self-important *echt*-Russian community in the city—largely bureaucrats and army officers and their wives—who socialized with the local Russified nobility. Excluded from this society, the Jewish middle classes created their own, supplying most of the clientele as well as impresarios for the Odessa musical, operatic, and theatrical scene. Eschewing both the Yiddish of their parents or grandparents and the Ukrainian of the local peasantry, they nonetheless spoke a version of Russian that was inevitably influenced by the cadences, syntax, and phonology of Yiddish and, to a much lesser extent, Ukrainian, which elicited a mixture of condescension and schadenfreude on the part of the local native-Russian speakers. Isaac Babel would later famously protest that "in

Odessa they murder the Russian language," a charge still repeated by Muscovites and Peterburgians in the late twentieth century.[1]

In this milieu, Jabotinsky's impeccable Russian, betraying not a hint of a Yiddish lilt or a southern twang, was central to his public persona— then as later. Indeed, it was also crucial that he did not "look Jewish" to his contemporaries; indeed, his rather odd physiognomy struck some as very Russian and others as vaguely Asiatic. Equally important was his utter self-confidence and assumption of a quasi-aristocratic hauteur, best typified by his insistence on using only the formal "vy" rather than the informal "ty" (the Russian versions of "vous" or "Sie" rather than "tu" or "Du") when speaking even to his intimates or children; this formality of address was the opposite of the easy familiarity regarded as all too Jewish. His columns proved popular with his readers, written as they were in his literary and yet accessible Russian style, combined with firsthand knowledge of Italian and other western European languages and cultures.

Yet the task of supplying his readers with a daily feuilleton filled with charm, wit, and Kultur exhausted even Jabotinsky's cocky self-assurance and quick pen. Many of his articles retain their interest today because they are wonderfully evocative of a fascinating time, place, and culture; all are marked by his dexterous and appealing way with words. But a very large number are forced and filled with fluff, obviously written to deadline rather than out of any conviction, however slight. Among the most successful are the many retrospective sketches of his years in Rome, penned with a keen sense of humor and a fetching evocation of the carefree life of the Italian capital, so different from the dreary reality on the gray shores of the Black Sea. In the most alluring of these feuilletons, entitled "Studentesca," Jabotinsky placed himself (or, rather, his literary alter ego, here named "Vladimiro," though in the genre of the feuilleton, the speaker and the author are assumed to be the same person even if in fictional situations) back in his wild, impoverished student days in Rome. Neither he nor any of his friends ever seem to be attending classes or studying anything other than how to avoid the landlady's demands for rent. Certainly no ideological commitment is expressed, other than a devotion to wine, women, and song. Young Vladimiro joins in the revelry and adventures of his debauched but compelling Italian mates, but only so far: he insists that he resisted the wiles of the women whose services were shared by his roommates, since "pleasures available to all are not to my taste, and in Italy I felt a duty to play the role of the cold

Northerner." Not only was he virginal; he was also conscious-stricken. While his friends delighted in eluding their debtors, hopping from one unpaid den of iniquity to another, he felt compelled to hawk his meager possessions to try to make up at least part of their collective debts. In a wonderful scene, Vladimiro's friends all go back home for Easter, to Sicily, Abruzzo, or other parts of Rome, and he is left alone to try to find some way to dig up some lire to pay the salary of Lina, their maid, cruelly abandoned by his friends without recompense or regret. Hat in hand, he tries all his acquaintances in Rome, freezing in the light summer coat that was the sum total of his remaining possessions. But to no avail; he knocks on Lina's door to admit his lack of success, to apologize for his inability to pay her before the holiday:

> Lina opens the door. I took off my summer coat, hung it in a corner, and said to her in my most serious sweet voice: Linetta, I'm very sorry. I couldn't get even one lira, and won't be able to tomorrow either.
> "And so, what will I do?" she asked angrily.
> "I don't know. I have nothing, not even a centime, I won't be able to move somewhere else tomorrow. . . ."
> Lina approached me in silence and put a hand on my jacket:
> "Don't be so sad, Signior Fladimiro," she said in a lively, upbeat voice. "Now, we'll eat, tomorrow we'll see, maybe you'll be able to hawk something. . . ."
> When Lina returned, she sang the following song—or rather not exactly this song but something like it: "O che tempi felici / O che belli momenti. . . ."
> I won't go on to describe to you how we dined together that Easter eve, what songs we sang, and what stories she told me about her life, or how I got money the next day, etc. Much of this I myself remember indistinctly, and much of it is not interesting. I only wanted to remind myself—and if possible, you as well—about these wonderful years and gay days that passed, never to return, to have waft over myself, and possibly over you, the resinous smell of youth. I wanted to remind myself of all this on this holiday of forgiveness—I am not a Christian, but love this holiday of forgiveness and absolution—in order heartfully and mournfully to absolve my youth and my future of these few happy years, beautiful days, that will never return.[2]

This remarkable passage, written in April 1902, was heavily censored in the Hebrew translation of Jabotinsky's feuilletons published in the 1930s in Jerusalem.[3] While the young Jabotinsky could retroactively be permitted his love of Rome and even his flirtation with the young Italian servant girl, his love of Easter and its promise of forgiveness and fulfillment could not be admitted, especially since it was precisely Easter that was canonized, in eastern European Jewish collective memory and nationalist discourse, as the most dangerous day of the year, the moment of the most intense antisemitic danger and Jewish fear. Indeed, Easter day the following year did witness the most famous pogrom in late Imperial Russian history, the Kishinev pogrom of 1903, thereafter connected in fascinating ways with Jabotinsky himself.

But to understand Jabotinsky as a Zionist one has to be able to understand his love for Easter in 1902 as much as his abandonment of that love in 1904 or 1905, not to speak of 1939. To censor this passage or the hundreds like it not only distorts the past; it rids that past of its very presentness, its most intriguing and beguiling complexity, so much like that of our own lives and times. For in this passage Jabotinsky revealed more to us than he undoubtedly intended at the moment of its composition. First of all, we cannot know for certain whether he (not to speak of his readers) understood the underlying pathos of this feuilleton, the pose of world-weary nostalgia on the part of a speaker barely into his twenties. Whatever nostalgia can possibly mean for a twenty-two-year-old—in David Lowenthal's words, "nostalgia tells it like it wasn't"[4]—we can see here, and in most of his columns and poems written in 1902 and 1903, a young man clearly at a moment of existential emptiness, yearning for a world of meaning and commitment, not knowing where to turn. Indeed, this lack of direction and meaning itself became the leitmotif of his daily feuilleton in *Odesskie Novosti*. In piece after piece he lamented and bemoaned the lack of ideals and causes, of meaning and purpose, in himself, his colleagues, his friends. "Our life is dull, melancholic, paltry, there is no joy. Everyone is searching for a laugh, for beauty, for light; where are they?" Even Art and Love are no longer the solutions they earlier promised to be; even Chekhov and Gorky fail to come up with palpable remedies for the collective angst. "I am unhappy, at the depth of my soul," he repeatedly lamented, "terribly unhappy."[5]

Second, and of equal importance, this Easter column was, to my knowledge, the first and only time in the hundreds of newspaper columns written by Jabotinsky before he became a Zionist when he revealed that he was a Jew, and there is some evidence that his readers were indeed not certain of Altalena's true name or ethnic and religious origin. But the essence of his Jewishness was not its content but precisely the obverse, its lack of content, what the jargon of today would call its "liminality"—its marginality, vagueness, and transitory and transitional nature. Indeed, he did not say, "I am a Jew," but—as the medievals would put it, *via negativa*—"I am not a Christian," which is reminiscent of Nordau's elusive self-definitions before *he* became a Zionist.

If it is possible to speak nonteleologically about being on the threshold, that is where Jabotinsky was during 1902 and 1903, just like so many of his contemporaries. This period in his life also witnessed a potentially traumatic, though in his case curiously unrepercussive, event—his imprisonment for six weeks in early 1902 in the Odessan municipal jail on suspicion of revolutionary sympathies. Unfortunately, the only testimony we have of this incarceration is the short notice he gave it in his autobiography, where he treats his time in the tsarist prison as a rather pleasant interlude in his otherwise boring existence, affording him the opportunity to enrich his Russian with the delightful slang used by his fellow inmates. (After the fall of the Soviet Union, scholars searched the archives of the tsarist police for Jabotinsky's file and found no material relating to this 1902 imprisonment, though they did find very confused, secret police reports about his later activities as a Zionist propagandist in Russia.)

In sum, it was by no means preordained that Jabotinsky would turn to his Jewishness as the tonic to his highly personal yet by no means idiosyncratic crisis of meaning and faith, or that his turn to Jewishness would take on the peculiar coloration it did. Indeed, Zionism did not enter and fill this void clearly and swiftly, as an ideological and existential deus ex machina that one fine day struck him and provided him with a clear goal in life. In fact, he came to Zionism slowly and rather hesitantly—and even more slowly and hesitantly did he attempt to transform it from the inside, to reshape it in conformity with his worldview, his culture, his Jewishly deracinated notions of right and wrong.

This is best documented by several columns he wrote for the *Odesskie Novosti* in 1902 and early 1903, at a time in which, according to his own recollections and those of others, he was totally aloof from Zionism and its internal squabbles. The first—and hitherto unexamined—column, entitled "On Zionism" and signed with his favorite pen name, "Altalena," was a defense of Zionism against a widely read and influential recent denunciation written by Joseph Bikerman, an equally young but far more knowledgeable Russian-Jewish intellectual. Published in *Russkoe Bogatsvo* (Russian Wealth), the leading legal organ of the anti-Marxian Populists, Bikerman's essay pithily attacked the various versions of Zionism formulated by Herzl, Nordau, and their Russian predecessors Leon Pinsker and Ahad Ha'am, pointing out the internal contradictions of Zionism and its version of nationalism, the similarity of its critique of the Jews with that of the antisemites, and the flimsy basis of its claim to represent the interests and deep-seated desires of the Jewish masses in eastern Europe. While from the vantage point of today, Bikerman's claims about the ahistoricity of Jewish nationalism and its difference from other contemporary European nationalisms is naive and itself ahistorical (and his firm conviction that it was impossible for the Jews to create a state of their own in Palestine or anywhere else obviously has been belied by history), for its time it was a highly intelligent and informed survey of the paradoxes and peculiarities of the nascent Zionist creed. Bikerman was not an "assimilationist" or a Bundist or a Bolshevik, but a typical, well-educated Russian Jew straight out of the shtetl, fully convinced that Zionism was a reactionary move back to the ghetto, that its nationalist propaganda in fact worked against the interests of the Jewish people and hence was fundamentally "antinational." His solution was an alliance of the Jewish intelligentsia with the "progressive" elements of Russian society, to forge a Russia more just, more pluralistic, more hospitable to difference.[6]

Altalena understood none of the subtleties of Bikerman's argument. His counterarguments were flippant, largely focusing on a straw man, the claim by supporters of Bikerman that Zionism is utopian and non-scientific. The first third of Jabotinsky's column "On Zionism" derides the very idea of a "scientific" view of history and society, debunking the essence of the positivist creed. Jabotinsky then moves on to Bikerman's central claim that Zionism is inherently a reactionary movement, a retreat to the ghetto in the name of progress; he responds that those who hold such a view

> want the whole world to reduce everyone to the same level, to pin the same label on everyone, to make everyone in the world as narrow, rectilinear, orthodox and ordinary as they are, unable to hold different opinions.
> There are no regressive elements in Zionism at all!
> Is nationalism regressive?
> Loving one nation more than all others is as natural as loving one's own mother more than other mothers.
> Just as a person is in the right to preserve and develop his own individuality, so too are nations in the right to value their own nationality. And if some oppressed nationality wishes to develop its own national individuality, as is happening now in Poznan, we all denounce its oppression and support its national awakening.
> We all regard nationalism as self-defensive.
> Such a nationalism is the highest form of progress.
> The only nationalism that is reactionary is that which tries to impose on

another nation its own physiognomy, its own language, its own customs. Does anyone claim that the Jews are seeking their own state in order to oppress or subjugate other nations? What a crazy idea of Zionism, of nationalism, of reaction![7]

He then moves on to Bikerman's assertion that Zionism seeks to remove Jews from universal civilization, from caring about other people's problems:

What a strange notion, as if all people must work on one and the same level! One may be a friend of all humanity but work for the benefit of one nation, since the happiness of one nation is part of the happiness of all of humanity. Does Zionism seek to tear the Jews away from spiritual closeness to Europe? No—Zionism seeks a place for the Jews, where they can maintain that closeness, develop it and enjoy it, without suffering degradation or persecution, not risking losing their own national essence.[8]

Much like the Easter story, this defense of Zionism reveals far more about Jabotinsky than he undoubtedly intended, if parsed carefully and in context, rather than with hindsight. Most important, nowhere in this piece does Jabotinsky speak about Zionism or the Jews from the inside, nowhere does he identify with Zionism personally and existentially; Zionism is here defended explicitly as if it were any other newly organized nationalist movement, like that of the Poles in Silesia. This aloofness was not his style in most of his feuilletons, which on the contrary were highly personalized and even autobiographical, revealing the delights and despair of their author.

It is such a highly personalized column, written six months later, that gives us an even deeper and more revealing glimpse of young Jabotinsky's mind—a feuilleton simply entitled "On Nationalism," written on January 30, 1903.[9] Here, speaking totally as a Russian, with no mention of Jews at all, he explains that both conservative and radical Russian ideologues misunderstand nationalism, arguing that it and progressive politics are totally incompatible. Both are wrong, for it is indeed possible to support the broad social ideals of contemporary civilization, to yearn for the fraternity of nations, and at the same time to be in favor of nationalism. Where the "progressives" err is in their conviction that progress will efface national idiosyncrasies; where the conservatives err is in their rejection of the inevitable progress of humanity. Progress, especially scientific and technological and hence economic advance, is both inevitable and salutary, but it will not make the Italian sky look like the Finnish, will not make Switzerland look like Russia or Russia like France. The progressives are correct to argue that in the present-day world, class differences are more important than national differences, that the Russian intelligentsia is further aloof from the Russian peasantry than from the German or English or Italian intellectual classes. But this class differentiation is temporary and contingent, not essential and permanent, and will itself inevitably disappear as progress progresses. But that is not true of national idiosyncrasies—these are essential and permanent and thus will only grow, or rather be more apparent and important, in the absence of class difference and class conflict. That, the twenty-three-year-old Jabotinsky concludes, rather grandiloquently, is the march of history, and it is for the better. Evoking a metaphor that to us is a tired cliché but was all too popular at the time, he explained that humanity is like a symphony orchestra:

> The more varied the orchestra, the more beautiful the symphony. The violin complements the flute, the clarinet is more beautiful when played alongside the harp. The entire symphony of the creative human spirit—the development of science, art, poetry—requires a rich and diverse orchestra, the more varied the better. Each instrument has its own timbre, and each nation its own spiritual cast. We must value these national timbres, not efface them; we do not want the violin to sound like the trombone, nor the Czech like the Frenchman. Life does not flourish in one register, but in diversity, in the harmony of a myriad of dissimilar individualities. Nationalism is the individualism of nations.[10]

This was a total reversal of the stance he had taken merely a year or two earlier, when he often and militantly denounced nationalism as reactionary, close-minded, and stifling of the individualism of the creative soul. What changed between 1900 and 1903 was not Jabotinsky's attitude to his dormant Jewishness, caused by a conversion to Zionism, but rather the beginning of the collapse of the cultural and quasi-political aspirations of the entire aestheticist generation. Many of the most famous Symbolists and Decadents in western Europe had already reversed their militantly apolitical stances, gravitating to leftist or rightist political movements, to anarchism, religion, mysticism, spiritualism, the various nationalist movements. In Russia this would happen en masse a few years later, but by 1903 the fin-de-siècle malaise was already past its prime, even in the provinces. Beyond the myriad cultural and artistic manifestations of this crash of sensibility and hope was a remarkable and unprecedented reorientation of Russian politics over precisely the same issues intriguing, depressing, and beguiling the young Jabotinsky. In early and mid-1903 the famous split over nationalism occurred in the Russian Social Democratic Party, centered on the role

of Jewish nationalism in the all-Russian party; the Second Congress of
the Russian Social Democrats met in June, resulting in the creation of
the Bolshevik-Menshevik split and the withdrawal of the Bund from the
party. At the very same time, another group of former Russian (and
Russian-Jewish) Social Democrats abandoned their erstwhile Marxist-
flavored positivism in favor of philosophical idealism, articulating a
metaphysical and religious foundation for liberal politics and founding
the Union of Liberation, Russia's first liberal party. Finally, at this same
moment, Russian conservative nationalism was beginning to organize
itself, with the newly founded Russkoe Sobranie, dedicated to counter-
acting the spreading cosmopolitanism of the upper classes by liberating
and awakening national feelings, publishing popular brochures, and
opening provincial branches and a student circle.[11]

In sum, just as his turn to Symbolism and Decadence in the late 1890s
was typical rather than idiosyncratic, Jabotinsky's abandonment of Symbolism and Decadence was also typical rather than idiosyncratic. A thoroughgoing atheist and rationalist, he could not, to the end of his days,
comprehend any mystical or religious sensibility or even any metaphysical philosophical stance, idealist or not. Thus even a turn to a full-
fledged neo-Romanticism à la Martin Buber or Y. L. Peretz or the
thousands of other young Russians, Poles, Germans, and Jews was not
possible for him. As a foreigner in Switzerland and Italy he had experienced viscerally the realities of national differentness and intense nationalist sensibilities, and he slowly if surely was increasingly attracted
to the psychological and political potency of nationalism as an answer
to his aching emptiness. The remaining question before him, however,
was which nationalism: which nation was he a part of, of which national
individuality did he partake, to which national cause could he hitch his
own wagon, given the tide of history as he perceived it?

There were in theory three options available to him: Russian, Ukrainian, and Jewish nationalism. Though clearly the Russian language and
culture were his language and culture, he was not an ethnic Russian.
More important, Russian nationalism was entirely the preserve of the
reactionary, antisemitic Right: the Russian liberal movement was still
dedicated to cosmopolitanism, albeit in a Russified mode. The Ukrainian
national movement had more of a liberal and even leftist presence,
alongside its chauvinistic Right wing, and Jabotinsky would from this
time on always feel close to Ukrainian nationalists and their cause—
later, in extremely controversial ways. But he was, in truth, an Odessan,
not a Ukrainian, and could not possibly feel comfortable identifying

himself as the latter. And so, virtually *faut de mieux,* there was the Jewish national movement. Since he was by no means a socialist, the Bund or various movements attempting to synthesize socialism and Zionism could not possibly attract him. And so, the invitation of a group of Odessan Zionists, eager to convert the well-known Altalena to their cause, to have him attend the Sixth Zionist Congress as one of their delegates, fell on attentive, if not yet committed, ears.

We have no reliable evidence of the details of this engagement with the Odessan Zionists, no contemporary letters or archival materials, but only recollections written thirty years later by Jabotinsky himself as well as by one of his closest comrades-in-arms, Solomon Salzman, who wrote his memoirs in 1943—three years after Jabotinsky's untimely death, and with full knowledge of *Sippur yammai,* Jabotinsky's autobiography, which Salzman cites in great detail.[12] As a result, while there are some interesting discrepancies between the two accounts, both proceed from the assumption that Jabotinsky's Zionism was latent from birth and had merely to be reactivated at the correct moment. Specifically, both aver that the core of his later beliefs—a militant and indeed militarist version of Zionism, which insists on force of arms as the sine qua non of Jewish national pride—was at the heart of Jabotinsky's Zionism from the get-go. Thus, both provide their readers with a wonderful story: that Salzman and Jabotinsky met at the Italian opera in Odessa and became friends due to this shared passion. In the course of their discussions about opera, Salzman revealed that he was a Zionist and then indoctrinated Jabotinsky into the movement. At the same time, and even before he became an active Zionist, Jabotinsky was instrumental in organizing the self-defense of the Jews of Odessa against the threat of a local pogrom (which thankfully never materialized). Not, both of them insisted, that Jabotinsky became a Zionist in response to persecution or pogrom. Jabotinsky, even more than Salzman, was especially eager to deflect any suggestion that he became a Zionist in reaction to the Kishinev pogrom, which broke out on Easter Day 1903. Since Jabotinsky would later become famous as the translator of the most important work of Hebrew literature composed in the wake of Kishinev, Hayyim Nahman Bialik's "In the City of Slaughter," it became common practice to associate his involvement in Zionism with the response to the Kishinev pogrom. Jabotinsky rejected ferociously such an association:

> It is strange: I do not remember the impression which [the Kishinev pogrom] that watershed for our life as a nation, had on me. Perhaps it actually made no impression on me. I was a Zionist even beforehand, I thought of Jewish

self-defense beforehand, and even the Jewish cowardice that was evident at
Kishinev was no new discovery to us at the time—not to me or to any Jew
or Christian. I've always had the feeling that events don't teach us anything,
don't surprise me at all; it is as if I've always known that something will
happen, and then it happens.[13]

Indeed, it is striking to note that nowhere in Jabotinsky's vast literary
output of that period is there any mention of Kishinev, not in his columns in *Odesskie Novosti* nor in his correspondence. In his autobiography he tells us that since his newspaper received many contributions
for the victims of the Kishinev pogrom—food, clothing, money—he
traveled to Kishinev as a representative of the paper to distribute alms,
in the process meeting the leaders of Russian Zionism who were gathered to investigate the pogrom, including Bialik. Jabotinsky confesses
that he is ashamed to say he had never even heard of Bialik before. Upon
his return to Odessa, he reports, Salzman introduced him to more members of the local Zionist intelligentsia, who were delighted at the prospect of the famous Altalena becoming a Zionist; Salzman then pulled
some strings to get him credentials to attend the Zionist Congress as a
delegate from Odessa. And so, in late August 1903 Jabotinsky returned
to Switzerland to attend the Sixth Zionist Congress in Basel, after which
he planned to revisit Rome.

There is only one extant piece of correspondence from this period
preserved in Jabotinsky's massive archive: before leaving for the West,
he wrote a most revealing letter to Maxim Gorky:

Dear Alexei Maximovich:

After much hesitation I have decided to send you, in your capacity as director
of *Znanie* [Gorky's publishing house], a collection of my newspaper feuilletons, which I ask you to publish as a separate volume.

I have been stuck in my newspaper work and it seems I will never break
loose from its bondage. Therefore, all those who predicted greatness for me
are now convinced that I am lost. I don't want to agree with them, since I
know that I invested much energy and true venom in several of these feuilletons. It pains me to think that because of their origin in journalism they
will be doomed to ignominy. Please do not refuse to glance at them; perhaps
you too will agree that the fate predicted for them is unjust.[14]

The pathos of this plea, which remained unanswered by Gorky, is
palpable: on the eve of his departure for Basel, the twenty-three-year-
old Jabotinsky had to confess to himself as well as to one of his literary
heroes that his longed-for career in Russian letters was all but a lost

dream—"those who predicted greatness for me are now convinced that I am lost. I don't want to agree with them." His ideological and spiritual crisis was now joined by a terrible, painful recognition that his most cherished self-conception, that of an artist, had no future. He was stuck: in provincial Odessa, as a newspaper columnist, as a deracinated Russified Jewish intellectual. Before him loomed the classic Russian dilemma—*Chto delat'* (What is to be done?)—made famous by Nikolay Chernyshevsky long before Lenin. In this mood of both professional and ideological disarray he left for Basel, where at long last he found the cause that could fill the gaping hole in his heart and mind, and the stage upon which he could develop his talents and ambitions.

In his autobiography, Jabotinsky tells the following story about his participation in the Sixth Zionist Congress:

> It would be possible to write a light comedy about my intervention at the Congress. . . . Several months earlier, Herzl had travelled to Russia and spoke with Plehve, the minister of the interior—Plehve, that is, who was thought to be the instigator of the Kishinev pogrom. A furious argument broke out among the Russian Zionists if negotiations with such a creature were permissible or not—but it was decided not to raise this dangerous topic at the Congress. I knew all this, but figured that I wasn't affected by this agreement, since as a veteran journalist in Russia I was able to discuss dangerous questions without raising the ire of the censor. My turn to talk came when speakers were already limited to fifteen minutes. But I never got to complete that quarter-hour; I began to argue that one ought not to confuse ethics and tactics, and the Opposition immediately knew what this unknown lad, with a black pompadour, speaking Russian so refined it sounded like he was declaiming a poem for a gymnasium exam—was talking about and they started screaming and shouting: Enough! Enough! On the dais chaos ensued; Herzl himself, who was in an adjacent room, heard the noise and rushed onto the dais and asked one of the delegates "What's happening, what's he saying?" By chance the delegate in question was Dr. Weizmann, who answered briefly and to the point: "Quatsch" (Nonsense). Then Herzl came up behind me on the podium and said to me "Ihre Zeit ist um" (Your time is up). And these were the first and last words I ever heard from his mouth. Doctor Friedmann, one of Herzl's closest advisers, explained these words to me in his native Prussian way: "Gehen Sie herunter, sonst werden Sie heruntergeschlept!" (Get off the platform or you'll be dragged off!) I descended from the dais without finishing my defense, unwanted by the person whom I rose to support.[15]

All of Jabotinsky's subsequent biographers have faithfully repeated this charming story. Joseph Schechtman, Jabotinsky's most trusted and talented biographer, not only provided a word-for-word recitation of the Herzl story, but referred the reader to its source, page 93 of a 1903 transcript of the Sixth Zionist Congress published in Vienna.[16] On the specific page Schechtman cites, there is, in fact, no mention of Jabotinsky, but on page 94, the following description appears: Delegate Jabotinsky rises to the podium and speaks in Russian. [The stenographer only transcribed those speeches declaimed in German or in what was called Kongress-Deutsch, a highly Germanized form of Yiddish invented on the spot by East European Jews trying to communicate with their German-speaking brethren. Speeches in other languages were simply listed with the name of the delegate and the language he was speaking.] The vice-chair of the session, Dr. Bodenheimer [Max Bodenheimer, the organizer and president of the Zionistische Vereinigung für Deutschland and future Revisionist Zionist], interrupts him, informing him that it was against the rules of the Congress to address the issue he was raising. Delegate Jabotinsky continues, however, amidst both applause and cat-calls. Frustrated, Dr. Bodenheimer intervenes again: "Please finish and sum up!" But Delegate Jabotinsky refuses to do so, leading to even more chaos in the hall. At this point, Bodenheimer takes the floor away from the obstreperous Russian: "Ich bitte den Redner, die Tribune zu verlas-sen. Ihre Zeit ist um. Das Wort hat Herr Rabinowicz." And the floor is indeed handed over to Mr. Rabinowicz.[17]

Given what we already know about Jabotinsky's autobiography, it is not too surprising to discover that it was not the stenographer who got the story wrong, but Jabotinsky; Herzl and Weizmann were not present at this time on the main floor of the Congress, and Dr. Friedmann was indeed Dr. Bodenheimer.[18] In other words, Jabotinsky's one and only conversation with Herzl never, in fact, occurred. This is perhaps the most evocative case of Jabotinsky's retroactive creation of his own myth, accomplished by transposing only a few details, a few names, a few facts. In later years Jabotinsky would put to good use this delightful and amus-ingly self-denigrating story of his one and only encounter with the man who would indeed become his subsequent life-long hero, Theodor Herzl.

While neither Jabotinsky's memoirs nor the official stenographic ac-count are very helpful in reconstructing Jabotinsky's reactions at the time to the Sixth Zionist Congress, it is possible to do so on the basis of a source never before analyzed in the literature: four articles about the Congress that he wrote in Basel and cabled home to the *Odesskie Novosti*. These reports reveal a great deal about his first encounters with Zionism, Herzl, and the inner workings of his newfound faith.[19] The first report was composed on the eve of the opening of the Congress, as the young Jabotinsky introduced his readers to the maze of *Vorkonfer-*

enzen, the preliminary caucuses of the various Zionist subgroupings gathered in Basel. With his typical light touch and sarcastic tone, Jabotinsky depicted himself groping his way through these meetings, comprehending little but gathering information and impressions of their proceedings. Finally he settled down in the "Ibria" assembly, composed of the promoters of Hebrew as the national language of the Jewish people and of the Zionist movement. Freely admitting that he could not really follow the deliberations since his Hebrew was so rudimentary, he nonetheless did not hesitate to make confident pronouncements to his audience back home about the Kulturkampf that so threatened to overtake and to derail the nascent Zionist movement. To him, it was obvious that Hebrew should be the language of the Zionist movement and the Jewish people since most Jews are educated in the heder—the traditional Jewish school—whether in Lithuania or (he believed) in Algiers or Bukhara. In these schools young Jews learn the Bible and hence biblical Hebrew, and for all of them to be able to communicate with one another, Hebrew is the only plausible medium. True, the heder is reputed to have flaws as a pedagogic institution, but that is not important, at least not in regard to the content of what is taught in these institutions. What is crucial is not content but form: the form of the Hebrew language, since the Ashkenazic pronunciation regnant in European Jewish schools is "mutilated, corrupted and unrecognizable" and, even more important, un-European sounding. The Sephardic pronunciation, on the other hand, is far more aesthetically pleasing to the European ear, "despite its oriental guttural 'kh' sound" and thus should replace the Ashkenazic pronunciation in all European Jewish schools and in the Zionist movement as well.

What is fascinating about these pronouncements is not just their utter superficiality, but also the insouciance of their author, so totally unaware of the frantic behind-the-scenes battle over what would soon become known as the Uganda affair, not to mention his apparent ignorance of the history of the decades-long Kulturkampf he was discussing, the debates over Hebrew versus Yiddish versus the vernacular and the desirability and possibility of the rebirth of Hebrew as a modern language. Jabotinsky came to this session of Ibria blissfully ignorant of not only the language spoken there but also the storms its rebirth had evoked over the course of the past century and a quarter: from the time of Naphtali Herz Wessely's pamphlet "Words of Peace and Truth" (issued in 1782), through the fights over Hebrew versus the vernacular in Germany in the early and mid-nineteenth century, to the ideological travails

of men such as Judah Leib Gordon, Peretz Smolenskin, Eliezer Ben Yehuda, and Leon Pinsker in the Russian Haskalah of the 1850s through
1870s. It is likely, moreover, that Jabotinsky was not yet even aware of
Herzl's controversial passage in his *Judenstaat,* advocating a Swiss-like
multilingualism in the future Jewish state, a suggestion that infuriated
Ahad Ha'am and his East European disciples. Certainly Jabotinsky at that
time could not have read Ahad Ha'am's incensed essays on language and
culture in their original language, a difficult and sophisticated Hebrew.

Jabotinsky came to this debate without the visceral experience of
most of the members of Ibria, East European Jews from the Pale of
Settlement, many of them now students in western European universities, who had been educated in the traditional world of Russian-Polish
Jewry and abandoned it, hating virtually everything that world stood
for, dedicated to its obliteration in a cultural revolution that was often
Nietzschean (or at least believed itself to be Nietzschean) in its call for
a total transfiguration of values, of language, of worldview. Jabotinsky
was reared in the Richelieu Gymnasium in Odessa, not a heder, and his
rebellion—recall his very first published piece—was against the values,
the culture, the grading system of that gymnasium and its ersatz-
aristocratic but really bourgeois pretensions. Unlike most East European
Zionists he did not have to struggle with the emotional pull of their
mother-tongue, Yiddish, a language he did not know, nor could he truly
empathize with the profound sense of cultural inadequacy on the part
of Yiddish speakers who had to struggle to learn Russian or Polish or
German as their certificate of entry into linguistic "civilization," always
burdened by their fear of a slip into a Yiddish phrase or intonation. His
views on Hebrew and the heder, then, were utterly superficial when not
factually incorrect. Lacking intimate knowledge of the nuances of the
cultural minefield he was entering into, he could come to simple, even
obvious, conclusions and accept them without hesitation or emotional
travail. For him the matter was all so simple: Hebrew was the language
of the Bible and (supposedly) of the heder, so Hebrew it ought to be;
and indeed, immediately after the Congress, he set about to learn Hebrew from scratch and would do so with remarkable, if tellingly idiosyncratic, results.

Similarly, his second August 1903 report from Basel was a description
of the meeting of the Mizrachi, the small Orthodox Zionist party
founded a year earlier in Vilna. This was a sympathetic, if emotionless,
piece of superficial reportage that could not have been written by any
Jew from the Pale of Settlement, whatever his or her background. Ja-

botinsky did not have a visceral experience of Judaism as a religion—as an all-encompassing universe of faith and praxis. Indeed, it is possible that as a child he was even farther removed from Judaism as a religion than the nonpracticing Theodor Herzl and the zealously antireligious Max Nordau, both of whom had at least been reared in atmospheres with greater Jewish religious content than Jabotinsky's (Hungarian Reform in Herzl's case, moderate traditionalist in Nordau's). Jabotinsky later claimed that he was taken to the synagogue as a young child to say kaddish for his deceased father (though in fact underage sons were not usually permitted to do so), but that even then he had no feeling for the rest of the prayer service and took no part in it. In other words, even in his later autobiographical self-construction, when he was in fact immensely popular among certain segments of traditional Jewish youth in Poland and the Baltic states, he did not try to invent even a superficial attachment to religious Judaism and admitted that the entire world of Jewish ritual, prayer, and faith were foreign to him. The extent of his natural and unremitting secularism was most famously articulated in his last will and testament, written in English in 1935, in which he instructed his heirs: "I wish to be buried or cremated (it is the same to me) at the place in which death shall find me"—thus evincing not a whit of concern about transgressing perhaps the ultimate and certainly the last taboo in Judaism, cremation, which is shunned and avoided by even the most alienated and atheistic Jews.[20]

It is crucial to understand, then, that unlike other secularist or antitraditionalist Zionists, Jabotinsky had no tradition to rebel against, no psychological animus against Jewish Orthodoxy that in many ways constituted the animating spur to Zionism for other Russian, Polish, and Lithuanian Jewish youths. Even Chaim Weizmann, later rather a moderate on this score, was at this stage in his development renowned in Zionist ranks for his militant anticlericalism.[21] In fascinating and subtle ways, then, precisely because of his lack of contact with Jewish Orthodoxy, Jabotinsky could be more sympathetic to its proponents within the Zionist movement than his fellow Russian Zionists!

And so he came to the meeting of the Mizrachi faction without any knowledge of its exceedingly precarious position on the modernist wing of the traditionalist world. He showed no awareness of the fact that by far the vast majority of traditional rabbis in eastern Europe vociferously opposed Zionism on religious grounds, condemning it as heresy for its rebellion against the messianic tradition and for being led by freethinkers and heretics. Indeed, the Mizrachi had been formed as a separate party precisely in protest against the embrace of the cultural goals of the secularist Zionists; its leaders had to insist that Zionism entailed no cultural modernization, not to speak of revolution, only the securing of a homeland for the Jews. As such, they made common cause with the political Zionists—especially Herzl and Nordau—who opposed the cultural program demanded by the Russian Zionists on both tactical and ideological grounds. (As discussed in the chapter on Lilien, the debates between the political and the cultural Zionists exploded at the Fifth Zionist Congress in 1902, at which the leader of the Mizrachi, Rabbi Yizhak Yaakov Reines, announced that "for us the cultural question is a misfortune. It will smash everything to pieces.") At the Sixth Congress, this tactical alliance with Herzl and political Zionism and against the cultural Zionists led Reines and the other Mizrachi delegates to vote *in favor of* the Uganda project, a vote often effaced in loyal Mizrachi scholarship and recollection. This alliance with Herzl against the so-called Zion Zionists only consolidated the opposition to the Mizrachi movement on the part of most East European Zionists, who moreover despised the Mizrachi's conservative stance on such issues as the status of women and other social questions.

All this Sturm und Drang was simply not part of Jabotinsky's experience as he strolled into the Mizrachi caucus in late August 1903. He had heard some harsh rumors about the obscurantism of this party, he reported to his readers back home in Odessa—that its delegates all wore yarmulkes and long *kapotes* and forbade women and bare-headed men at their meetings; that they were cowed into strict obedience to their leaders and were dedicated to the extirpation of freethinkers within the Zionist movement as a whole. Most of this was not true, he was happy to discover. While the men all did wear what he took to be traditional Jewish garb and did display great discipline in their caucus, they appeared far more liberal and pluralistic than he expected. Most impressive was Rabbi Reines, who, he reported,

> is an interesting old man. Under his yarmulke there is without doubt far greater tolerance and understanding of the Zeitgeist than under the other hats on the dais. It seemed to me that when the speakers were holding forth angrily about the battles between the orthodox and the freethinkers, his face clearly revealed the line of the book of Kohelet: vanity of vanities, all is vanity. You think one way, I another; in fact, in my heart I am not such a believer in my beliefs and you in yours. Everyone is babbling, throwing ideas back and forth, but the only important thing is the anguish of a homeless people who need a homeland, that is the only matter of importance.[22]

This remarkable (and completely counterfactual, needless to say) projection of pluralism onto the visage of Rabbi Reines was extended to Jabotinsky's reporting of the controversial issue of the status of women in the Mizrachi movement. A place at the back of the hall was reserved for visitors who were not members of the party. Some guests, including several women, made their way to the middle of the hall and found themselves sitting among Orthodox men. The latter didn't protest, but since the movement of the guests had made a lot of noise, the vice-chair of the meeting, "a student at Bern University but in a yarmulke," lost his patience and said: "I wish to bring to the attention of all present that according to the statutes of the Mizrachi movement, women are not allowed to sit alongside men." At this, a ruckus broke out: someone screamed "pfui," others began to stomp their feet, to protest. Rabbi Reines then rose to his feet and explained that his young colleague had not expressed himself correctly; while it was true that the statutes of the Mizrachi required women to meet separately from men, that did not apply to guests.

Jabotinsky remarked:

> As an observer from the sidelines I concluded that this made a very positive impression on me. Without a doubt, in fact the erroneous interpretation was made not by the vice-chair but by Rabbi Reines, since the statutes of Mizrachi clearly forbid the mixed seating of men and women. Reines made a concession, and one in consonance with the spirit of the times. . . . The Orthodox cannot not be Orthodox; but the recognition of other points of view and ways of life alongside their own is a huge step forward from fanaticism.[23]

However, he continued, both Mizrachi and the political Zionists are wrong to deny the importance of culture in Zionism, since educational and literary efforts are central to the goals of the movement as a whole and cannot be abandoned to the opponents of Zionism. Thus, every effort must be made to advance the cultural program enunciated by Ahad Ha'am and his supporters, as well as the excellent idea of a Jewish university promoted by Chaim Weizmann.

To Jabotinsky—unlike virtually any other delegate at the Congress— these did not seem to be contradictory goals or points of view, precisely because he was an outsider, an observer from the sidelines not only of the Zionist movement but, more important, of Judaism and the Jewish community as a whole, much as Herzl and to some extent Nordau had been a decade earlier. Jabotinsky was gradually becoming converted to the idea of Zionism but remained aloof from its internal, highly emotional, and profoundly ideologized struggles, redolent of the deep divides and hatred of Jewish society. His reactions, then, were a mix of ignorance and common sense, entirely devoid of any passion. Rabbi Reines, Chaim Weizmann, Martin Buber, Ahad Ha'am, all were at this point neutral figures in his psychic universe and personal experience; he could view them all, and the divisive ideologies they represented, with equal dispassion, picking and choosing what seemed to be logical in their stances, even if to other Zionists his conclusions were incommensurable or based on utter ignorance. Indeed, in this final piece of reportage on the 1903 Congress, Jabotinsky went on to predict that despite all the internal squabbles, the movement was essentially unified, the various subgroupings all dedicated to the same goal and capable of working together in harmony. As he was to learn immediately upon the formal opening of the Sixth Zionist Congress, this prediction of unity amid diversity was totally in error, for within the very next few days, Theodor Herzl would present to the Zionist movement the British offer of a Jewish protectorate in Uganda, and all hell would break loose.

Jabotinsky reported on this shocking development and the furious split it engendered in two columns dated August 27 and 28, the last two days of the 1903 Congress. In the first piece, Jabotinsky began with his first live impression of Theodor Herzl:

> He has the most interesting looks of anyone I've ever seen, at once extraordinarily masculine, hard, and graceful. A profile of an Assyrian emperor like those engraved on ancient marble slabs; the manner of a man confident in his next ten years, if not accustomed to ruling then prepared immediately to do so. I listened to and thought a great deal about this man: the Zionist movement has deep roots and does not depend on one man, but its entire leadership, its entire direction, its entire responsibility falls on Theodor Herzl. When one thinks of the Zionist movement, one thinks of him. If he should die, it would take many months to convince onlookers that the movement as a whole has not died along with him. The life of the Zionist movement is not dependent on Herzl, but its future is entirely in his hands. The success of the movement at this time is entirely synonymous with the success of Herzl. All the stakes of Zionism rest on him, so it is crucial to understand him correctly.
>
> I know what everyone around him says about both his good and bad points, and I'm able to look at him coldly and dispassionately and conclude that he is one of the most remarkable personages of our age. Precisely what his power consists in is hard to define: he is far from being a great writer, though he has an excellent style and is able to express precisely what he has to say; he is not a great orator but manages to say exactly what needs to be

said, and when. He is astonishingly at one with himself, totally self-possessed—he creates the impression of a man who is not capable of a false, calculated gesture; a man capable of course of making a mistake, but not of stumbling into error. He is never abrupt but always overwhelming; many maintain that he has hypnotized them. *En détail* he seems to be a man of middling talents, but in sum he is an extraordinary figure, perhaps not talented but a true genius.[24]

It does not take much psychological ingenuity to see how transfixed the young Jabotinsky was by Herzl. This description goes beyond the realm of lionization to something far deeper and hence far more impervious to simple categorization. Without resorting to any irresponsible "psychohistorical" hypotheses, suffice it to recall only the bare facts of Jabotinsky's life to this moment: his father died when he was six; he was raised by his mother and sister as the apple of their eyes, convinced that he was to be a great writer and a great man; he was an extremely precocious adolescent, becoming a professional author at the age of sixteen. But now, seven years later, after much—perhaps, indeed, too much—success, Jabotinsky felt stuck and hopeless, both ideologically and professionally, and was looking to the Zionist movement and a still inchoate Jewish identity that he had only discovered a few months before perhaps to give meaning to his life. Into this vacuum stepped Theodor Herzl, a leader of the Jews but distinctly un-Jewish in his looks, actions, and bearing; a man of enormous self-possession, self-discipline, and pan-European culture, embodying the fin-de-siècle ideal of elegant masculinity, at once hard, strong, elegant, and yet understated, enormously powerful, forceful and compelling but without the need to raise his voice, to lower himself to the level of his opponents, since he was in his very essence above the fray, a natural ruler even without a kingdom to rule. It is obvious that this was the template that would guide Jabotinsky for the rest of his life: ultimately, he would become—or at least seek to become—the second Herzl, formed in the precise image of the first. His subsequent lifelong cult of Herzl and call for a "return" to pure Herzlian Zionism, the essence of Revisionist Zionism, was as much a psychological as an ideational return—though an orthodox Freudian might choose to use the term "repetition compulsion."

To be sure, in late August 1903, this process was only in its first and very precarious stage, complicated from the start by the fierce battle over the very meaning of Zionism engendered by the Uganda controversy. Given his reaction to Herzl, how would Jabotinsky vote on Uganda? In his autobiography, he says the following, immediately after his description of the fictionalized encounter with Herzl:

> I understood that my task in this Congress was to keep quiet and to observe, and so I did. There was a ton to observe. The Sixth Congress was, after all, the last in Herzl's lifetime, and perhaps the first of *mature* Zionism. The test of maturity was the famous name: Uganda. I was in the minority that voted against Uganda, and together with the other Neinsagers I left the hall in protest. To myself I wondered at the hidden impetus in the depths of my soul that led me to vote no. . . . I had no romantic love for the Land of Israel then—indeed I'm not sure that I have that now; and I couldn't know if there was a danger that the movement would split—I didn't know the [Jewish] people, I saw its representatives here for the first time and didn't even dare to speak with any of the leaders. The majority—even the majority of those who came from Russia—voted "yes" [that is, in favor of a protectorate in Uganda]. No one urged me to vote the way I did. . . . I can still hear Herzl's ringing oath at the end of the Congress—"If I forget you, O Jerusalem"— and I believed that oath, everyone believed it. But I voted against him, and I don't know why: "Just because"—that "just because" that is stronger than a thousand explanations.[25]

This fascinating passage has often been cited, not only as a supposed explanation of his vote in 1903 but also because of his enormously revealing confession, thirty years later, that he still bore no "romantic love" for Palestine. But as an accurate reflection of his feelings at the Sixth Congress it is also utterly misleading—a fact hinted at by his erroneous recollection that the majority of Russian Zionists voted in favor of Uganda, which was not so. In fact, in 1903 Jabotinsky knew better and knew very well why he voted the way he did: in his reportage from Basel, he announced to his readers that Herzl's opening speech at the Congress was "perhaps the turning-point in Jewish history," the first real chance to undo the millennial Exile, to bring the Diaspora to a close, and, especially in the wake of the Kishinev pogrom, to "save 11 million people." But he explained, "the more I think about East Africa, the more I comprehend the tragic aspect of this moment," because for him as well as for the vast majority of East European Zionists, Zionism was inconceivable without Zion. There is a fundamental difference, he struggled to understand and then to explain, between Zionists in western Europe and in the East, unknowingly repeating the leitmotif of many of Max Nordau's speeches and articles on Zionism from 1897 on, but now against Nordau's own position. In western Europe, Zionists are not only free men (that is, emancipated citizens of modern nation-states); they are mostly doctors of philosophy, and "doctors of philosophy are not for Jerusalem":

> They simply need a territory—the best one will do—where they can feel themselves to be first-class citizens, as Nordau put it here. Regarding any spiritual ties to Palestine, doctors of philosophy are too skeptical, too surface-oriented, to care about all these fables and dreams. Certainly if Palestine were available to them, they would prefer it over Africa, but if they were given the choice to settle, under conditions of autonomy, either Wiesbaden or Jerusalem, who knows?[26]

Russia is a different case, and Russian Zionism is a different movement:

> I consider Russia an amazing country: there live the best Slavs and the best Jews. Best in the sense that they are entirely whole, entirely devoid of that superficiality that Ahad Ha'am decried in western "Israelites" as "Slavery in freedom." Precisely because the Jewish masses in Russia live in such density, and their situation is one of such hopelessness, their dreams and aspirations are so bold.[27]

In Russia, Jabotinsky instructed his readers back home in Odessa, Zionism is a movement of the masses, even if those masses are actually unaware of their innate Zionism, ineluctably redolent of Judaism, Jewish symbols, Jewish memory, and naturally transmutable into political action. In Russia, Jabotinsky insisted:

> Zionism—Palestinian, not African—is an innate feeling of the masses, an emancipation of national strivings and the people's will. The masses are silent, they do not speak but they do think, and Zionism articulates their thoughts. Indeed, it is not difficult to articulate their thoughts. In times of grief, in exile, what can people dream of but of a homeland, prayed for and yearned for in all their holy books, endowed with miraculous expression, preserving the ruins of holy places, given to their forefathers, taken away from their grandfathers and promised to their grandchildren. One must *want* not to understand in order not to understand the inevitable, elemental necessity of this national dream.[28]

To understand Jabotinsky here one must attend carefully to the specific language he used, difficult to translate because of its specific fin-de-siècle Russian resonances. In arguing that Zionism was "the elemental expression of the people's will," Jabotinsky used two of the most evocative stock phrases of the Russian leftist lexicon, in either its populist or Marxist variations: *stikhiinost'*, meaning "spontaneous and innate," and *narodnaia volia*, meaning either "popular will" or "national will."

From the latter phrase comes, of course, the name of the first revolutionary terrorist organization in Russia, responsible for the murder of Alexander II. More broadly, the phrase "narodnaia volia" connotes an innate, freedom-seeking quest of the masses, the Russian word *volia* meaning both "will" and "liberty." In crucial ways, then, Jabotinsky's nascent understanding of Zionism in 1903 was—quite naturally, given his intellectual and cultural background—expressed in and through the language and the thought patterns of the Russian leftist intelligentsia, a worldview not reducible to or synonymous with any particularly rigid ideology, thus frustrating future historians. We have seen Jabotinsky flip and flop through this weltanschauung, challenging some of its basic premises while retaining its formative ideas, following its shifting fads and fashions while slowly and inchoately cutting out his idiosyncratic path. Here, he even conjures up what one might call a populist-Zionist variation on the Marxian concept of "false consciousness": Russian Jews, even if they reject the Zionist movement or ignore it, are deemed to be innate Zionists, since Zionism is the ineffable expression of their millennial yearning for a homeland. It is probably unnecessary to repeat here that Jabotinsky had absolutely no firsthand knowledge of East European Jewish society and its innermost strivings and hopes, no true understanding of the exceedingly complex relationship between the messianic longings in traditional Judaism and the goals and rhetoric of the Zionist movement.

But on the basis of this emerging "populist" perspective, he concluded, he had no choice but to vote against the Uganda plan, even if it meant voting against Herzl. And so he joined the "Neinsagers" in the (losing) vote on Uganda, unlike the delegates of either the socialist or the Orthodox Zionist streams in Russian Zionism (who voted for the East African plan); Jabotinsky voted on the basis of his belief, as he concluded his reports from Basel, that "the roots of Zionism lie in the depths of the Jewish soul, and hence Zionism leads to Palestine."

With this newfound conviction, Jabotinsky left Basel and returned to his beloved Eternal City, to revisit his friends and the site of his youthful happiness. As soon as he arrived in Rome, he did what he had never done before during his previous long stay in the Italian capital: he visited the Roman ghetto and sought out the Roman Jewish community. In three long feuilletons cabled from Rome to *Odesskie Novosti*, he struggled with the meaning of Jewishness and hence of Zionism through the looking-glass of a newfound Jew and a newfound Zionist wandering through the streets of the Roman Jewish quarter, trying to sort out the complex identity of the Jews of this most ancient community of the Diaspora.[29] The result is a curious mixture of acute insight and astonishing hubris. His starting—and startling—position is an explicitly autobiographical lament:

> I lived in Rome for almost three years, wandered through its backstreets, acquainted myself with the most varied parts of its population, knew all the city's gossip, nicknames, jokes, double-entendres.
>
> But in those three years I never came to know the Roman Jews . . . literally never heard the word "ebreo" in print or in daily speech, even though today I know that many of the articles I read were written by Jews and indeed many people I met were Jews.[30]

Why was this? Not because during his years in Rome Jabotinsky had no interest in things Jewish, never tried to visit the synagogues or read the newspapers or publications of the thriving Italian-Jewish community, but rather, he claims, because of the pathetic self-abnegation of Roman Jewry—"because they concealed and fled from any mention of their nationality." Now that he was armed with an assertive understanding of the very essence of Jewishness—Zionism—he visited the old ghetto, interviewed Jews from all parts of life, confidently judging and dismissing their complex synthesis of Italian, Roman, and Jewish identities. On his first Friday night, he attended services at the Liberal temple in Rome and then complained that it had an organ and women sitting alongside men—"just like a church." The next morning he visited the old Sephardic synagogue, where he tipped the attendants, not knowing of the prohibition of the use of money on the Sabbath, and in synagogue no less. When he asked one Roman Jew how many Jews there were in all of Italy, he laughed at the ignorant response "I don't know, probably millions," disdainfully informing his readers that there were actually "a maximum of several hundred thousand"—a figure that was off by more than ten-fold. Of far more interest is that Jabotinsky in these columns misrepresented the history of the Zionist movement in Italy, informing his readers that there were no Zionists in Italy, that he could only find one secretive Zionist in Rome, a fellow who had no comrades-in-arms, given the self-denial on the part of Italian Jews of Jewish nationality. In his retelling of this story, Joseph Schechtman compounded the error by explaining that "the sole Zionist in Rome was at that time a certain Izzaco G. (Jabotinsky did not dare to reveal his full name.)[31] In fact, the Italian Zionist movement was founded in 1899 by Felice Ravenna, a lawyer from Ferrara who had attended the Second Zionist Congress a year earlier and who was a friend and early confidant of Herzl. At the very moment that Jabotinsky was in Italy, lamenting the lack of Zionist consciousness because of the ostensible false self-conception of Italian Jewry, *L'Idea Sionnista* was being published monthly by the Zionist Federation of Italy, and the older and more established Jewish newspaper *Corriere Israelitico* was disseminating Zionist ideas to the Jews of Italy.[32] Indeed, Italian Zionists even played an important role in the battle fought in Basel, which Jabotinsky had just witnessed and participated in: the Italian delegation had voted for the Uganda plan, and one of its members, Bernardo Dessau, a professor of physics at the University of Bologna, was elected to the commission to prepare an expedition to East Africa after Herzl's Pyrrhic victory at the Sixth Zionist Congress.

Of all this Jabotinsky was unaware, or at least chose not to disclose to his readers back home in Odessa, in order to make the overarching point that, in his eyes, Italian Jews were deeply ashamed of their Jewish nationality and instead naively believed that they were "Italians of the Mosaic religion." Walking in the Jewish quarter with a friend who was an Italian Catholic, he remarked that the people in the street obviously did not look Italian:

> "What do you mean, they're not Italians?" he said. "Then what in heaven's name do you think they are?"
> "Jews."
> "What does that matter? There are Methodist and Lutheran Italians and many other denominations, but they're all Italians."
> "But are Jews of the same race as you?"
> Then he understood and answered:
> "In that case you wish to say that they are not of the Latin race. That's true, they're not Latins, but they are Italians."
> I met the same response from everyone I spoke with about Jews—the Jews themselves and native Italians. They completely expunge the national element from the concept of "Israelites."[33]

Like Chaim Weizmann in Germany, Jabotinsky could not comprehend— and hence could not accept—this synthesis between Judaism as a faith and Italianness as a nationality, since it countered both his emerging notion of Jewishness as a national identity and, equally important, since it differed from his own experience in Russia, which he took to be definitive of Jews everywhere:

> In Russia, the defining difference between the two entities is expressed as follows: "This is a Jew; this is a Russian." Here they say "This is a Jew. This is a Catholic." The entire difference is held to be religious. And since religion plays such a limited role in the life of a contemporary Italian, he notices no

fundamental difference between himself and a Jew, and the Jew himself ceases to be conscious of the distinction.[34]

This is a fundamental and fatal error, Jabotinsky now concluded: the Jew who regards himself as a Jew by religion is quite simply wrong, for Jewishness is not a religion but a nation; to confuse the two is not simply an error; it is a self-denying, self-deluding error. That erroneous stance, moreover, is known by a simple word—"assimilation." An "assimilated Jew," or an "assimilationist," is one who denies the essential *nationality* of the Jews, whatever their level of religious belief or affiliation. Thus, a fully Orthodox Jew who considers himself to be a German or Italian or Frenchmen of the Jewish faith and who denies the nationality of the Jews is as "assimilated" as a Jew who observes no religious ritual. And so, concludes Jabotinsky, Italian Jews, however pious, are to be condemned for the error of their "assimilation":

> [The Italian Jew] is assimilated, indeed so assimilated that he regards debates about assimilation as irrelevant . . . he sees no difference between himself and other Italians except for religion . . . and thus can think of himself at one and the same time as a Jew and an Italian!
> The syllogism is so intricate it is virtually Talmudic: an Italian is nonetheless a Jew![35]

It is crucial to understand that for Jabotinsky in 1903, this statement was self-evidently syllogistic (that is, logically and inherently wrong, regardless of external context); the statement was independent, in other words, of the degree of receptivity or antagonism to Jews in the society or culture in which they lived. Thus, it is wrong and assimilatory in Italy as much as in Russia, despite the fact, as he notes, that "in Italy there is no antisemitism, there is no 'Judennot,' Jews are considered citizens not only on paper but de facto as well." Antisemitism is thus irrelevant to his conception of Zionism: Jews in Italy can serve—as they did in 1903—in the highest rungs of Italian politics, culture, or society, without trammel or opposition and still not be, in his conception, true Italians, for they are not, ontologically, Italians. This difference he sometimes explained by using the term "race," but—as argued in regard to Nordau—one must be careful not to confound his and other fin-de-siècle writers' use of the term with the pseudoscientific racialism of either the 1870s and 1880s or our own time. For Jabotinsky and other non-racialist nationalists in 1903, there could exist a "Latin race" and a "Slavic race," as well as a "Jewish race" (even with obvious, physical dissimilarities), without their embracing an underlying theory of immutable biological or genetic difference, not to speak of superiority. Indeed, for the rest of his time in Italy, and hence in the rest of his newspaper series from Rome, Jabotinsky tried mightily to articulate the difference between Italian Jews and Italian non-Jews, without engaging in quasi-scientific babble but also without accepting his interlocutors' conviction that religion was the basis of that difference. Consciously extrapolating from the Russian reality to that of other European countries, he believed that Russianness, Italianness, and Germanness were national categories that could not include Jews, regardless of the existence or degree of antisemitism in any given society. Even in the absence of antisemitism or political persecution, there persisted a semiconscious feeling of differentness, extremely complex because it could often be reified in the shared desire among Jews and non-Jews that the differentness not be manifest—that Jews not make a point of talking about themselves qua Jews or acting "too Jewish." And this semiconscious, only half articulated differentness could be present even in a society such as Italy's, in which Jews had lived for two thousand years (thus he corrects his previous error about their origin in the expulsion from Spain) and in which they were not excluded from public life or oppressed in any overt fashion at all.

Most important, he concluded, not recognizing and acting upon this differentness takes an internal, psychological toll on the Jews themselves:

> I have come to the conclusion that this game of hide-and-seek, played by people who enjoy all the rights of political freedom, has so much internal servitude, so much cowardice, treachery, and insufficient consciousness of self-worth, that a true and rational friend of the Jewish people would rather wish it a proud and hungry death than such a dishonest existence—much like that of a fish cast onto the dry land who tries to demonstrate to its masters that it is delighted to be on dry land.[36]

This rather poor metaphor, just like the errors of omission and commission in his facts and argumentation, should not obscure the acuity of Jabotinsky's newfound conclusions about the Jews and Zionism. In Basel and then in Rome he developed his own understanding and formulation of the Zionist creed, a version of Zionism informed by his experiences as a deracinated, areligious Russian Jew now defining himself anew as a Jew; a fin-de-siècle intellectual still speaking the language of the cosmopolitan leftist milieu but now convinced of the unassailable ontological truth of national divides; and an extraordinarily talented young man now recognizing that he has come to the end of his road as a Russian litterateur but who has found a new canvas on which to sketch a grand future for himself.

From Rome, Vladimir Jabotinsky returned to Russia and to full-time engagement as a Zionist activist.

CHAPTER EIGHT

Jabotinsky's Early Zionism

From "In the City of Slaughter"
to Alien Land

From Rome, Jabotinsky returned to Russia, but he stayed only briefly in Odessa before moving to St. Petersburg, where he entered full-time Zionist work as a correspondent for the newly founded journal *Evreiskaia zhizn'* (Jewish Life). After years of longing to find a permanent way out of Odessa, he finally made it to the big time, the capital of all the Russias, not as an aspiring Russian litterateur but as a Jewish activist, eager to spread his new faith throughout the empire.

For many years he made his base in St. Petersburg, traveling as a Zionist speaker and propagandist throughout the Pale of Settlement, even twice standing for parliament, unsuccessfully, on the Zionist ticket after the Revolution of 1905. Odessa would never again be his home, though he visited it frequently and continued to work as a correspondent for the *Odesskie Novosti* through the First World War. His writings, both Zionist and general, provided him with a meager livelihood, especially needed after his marriage in 1907 to Ania Galperin, an agronomy student from Odessa.

The story of his emerging career as a Zionist leader has been amply detailed in the scholarly literature on him and the early years of the movement. Schechtman's two-volume biography, with all its shortcomings, especially its overreliance on Jabotinsky's autobiographical accounts, is still the most useful chronicle of Jabotinsky's public career, supplemented by Jacob Shavit's study of the Revisionist Zionist movement Jabotinsky founded.[1] My concern here is not to reprise these accounts but rather to probe between the lines of his public and private lives, to understand more deeply the continuing relationship between Vladimir Jabotinsky the Zionist and Vladimir Jabotinsky the cosmopolitan Russian intellectual, a synthesis that defined the rest of his life and the deepest layers of his Zionist thought. As with Nordau's Zionism in chapter 4, I shall not attempt here to summarize Jabotinsky's massive Zionist oeuvre but instead will focus on a small number of salient texts written between 1904 and 1914, most of which have never been studied in any depth.

The first such text is a long and substantial article published in the second volume of *Evreiskaia zhizn'* in February 1904, entitled "Zionism and Palestine," which on the surface merely responded to the debate between the "Zion Zionists" (those who insisted that the goal of the movement had to be Palestine) and the "Territorialists," who argued that any territory available for Jewish autonomous settlement ought to be taken, given the plight of the Jews and the problems associated with the Holy Land.[2] But on a far deeper level, in this piece Jabotinsky expanded on his views about the very essence of Jewish identity that he had set forth in his reports from Basel—views that must be understood in their crucial, but largely overlooked, Russian and fin-de-siècle ideational contexts.

At the very heart of his argument lay the claim that the Zionist movement had not hitherto sufficiently explained its commitment to Palestine but had merely repeated the Romantic clichés of the Love of Zion movement of the 1880s. What was necessary was a clear-headed demonstration that "the tie between Zionism and Zion is for us not only an ineradicably strong instinct, but also an empirically proven consequence of strictly positivist study" (*probnyi, zakonnyi vyvod strogo-pozitivnogo razmyshlenie*).[3] This last phrase was fatefully mistranslated (or misunderstood) in the Hebrew version of this article published by Jabotinsky's supporters in Palestine in the 1950s, where it was rendered as "a legitimate and crucial conclusion resulting from purely positive considerations."[4] But the Russian *pozitivnyi* here meant positivist, that is, "scientifically demonstrable," not the opposite of "negative"; *probnyi* and *zakonnyi* meant "empirically proven," not "legitimate and crucial." These differences are not incidental, but central to Jabotinsky's analysis and to his worldview. As discussed in chapter 7, only a few years earlier and before he became a Zionist, in his response to Bikerman's anti-Zionist tract, Jabotinsky had derided the very idea of a "scientific" view of history and the positivist conception of human society. Now he turned full circle: anyone disposed of a "contemporary scientific weltanschauung," he argued, could see that "history is made not by the inventions or schemes of leaders, but by inexorable processes independent of us but directly determinative of the national will of the masses."[5] The problem, however, is who can decipher that "always unerring national will," since the masses themselves, given their state of unenlightenment, are incapable of understanding their own innate desires. They are like a man with a cataract in his eye who, forced by his doctor to stay in a dark room for several days after surgery, keeps on shouting, "I want light! Let me out of the dark." The doctor knows that this is not his patient's true desire, which is for a total recovery; if the doctor does not succumb to the understandable, but subsidiary and counterproductive, pleas of his patient, "he has obeyed the true, organic will of his patient." The same is true in regard to "national wills"—the true leader does not listen to what "the people" say, how they explain or articulate their predicament, and does not succumb to the seemingly palliative, but scientifically counterproductive remedy demanded by the masses or their unenlightened leaders. The true leader studies the problem scientifically, with all the strictly objective tools of empirical observation, analysis, and conclusion. In the case of the Jews, objective analysis yields the conclusion that for two millennia Jews have been fundamentally misled by their supposed leaders into believing that they were adherents of a religious faith that provided the solution to their persecution and overarching agony. But they could not understand that their religious faith was only a primitive, time-bound, and regressive ideological force that actively discouraged the natural evolutionary differentiation of their national organism. Judaism ought to have developed, as did Christianity, in line with the progress of world civilization and scientific knowledge, but it did not do so because of one and only one empirically observable factor: its displacement from its fatherland, its native soil:

> It is an inarguable fact that from the first day of its Exile, the internal progress of Judaism was brought to a halt—the religious "creativity" of Exile devolved into pointless exegesis upon exegesis. . . . Judaism did not progress, it did not follow the laws of evolution. As soon as the Jewish people lost its land, Judaism stopped changing, developing, progressing . . . Jewish religious and ethical thought, which had previously been advancing to a higher stage, preparing the ground for Christianity, began to ossify, to reject any change. . . . In this way, Judaism died, for a being that does not develop dies.[6]

This leads to one and only one scientifically sound conclusion: that the lifeblood of the Jewish people was its historic land, to which it was attached organically, biologically, physically, and psychically. The irreplaceable core of its "national individuality" was the soil of Palestine, without which it simply could not flourish. Exile resulted, quite naturally, in atrophy and almost in death. The saving grace was the immutable, biologically determined "national will" of the Jewish people, which led, if ever so unconsciously, to a never-ceasing yearning for its homeland, its native soil. This national will was misread, misunderstood, misarticulated by its ostensible leaders, who transmuted it into a desiccated, hyperspiritualized, messianic belief system that merely collaborated in and exacerbated the illness of their followers, justifying their anguish-laden residence in alien climates and alien soils, in which they could not flourish. The only viable solution to their plight, both biological and psychological, is quite literally their transplantation back to their native soil, in accord with the innermost dictates of their immutable *Volksgeist*. The commitment of Zionism to Zion, then, is not a Romantic idyll, but "an empirically proven consequence of strictly positivist study" of their past, present, and future. The centrality of Palestine to the Jews is not something to believe in, Jabotinsky concluded, but to *know:*

> Do you believe that after February comes March? You *know* it, for it cannot be otherwise. Thus it is irrefutable to me, on the basis of irresistible and immutable laws and processes, that Israel is preparing itself for a rebirth in its native Palestine, and my children and grandchildren will vote there for their own Constituent Assembly.[7]

This remarkable piece of writing had some precedent, to be sure, in earlier Zionist thought, both in Russia and in the West. Although it has not yet been subjected to a truly contextual analytic study, Leon Pinsker's 1882 "Auto-emancipation" employed similar organicist explanations for the ostensible "death" of Judaism and, in Pinsker's case, for the potency of antisemitism. But in that pamphlet Pinsker argued that any territory outside of Europe was a viable national home for the Jews, and hence he did not make an ecologically determinist case, as it were, for the return of Jews to Zion. Both Herzl and Nordau used similar post-Darwinian language in their diagnoses of the *Judennot,* but neither drew out a positivist case for Palestine and against Judaism as the abiding core of Jewish history to quite this extent, and for good reason: they were far less committed to Palestine than Jabotinsky and for tactical reasons tried publicly to mute their antagonism to religious Judaism. On a theoretical level, Jabotinsky's positivism here is in crucial respects similar to Nordau's Social Darwinism, though there is no evidence that he read the latter's pre-Zionist works. But Jabotinsky's "Zionism and Palestine" can only be understood against the backdrop of the highly intense contemporary Russian debate over positivism and its implications for nationalist and socialist thought that all but obsessed the Russian intelligentsia at precisely this time. As Richard Pipes explained in his study of one of Jabotinsky's contemporaries and soon-to-be-opponents, Peter Struve:

> Positivism had two features which particularly attracted Russian intellectuals. One was its denial of a qualitative difference between nature and society, with the corollary proposition that identical laws explained the operations of both. The other was the definition of human progress as progress of enlightenment, understood to mean the transition from "theological" and "metaphysical" ways of thinking to the scientific or "positive" one. Positivism put a premium on knowledge and extolled the intelligentsia as its carrier. It made the latter the prime mover of history, teaching that an intellectual, by the simple fact of converting his way of thinking to the "scientific" mode, made a decisive contribution to the advancement of the human race. It was an outlook admirably suited to a large and ambitious elite long on education but short on wealth and political influence.[8]

However, both Struve and Jabotinsky (as well as thousands of other fin-de-siècle Russian intellectuals) struggled with the implications of such a worldview on political action. Like Struve, but without the latter's interest in and capacity for metaphysical speculation, Jabotinsky had seen all too clearly that positivist ethics could easily lead to a mindless hedonism, a stance he rejected for its emotional and existential vapidness as well as its political impotence. Like Struve, but à la juive, he had come to see nationalism as the tonic to his—and "his people's"—crisis of meaning and of destiny. On a substantially higher level of philosophical discourse, Struve and other philosophically inclined Russian thinkers such as Nicholas Berdaiev confronted the inevitable contradictions between the positivist and nationalist points of view, and resolved these by embracing "a dualistic philosophy with two parallel realms, one empirical, the other transcendental."[9] Jabotinsky, always immune to any transcendental arguments, failed to see, or did not care about, the contradictions between the blatant Romanticism of the nationalist idea and scientific empiricism and here conjured up a rather vulgar positivist conception of Jewishness based on an immutable, "organic" connection with the soil of Palestine. In this view, not only was Judaism as a religious faith rejected on the grounds that it was superseded by history or science; it was dismissed as a dead irrelevance, a primitive misunderstanding of the Jewish national will that had become ossified, and hence superannuated, in 70 A.D.

The ultimate irony, of course, was that Jabotinsky's "organic" analysis of the Jewish *Volksgeist* was deeply rooted in and dependent upon fin-de-siècle Russian notions of science, truth, culture, religion, and nationhood. It was totally oblivious to the constitutive dilemma of internal Jewish intellectual life since the time of Moses Mendelssohn, the possibility of a synthesis between Judaism as a living system of belief and praxis based on an ongoing exegesis of divine revelation and modern conceptions of the true and the just. This dilemma continued to define the inner struggle of the Jewish intelligentsia, both East and West, and lay at the heart of the Zionism of virtually all of Jabotinsky's Russian comrades, who came to Zionism not from the outside, as he did, but from the inside. They were heirs of, and in some cases former contributors to, the Haskalah movement and continued to ponder the central problems of Jewish faith and identity debated for over a century in the Hebrew, Yiddish, German, and, more recently, Russian and Polish writings of the Jewish Enlightenment. Whether now advocates of Ahad Ha'am or Theodor Herzl, Max Nordau or one of the new socialist Zionist thinkers, they continued to grapple profoundly with the residue of their rejected faith, the push-and-pull of their inescapable embeddedness in the culture and traditions of historic Judaism, however deep their modernist pretensions.

Not so Jabotinsky, who knew nothing and cared less about this Jewish Enlightenment tradition and the religious faith it aimed to supersede. His positivist Zionism was not only unconcerned with issues of ultimate spiritual truth and meaning; it was totally deaf to their incessant and insistent resonances in the prose and poetry of his contemporaries, even within the Zionist movement. Thus, when he came to produce his most widely read and least studied Zionist work, his translation into Russian of by far the most famous Hebrew poem of the period, Hayyim Nahman Bialik's "Be-ir ha-haregah" (In the city of slaughter), the result was, to say the least, highly idiosyncratic.

Schechtman notes, as have others, if only in passing, that Jabotinsky's rendition of Bialik was substantially different from the original:

> [Jabotinsky] put into this translation all the deep feelings of his own soul, all the fire of his indignation, and all the intensity of his pride. So imbued was this Russian version of Bialik's poem with the spirit and personality of its translator that it came to be regarded as an original poem of Jabotinsky's rather than the translation it was supposed to be.[10]

Indeed, there is much contemporaneous evidence that Jabotinsky's Russian translation was read far more widely than the original and may well have been the main conduit of its popularization and putative message to a readership far broader and deeper than those with sufficient Hebrew to decode the brilliant, but highly complex, original. Although we cannot estimate with any degree of precision how many Jews in the Russian Empire could read either literary Hebrew or literary Russian, it seems fair to assume (though it goes against common stereotypes) that by 1903–1904, the latter far outnumbered the former, for the simple reason, first and foremost, that half the Jewish population, the women, were for the most part not trained in Hebrew to any serious extent but were becoming more and more literate in Russian. Moreover, the twin processes of Russification and embourgeoisement combined substantially to increase the number of Jewish males as well who learned Russian in the fin de siècle. In addition, of course, there was the vast non-Jewish Russian reading audience as well, and many prominent Russian authors read Bialik's poetry in Jabotinsky's translations.[11]

Jabotinsky often claimed, in fact, that he decided to learn Hebrew because of Bialik's poem and used it as his primary text in studying the language. His comment "if such poems are written in Hebrew, it's worthwhile learning the language"[12] has been cited countless times by students of his life and Bialik's poetry, but no one has stopped to ponder its multiple implications. To be sure, Jabotinsky may well have been speaking here in his typically jocular and ironic style, but beneath the mannerism there lurks the quite serious and highly revealing confession that to him Hebrew was worth learning only because a highly modern and sophisticated poetry was being written in it, not in order to gain access to the Bible or the massive literature of Jewish intellectual, cultural, and religious creativity over the past two thousand years, of which he remained basically ignorant for the rest of his life. Equally significant but more elusive to historical analysis is how one could in fact translate such a dense and multilayered poem without really knowing the language it was written in, and, on a deeper level, how this lack of linguistic and cultural competence was expressed in the ultimate result, both on the semantic level and on the more subtle planes of prosody and rhetoric.

Before addressing some of these issues, a bit of background to Bialik's poem. The Kishinev pogrom broke out on April 6, 1903, according to the Russian calendar, which that year marked both Easter Sunday and the last day of Passover. The pogrom lasted two full days and was by far the bloodiest until then in Russian-Jewish history, resulting in the deaths of 49 Jews, the wounding of at least 456 others, and the destruction of some 700 homes and 600 places of business. Virtually all contemporaries, Jewish or not, believed that the attack was planned in advance, or at least condoned and encouraged, by the Russian government as part of the overall antisemitic policy of Nicholas II and his minister of the interior Viacheslav Plehve. In this view, the tsarist army (often represented in literary sources and in subsequent popular culture as Cossacks) and the local police either participated in the rioting, killing, raping, plundering, and looting or idly stood by as the horrors took place.

Recent scholarship has largely disproved the culpability of the Russian authorities in the Kishinev pogrom or the existence of a government-run conspiracy at its heart. An excellent study entirely devoted to the events of those three days, *Easter in Kishinev: Anatomy of a Pogrom*, by Edward Judge,[13] demonstrates that the local civilian, army, and police officials (there were in fact no Cossacks involved here, nor in the pogroms of 1881–1882) were incompetent rather than deliberate in their actions (or inaction.) Their response to the violence was inept and uncoordinated rather than motivated by sympathy with the attackers, and the St. Petersburg authorities were not any more competent. Contrary to the received tradition, the tsarist regime hated and feared pogroms as uncontrollable expressions of mob behavior upsetting law and order, possibly at the service of the revolutionary movement. But in Kishinev, as before and later, officials from top to bottom mishandled orders to the provinces and made matters worse in their bungling attempts to blame the pogroms on the Jews themselves or, in some cases, to use the pogroms as fodder for rivalries within the government and to advance personal political ambitions.

But such retrospective historical understanding is of course irrelevant to the massive and immediate response among the Jews of the Russian Empire and their supporters at home and abroad. In the three languages of their literary creativity, Yiddish, Hebrew, and Russian, Jewish writers throughout the empire wrote reams of prose, poetry, and journalism decrying the events of Kishinev.[14] In Odessa, Bialik first wrote his searing poem "Al ha-shehitah" (On the slaughter), a title that evoked both the traditional blessing pronounced by a ritual slaughterer when cutting the throat of an animal and the well-known tale of the Hebrew Crusade Chronicles recounting the martyrdom of Jewish parents who recited the same blessing as they killed their own children rather than allowing them to be converted to Christianity.[15] At the same time, a group of

intellectuals led by Ahad Ha'am and the historian Simon Dubnov sent
out a call to Jewish youth to organize self-defense units in the event of
another bloody pogrom anywhere in the empire and set up a historical
commission to travel to Kishinev to chronicle the precise details of the
Easter massacre. At the behest of and with the financial support of this
committee, as well as the editor of the St. Petersburg Hebrew journal
Ha-Zeman (The Times), Bialik spent a month in Kishinev interviewing
eyewitnesses, with the intention of publishing a book on the subject.
From Kishinev he retreated to his in-laws' home in the village of Gu-
rovshchina, where he was supposed to edit the material he had collected
but instead wrote what would become his most famous poem, "In the
City of Slaughter," first published in late 1903 in *Ha-Zeman*.[16] Remarkably, it took almost nine decades for his source material itself to
be published in full, in a 1991 volume entitled *Eduyot nifgiei Kishinev*
(Testimony of the wounded in Kishinev).[17]

   This is not the place to enter into a full-scale analysis of Bialik's remarkable poem, whose publication has been called the most important
event in Jewish literary history in modern times. The critical literature
on this poem is substantial, although one prominent Israeli literary
scholar, Uzi Shavit, recently lamented that it is much thinner than might
have been expected, given the prominence of this poem in the canon of
modern Hebrew literature:

> It seems that there are two factors at play. The first is the feeling that this is
> a work that is *more* than a piece of literature, and therefore it is superfluous
> or even inappropriate to approach it with literary tools, as a classic piece of
> writing. The second is the opposite: the feeling that from a purely artistic
> vantage point "In the City of Slaughter" is not a totally complete work, and
> therefore there is no point in analyzing it aesthetically, solely as a work of
> literature. Both these feelings mixed together, it seems, in the minds of many
> . . . and led to a strange ambivalence in regard to the poem.[18]

   From the time of its publication, literary critics with impeccable Zionist credentials expressed this ambivalence by warning that Bialik's
poem must not be read solely on its surface level as a realistic description
of the massacre or a straightforward ideological call for self-defense.
Though, to be sure, such a reading was plausible, it ignored the fact that
Bialik deliberately avoided realism in the poem, resorting to a highly
stylized and often metonymic style. Some noted (or objected) that to
achieve his complex poetic goals, Bialik had in fact intentionally disre-
garded the existence of armed Jewish resistance in Kishinev. The "true"
message of the poem, many concluded, was an indictment not of Jewish

passivity in the face of attack, but of the root cause of that passivity, traditional Jewish theodicy and eschatology. Carefully analyzing the morphology of the poem, critics recognized its complex intertextual evocations and subversions of the text of Ezekiel, Isaiah, and other parts of the Holy Writ and Jewish liturgical writings; hence it was categorized as a powerfully ironic mock-epic, a despairing and sardonic burlesque of the Jewish martyrological tradition as a whole.[19]

Such powerful literary readings of the poem are entirely convincing but had virtually no effect on its broad public reception, including its use by historians. Here there has reigned an unambivalent conviction that "In the City of Slaughter" was a "poem of rage" in the narrower, ideological sense, an all too realistic depiction of the slaughter at Kishinev aimed at attacking the passivity of Russian Jewry in the face of external assault. To contemporaries and then to historians, this poem was indeed "more than" a poem, for it served a crucial function in stirring young Jews to take up self-defense in the face of pogroms, as indeed happened soon after Kishinev in the city of Gomel. Thus, even highly sophisticated historians have widely used this poem as an unmediated firsthand description of the Kishinev pogrom and an uncomplicated hortatory call to self-defense.[20]

Without overstating the case, it is highly likely that the person most responsible for the spread of such a reading of "In the City of Slaughter" was none other than Jabotinsky, who beginning in 1903–1904 propounded this view in his poetic introduction to his translation of the poem, in the Russian translation proper, and in his various writings over the subsequent decades. Jabotinsky seems to have begun to work on translating Bialik's poem into Russian immediately after its first Hebrew publication in late 1903, possibly with the help of his former Hebrew teacher, Y. H. Ravnitsky, who was also a close friend of Bialik, his publisher, and the owner of the bookstore in Odessa that was the primary distributor of the poet's works. After Jabotinsky moved to St. Petersburg, he studied the poem line by line with Ben-Zion Katz, the editor of *Ha-Zeman*, who translated the difficult Hebrew for the young ingenue (or so Katz claimed in his memoirs).[21]

In late 1904, almost two years before the translation was first published, there appeared in *Evreiskaia zhizn'* Jabotinsky's poetic introduction to "In the City of Slaughter," entitled "H. N. Bialik: March 1904, before Passover."[22] The epigraph to the poem is "Im en ani li mi li" (If I am not for myself, who will be for me), which is the part of Hillel's famous dictum most often cited by nationalists, as opposed to its continuation:

"Ukheshe-ani le-azmi az mah ani" (When I am only for myself, what am I). Jabotinsky's poetic prologue is worth citing in full:

My older brother in spirit, magician
And master of that musical tongue
That my ancient ancestor called his own
And my grandson will master as his own
Please forgive the many shortcomings
Of this hurried and agitated work.
I'd be proud and joyful if I could only
Reproduce in this language of exile
All the depth and might of indignation
That thunder out of your every line
But there's no time, the hour is short
The storm threatens, the enemy is nigh. . . .

Awake! Tribe of Judah!
Nature beckons with the Spring
Passover beckons, the day of Exodus
Liberation from our chains
    They're threatening us once more
    As before, in days of yore
    Pharaoh's chariots filled
    With our enemies' hordes
    All our friends have disappeared
    We're all alone on the battle field
    "Mi li mi li im en ani li" [Who, oh who, is with us but us]
    Together, brothers, forward march!
Hear O Israel!
Your one and only hope is you yourself
There's nothing worse or more worthy of shame
Than being the object of attack
    Throw away your despicable abasement
    So that in its place will grow
    Strength in your muscles
    Manliness and pride in your heart.
        Whoever's not on our side, cast them out
        They deserve nought but torture
        Mi li mi li im en ani li?
        Together, brothers, forward march!
Our history till now
Was created by others, not by us
Our chronicles were compiled
With others encircling us in chase
    March forward into the arena
    From now let our fate
    Our enslavement, our will
    Be in our own hands!

> The past we have laid to rest
> Our future we will forge
> Mi li mi li im en ani li
> Together, brothers, forward march!
> . . . .
> . . . . [ellipsis in original]
> There's no time to wait, the time has come
> To set forth boldly in the fight
> If but a faint echo of your reproach
> Your great reproach and mighty call
> Reaches the former downtrodden slaves
> Let them read your words of wrath
> And may the seed you planted
> Blossom in their hearts. . . .
>> And yet, besides you
>> (I must remind you of this)
>> Another poet has written of this terrible pogrom
>> A shocking tale of woe.
>> Yours is full of might and power
>> But his is stronger still.
>> Once, in a garbage heap
>> In that very same town
>> I saw a piece of parchment
>> From a torn Torah scroll.
>> I picked it up and wrapped it in my handkerchief
>> Carefully blew off the dust
>> And read: "be-erez nokhriah"
>> "In a foreign land."
>>> I nailed these words to my walls
>>> For in these two words of Genesis
>>> Is told the story of this pogrom.[23]

As any heder-schoolboy could have told him, the climax of this poem was based on an elementary error: the words "be-erez nokhriah" appear only in the Book of Exodus, never in Genesis. Not surprisingly, this startlingly revealing mistake was effaced in the later Hebrew translation of this introduction, as was Jabotinsky's deliberately blasphemous mutation of the Shema Yisrael from a credo of unmitigated monotheism to a call to arms.[24] But no knowledge of Russian or subtle literary analysis is required to see that what Jabotinsky has done in this prologue is quite simply to read into Bialik's cri de coeur not only his own recently expressed positivist conception of Jewish history, but also Max Nordau's call for a "Muskeljudentum." Comprehending the complex and multi-layered "In the City of Slaughter" on its most superficial, ideological level, Jabotinsky conscripted Bialik as "his older brother in spirit," bidding the Jews to remake themselves with "strength in your muscles, manliness and pride in your heart"—in other words, to refashion their Jewishness in the image of fin-de-siècle conceptions of masculinity and valor. Indeed, Jabotinsky went further than Nordau, who disdained the Bible as a work superseded by science. In line with his positivist theory, Jabotinsky maintained that the Book of Books continued to inspire and teach its lessons to the Jewish people, but that lesson was that they must take history into their own hands and rebel against their exile in an "erez nokhriah," a foreign land.

Jabotinsky's translation itself was a far more subtle, sophisticated, and masterful work than his introduction. In general, his poetry translations—whether of Poe, Verlaine, D'Annunzio, or Bialik—were far more successful than his own attempts at verse. Paradoxically perhaps, his later translations into Hebrew, most famously his renditions of Poe's "Raven" and "Annabelle Lee," were much better than his translations of these same poems into Russian, a language he knew far better than he ever would Hebrew. A phenomenally talented student of languages, he learned Hebrew rather quickly—by the late summer of 1904 he was able to write Ravnitsky in halting Hebrew and had begun to try his hand at Yiddish as well.[25] Although to the end of his life he admitted feeling uncomfortable with the Hebrew alphabet, and hence called for a Romanization of Hebrew script, soon enough his grasp of Hebrew and Yiddish, both active and passive, was remarkable for one not trained in these languages from childhood. His writings in both tongues were fluent and highly effective and at times quite eloquent and beautiful, and his fame as a spellbinding orator in Hebrew and Yiddish as well as in Russian and many other languages was legendary.

On a deeper level, however, both his Hebrew and his Yiddish were marked by a pitch and a semantic range almost entirely devoid of Jewish cultural and religious resonances such as so naturally and unconsciously occur in the writing and speech of native speakers or those trained in traditional Judaism. There is a wry Yiddish expression for such a linguistic register: "er redt vi an orel"—literally, he speaks like an uncircumcised one, that is, a Gentile. This might be the most apt description of his translation of "In the City of Slaughter," which he called in Russian *Skazanie o pogrome* (Tale of a pogrom).[26]

In its original version, first published in 1906, and even more so in its reworking in 1911 in a collection of his translations of Bialik's poetry,[27] *Skazanie o pogrome* was a tour de force, a gripping, taut, and at times dazzling transmutation of Bialik's masterpiece into a fiercely combative and emotionally inspiring Russian poem, a Zionist companion piece, as it were, to Aleksandr Blok's "On Death," written at roughly the same time ("I wander more and more about the city / More and more see Death. And I smile").[28] But quite literally from its first word to its last, Jabotinsky's translation succeeded by muting, and all but eliminating, the deeply layered and omnipresent evocations of biblical and post-biblical Jewish culture so central to Bialik's poem and his worldview. Fully to chronicle this claim would require a long and highly technical apparatus that is not appropriate here. Suffice it to cite the opening line of the poem: *Kum lekh lekha el ir ha-haregah* (Arise and go forth to the city of slaughter). The first three words compress in an explosively evocative phrase God's command to Abraham to abandon his father's home for the Promised Land (*Lekh lekha*) and His call to Jonah to "arise and go forth to Nineveh, the big city" (*Kum lekh el nineveh, ir ha-gedolah*).[29] Jabotinsky's first Russian version renders this as *Vstan', i proidi po gorodu pogroma* (Arise and pass through the city of the pogrom), an almost deliberate flattening deflation of the original's textual associations and a problem Jabotinsky tried to amend in his later version by changing the Russian to read *gorodu rezni* (the city of slaughter). But this was just the opening gambit in a long (272 lines in the original Hebrew, 237 in Jabotinsky's Russian) conversation between the two texts in which virtually every single reference to traditional Jewish culture, whether biblical, talmudic, or liturgical, is either omitted entirely or neutralized by under-translation.

To be sure, every translator of Bialik's verse in general, and of "In the City of Slaughter" in particular, has had to face the problem of coping with his dense and often oblique but always indispensable plays upon biblical and post-biblical Hebrew. Both Bialik himself and Y. L. Peretz confronted this dilemma when they translated the poem into Yiddish at the same time that Jabotinsky did so into Russian, and their Yiddish versions are also very different (and, to my ears, far less successful) poems.[30] But Jabotinsky's resolution of the problem was an extreme one: not only a de-biblicization of the poem's lexicon but a de-Judaization of its entire symbolic and semiotic systems. This was not the result of a technical problem, the difficulty in finding Russian equivalents to Bialik's biblical allusions, as Jabotinsky later apologetically claimed in his introduction to his 1911 collection of Bialik's poetry. Had he so desired, Jabotinsky—like many other translators of Bialik into other tongues—could easily have attempted at the very least to mimic the High Biblicism of the original or to render into poetic Russian recognizable

allusions to extremely well known Hebrew liturgical texts evoked by Bialik, such as the confessional prayer of the High Holiday liturgy. By the
turn of the century there were ample translations of the Bible into Russian, as well as bilingual editions of the mainstays of traditional Jewish
liturgy. Thus, to cite another simple example, Jabotinsky could easily
have found a way to translate into Russian Bialik's poetically crucial references to the Shekhinah, the feminine emanation of God, invoked in
critical moments in the poem as the aspect of the divine closest and most
sensitive to human, and particularly Jewish, suffering. But Jabotinsky
did not—the Shekhinah is rendered as a vague male spirit, with no particular connection to any symbolic tradition, Jewish, Russian, or other.

The conclusion one reaches is that because of his lack of Jewish
knowledge and cultural references, combined with his studied conviction that Judaism was fundamentally irrelevant to the Jewish past and
the Jewish future, Jabotinsky simply did not understand Bialik's multi-
layered allusions, could not parse the Judaic metonyms and metaphors
in Bialik's verse, could not recognize the evocations of highly familiar
but to him totally obscure Hebrew prayers or post-biblical canon. (As
we have seen, at this stage his knowledge of the Bible itself was pretty
scant.) To some extent, his 1911 reworking of the translation attempted
to redress this problem, though the overall effect is the same, despite the
fact that by then he had spent more time in Zionist work, learned more
Hebrew, and become more conversant with some of the basics of Judaism and the Jewish tradition.

As a result, Jabotinsky's influential Russian rendering of "In the City
of Slaughter" succeeded most strikingly in subverting the highly sub-
versive ideational core of Bialik's original. The reader of the Russian
version could only with enormous difficulty, if at all, make out what
becomes all too clear in the Hebrew or Yiddish (or A. M. Klein's masterful, if far from perfect, English translation).[31] The biblical locutions,
snippets of common Jewish liturgy, citations from talmudic accounts of
Jewish martyrdom and woe—all are twisted and turned in a frantic,
often grotesque, and always macabre subversion of their original contexts and theological connotations. Unlike the Hebrew (or Yiddish or
English) reader, the Russian reader cannot understand that the speaker
in the poem is God, not the poet himself or an implied human narrator;
Jabotinsky's speaker sometimes refers to God in the first person, but
more often in the second or third. Nor can the Russian reader easily, if
at all, come to see that God is deliberately invoking the precise language

of His most direct means of communication with human beings, that of prophecy. And not just any prophet, but specifically Ezekiel, the prophet who saw God most clearly after Moses, described Him in the terrifying image of the divine chariot, and then in His name castigated the Jewish people for their sins, detailed their doom and perdition, and only thereafter was able to console them in their agony. Bialik's evocation of Ezekiel is hardly subtle or encoded in esoteric or oblique language: the Divine narrator addresses his presumed interlocutor directly and frequently as *ben-adam* (Son of man), a phrase with almost as culturally embedded a reference to Ezekiel (and thence to the New Testament) in English as in Hebrew. Jabotinsky seems totally to have missed the point, rendering this phrase either as *syn Adama* (son of Adam), which is the literal translation of the Hebrew, or simply as *chelovek* (the neutral Russian for "man"). By 1911, he understood the blatant error here and substituted *syn chelovecheskii,* the obvious Russian equivalent ubiquitous in renderings of Ezekiel into Russian, when doing so was possible given the rhyme and metrical scheme of the translation.

In the end, then, not only are Bialik's Hebraic and Jewish references lost in the shuffle; their parodic but profound theological heterodoxy is totally elided. The literary scholar Alan Mintz wrote with much insight of the original:

> ["In the City of Slaughter"] is neither an epic nor a mock-epic. It is rather an anti-epic, which proposes its own, negative, principles of meaning. The indirection of metonymy . . . enables Bialik to eliminate the enemy as a touchstone of antipathy and abomination and to force the reader to transfer those emotions to the interior drama of Jew and Jew, God and His people, the poet-prophet, his sender and addressee. The refusal to allow the reader egress from this impacted family scene is one of the greatest autocratic coercions of the poem.[32]

In Jabotinsky's version the reader is never introduced to this impacted family scene and is left without any indication whatsoever of Bialik's negative principles of meaning. His "Tale of a Pogrom" is simply that, a starkly lyrical and horrifying positivist pogrom poem, a beautiful, tendentious denunciation of the unmanly weakness of the victims of the attack. They alone are to blame for this state of affairs, not their superannuated and emasculated God, whose cosmically pitiful cries *elohehem azavam* (their God has abandoned them) and *elohekhem ani kemot-khem, ani hu be-hayekhem ve-kal vakhomer bemotkhem* (yours is a pauper-Lord, poor during your life, poorer still at your deaths) do not appear at all in the Russian translation. In fact, in the introduction to the 1911 collection of Bialik poems, Jabotinsky laid out this view in clear prose:

> Bialik was a rebel, but on a deeper level. His hammer was waged not at the external enemy . . . [but] at the internal one, the Jewish head and the Jewish heart. To him, the only guilty party was the Jewish people—it is guilty, because it tolerates, nay, agrees to suffer.[33]

A decade later, rewriting this introduction for a collection of translations of Bialik into English, Jabotinsky repeated this claim and spelled out even more clearly what he took to be the "highest point" of Bialik's poetic "trajectory":

> The Ghetto despised physical Manhood, the principle of male power as understood and worshipped by all free peoples in history. Physical courage and physical force were of no use, prowess of the body rather an object of ridicule. The only true heroism the Ghetto acknowledged was that of self-suppression and dogged obedience to the Will above. Bialik revolts, and becomes a singer of triumphant, invincible, rebellious Manhood, of the arm that wields the sword, of muscles of granite and sinews of steel.[34]

This breathtaking "Nordau-ization" of Bialik, already fully formed in 1904, lends a somewhat ironic twist to the oft-told but largely misunderstood story of the intervention of the Russian censor in the publication of "In the City of Slaughter." Bialik's original title for the poem was simply "Masa," a biblical synonym for prophecy, thus clearly announcing at the outset his overt evocation of the prophetic genre. Both the editor of *Ha-Zeman* and one of his subordinates later claimed that they suggested the title be changed by adding the word "Nemirov"(which is the name of a city where a famous massacre of Jews occurred during the Chmielnicki rebellion of 1648), since they were certain that the government censor for Hebrew would never allow a poem with such a bold and explicit relevance to the events of Kishinev to be published. In the event, when the censor—a Habad Hasid who had converted to Russian Orthodoxy—was confronted with Bialik's poem, he objected not to its obvious contemporary relevance or Zionist message, but to what he took to be blasphemous statements about God's impotence and decrepitude. These offended his own (rather idiosyncratic) theological beliefs, and he would not permit their publication, as offensive to public morality, both Christian and Jewish. To be sure, as with so many censors past and present, his literary prowess was limited and so he missed most of the highly heterodox allusions in the poem. But when it was published in 1903 as "Masa Nemirov," three and a half lines and several other phrases deemed unpublishable to the censor were indeed omitted, much to Bialik's chagrin.[35] A longer segment—in which the Jews are depicted cramming the bones of victims of the pogrom into knapsacks and selling them as precious wares in the marketplace, in order to evoke sympathy from the Gentiles—was excised as well, not by the government censor but, as the editors of the most recent scholarly edition of Bialik's works claim, most likely at the behest of Ahad Ha'am, who regarded the scene as too incendiary to Jewish sensibilities. Thus, the culminating phrase of this passage, *vekha-asher shenorartem tishnoreru* (just as you have always been beggars, you always will be beggars), which offers a chillingly brilliant Hebraization of the Yiddish word "shnorer," did not appear in this or several subsequent publications (or in Jabotinsky's Russian renditions, either in 1904 or 1911).

However, the fact that Jabotinsky's poetic introduction to "Tale of a Pogrom," including its overt incitement to Jewish armed rebellion in the face of attack, was published in 1904, and in Russian no less, in a legal Zionist journal printed in St. Petersburg, speaks volumes about the actual (as opposed to mythologized) dynamics of censorship in Russia at this time. The issue of tsarist censorship was raised in a fascinating way when *Skazanie o pogrome* was first published in 1906, as a small volume put out by the Zionist press Kadimah, which also issued in the same format Bialik's Yiddish translation of the poem. An anonymous foreword, probably written by the owner of the Kadimah press, Jabotinsky's Odessa friend Solomon Salzman, preceded both the poem itself and Jabotinsky's prologue.[36] It alerted the reader that the Hebrew title of the original was changed to "The Tale of Nemirov" because of the notorious censorship that ruled in those not too distant days—allowing the reader to conclude that this was an act by the government censor at the behest of the Russian authorities, rather than by the publishers themselves in a preemptive move. The foreword then cites Nekrasov's famous line, "The scene changes to Pisa, and a multivolume novel is saved." This is an especially noteworthy invocation, in that it aimed rhetorically to situate Bialik's poetry, and thus Zionism as a whole, firmly within the tradition most sacred to the turn-of-the-century Russified Jews who were the potential readers of this volume—the tradition of the Russian intelligentsia and its antigovernmental struggle. Neither Bialik's original title nor Jabotinsky's translation, it claimed—counterfactually—could have been published in Russian because of censorship rules, but the latter circulated privately, in what would later be called *samizdat,* along with his poetic introduction, in advance of an expected pogrom in Odessa on the eve of Passover, 1904. That pogrom did not occur: "It was postponed, until that other bright and festive day, a day not of religious [but] of political resurrection—they came to kill the children and the women." The reference is to the pogroms that broke out after the 1905 Revolution, especially in the aftermath of the October Manifesto of 1905, in which Nicholas II was forced to concede constitutional liberties to his nation:

> The fearful images of the Kishinev-Nemirov tale were now repeated, multiplying their horror and their bloody hopelessness. From Russia's political depths arose new dark forces, which in a loathsome combination with newly awakened popular brutality, descended at arms upon the Jews. But in this new black and red, blood-stained image of Jewish sorrow, we see some brighter shades which were not visible in Bialik's terrifying jeremiad.
>
> In these new torturous trials there is no shame, that quality worse than anything else that compelled the poet to spill tears "not of bitterness but of fury." The sorrow of the people is still horrible, but it is only sorrow, not shame. Yes, they have arisen—"the children of those whose ancestor was Judah, lion of the Maccabees." They have indeed arisen and washed away with their own blood the shame which previously stained and humbled dying Jews. They no longer cringed "seven to a hole," but died one against seven, against seventy—and only by stepping over the corpses of our heroes who died in self-defense could the vile animals torment our defenseless wives and children.
>
> To them, the fallen heroes, we dedicate this little book. Aside from its own great artistic merit, these "pages of wrath" are an important historical document which is luckily already history. This book bears witness to how quickly "the carefully nourished seed" bore fruit, to the gigantic steps in the growth of national consciousness, national dignity, national honor. And this honor powerfully demands that our people deliver themselves from the humiliating and self-destructive "expectation" of pogroms. It calls forth our youth to other, more creative work, the task of "auto-emancipation."[37]

Here we have one of the earliest examples not only of an archly politicized reading of "In the City of Slaughter," but also its defanging through historicization. In late 1905, when the Kadimah press's volume was approved by the far more lenient censor, "In the City of Slaughter" was presented to Russian readers as a text with a simple, time-bound, Zionist message, a call for Jewish self-defense rather than a poignant and pained threnody on the self-defeating uselessness of Jewish conceptions of God and of Providence. Moreover, in this reading, the message of the poem had been already heeded, the malady redressed through the creation of Jewish self-defense forces, a Jewry—or at least some Jews—of muscle.

Only a few months after "The Tale of a Pogrom" was published, Jabotinsky put the finishing touches on a new play whose title connected it to his prologue to Bialik's work—*Chuzhbina* (Alien land). Unlike his first two pieces for the theater, this play was never produced on the stage; it was published in its original Russian in Berlin in 1922, and in a problematic and bowdlerized Hebrew translation in Jabotinsky's collected works.[38] Despite the importance of this work to Jabotinsky's worldview and its availability in Hebrew, it is has not to my knowledge been analyzed in any serious scholarly fashion by anyone. Schechtman, for example, devoted a mere two pages to an extremely unsatisfactory summary of the play, which misrepresents not only the plot but also the overt message and fascinating complexity of its point of view.[39]

Alien Land, unlike its predecessors, is a very long play—five acts, almost all in verse, with much Odessan dialect, covering some 240 pages. The plot, involving thirty main characters plus a chorus, is rather convoluted, but reducible to the following outline. In a city very much like Odessa, a group of Jewish revolutionary socialists hold a meeting to protest the beating by a Jewish factory owner of one his workers. To this meeting come not only committed Jewish socialists but a cast of other characters: an upper-middle-class Russian woman named Natasha; a variety of more-or-less traditional Jewish business-and-synagogue types who speak in a wonderfully amusing mixture of Russian and Yiddish; and two alienated Jewish intellectuals, of radically different miens. One, named Gonta (which is the name of an important Ukrainian Cossack military leader implicated in the massacres in Uman in the late eighteenth century), is a former revolutionary who, after witnessing the Kishinev pogrom, despaired not only of his socialism but his Jewishness as well, went off to New York to find his bearings, and has returned to fight against Jewish socialists in the name of a liberated and proud Jewish nationalism. The other intellectual, Extern Abram, is the secularized son of a Hassidic zaddik, who hovers elliptically over the whole play, at least until its last scene, as the characters' authentic, if deracinated, Jewish conscience.

As the protest over the humiliation of the worker evolves into a strike, we learn that after Kishinev, Gonta (the ex-socialist nationalist hero) had a brief fling with Natasha (the liberated emblem of Russian womanhood), in which he pretended not to be a Jew. Now, serendipitously, they meet again, the inevitable sparks fly, and despite his newfound nationalistic consciousness, he succumbs not only to her but to the attendant allure of forgetting his Jewish sorrow, reveling in the liberation of unadulterated humanness (much like the hero of the mock epic "Noella" in Jabotinsky's earlier play *Ladno* (All right).

Meanwhile, the strike has taken on greater proportions than ever anticipated, and the revolutionaries begin to hope that their longed-for apocalyptic battle with the bourgeoisie has finally come, as the non-Jewish urban masses swell the ranks of the protesting Jewish proletariat. Soon, however, politics are overwhelmed by vodka, and the strike snowballs into a riot, and then into a pogrom against the Jews. The revolutionaries scatter in disarray and despair, interrupting the Shemoneh Esreh prayer in the synagogue to hold an emergency meeting, where the assembled flock discuss the possible solutions to their plight: a renewed commitment to internationalist or Bundist socialism, self-defense, Palestine, Labor Zionism, or Gonta's newfound proud, pure, and hard-nosed Jewish nationalism. Gonta seems to be gaining the most ground, but he is shooed off the stage and humiliated by Extern Abram, who waves a compromising, mysterious letter testifying to Gonta's essential hypocrisy; the audience is expected to deduce that this is a love letter from Natasha detailing their consummated love—and so Gonta must retreat in shame. Finally, Extern Abram abandons his silent role as observer and launches into a scathing attack on all the characters and ideologies he has witnessed, from left to right and in between, a rather shocking denunciation of what he lambasts as the pathetic gallery of Russian-Jewish types. His only solution is rank cynicism—all hope is lost; the only recourse is wine, women, and song. With this, he too is chased out of the synagogue and off the stage, and, as the other characters retreat, the scene freezes on the old Jewish businessmen who know they have lost the battle and their children but have no recourse but to resume their evening prayers, as the sounds of the Shemoneh Esreh prayer reverberate through the theater and the curtain falls.

On its simplest level, *Alien Land* is a dramatic reflection of Jabotinsky's public polemics of these years, especially his many essays arguing against Jewish socialism—most importantly, against the Bund. Throughout the whole play, the radical students and revolutionary organizers are depicted by Jabotinsky with a scorching sarcasm that reduces most of them to pathetic dupes, pitiful parrots of a party line that defies reason and reality and serves only to harm the interests of their ostensible allies, the Jewish working class. Perhaps the most searing in-

dictment occurs at the very beginning of the pogrom: when the news
comes back to the Jews that the protesters are turning to violence and to
drink, two of the revolutionaries—one is appropriately named Kautsky—
engage in a debate over whether the incipient pogromshchiki are stevedores or porters, for there is, they believe, a crucial and scientifically demonstrable class difference between the two groups. It turns out, of
course, that it is both the stevedores and the porters and everyone else who
is running wild through the streets, screaming, "Beat the dirty Jews." The
most intelligent and sympathetically portrayed revolutionary, Makar,
early on in the play delivers one of its most interesting speeches, in which
he denies the importance of his Jewishness and proclaims his solidarity
with the Russian working class, even though he understands that ultimately he and the other Jewish intellectuals will be swept aside by the
longing of the non-Jewish masses for a leader from among their own
ranks, "a new ataman," but one serving the Revolution.[40]

On the same level, we see enunciated here in a fascinating form Jabotinsky's incipient new positivist ideology of Jewish nationalism, one
that totally rejects traditional Jewish forms and content (of which
Gonta, its representative and obviously its author's alter ego, is largely
ignorant). More than that: Gonta, with some assistance from Natasha,
viscerally and vociferously rejects with undisguised contempt the bearing, demeanor, and deeply etched impotence of East European Jewry,
whether traditional, revolutionary, or in between:

> Let me introduce myself: to cite Christ—
> I am a guest at your feast, but not in festive attire . . .
> I do not believe in your idols, I do not believe in you:
> When a bottomless sea rages all around you
> Flinging you about in powerful tides—
> You pretend that you yourselves made the storm
> You, petty droplets on other peoples' waves;
> Not powerful enough to ignite or to extinguish
> The flame of worldwide fire.
> In a muscle-less arm you hold a harmless sword
> You are superfluous in the battle!
> By the boot of History you were kicked into exile
> Running away, like scared little boys, from the fight
> Believing all the while, that your pathetic nation
> Was the hope and leader of all mankind.
> You ought to have stood, my nation, like a rock,
> But instead you skulk around, . . . a nation without pride
> I have nothing to say to you—I don't give a damn![41]

But of course he does, and time and time again he returns to save the Jews with his newfound vision; near the end of the play, after all that has happened, after the Zionist handwriting should be clear on the wall, he screams out:

> I call on you to stop lying to yourselves
> To know that we live here in the lions' den
> All our truths and words and beliefs are in vain.
> We must cut off once and for all
> The bridge between us and this alien land
> Curse it for good, and go on—
> Never looking back at others' beauty and riches
> Striding forth proud of our disheveled rags
> The pride that once was that of a king.[42]

Yet despite the force of Gonta's new nationalistic fervor, he does not carry the day; he is unmasked—right at this moment—by the revelation of his essential dishonesty and hypocrisy. For what Jabotinsky was able to convey in a powerful and complex manner through the medium of drama—which perhaps it was not possible for him to convey in his polemical and ideological writings—was the wrenching pathos that he knew, in his heart of hearts, lay at the core of his new faith. While steadfastly maintaining this new belief, which would, in due course, become fully articulated as the concept of *hadar* (Jewish pride) at the core of Revisionist Zionism, he grappled in *Alien Land* with his own consciousness of the artificiality and inauthenticity of his hero and alter ego's solution, their formidable but inescapable existential plight.

As we have seen so clearly, Jabotinsky knew only the externals, not the inner core, of Judaism—as Extern Abram puts it in *Alien Land*, only the prose, not the poetry, of his people. On a far deeper level than Herzl or Nordau before him, however, he recognized that his hard-nosed, proud, self-conscious Jewish nationalism was, at its core, but an attempt to mimic the non-Jews he was ostensibly urging the Jews to reject, a replication for the Jews of the natural, unself-conscious, proud bearing of the Gentile. Early on in the play, Natasha confesses her profound distaste for Russian Jews:

> You are strange, somehow all sick
> All this fuss and bustling about
> No quiet, none of that crucial silence—
> The pride that inheres in calm.[43]

Indeed, perhaps the most revealing moment of this play is Gonta's re-statement of this indictment in his monologue detailing his reaction to the Kishinev pogrom:

I was in Kishinev (Gonta explains)
There for three days . . .
On the third day I left—I thought
I would choke and suffocate. I thought, people were
Jeering and pointing their fingers at me
Saying: look, there's a Jew
A beaten-up kike.
I hid in a corner
Never went out,
Tried not to talk, not to think, not to move,
And yet to go forward.
And then I heard that phrase—the pride of calm—
. . . from a Russian girl, with whom I was cavorting
And do you know what? I told her
I wasn't a kike, but a Russian
I went over and talked, like an equal, like a free man.
O it was so easy, I could breathe deeply and fully
No hate, no disdain—my soul became so pure
As if I had left a putrid Jewish tavern
For the pure air of God's open fields
Or as if music had transported me to a fairy-tale kingdom and given me a
    crown.
The next morning the girl left, I don't remember where to.
I felt ashamed, ashamed to the depths of my being.
But were it not for that night, were it not for that princely sleep
I would have gone mad.
And then, I learned the only solution to the riddle of this world:
The commandment of pride, the cold,
Implacable, insurmountable, callous,
Bottomless, pride of a king
Deprived of his throne and his crown.[44]

Though spoken by a fictional character, this monologue on Kishinev can without difficulty be read as revealing the innermost thoughts and struggles of its author. Jabotinsky, in 1907, was already in the fascinat-ing position of being convinced that Zionism was the only possible an-swer to the Jewish plight, but because he was who he was, precisely because he had breathed the air of a free man, he believed that he saw through the clichés, the jargon, the ethnocentrism, what in Yiddish is called the *kleynshtetldikeyt* (the small-town provincialism), of East

European Jews and East European Zionism. He was not willing to follow Abram into cynicism and despair or Bialik into a self-imposed existentialist silence. Rather, he proceeded to create a version of Zionism that consciously attempted to destroy the traditional stance of East European Jewry not through what he took to be the self-defeating strictures of socialism, of which the Jews, he believed, would inevitably be the victim. Like Max Nordau, but within the East European Jewish world itself, in Russian and increasingly in Hebrew and Yiddish as well, he argued steadfastly that the hunchbacked, stooped, weak, and sniveling East European Jew must be reformed into a hard, cold, dignified—indeed, Aryan—new kind of man and Jew, imbued with a militant and cold patriotism reminiscent of Minister Gamm in Jabotinsky's pre-Zionist play *Krov'* (Blood).

But unlike the far less self-conscious Nordau, Jabotinsky acknowledged, at least to his private self, in the plays and poetry he wrote and sometimes shelved, the ironies and self-contradictions, if not the inauthenticity, of his own response—even as he became a central, and soon the most controversial, Zionist leader of his time.

CHAPTER NINE

Vladimir Jabotinsky, Cosmopolitan Ultra-Nationalist

In the late summer of 1912, Thomas Mann put the finishing touches on the novella he had been working on for most of that year, *Death in Venice*.[1] Only a few weeks earlier, readers of *Odesskie Novosti* had encountered in its pages a short story on the same theme, the unrequited but obsessive love of an aging German intellectual for a youngster he met at a foreign seaside resort. To be sure, the Russian story, entitled "Edmée,"[2] was artistically far less dazzling than Mann's masterpiece, and the subject matter slightly less shocking, in that the object of its romance was a young girl rather than a boy. Nonetheless, even sophisticated readers may well have been perturbed by its tender depiction of pedophilic obsession:

> Her figure was childish, but her gestures, her carriage, her way of stooping, of rising on tiptoe, of halting suddenly in the chase—all that suggested a richer age. As I got to know her better it struck me that this is perhaps the most beautiful stage in women's development. Not all women, of course: there is also that well-known type of girl with red hands and awkward manners, but I assure you that one meets that type less the further west ones goes and the higher up on the rungs of civilization. There you find natures in whom the transition to womanhood slides unobtrusively, inwardly, under the skin. In them, adolescence is *the* age, the most charming, the most lyrical, the most fragrant. In general I am of the opinion that dawn is better than morning or mid-day, that April is better than May. Just where Nature insensibly works her mystical transitions from stage to stage, there you can more tangibly breathe the balm of elemental sacrament, feel the fanning touch of

God passing by with a magic wand in His hands. There you can dimly perceive miraculous possibilities, none of which will probably be realized. God created three beautiful things: childhood, youth, and woman. Imagine how sublimely exquisite must be the moment when these three beautiful things unite, when in the soul and body of a woman childhood glides into youth. But for my fear that you may take me, *Gott bewahre*, for a lover of paradoxes, I should say that strictly speaking, a woman begins to get old after fourteen.[3]

The author of "Edmée" was, of course, Vladimir Jabotinsky, and this story might have been a reworking of the novella he had sent, a dozen years earlier, to Vladimir Korolenko, who dismissed it as decadent pornography.[4] By 1912 Jabotinsky had changed in many ways, but, as "Edmée" so beautifully exemplifies, his turn to Zionism had not replaced or superseded his decadent fin-de-siècle sensibility. Rather, at its core his Zionism was itself built upon that sensibility, now summoned to the service of the Jewish people. "Edmée," like *Death in Venice* (and of course *Lolita* much later), transmuted the conventional fin-de-siècle topos of the unkindled eroticism of pubescent sexuality into a work redolent of its author's idiosyncratic weltanschauung—in this case, a decidedly decadent Zionism.

The story, a monologue spoken to someone very like Jabotinsky, begins with the announcement of a German-Jewish professor of anatomy who has recently been denied a university chair in Prussia because of his Judaism: "The East? It is entirely foreign to me. Here you have a living refutation of your theories about race and the call of blood."[5] He then begins to unravel his tale. Despite the "tell-tale shape" of his nose, he feels himself totally to be a Westerner, a man with no religious commitments, no connection with the Jewish community. Still, he refused to convert to Christianity in order to win an academic promotion— "there are certain things that repel me esthetically, and apostasy is one of them." To heal his wounds, he decided to have a look at the Orient— to return to the East, since he was the victim of prejudice against the East. He got as far as Istanbul (or rather, Constantinople), which he hated: the "crude brilliance of the sun," the dirt, the crowds, all repelled him as far inferior to "our Hartz or Schwarzwald." He took refuge on the island of Prinkipo, which, he explains, "I do not deny . . . is a pretty island, but it ought to be taken away from the Turks and made to look like something respectable—a sort of Ruegen of the South."[6] Here, on Prinkipo, in the Hotel Giacomo, he met her: "Her name was Edmée and she was twelve years old." Her father was the French consul in a small provincial port, both her parents were Parisians, as was she, though she only lived there until she was four—long enough for "the stamp of the West" to be all over her; indeed, "she seemed an embodiment of refined Occidental culture *in partibus infidelium.*" But our professor is no Humbert Humbert *avant la lettre*—he is "a die-hard bachelor who has scarcely seen any women in his time," and he never does anything even remotely ungentlemanly with Edmée. But like Mann's von Aschenbach, he becomes completely transfixed by the object of his attention, so alluringly innocent, so freshly pubescent, so "aromatic." They become friends, they spend hours talking, he is totally enraptured with her stories, her voice, the tales she spins of childish gossip and womanly intrigue. He even introduces her to two friends who come to visit from Russia (which he knows is his silent interlocutor's home), to whom she acts quite naturally as the charming hostess of a salon—coquettish, yet demure. But then, a week after their meeting:

> Edmée came into the garden with her doll and her hoop and told me they were leaving the next day. I felt inexpressibly sad, so sad that I had to scold myself inwardly. What nonsense! I was 52, I could not have fallen in love with that baby; on the other hand I was not yet as decrepit as our King David of old, in whom only the warmth of another's youth could keep up the pulsation of life.[7]

He was hurt, and Edmée sensed it, admitting that she too would miss him, her only friend on the island: "I confess, I almost made a move to kiss her hand, but drew back in time . . . I did not even stroke her hair." But he did say, just to say something, didn't she have other friends in Prinkipo, what about the other little girls he saw her playing with? What about Cléo?

> And then she answered me like this . . . the words, as they say, still ring in my ears. I begin, however, to hesitate to repeat them to you: you are likely to make use of them for one of your favorite harangues about the sacrosanct hedges cutting humanity into sections. Well, never mind, since you know the story you may as well know the end. She said:
> "Oh, Cléo . . . You see, she is a Jewess. What I hate about Prinkipo is that there are so many Jews about. They are so vulgar. I cannot bear it, can you?"[8]

With this, the story ends. Its moral is clear, even if the narrator does not want to accept it, though he himself has suffered from its consequences. Edmée's antisemitism is not mean-spirited—how could it be, given her purity, her good breeding, her tenderness. Rather, it is endemic, involuntary, as unself-conscious as her budding sexuality. She

cannot escape her culture, her heritage, her apparently biologically innate antisemitism. Like a medieval cleric afraid to speak of God's positive attributes and therefore able to describe the divine only *via negativa,*
the professor hesitates to tell the end of the story to his unseen interlocutor, to provide grist for the mill of the latter's "favorite harangues about
the sacrosanct hedges cutting humanity into sections." Despite everything, the professor still wants to continue believing that he is a German,
a Westerner, to whom the climate and geography of the Harz mountains
or the Black Forest are native. But he, and we the readers, must learn
the lesson of Edmée.

Given Jabotinsky's subsequent fame, it is not surprising that this story
was often reprinted, both in Russian and translated into other languages.
The first Hebrew version appeared in 1920, Yiddish in 1928, German
in 1935, and Polish in 1937.[9] A first-rate English translation appeared
in the collection of Jabotinsky's short stories entitled *A Pocket Edition
of Several Stories, Mostly Reactionary,* published in Paris in 1925. This
wonderful title, undoubtedly provided by Jabotinsky himself in a typical
ironic gesture, underscored the fact that by the mid-1920s he was an
extraordinarily well known and controversial figure within the Zionist
movement and throughout the Jewish world. By then, neither his followers nor his opponents quite knew what to do with "Edmée" and his
other literary works: although the other major leaders of the Zionist
movement such as Chaim Weizmann, David Ben-Gurion, and Berl Katznelson were brilliant politicians and extremely erudite and worldly intellectuals, it is impossible even to imagine any of them penning a story
such as "Edmée." How could that story and Jabotinsky's mature literary
oeuvre as a whole fit into the life and thought of this increasingly strident
ultra-nationalist?

Exactly as had been done with the works of Herzl and Nordau before
him, "Edmée," and anything else Jabotinsky wrote regardless of genre
and context have usually been treated as unmediated expressions of his
own life and thought: a 1999 volume, entitled *The Political and Social
Philosophy of Ze'ev Jabotinsky,* promiscuously identifies as his own beliefs passages spoken by a variety of fictional figures in his novels and
short stories.[10] Thus, it is not at all surprising to find Schechtman summoning "Edmée" as evidence of Jabotinsky's inner thoughts after the
failure of his first foreign Zionist mission, to Istanbul, where he became
embroiled in his first contretemps within the Zionist movement when
he objected to the circulation in Turkey of a book that clearly called for
the creation in Palestine of an autonomous Jewish state.[11] This led to a

confrontation with David Wolfssohn, Herzl's successor as president of the movement, who demanded that Jabotinsky heed orders from his superiors and then issued a formal censure of the young Russian upstart, who promptly resigned from the executive committee of the Zionist movement and left Istanbul. Schechtman was uncomfortable with his hero's position here, since it contradicted his later ideological core, and obviously could not present this departure as a failure on the part of Jabotinsky. As a result, he explained it away in the following manner:

> There can, however, be no doubt that, notwithstanding the striking success of his journalistic and oratorical activities in Turkey, Jabotinsky was not only far from smug self-satisfaction but was getting increasingly unhappy in Constantinople. For this there were several reasons.
>
> In the first place, he violently disliked the Orient in general and Constantinople in particular. We read in his short story "Edmée:" "The East? It is entirely foreign to me. . . . Mine is a Westerner's mentality. . . . I must confess that I did not like Constantinople at all. To begin with the celebrated Bosphorus.[12]

This blatant confusion of the words of the fictional "assimilated" German-Jewish professor and Jabotinsky's own thoughts and convictions is noteworthy merely because it exemplifies how utterly unseriously his belletristic works have been taken by even his most dedicated followers. No one who has read "Edmée" carefully or given it any sustained consideration as a piece of fiction, of whatever literary quality, could make this sort of elementary error. This attitude to Jabotinsky's art is doubly unfortunate, since, as was evident in *Alien Land,* he often did reveal his innermost self in his literary works, lifting ever so slightly the mask of supreme self-confidence that dominated his polemical writings. For obvious psychological reasons, this outlet became only more important after he became the most controversial figure in the Zionist movement.

Here, too, some context is necessary: although the incident in Istanbul caused some ripples with the leadership of the Zionist movement, before the First World War Jabotinsky was not a figure of any great controversy either within or without the Zionist world. A strange piece of evidence has recently surfaced to reinforce this point: as with so many thousands of political activists in Russia, Jabotinsky's whereabouts were tracked by the Okhrana, the tsarist secret police. But his files were filled with totally inaccurate information—or perhaps the police confused him with someone else: both in 1912 and 1915 he was listed as having been an active member of the Russian Social Democratic Workers Party since the turn of the century, and that party's representative for the Dal'nitsky region as well as being a delegate to various Zionist congresses.[13] To be sure, the Russian secret police were often inept, but this degree of mistaken information was unusual, betokening Jabotinsky's modest public profile at the time.

Soon after the start of the war, however, acute controversy did begin to swirl around the decidedly non–Social Democratic Jabotinsky, as he began an intense international campaign for the creation of an armed Jewish fighting force within the Allied armies. This idea was strongly opposed by many Zionists: those who urged the movement to remain neutral in the war; those (especially in Germany and Austria) who supported the Entente; and those who regarded Jabotinsky's unadulterated militarism as harmful and foreign to the ideals and culture of the Jewish national renaissance. The old debate between Max Nordau and Ahad Ha'am came to a head once more, as Jabotinsky ever more stridently lobbied for the absolute centrality to the Zionist cause of manly, physically fit Jews, now outfitted as soldiers able and ready to fight for the liberation of their historic homeland.

As is well known, this campaign had significant results. First, it aided in the creation of the first Jewish fighting force within the British Army, the Zion Mule Corps, which saw action at Gallipoli. Soon thereafter, Jabotinsky was instrumental in the founding of the Jewish Legion, the Judaeans, who participated in the British conquest of Palestine in late 1917, and in which he was commissioned as a lieutenant. After the war, he remained in Palestine for a while, where he helped organize the Haganah, the self-defense force of the Jewish community. As head of the Haganah during its resistance to the Arab riots of April 1920, he was arrested by the British authorities and sentenced to fifteen years penal servitude. Now, for the first time he became the object of intense lionization in Zionist circles around the world: *The New Palestine,* the organ of the Zionist Organization of America, reported that London newspapers were calling him "the Jewish Garibaldi" and commented that he "deserves this distinction and will wear it nobly." While imprisoned in the Acre prison, he wrote his famous Hebrew poem "Song of the Prisoners of Acre" in memory of his friend Joseph Trumpeldor, the one-armed Russian military hero killed in defense of the Gallilean settlement Tel-Hai, who was said to have uttered as he lay dying, "ein davar, tov lamut be'ad arzenu" (no matter, it is good to die for our country).[14] Subsequently, this refrain would become inextricably linked with Jabotinsky himself, as the opening couplet of the anthem of his youth movement, named Betar, both after Bar Kochba's town and as an acronym for Brit Yosef Trumpeldor, the Order of Trumpeldor: "Tov lamut be'ad arzenu, Jabotinsky manhigenu" (It is good to die for our country, Jabotinsky is our leader).[15]

Amnestied and released from prison by Sir Herbert Samuel, the Jewish first High Commissioner for Palestine, Jabotinsky returned to Europe and promptly stirred up even more fury by entering into negotiations with representatives of the Ukrainian government headed by Simon Petliura—widely if incorrectly blamed for the massive pogroms against the Jews of Ukraine during the Civil War—for the creation of Jewish police units within the anti-Bolshevik Ukrainian army. Consistent with his views of nationalism as a whole, Jabotinsky had long supported the Ukrainian national cause and its call for independence from Russia, and he now defended the integrity of the Petliura regime. Moreover, in response to criticism of his actions he retorted, in another famous phrase, that to defend Jewish lives and honor he would be prepared "to negotiate even with the devil." Soon thereafter he resigned from the executive of the Zionist movement and founded his own Zionist party, the Revisionist movement, calling for a return to the true, Herzlian principles of political Zionism, demanding an immediate Jewish majority on both sides of the Jordan River and the militarization of Jewish youth both in the Holy Land and in the Diaspora. In response to these positions, he became the bête noire of the mainstream liberal Zionist movement headed by Chaim Weizmann and the object of especially virulent hatred on the part of left-wing Zionists (as well as non-Zionists), who persistently attacked him as a fascist and compared him to Mussolini. The head of the Palestinian Labor Zionists, David Ben-Gurion, later went so far as to dub him "Vladimir Hitler."[16]

All this is, of course, the subject of a huge scholarly and popular literature. Most reasonably objective analysts have understood that even at the peak of his extreme nationalism, Jabotinsky was by no means a fascist, in any ideologically meaningful sense of the term. Although the definition of fascism has itself yielded a highly complex and contentious scholarly debate, no reasonable version of that ideology could encompass Jabotinsky's uncompromised support for personal liberties and constitutional democracy and his opposition to totalitarian dictatorship. Though some of his followers did cross the line from integral right-wing nationalism into fascism, Jabotinsky himself never did, leading to a famous split within the Revisionist movement itself in the mid-1930s.[17]

But the clichéd retort to the charge of his fascism—that he was a liberal, in the "classic nineteenth-century meaning of the term"—is also inadequate and highly misleading, even though whole books have been written arguing the point, based first on an uncritical acceptance of Jabotinsky's own autobiographical self-construction and second on ignorance of the European and Russian intellectual contexts of his thought.[18] In *The Story of My Life,* Jabotinsky maintained that both before and after he became a Zionist he was able seamlessly to merge radical individualism and integral nationalism, that he always maintained the belief that "every individual is a king." As has here already been established, this claim was historically false, belied by dozens of his writings from 1896 to the mid-1930s. Early in his adulthood he had passionately opposed nationalism of any sort and espoused the typically jaded and cynically solipsistic individualism of the fin-de-siècle Russian intellectual, but, like so many other members of the Silver Age intelligentsia, he soon abandoned that stance and hitched his ideological and personal wagons to the cause of nationalism, interpreted through distinctly illiberal and anti-individualistic, if putatively positivistic, lenses. At the core of this mélange of populism and biological determinism lay the belief that neither the will of the individual nor the conglomerate of individuals in a society can be trusted, unless they are deemed to be in accord with the innate forces that determine the distinctive history of every nation. These immutable (in Russian, *stikhinnii*) laws of national development are entirely independent of human agency and can only be perceived by an intellectual elite that sees through the false consciousness of the masses. Moreover, in an argument parallel to Lenin's, Jabotinsky held that this elite well understands that the axioms of the liberal Enlightenment tradition are fundamentally flawed, since its universalism traduces the distinct deep structure, the unique *Volksgeist,* of each nation, determined by genetic and biological dispositions that cannot be changed, though they can be transgressed against by bad leaders. Thus, Jabotinsky had argued that the self-conception of individual Jews, their commitment, say, to being politically liberal Germans or Frenchmen of the Mosaic persuasion or Bundist socialists, was wrong, not because their views of European or Jewish society were unacceptable, but because they were expression of false consciousness scientifically contradicted by the "national individuality" of the Jewish people. Though he was not prepared to ban these opposing points of view, he was also not ready pluralistically to grant them even a theoretical or rhetorical legitimacy.

By the mid-1930s, under increasingly furious attack as a fascist, Jabotinsky began to retort that he was, after all, but a nineteenth-century-style liberal—that there was no contradiction between his brand of integral nationalism and liberal individualism:

> it is better for an individual to sin against the collective than for society to sin against the individual. Society was created for the individual, and not vice versa, and the future end of the days, the messianic era, will be a paradise for the individual, a glistening state of anarchy. . . . You might assert that there is a contradiction between this view and my nationalistic pronouncements; one of my friends, who read this manuscript, said that he heard another theme from me—In the beginning, God created the nation. But there is no contradiction between these two views. I developed the second theme in opposition to those who assert that in the beginning "humanity" was created. I believe with perfect faith that in a contest between these two views, the nation must take precedence; and similarly, that the individual comes before the nation. And even he who subjects his whole life to service to the nation, that is not a contradiction in my eyes—he does so voluntarily, not by force.[19]

Though rhetorically clever and oft-repeated, this claim was philosophically incoherent. The tension between an individual's freedom and his or her duties to a higher collectivity was, of course, one of the oldest dilemmas of political thought, and Jabotinsky could not have been expected to contribute anything original on this score. And he did not: like virtually all modern nationalists, he believed that national divides were both ontologically and sociologically primary, superseding other ties and loyalties—regional, religious, tribal, even familial. On this view, one could not authentically opt out of one's nationality on the basis of a claim of untrammeled freedom of the individual nor claim exemption from the consequent responsibilities by dint of allegiance to countervailing loyalties or by a self-definition as part of a nationally undifferentiated humanity. His claim that voluntary "service" to a national cause resolves the problem of the inescapable subordination of the individual to the collective is at best a non sequitur, at worst nonsensical.

But neither was it original: like most of his mature political and economic views (insofar as they did not relate to the Jewish question), it was based on the writings of an eccentric and eclectic, if quintessentially fin-de-siècle, thinker, Josef Popper-Lynkeus. A Viennese Jewish sociologist, scientist, and inventor much influenced by Herbert Spencer as well as by Karl Marx and Friedrich Engels, Popper-Lynkeus dedicated his life to what he believed to be an updating of Voltairianism after the advances of Charles Darwin and nineteenth-century physics.[20] Trusting that science could show the way to a harmonious solution to all the problems of human life and modern society, he concentrated his scientific research on applied physics, specifically electrical engineering, and his sociological meditations on the problems of inequality and liberty in modern society. In his early years he tended toward anarchic individualism, and in 1878 he published a book entitled *Das Recht zu leben und die Pflicht zu sterben* (The right to life and the duty to die), in which he opposed universal military conscription as an unjustifiable intrusion by the state on individual freedom. Instead, he proposed an entirely volunteer army, arguing that voluntary submission to military discipline elides the necessary relinquishment of individual freedom in an army or any other regimented social organization.[21] In subsequent decades he more and more pondered the problem of inequality in modern society and was attracted to the idea of a "scientific socialism" but was troubled by the socialists' attitude toward private property and most of all by Marx's identification of the proletariat as the avant-garde of a just state and economy. Well ahead of others, Popper-Lynkeus argued that faith in the industrial working class as the motor of history was belied by the scientific and technological revolution of modernity, which pointed the way to a future economy in which the laboring classes would more and more be supplanted, and ultimately rendered all but superfluous, by the advance of machine-based production. In the first years of the new century he began to work out what he believed to be an all-encompassing solution to the contemporary dilemma of economic and social inequality, as explained in his major work *Die allgemeine Nährpflicht als Lösung der sozialen Frage* (The general subsistence-duty as solution to the social question), published in Dresden in 1912.[22] Here he insisted that the state had the obligation to provide every individual with a guaranteed minimum of subsistence—food, clothing, housing, and employment. To fund this extremely centralized welfare state, Popper-Lynkeus proposed two sources of state revenue: first, the nationalization of all essential industries, and second, the creation of a compulsory civil "army," in which all eighteen-year-olds, male and female, would serve for an eight-year term, to build the requisite housing, grow the needed food supply, and create the necessary clothing for the population as a whole. Arguing that his proposed solution was both less utopian and more scientific than socialism, Popper-Lynkeus wrote:

> The Marxist Party should, it were logical, support my system entirely, in that I accept its call for the collectivization of the means of production, and after experiencing my system would come to the conclusion and desire that some degree of a free economy and supply of luxury goods be permitted, elimi-

nating the need for the impractical socialization of all private enterprise, as the International Social Democratic party now proposes. . . . It is regrettable that because of their one-sided obsession with industrial workers that party cannot win the support of artisans and other middle classes.[23]

Here was the key to a "scientific" organization of the future: the bourgeoisie (or at least the progressive part of the bourgeoisie), if properly organized, heavily taxed, and substantially restrained by the state, could fund the requisite minimum requirements of a just society, providing basic equality to every citizen while permitting just the right amount of free enterprise and luxury consumption to encourage individual incentive, but only to the extent that it did not lead once more to too egregious a distinction between rich and poor, in which case the state would have to step in and reduce this gap through a further redistribution of capital and property.

True to his notion of unmitigated positivism, Popper-Lynkeus rejected all nationalist movements (including Zionism) and religious faiths as reactionary and withdrew from the Viennese Jewish community, registering himself as "konfessionslos." But this did not stop Jabotinsky from accepting virtually wholesale Popper-Lynkeus's philosophical, social, and economic ideas—once more rather blatantly if idiosyncratically adapting fin-de-siècle European thought to the cause of Zionism.

First, the notion that if "service" to one's nation is entirely voluntary, the "contest" between individualism and nationalism is resolved: several years before repeating this claim in his autobiography, he argued, in a fascinating Yiddish article entitled "Vegn militarizm" (On militarism), written in the fateful year 1933, that voluntary enrollment in a militarist organization or machine-like armed force did not infringe upon the individuality of any participant. Hence, membership in Betar and utter submission to its rigid code of discipline could not be considered a breach of individual liberty.[24] One wonders how long Jabotinsky would have maintained this position had he ever had real political power in a Jewish state requiring an armed force to sustain itself. But in the absence of such a real-life challenge, the rhetorical device of "voluntary" submission to a militarist national discipline allowed Jabotinsky to mask his distinctly illiberal anti-individualism as its opposite.

More central to challenging his claim to liberalism, Jabotinsky followed Popper-Lynkeus in rejecting absolutely the alpha and omega of classic nineteenth-century liberalism, the "invisible hand" theory of the market and its corollary commitment to an economic system untrammeled by governmental intervention. In a peculiar speech entitled in its original Yiddish "Perokim vegn sotsialer filosofye fun tanakh" (Chapters on the social principles of the Hebrew Bible), Jabotinsky attributed a biblical origin to his economic views, taken straight out of Popper-Lynkeus's *Die allgemeine Nährpflicht*:

> The essence of [my] concept is that society must not leave the employee at the mercy of the employer, permitting him to force the pauper to do whatever he desires. The Bible allows no "free contract," does not recognize the "iron law" of nineteenth-century economists stipulating that the conditions of proletarian labor are determined by the effort and hunger of the laborer. . . . The relationship between employer and worker is not a private matter but a divine one, determined by the highest rungs of human conscience, not by the appetites of one side or the other, but according to the ethical and material "pathos" of a society. . . .
>
> Before the War, a Viennese Jew, Popper-Lynkeus, wrote a book *Die allgemeine Nährpflicht* which is an attempt to advance the Biblical concept of "Peah" to its ultimate end. According to Popper-Lynkeus's plan, the state must free all its citizens, both rich and poor, from the three most elementary cares of life: food, clothing, and housing; the state must provide food, clothing and housing to all. This plan is set forth in intricate detail in the book, including how many people must bear the "alimentary obligation" every year in order to provide the requisite amount of food, housing, and clothing. I am not expert in all the details of this plan and its economics, but I do believe that however utopian it sounds today, its essence will be realized—that society must provide the elementary material minimum to all, just as today it provides the spiritual minimum—the public elementary school. Hunger, cold and homelessness will disappear, just as illiteracy has disappeared in several cultured countries—only a hundred years ago, this was also thought to be utopian.
>
> I seriously believe that this will not take a century. Perhaps the huge amount of taxes that every contemporary state extracts from its citizens would suffice to provide the population with Popper-Lynkeus's elementary minimum, were it not for the millions thrown away for rifles and battleships. . . . And I strongly believe that the children of today's generation will know a world without war. And then they will liberate enormous sums for purely social goals. . . . They will see a world in which the word "hunger" will sound like a legend from days of yore, a world in which the difference between rich and poor will lose ninety percent of its contemporary tragic bitterness; a world in which no one will have to worry about widows or orphans, unemployment, or downward mobility—since no one will be able to fall very far down, society will provide everyone with the soft, warm, and full "floor" from which everyone can rest and from which they will be able to lift themselves up again. . . .
>
> But the difference between rich and poor will still exist—though far from

the pained and embittered difference of today. But there will still be a difference, and this difference will also spur people, continue to motivate them to compete against one another and demand from society a continuing process of leveling, so that the gap cannot become permanent or unjust. [25]

This was the difference, Jabotinsky continued, between his—and Popper-Lynkeus's—proposed economic system and socialism. Moreover, although socialists of all stripes claim that their ideas were rooted in the views of the Hebrew Prophets, it was Popper-Lynkeus's celebration of the bourgeoisie and his synthesis of capitalism and the state's nationalization of the means of production that was authentically Hebraic—an updated articulation of the biblical ideals, especially the concept of the Jubilee. Thus, in several articles entitled "The Idea of the Jubilee," Jabotinsky proposed an economic system in which free enterprise and the accumulation of wealth is permitted, but only in fifty-year cycles, after which a redistribution of property is enforced by the state, which sees to it that the cycle of moderated class differentiation begins again but never reaches the level obtained either in free market or socialist economies.[26] This was but a reworking of one of the core ideas of Herbert Spencer's positivism, which called for a totally free market economy permitting unlimited accumulation of wealth, but only until an individual's death; thereafter, all the capital would revert to the state, with no inheritance of wealth allowed. Thus, even without going into a more technical discussion of Jabotinsky's rather muddled economic proposals, under no rational definition of "classic nineteenth-century liberalism" can his social and economic positions be so labeled.

But Jabotinsky's debt to Popper-Lynkeus's restatement of Spencerianism goes even further: although of course the notion of "Monism" was a classical philosophical concept, the ideological cast Jabotinsky gave to this term, which he increasingly used to define his entire political system, was lifted straight out of the lexicon of Popper-Lynkeus and his fellow fin-de-siècle utopians such as Ernst Mach and Ernst Haeckel. Their followers founded the Austrian "Monistenbund" (Monist Federation) before the First World War and later Monist organizations in Germany, Hungary, and the United States. Advocating strict adherence to the scientific worldview of positivism and materialism, the Monist Unions attracted thousands of members throughout central Europe, and admirers as distinct as Albert Einstein and Sigmund Freud, both of whom wrote laudatory articles in memory of Josef Popper-Lynkeus in the federation's publications. By the early 1930s, the Monists focused their attention on the increasing attraction of irrational ideologies, both political and religious, calling for a renewed commitment to the late nineteenth-century belief in science as the motor of human progress. With increasing pessimism and at times pained despair, they steadfastly opposed religion, nationalism, theosophy, and any philosophy based on "intuition" rather than scientific observation and analysis.[27] What Jabotinsky did was to take up both the vocabulary and the basic weltanschauung of this late nineteenth- and early twentieth-century movement and apply it to Zionism, with the requisite disregard of the Monists' rejection of nationalism as unscientific. On the surface, as Jabotinsky repeatedly explained, "Monism" to him meant an unvarying commitment to one unitary goal, the creation of a Jewish state in Palestine, regardless of the class or ideational divides within Jewish society. On a deeper level, this unilateral goal was premised, just like his cultural and literary writings and his social and economic views, on a commitment to the eternal verities of fin-de-siècle European culture and thought, now melded with integral nationalism of a distinctly illiberal, interbellum variety. More and more Jabotinsky's nationalism came to resemble other versions of extreme right-wing nationalism that flourished in Europe in this period, from the Polish Endecja to the French chauvinism of Maurice Barré, but without their culturally xenophobic and economically reactionary sensibilities. Thus, Jabotinsky's Zionism, neither fascist nor liberal nor classically conservative, never truly departed from its fundamental cultural cosmopolitanism and its deep-seated philosophical and intellectual roots in the European fin de siècle.

These continuities may be seen most clearly by examining the persistent centrality in Jabotinsky's Zionism of the stereotypically turn-of-the-century concept of "Muskeljudentum." In his Yiddish article "Vegn militarizm," he directly and dispassionately took on his opponents' attacks on him as too militaristic:

> "Militarism" is an ugly word. But adults ought not be put off by a sound, but rather should be expected to analyze a concept and to discern the good and bad in it. War is bad, the murder of young and innocent souls. This we all agree on, and hope that the day will come when war will be impossible, as impossible in civilized societies as already now are cannibalism or physical torture as practiced before the French Revolution. But is this the true defining content of army life? . . . Every idealistic movement in the world takes at least half of its technical vocabulary and three fourths of its rhetoric from military life. Apparently, not everything in that life is so bad.
>
> The truth is that only war is ugly; military life per se has many beautiful sides which we yearn for in civilian life but cannot, to our regret, fully

achieve. First, the fraternity of army life, its Spartan simplicity, and equality between rich and poor; second, the hygienic benefit, the fresh air and bodily fitness; thirdly, military discipline itself—a matter that merits special deliberation.[28]

Citing (imprecisely, to be sure, but that is not the point here) Jan Masaryk's recollection that he was never so stirred as when he witnessed in his youth the first public demonstration of the Czech Sokol movement, Jabotinsky remarked,

> It is a well-known fact that you can take even the most assimilated Jew and hypnotize him (at least for a while) with nationalist enthusiasm by means of a simple technique: take a couple of hundred Jewish youths, dress them all alike, and march them in his clear view in a well orchestrated parade, each step of the two hundred lads clicking in unison like the well greased wheels of a machine. Nothing in the world can make such an impression upon us as the ability of the masses, in particular moments, to feel and to act as one unit, with one will, working at a steady tempo. This is the difference between the "masses," the "riff-raff" and a nation.[29]

For the Jews, Jabotinsky continued, the experience of military discipline is even more essential than for any other group in the world:

> There is one other benefit to military discipline which usually is responded to by us with a "feh" but which we all know in our hearts is so essential and so bitterly lacking among us Jews, in all realms of life—this is ceremonial [in Yiddish, "dos tseremonial"]—the precise and clear rules of how to stand, how to greet one another, how to speak to a friend and how to speak to an official. We Jews suffer from a *lack of form:* the old ghetto had its own social ceremonies, albeit peculiar to it; but recently we have lost this form of ceremonial and have not replaced it with a new one. The average Jew has no notion of beauty in his mode of walking, of dress, of eating, of dealing with other people. This shortcoming is most evident any time he deals with any sort of hierarchy, when he speaks with an important "lord" or even with a rich Jew; he wishes to display some sort of honor but does not know how to do so without losing self-respect, and the result seems either arrogant or obsequious.[30]

This is a breathtaking paragraph in the context in which it appeared. Jabotinsky was speaking here mostly to Polish Jewish youth, who in the early and mid-1930s were increasingly desperate about their futures and hence were drawn in their hundreds of thousands away from mainstream liberal, religious, and Zionist ideologies to his radical Revisionist movement, to the newly invigorated socialist Bund, or to the steadily growing, if still illegal, Communist Party. Most of his audience were children of traditional, petit bourgeois Jewish homes, whose least problem, one might have thought, was the lack of "ceremonial" in their lives. But Jabotinsky brilliantly zeroed in on their aching need for at least the appearance of power and agency in their progressively more and more impotent lives, caught between the collapse of traditional Jewish norms and the now largely unattainable dignity of embourgeoisement and upward social mobility. Like Nordau's original concept, Jabotinsky's embrace of Jewish militarism as the sine qua non of self-liberation overtly played upon stereotypes of Jews' weakness and incivility, shared by their detractors and enemies. But Jabotinsky far more astutely than Nordau intuited his audience's profound ambivalence in regard to the past they were in the process of rejecting. Thus, he threw a rhetorical sop to the "ceremonials" of the old ghetto, however "peculiar"—akin to his extraordinarily controversial but politically wise move of adding a pro-religious plank to his movement's platform, despite his own unchanging atheism and profound Popper-Lynkeus-like anticlericalism. With the façade of an insider, however, he could proceed to attack the fundamental institutions of East European Judaism with a lacerating critique:

> The lack of form, the absence of reinforced ceremonial, is felt in other realms as well, even among those with purely spiritual natures. Listen to the sermon of an old preacher in synagogue: intellectually he is superior to even ten Gentile philosophers, but he has no clue how quietly to develop an idea from beginning to end, he jumps from one subject to a third, and worse, this very attribute finds favor in his audience. They have lost the need for order, for constancy, for the ability to discern the beginning, middle, and ending—as in an army on a march.[31]

This from a man who had probably never really heard one of these sermons and could not follow its internal arguments, however logically or illogically presented. But this was precisely his strongest card, even more potent than the similar stances of Herzl and Nordau before him, who were so clearly western European Jews, overt products of Emancipation and embourgeoisement—doctors of philosophy or of medicine who one could not imagine, in the wildest of one's dreams, wowing an audience of Polish Jews in their native Yiddish, however learned or mannered. It has become trite to note that the most effective leaders of nationalist or class-based movements often come from the periphery of the groups they claim to represent, and indeed Jabotinsky could and did play both sides of the "Ostjudenfrage" to his advantage. He was indeed an East European Jew, born and bred, but the most Gentile-like East European Jew one could possibly imagine, far more cultivated, gentlemanly, sophisticated than his followers could ever hope to be, but still undyingly committed to his people, sacrificing his life to them and for them. Earlier, in the fin de siècle, the Bund had such a leader: Vladimir Medem was not only a native Russian speaker born to a bourgeois Jewish family, but trumped even Jabotinsky in his remove from traditional Jewish life—he had been baptized as a child and famously had to "return to the Jewish people" and reject Russian Orthodoxy. Medem died in 1923 after emigrating to America and was replaced by a new cohort of leaders who were highly educated and sophisticated but, at the same time, like the leaders of liberal and socialist Zionism, patently secularized sons of traditional East European Jewish fathers. Jabotinsky stood alone as the most un-Jewish Jew undyingly committed to Jewish nationalism: the personification of cosmopolitan ultra-nationalism.

Thus, a year after the publication of "Vegn militarizm," Jabotinsky went even further along these lines in his extraordinary Hebrew manifesto "Ra'ayon Betar" (The idea of Betar). Here, under the heading "Betar Discipline," he expanded the Popper-Lynkeus theme that voluntary submission of individual will to a cause obliterates the stain of authoritarianism:

> The structure of Betar is based on the principle of discipline. Our goal is to make it a worldwide organism that will be able, upon an order from the central command, for tens of thousands of its members simultaneously to carry out the same action in every city and state. Our opponents claim that this contradicts the honor of free individuals and makes them into a "machine." I advise you proudly and without shame to answer: yes, a machine.
>
> For the greatest accomplishment of free men is the ability to work together in precise unison, like a machine. This is possible only for free men imbued with high culture . . . When we listen to a choir or an orchestra, and one hundred musicians punctiliously heed the orders of one conductor, impressing us as working totally in unison, that is proof that each individual musician has dedicated his utmost effort to the result; it is not the conductor who has forced him to do so but he himself, his own desire for unity. This is the sort of "orchestra" we want to make out of the entire Jewish people, and the first step toward this goal is Betar.[32]

The essence of this new Jewish personality, Jabotinsky continued, is contained in the word "hadar," which, he explained,

> is a Hebrew word almost impossible to translate into other languages, encompassing at least twelve separate concepts: external beauty, pride, politesse, loyalty. . . . But its true "translation" in everyday life ought to be the Betar member himself, when he goes out and when he comes in, in his actions, his speech, behavior and thoughts. It is self-evident that we are far from this goal and cannot even reach it in one generation. But this "Betar-hadar" must

become the ultimate goal of every one of us—every step we take, every hand motion, every slight sound, every movement and even every thought must be stubbornly guided by the notion of "hadar."

This is crucial not only because every human being ought to strive for "hadar." It is especially crucial for us Jews. We have already noted that our life in Exile has excessively weakened the healthiest instincts of a normal nation, and this is most apparent in regard to our external bearing. Everyone knows, everyone privately laments that the average Jew pays no regard to his manners, to his external appearance. This is not a trivial matter, but one of the essential aspects of self-respect. Just as a man must take care of his physical hygiene, not out of concern for what others will say about him, even if he is a Robinson Crusoe, simply out of his own self-respect, so too must he educate himself that every word he utters, every step he takes, must accord with his own supreme self-worth, his own majesty, since everyone is imbued with his own royalty, his own majesty. If the "aristocrat" has any meaning it is this: that one's father and father's father and so on were always, for generation upon generation, men of culture, i.e. men who lived not according to the notion "anything goes" but in deep appreciation of aristocratic notions and in dedication to noble ideals. And we are the most "aristocratic" nation in the world—even the oldest royal dynasty cannot claim more than twenty or thirty generations of civilized life—somewhere, not too far back, is some half-savage farmer if not a bandit. But not us Jews: behind each one of us there stand at least seventy generations of literate men, who studied and spoke about God and history, about nations and kings, about ideas of justice and righteousness and about the problems of humanity and the future. Every Jew is in this sense, a "prince."[33]

This rather histrionic appeal to national vanity is immediately followed, in a remarkably telling rhetorical and substantive stroke, by a call for Jews to learn how to emulate the manners and mores of the cultivated European bourgeoisie:

Betar discipline is one of the best ways to learn "hadar." But this is not at all sufficient. Everyone must train oneself to filter and refine his ways. Hadar is comprised of a thousand "trivialities" that define our daily existence: Eat quietly and in moderation; don't lean on your elbows when you eat; don't slurp your soup with a noise that can be heard at a distance; when walking on the street with your friends, don't hog the whole sidewalk; when you go up the stairs at night, don't make noise or wake your neighbors; give way to a woman, an older person, a child, indeed to anyone—just because someone else is rude, don't you be—these and an endless number of other seeming trivialities that add up to "Betar hadar."

But most important of all is ethical "hadar"—you must be generous—so long as something does not concern a crucial matter of principle, don't stand on ceremony for petty matters, it's better to sacrifice yourself than to demand someone else do so. Every word you utter must be a "word of honor, " and your word of honor must be tougher than flint. So that the day will come, when every Jew who wants to express the highest rung of human honesty, of dignity and honor, will say, not like today—"that's a true gentleman," but "that's a true Betari."[34]

Not far under the surface of this call there lay a very thinly disguised (or, as Freudians would say, "cathected") intense contempt for the manners and mores of traditional East European Jewry. This was, of course, the underbelly of all such self-criticisms of traditional Jewish life, from the earliest stages of the Jewish Enlightenment movement with its Hebrew translations of Benjamin Franklin's principles of self-improvement, its biting Yiddish parodies of shtetl vulgarity, its German primers of correct behavior and thought. But the point of that enterprise had been precisely to effect an internally coherent synthesis, true to both sides, between Judaism as an ongoing and vital religious civilization and bourgeois European culture. That was the meaning of the famous, if oft misunderstood, motto of the Hebrew Haskalah, Judah Leib Gordon's line "Be a man on the street and a Jew at home."[35] Unlike Weizmann or any of the other East European Zionist leaders or even the adherents of Nietzscheanism within the Hebrew revival movement, Jabotinsky had no grounding or interest in that internal discourse. His scattered comments on the Haskalah and its offshoot the Love of Zion movement reveal not simply contempt for their philosophical and political feebleness, but also a fundamental miscomprehension of their basic ideational and cultural goals. As a result, his concept of "hadar" did not emerge from within Jewish intellectual and cultural history but was self-evidently a translation into Hebrew of western European and Russian fin-de-siècle notions of bourgeois manliness. Jabotinsky did not even bother here to invent a mythologized biblical origin for this Hebraized but internally de-Judaized gentleman soldier, a bourgeois "muskeljüdische" cadet immune to and ignorant of the superannuated effeminacy of the ghetto.

In one crucial piece of writing, however, Jabotinsky did indeed turn to the Bible as a source for such a hero—his novel *Samson the Nazarite,* first published serially in the Russian-language Zionist journal *Rassvet* beginning in 1926 and then as a separate novel in 1927.[36] Like his earlier plays, poetry, and short stories, *Samson* can be read as revealing Jabotinsky's most intense internal struggles, his grappling with the tensions and contradictions in his public and private lives. Unlike the rest of Jabotinsky's literary oeuvre, his novels *Samson* and *Piatero* (The five) have been the object of some very good scholarly analysis, particularly by the Russian literature specialist Alice Nachimovsky.[37] But they have not been sufficiently examined against the backdrop of his overarching intellectual development and lifelong embeddedness in fin-de-siècle politics and culture. In this light, first and foremost, *Samson the Nazarite* ought to be read as one of the small but fascinating group of decadent early twentieth-century novels on biblical themes, a genre that culminated most famously in Thomas Mann's *Joseph and His Brothers* and in the annals of Jewish writing in Sholem Asch's highly controversial Christological trilogy. In this group, *Samson the Nazarite* reads as an artistically middling but not unimaginative piece of writing that departs from the mold not so much for the inevitable liberties it takes with the biblical original, but in its extreme desacralization of the entire scriptural script. As others have noted, the biblical Samson may be regarded as one of the most "un-Jewish" Israelite leaders, though this of course is inevitably the result of a circular perception of what constitutes innate Jewishness. But Jabotinsky's Samson is not simply a military hero or a proto-Muskeljude—one who urges his followers to "take up iron" in their defense, the line most often cited by commentators who read the novel as a simple call to Revisionist Zionism. More to the point, the entire story depends upon a thoroughgoing purge of every supernatural motif in the original tale, save one—the Israelites' worship of pagan gods. In the Book of Judges, the Samson cycle begins with the verse "And the Children of Israel continued to do wrong in the name of the Lord, and the Lord gave them in the hands of the Philistines for forty years" (13:1). But the Lord, or any of His agents, is fundamentally absent in and irrelevant to Jabotinsky's story, just as in his translation of Bialik. Here, not only the Israelites in general are pagans, but—shockingly—Samson and his mother are as well; indeed, the latter is a devout idolater who maintains a whole stable of gods and goddesses, including the God of Israel, and hires a Levite to conduct regular worship service in her expansive private pantheon. One of the most florid paragraphs in this otherwise sparsely written novel occurs near the beginning, when the narrator describes Samson's mother's polytheistic temple:

> Under a sloping roof, idols of various sizes were standing on stone pedestals on the clean-swept ground. An archeologist of today would have given half his life for half an hour in this shrine . . . the collection in her temple reflected the religious beliefs of the whole of Canaan, Transjordania, the desert, Lebanon, the Mediterranean coast and the Aegean islands. There were horned Astartes, Astartes with doves, naked Astartes—now dressed in little frocks;

a goddess holding a cross in her hand, another with a curly beard; a little god with a fish's tail; several with goat's legs, pointed ears and horns; a calf with a turquoise in its forehead and gold leaf peeling from its body; a fat, seated male figure, with a great naked belly, an excessively large head and terrific jaws; a winged girl with flowing hair—a beautiful bit of carving in ivory; an idol with a hawk's head; a dwarf standing on one leg, with a tail shaped like a leech; dragons and serpents; a scaly, curly-haired idol, half animal, half man, eyeless, but with a huge eye in its breast; two handsome naked youths, foreign work, each equipped with a woolen apron for propriety's sake; little men with a gnat's sting in their mouths. On a special stand draped with panther skins and cloths of silk, stood the household gods, seven in number, crude handiwork of a native craftsman: they consisted of the figures of two men and two women in red clay, and two men and one woman in stone. One of the male figures in stone had on his head something like a tightly filled sack, which hung down his back, and was evidently intended to represent the long hair of a Nazarite. . . . It was arranged that sacrifices should be made only before the golden column, to Jehovah, while the rest of the idols were to content themselves with prayers.[38]

This is crucial to the plot since the core of Samson's national and cultural ambivalence, the heart of the novel, is his uncertainty about his national and religious origins, whether his birth father was an Israelite or a Philistine—hence, perhaps, his attraction to the latter culture and especially to its women. The transcendental core of the biblical story, that Samson's mother was visited by an angel of the Lord who promised her a son on the condition that he be pledged to God as a Nazarite, is laughingly dismissed as but a patently absurd cover-up for her adulterous amour with a mysterious stranger that left her with child. And the child of sin is himself a defiant sinner, sexually insatiable and promiscuous, his couplings and near-couplings described in extremely graphic detail typical of decadent fin-de-siècle writing. But even more centrally, the very essence of Samson's life, his election as a Nazarite, is meaningless to him and devoid of any theological import, either when he obeys the rules of his dispensation or when he flaunts them in public. Indeed, any reader unaware of the biblical concept of the Nazarite—a *nezir elohim*, an abstinent monk dedicated to divine service—could easily come away from this novel not only missing that point, but thinking that "Nazarite" is but an unexplicated toponym. Even Samson's ultimate downfall here results from acts wholly independent of the abrogation of divine rules: in Jabotinsky's story Delilah still cuts Samson's hair (or rather, more melodramatically, shaves his head bald) but that is incidental to his defeat or to his eventual suicide and last act of bravery. At the climax of the biblical account the blinded Samson, surrounded by all the lords of

the Philistines, three thousand men and women, calls out to the true
Lord: "O Lord God, Please remember me and give me strength just this
once, O God, to take revenge of the Philistines, if only for one of my
two eyes." But Jabotinsky's Samson never prays to God, never invokes
His name as the catalyst for his victories or his defeats. In a remarkable
scene, while serving as a judge in Israel, Samson is confronted with a
prophet who instructs him that it was against God's law for Israelites to
wed foreign wives—"Jehovah Himself, Moses His representative, and
that famous general, Joshua the son of Nun, had forbidden the tribes to
wed with Canaanitish women."[39] However, concurring with modern
biblical critics who hypothesize that the Book of Judges may well have
been written long before the Pentateuch, Jabotinsky writes:

> Samson had never heard of Moses, though someone had once told him some
> story about Joshua. He said, with a yawn: "All kinds of people forbade things
> before ever your grandfather saw the light, but we must know the reason."
>   "Foreign girls have brought foreign gods among you!" screamed the
> prophet from among the crowd.
>   "Hey, you good-for-nothing," cried Samson, turning to him. . . . "Why
> do you interfere, while Jehovah Himself puts up with the Astartes and house-
> hold gods?"
>   The crowd, among whom there were many natives, laughed at this apt
> reply.[40]

After he is snipped by Delilah's scissors and then has his eyes cut out,
this Samson has every means and opportunity to end his subordination
to the Philistines and to return to his people as a military hero or a judge.
But he freely chooses not to do so, in order to fulfill his mission, which
is a trouncing of the Philistines for purely personal and nationalistic, as
opposed to prophetically driven, reasons. He therefore voluntarily continues in his servitude to the Philistines, and the narrative continues in
rather muddled chapters, which tell of hidden long-lost loves, unheard-
of children, and rambling travels to nowhere in particular. Perhaps Jabotinsky realized that he was losing the thread of his story and ended it
all with a corny and rather messy denouement related in the most hack-
neyed narrative exit device possible, an epistolary epilogue, here penned
by a previously unknown character, an Egyptian chronicler, who tells
of Samson's tragic but noble demise.

   Thus, Jabotinsky's Samson, bereft of any divinely inspired belief either in life or in death, drifts through the novel as an all but unconscious
sensualist, but one torn, in the depths of his soul, by a tormenting psychological dilemma: a deep-seated attraction to the ways of the Philis-

tines matched only by a profound alienation from the people—or rather the People—he is fated to serve and to lead. Tortured by this divided loyalty, he knows in the deepest depths of his being that he is passionately entranced by the ways of his supposed enemies:

> Delilah's caresses were so different from the bovine surrender or the shrill lust of his native concubines. . . . Women were no strangers in Samson's life. In Dan, the land of his Nazarite vow, he kept himself apart from the intoxication of love; but in Philistia, the daughters, wives and sisters of the natives hung upon his nod, and they were often members of the most beautiful races in Canaan. He was accustomed to think himself satiated; but now he realized how completely he had been starved. Samson loved to drink from hammered cups rather than earthenware bowls, even when the drink was the same. That is why he loved the Philistine way of life.[41]

Further, he explains:

> I know the [Philistines'] lilting speech, fine clothes, courteous manners. And I know things of greater moment: you have rules for all the affairs of life, for the gravest and the most trivial; you conduct yourselves with order and dignity in warfare, religion, and municipal matters. And I know something weightier still about you, your sated hearts. . . . I have always admired your judges, governors, and captains . . . because they perform their duties with such skill and promptitude, but when their work is done they go to a harlot's house and make jest of it.[42]

Indeed, Samson continues, his love of Philistine ways is paralleled by his hatred of the Israelites:

> I love you . . . and that is why I do not love Dan, and why I hate Dan's kinsmen. Everything there is different. When a man reaches the age when he can take part in the meetings of the elders at the town-gate, he becomes unbearable in his own household. . . . Their life is like sand, made up of the tiniest grains, and they are ready to quarrel over each grain, to be immoderately happy or immoderately downcast. You insist on order even in the fields of the natives. Under your supervision the native ploughs in regular strips. But in Dan there is no supervision: Dan's husbandmen plough for themselves, hurriedly and even haphazard. Dan envies its neighbours; envies even the natives; everywhere there is someone in front who must be overtaken, and therefore Dan throws out its nets in all directions and sows its seeds on all sides. In Dan there is neither order nor rank; it is a chaos of towns, altars, and ideas. The husbandmen hate the shepherds, Benjamin hates Judah, and the prophets hate them all. But beyond all that they have one thing in common—the hungry heart. A greed for all things, visible or invisible. Every soul is in revolt against what is, and cries for something else.[43]

Beyond the obvious parallels to the heart of Jabotinsky's polemical call for a revolution in Jewish mores and manners, anyone who has carefully read Jabotinsky's earlier play, *Alien Land,* can recognize in these words Natasha's searing condemnation of East European Jewry as frenzied, disorderly, lacking the "pride that inheres in silence." But although the words are virtually the same, in the intervening decade their author had moved from the margins of Jewish life to its very center, and these words are now placed in the mouth not of an outsider but of a Hebrew hero, who is fully cognizant of his own near-hatred of his own people and also of his inability to be anything but their leader. He cannot be a Philistine, even if he wants to be one. Belonging to a nation is not a matter of feeling, of cultural choice. The wise Philistine leader to whom Samson reveals his innermost plight cannot understand his angst: "If a man loves one nation and hates another, if in one nation he has friends and in the other betrayers, then his place is among his own people and against the foreigners." To which Samson angrily retorts:

> "Loves"? "Does not love"? . . . You are a wise man and yet you speak to me in the language of women. Does love decide what is yours and what is alien? . . . I am not one of you! Invite me to your feasts, Philistine, and I will come and help you to pass the time pleasantly, even if the feast be held round the place of my execution. I will drink and jest with you gladly but . . . I don't believe in you.[44]

Crucially, this pledge of undying commitment to the people of Israel is made before Samson learns the truth about his birth-father—that he was, in fact, an Israelite and not a Philistine. When Samson hears this news, he simply laughs—he has been condemned as an outsider by enemies within the Israelite fold, and it is too late to undo the damage. But what others believe about him is as incidental to his immutable calling as is the revelation of his father's origins. National belonging is neither voluntary nor merely biological; even if his father had turned out to be a Philistine, Samson could not have been anything but an Israelite, raised among the Israelites by an Israelite woman and her Israelite husband who devoted themselves to their son and his mission to lead his people and defeat their enemies, whatever his own desires or cultural preferences.

As in "Edmée," the overt moral of the story is given in its last lines, here spoken by the Egyptian chronicler:

> There is surely nothing more mysterious, nothing more august than that intangible quality, dwelling in the soul of a whole people, that distinguishes it from all other nations of the earth; the most insoluble of all enigmas, revealed to me that night both by that unaccountable man himself, and by the people that loved him, blinded him, and perished with him in the same fire.[45]

Under the surface, however, one can hear the inner turbulence of the author himself, the ultra-nationalist leader keenly conscious of his own profound plight: an undying dedication to a nation that repelled him.

This dilemma was pursued even more assiduously by Jabotinsky in his second and last novel, *Piatero* (The five), first published in toto in Paris in 1936.[46] Unfortunately, the Hebrew translation of this novel included in Jabotinsky's collected works in the 1950s is an extremely poor rendition of the original, almost totally effacing its highly stylized tone and narrative voice, and no translation into English or any other European language has ever appeared.[47] *Piatero* is a very different novel from *Samson*: it is overtly cast as an autobiographical novel nostalgically describing the Odessa of Jabotinsky's youth and especially depicting the tragic and fruitless "assimilation" of its Russified Jewish population. Most commentators have therefore seen no similarity between it and *Samson*.[48] But, in fact, *Piatero* can be read as a continuing meditation on the very same theme as its predecessor, the abiding and irresoluble inner struggle of a profoundly self-conscious national leader grappling with the tensions and contradictions of his idiosyncratic mélange of cosmopolitanism and ultra-nationalism. Indeed, in many ways, *Piatero* is both the most literarily successful and the most psychologically revealing of Jabotinsky's adult writings, if it is read with extreme sensitivity to its very complex genre. Literary critics have long pondered and debated the ways in which ordinary, ostensibly factual, autobiographies are in many ways akin to the novel, in that they are eminently self-conscious retrospective narratives that tell only the stories that their authors want read or remembered, highly selective constructions and manipulations of the self that cannot be read—as their authors usually insist—as "objective" or "true-to-life" depictions of reality. That is why the student of autobiography cannot be shocked when the newspapers announce the latest revelation of a fabricated autobiography; to varying extents, all autobiographies are fabrications. When the author identifies his or her work as autobiographical fiction, clearly yet elusively adding another filter, only semi-opaque, between subject and object, then the problem of "Dichtung und Wahrheit," the problem of discerning fact from fiction, is immensely compounded. Paradoxically, however, for some authors the screen of fictional distortion can be liberating, serving to mute or even entirely to remove the terror of truth-telling. The reader is at one and the same time urged to believe and not to believe that what is described actually happened, that the characters depicted once lived and acted as they do in the story, that the narrator is the same person as the author. Thus shielded, the storyteller can perhaps allow a more nuanced truth to seep through than in an ostensibly "non-fictional" autobiography. For such a highly public and controversial figure as Vladimir Jabotinsky, the armor of fiction permitted him to do in *Piatero* what he could not do in his "real" autobiography. As we have seen, *The Story of My Life* is a steadfast and coherent (if historically fallacious) narrative with no zig-zags, no doubts, no tortured crises of faith or self-perception. In sharp contrast, in *Piatero* Jabotinsky more than ever before lifted the veil of unmitigated conviction, by creating a narrator (whom we are urged to identify as his alter ego), situated in his own place and moment of ideological rebirth—Odessa, 1902–1903; the narrator is a Russified Jewish journalist who has recently studied in Rome and Bern and has taken part in the organization of Jewish self-defense units in Odessa. Rather than telling his own story, the narrator depicts his interactions with the Milgroms, a typical haute-bourgeois Jewish family in Odessa. The father, a grain dealer born in a shtetl, has worked his way up the economic and cultural ladder and can speak proper Russian and play the part of the *kulturnyi* pater familias, though on occasion his native Yiddish breaks through as he bemoans the radically different life he has worked so hard to provide for his wife and children; left alone, he is happiest with the Romantic German poets that guided his passage from ghetto rags to upper-middle-class riches. His wife is a beautiful and gracious grande dame straight out of Turgenev, regally presiding over a salon of intellectuals and semi-intellectuals, obsessed with her children's welfare but never meddling in their affairs. She is as far from a stereotypical Jewish mother as possible and is the narrator's confidante. Her five children, three sons and two daughters, cover the ideological gamut of their time, from decadent sensuality to asexual Marxism, from neo-Romantic experimentation with Hinduism and Buddhism to conversion to Christianity for reasons of unabashed upward mobility. None of the children take the path of their friend, the narrator; Zionism is just about the farthest thing from any of their minds or the lives they ultimately create for themselves. In the end, of course, they are all lost to their family and to the Jewish people: two die senseless deaths before their time, one becomes a Bolshevik secret (or perhaps, double) agent, and one rationally considers his future and is baptized.

What is wonderful about this novel is that all these characters and their choices are portrayed lovingly and with extraordinary empathy by Jabotinsky, who in his thousands of polemical works attacked and derided such un-Zionist Jews with ceaseless and often venomous condemnation, on the basis of his pseudo-scientific positivism. Here the Zionist message is interstitial: we the readers know that the author of this novel is the famous Vladimir Jabotinsky and that the narrator has recently become a Zionist, but the latter barely even hints at his Zionism in the text, never "corrects" his interlocutors, not even when their actions lead to disaster or despair. He is omniscient but nearly invisible, irrelevant to the story he tells, merely the agent of the author's nostalgic retrospection. This is not the story of a simple longing for a world that is no more, but a highly self-conscious attempt on Jabotinsky's part to sort through, seemingly as much for himself as for his readers, the roads both taken and not taken from fin-de-siècle Jewish Odessa to the present—the mid-1930s.

To be sure, this unmediated self-examination is itself but a fictional ploy, a narrative device meant to draw the reader into the author's confidence, but in the process one feels nonetheless that the inner voice of the real Jabotinsky comes through more clearly than in his other work, a voice that is allowed to reconstruct the Odessa of his youth without the tendentious and counterfactual posturing of his allegedly more realistic memoirs. Thus, early in the novel he ponders the unsystematic political radicalism of his Odessa circle of friends, who somehow identified literature with "progressive" politics but didn't really know why:

> True sedition was not to be found among us, but we all were all like trained seals who would never tolerate words such as "autocracy" or "constitution" in our public discourse. But everything we discussed, from the organization of the zemstva to Hauptmann's *Sunken Bell*, was filled with rumblings of sedition. Chekhovian ennui was perceived by us as a protest against the regime and the dynasty . . . Political parties didn't yet exist, except underground, and Legal Marxists and Populists didn't really know how they differed from one another, since everyone, including the future Kadets, belonged to the "progressive" camp.[49]

This was a far more accurate accounting of his real political views before he became a Zionist than the picture he painted in *The Story of My Life*. Not surprisingly, at this point the narrator disappears, and the author intrudes with his self-conscious, retroactive analysis:

> Looking back on all this thirty years later, I think that the most curious thing about our group then was the peaceful fraternity of nationalities. All the eight or ten tribes of old Odessa met together in that club, but it never entered into anyone's mind to identify, even silently to oneself who was who. About two years later all this changed, but at the turn of the century, we all got along famously. It's strange: at home we all lived—I think—among our own kind,

Poles visited and entertained only Poles, Russians Russians, Jews Jews, with rare exceptions, but we didn't really wonder about this at all, unconsciously considered it a temporary oversight and the Babel-like confusion of our club a symbol of a beautiful future. Perhaps the best expression of that attitude—its conciliatory superficiality and underground menace—was an honest but stupid drinking-buddy of mine, a opera tenor with a Ukrainian family name, who, drunk one Saturday night, came over to me to congratulate me on some dinner-table speech:

—You really grabbed me tonight—he said, kissing me thrice—nothing can separate us, we're brothers for life. It's terrible that people still divide people by religion—this one's a Russian, that one's a Jew. What's the difference? Let everyone be united in soul, like you and me. But that X—he's something else—he has a Jewish soul. A mean, base soul . . .[50]

This moment is exceedingly revealing of Jabotinsky's subtle machinations in the novel as a whole: the clichéd iteration of the moral of "Edmée" is here deemed but retrospectively clear, though the incident itself could not have had any other contemporaneous interpretation. When "in fact" did the narrator realize the errors of his cosmopolitan ways, when did he discern the *stikhinnii* dialectic of nationalism? The distinction between present and past is deliberately effaced.

Indeed, the author's longing for the Odessa that is no more and to which he can never return is so stylized that it all but approaches parody of nostalgia rather than the ostensible real thing. The most extended description of Odessa is relegated to a chapter that occurs immediately after the most intense episode in the novel, the narrator's single night alone with the bewitching Marusya Milgrom, during which she pours out her heart to him, sharing with him a far greater intimacy than if she had slept with him, as she had with so many other lovers. Entitled "An inserted chapter, not for the reader," it begins with a fascinating, if self-obliterating, claim:

In all candor: I'm writing this chapter only out of pure cowardice. I've already tried about three different continuations of that night, but to no avail: I'm afraid. I've just torn to pieces three pieces of paper. To take a break, I'll now write about something else. One critic, reviewing my work, chided me that it has a grave insufficiency—no descriptions of nature. This was ten years ago, but my ego was bruised: I must try to repair that fault. Of course, such a chapter is not for the reader, who doesn't actually read descriptions of nature; I, at the very least, always ruthlessly skip them when reading. Due to the above-mentioned pride, I could at many points in this story have filled the pages with dozens of descriptions of the scenery, but that would have been a trap: in good conscience, the only thing to do is to put them all in a separate chapter (even more so because I'm afraid and want a break), and this chapter ought really to be called "Take it or Leave it."[51]

Humorously playing on the stereotype of Jews' remove from nature—
and to some extent, from guilt-free sexuality—the narrator tries to continue on to a description of nature but keeps interrupting himself in a
paragraph that reads (especially in the original Russian) like a parody
of Jewish humor, a page out of (a stereotypically misunderstood) Sholem
Aleichem:

> In the summer, our seashore—in the summer, what it was like in the winter,
> I don't want to know. In general, I love life, and especially love my own life
> and love to recall it, but only from April to September. Why God created
> winter I don't know. In general He, the poor thing, made a mess of a lot of
> things, and created many things that are superfluous. Most of my acquain-
> tances claim that they love snow—not just decorative snow, the summit of
> Mount Blanc, beautiful white snow in a painting, that one can love and turn
> away from—no, they like real snow, on the streets and the ground; to me,
> snow is but tomorrow's slush. I only remember summers.[52]

Only then does the nature description begin, but at first it is rather pathetic:

> In the summer, our seashore, walking along the water, looks like a mixture
> of only two colors, yellow and green—or, more precisely, red-yellow and
> gray-green. The coast is high, one solid wall of rock that goes on for tens of
> miles—I can't tell precisely how high, whether it reaches two hundred feet
> or not—just high . . . There was, of course, a third color, that of the water;
> but what was it? I don't quite remember it as blue, just dark-green, with a
> golden lining on striped shoals. Someone expressed surprise in my presence,
> that it was called the Black Sea, but I have seen it black with my own eyes,
> under my own paddles, not on a stormy or overcast day, but in sunlight.[53]

Now the author's ability to describe nature with great precision comes
into its own, only to be interrupted when it becomes too lyrical, too
successful:

> But one should gaze at our sea when it is white. You must get up one hour
> before dawn, sit in the water itself on the prickly rocks and watch the sun
> rise—you must only pick a quiet morning. Then there is one quarter of an
> hour when the sea is white, and the milky surface is rippled with undulating
> and shifting waves that are white, but of a different whiteness, some with a
> tinge of steel grey, others of lilac, and very rarely of sky-blue. Slowly the
> dawn begins to open the curtains over the horizon to allow in the first hint
> of the sun—reddish, orange, emerald—God help me, I don't know how to
> express these things in Russian.[54]

The authorial "I" must intrude at this point, disrupting the idyll, first
with self-consciousness and then with more than a hint of parody: the

most beautiful creature in Odessa, he continues, is the lizard—there are nice lizards throughout Europe, but our Odessan lizards are the nicest, the best, the most colorful, as are our second-best creature, the crab. Like Lilien's vipers gnawing at the corners of his scenes of Jewish exile and Zionist redemption, Jabotinsky's attempt at a nostalgic, verbal still-life of "Dawn over Odessa" is cut short by the author's far from nostalgic sensibility, his retrospective recognition of the grotesque amid the beauty, the dangers lurking just under the surface of the innocent white surface.

Only a few pages later, another sort of innocence is disrupted by subterranean realities: the Russo-Japanese war breaks out, and no one in the Milgroms' circle is too disturbed. Japan they know only as a land of mystery and elegance from children's storybooks, and when it turns out that the real Japan is a military might overcoming Russia, they all but celebrate their homeland's defeat, convinced that any blow to the tsarist regime is a step forward to liberty and freedom. The narrator tells us that he, too, shared in that consensus way back when: "Only now, looking backwards, do I feel how strange this all was, how many layers of alienation had to accrue to pervert the most basic, involuntary, innate response of a national organism to a thorn thrust in its side."[55] But this restatement of the moral at the end of *Samson* and the notion of a national "organism" is not left to stand unchallenged. Soon, in a critical chapter called "Gomorra," the narrator seeks the advice of a noted Odessan lawyer, after one of the Milgroms' sons has been arrested for a Bolshevik-like "expropriation" of money from a friend. The lawyer responds that the true cause of this crime is not the accused's character or his ostensible ideology but something far deeper and far more common, his entire generation's lack of moral convictions, their collective and individual inability to conceive of a clear response to the eternal question "Why not?"

> I assure you that no powerful ideological agitation can ever compare with the power of this one question. The moral balance of humanity has always depended on the existence of axioms: there are some doors that are shut with a sign saying "forbidden." Just "forbidden," with no explanations, and the doors stay closed, the ground does not crumble, the planets continue their orbit as they always have. But just once raise the question "why forbidden" "why not?" and the axioms evaporate. It's a mistake to think that axioms are self-evident and therefore it's pointless to prove them. No, axioms are suppositions that are impossible to prove. . . . But now, there's no more "forbidden" everything is "possible,"—not just the laws of basic morality like "Do not steal," "Do not lie," but the most unconscious, involuntary reac-

tions of human nature (as in this case)—shame, physical squeamishness, the voice of blood—all these disintegrate into nothingness.[56]

This was the standard—and vastly influential—critique of the Russian fin-de-siècle intelligentsia by its most severe critics from within. But here, the object of criticism is not all of the Russian intelligentsia, but specifically its Jewish component. The lawyer is an ex-Jew, a convert to Christianity who confesses that he has no right to criticize his former community but understands something profound about it:

> As you know, I do not agree with you—I believe in assimilation and sincerely want it to come about. But one cannot close one's eyes to the fact that the first stages of mass assimilation are a painful time. Russian culture is as great and bottomless as the sea, and just as pure, but when you first enter into the water from the shore, you must swim for a while in the muck, amidst twigs and garbage . . . Assimilation begins with the abandonment of old superstitions, and superstitions are holy things. . . . Perhaps all moral truths, including the very idea of civilized culture, is made up of superstitions; but such superstitions are unique to every culture, and the transition from one set of superstitions to another requires a long time, while the old ones fall away and the new ones are not yet ensconced—at least one generation, maybe two, perhaps even more. Do you know what? You're known as the greatest local lover of Odessa, which I love too but still know the truth—that in all of Russia, there is no greater site of this moral vacuum than our merry Odessa. I'm not just speaking about the Jews—the same thing is true of the Greeks, the Italians, the Poles, even the "Russians"—most of whom are Ukrainians pretending to be Russians—but this is clearest among the Jews. They lend the place its effervescence, its buzz, which all of Russia mocks and which you and I love so much. But often a period of brilliance turns out really to be a time of disintegration of values; that's the source of our collective dishonesty and roguishness, our affection for lies, both domestic and commercial, and the fact that nine out of ten daughters of our respectable homes are "demi-virgins" and the tenth one not a virgin at all.[57]

The crisis of Jewish "assimilation" is now slowly but surely understood to be not merely or even especially political or ideological but moral—a spiritual and ethical void that inevitably results from the voluntary abandonment of received traditions, of the necessary "superstitions" that make life bearable. Our narrator is thus driven—for the first and last time in Jabotinsky's written record—to ponder the imponderable, to examine the meaning of life and death, and the teachings of Judaism on these ineffable matters, as opposed to plumbing Jewish sources for a "scientifically" rooted economic policy or an ostensibly Hebraic political theory. After Marusya's tragic and senseless death, the narrator visits the Milgrom home, where the father is sitting shivah in

the traditional style, unshaven, on the ground, reading the Book of Job.
He says to the narrator:

> An amazing book. Of course, only now do I understand it properly. Its main
> point is the question: if something like this happens, what should one do—
> rebel? Put God on trial? Or, like a soldier stand at attention, salute, and bark
> out so that everyone can hear: Yes, sir, at your command, sir! The question
> I think is not one of justice and injustice, but of pride—human pride, Job's
> pride (which he, of course, said in Hebrew—"Iyov"), mine, yours. Do you
> get it? What is the more honorable path—rebellion or submission? What do
> you think?

To which the narrator can only reply, like Samson regarding the Law
of Moses:

> I, of course, did not "think"—I had never read Job, and since I had no
> answer, he answered for me:
>   Here the answer is submission. Why? Because if you rebel, the only answer
> to your pain is meaninglessness—evil happens at random, like a garbage-
> cart running over a snail or a cockroach. All of your suffering, indeed you
> yourself, are a chance trifle—no more than a cockroach.
>   I began to listen more closely. . . .[58]

A few days later, the narrator gets a call from the last remaining
Milgrom child, Torik, who confides in him his decision to convert to
Christianity and asks him to help prepare his parents for this news. Until
this point, Torik has been all but absent from the story—a quiet, stu-
dious lad whom the narrator espied years earlier studying Hebrew and
reading Heinrich Graetz's *History of the Jews*. But Torik has grown into
the most rational of his siblings, the only one not inclined to extremist
politics or dangerous personal experimentation. His decision to convert
was made long ago, he explains, a rational calculus after considering all
options and realizing that Jewishness is a hopeless cause, a rotten, sink-
ing ship. But you haven't really known the Jews from within, the narrator replies, why don't you give it a chance before abandoning it? But
I have studied it, replied Torik, not so much from books as from all
those tutors from the Pale whom my father hired to teach me Hebrew
and Jewish history, all those pathetic creatures who fled from their provincial homes and provincial wives—I have learned more from them
than I possibly could from the real thing, just like a pathologist learns
more from a corpse than a doctor does from a living patient. And my
diagnosis is clear and final: putrefaction, the Jewish people is disinte-
grating, and there is no solution. What about Zionism, our narrator
interjects, or perhaps even the Bund? From a medical point of view,

Torik answers, the two are the same, the Bund is but a preparatory class for the gymnasium of Zionism—as Plekhanov put it, Bundists are just Zionists afraid of seasickness. And Zionism?

> Zionism is like a gymnasium, a preparatory stage before university. And what is the university, that both of them are unconsciously leading to? Assimilation—gradual, reluctant, unhappy, even temporarily unsatisfying but nonetheless inevitable assimilation which, along with baptism and mixed marriages, will lead inevitably to the disappearance of the race; there is no other way. The Bund puts its hopes in Yiddish . . . but in twenty-five years Yiddish will disappear. And Zionism is no solution either: all that will remain will be the desire to "be like all the nations."[59]

Shockingly, our narrator has no answer for Torik—he knows that queries about religion or antisemitism will yield nothing, that there is no argument that can sway Torik from his path; all he asks is which denomination of Christianity will you adopt? To which Torik replies that he's considered this carefully as well and has chosen Lutheranism. With this the chapter ends, a pregnant silence on the narrator's part betokening the fact that there is, indeed, no answer that can sway Torik from his path.

The Milgrom family, and thus the Odessan Jewry it is meant to represent, has no future, only a past. And so the story comes to an end, the last chapter entitled "L'Envoi." The narrator now all but melds with the author, for we are back in the future, merely remembering the Odessa that is no more. The opening of this "envoi"—"Veroiatno, uzh nikogda ne vidat' mne Odessy. Zhal', ia ee liubliu"—is difficult to render effectively into English, as its very syntax and rhythm convey a peculiarly stylized nostalgia, an almost passive retrospection (or, perhaps, a retrospective passivity) not conveyed in the simple English translation: "Most likely, I shall never see Odessa again. Too bad, I love her."[60] This is important, because the narrator as Jabotinsky (or Jabotinsky as narrator) concludes his story with a jarring ideological passivity in regard to the very essence of the real-life creed and the real-life, indeed life-and-death battles of Vladimir—now also known as "Ze'ev"—Jabotinsky. Returning to the theme he raised at the beginning of the novel, he ponders again the multiethnic and multinational complexion of fin-de-siècle Odessa, but now with a far less certain retroactive ideological conviction:

> Ten tribes together, and all well-matched picturesque ones, one more amusing than the next: they began by laughing at one another and ended up laughing at themselves, at everything, at what they hate and what they love.

Gradually their customs rubbed off on one another, causing them not to take their own traditions totally seriously; gradually they became accustomed to a very important secret of the whole world: what is holy to you is nonsense to your neighbor, but that neighbor is neither a thief nor a bum—perhaps he's right, perhaps not; killing one another over such things is senseless.

Torik said: "disintegration." Maybe he was right, too . . . maybe periods of decay are the most charming, the most fascinating. Who knows? And maybe not just charming and fascinating, but advanced, as well. Of course, I am in the camp that rebelled against that very decay, that very disintegration, not wanting neighbors, calling on each group to settle on its own island; but—who knows?[61]

This twice-repeated and seemingly so anti-Jabotinskian "Kto znaet?" (Who knows?), which calls into question and deliberately does not defend the very essence of Jabotinsky's worldview for the past thirty years, hovers elliptically over the remaining pages of the book, in which the Milgroms and the Odessa they inhabited and personified are summoned one last time, before being parted with for good. The narrator/author returns in his mind's eyes to Odessa in dreamlike passages totally out of sync with the realistic tone of the rest of the novel: Marusya, he imagines, he would not see anywhere but in her old home; he wouldn't dare to ring the bell and enter the house but just doff his cap and pass by; the road is covered with straw, so as to muffle the noise of the wheels passing by:

> For silence is appropriate to this place, a place of deicide, pointlessness, purposelessness and profound pain. Above, on the second floor, a bedroom is decked out in the sweet and naïve style of the fin de siècle: from the pillow two dry eyes stare directly at the chest of drawers, which has five photos on it, of five youngsters decked out in short skirts or in trousers down to their knees, and each photo has sticking out of its middle, a rusty knife.[62]

This jarring image—the rusty knife lacerating the photos of beloved children—is, of course, a typical fin-de-siècle image brilliantly evoked here to bemoan the eclipse of that culture. In Russian, of course, the word "five" also summons up the notion of perfection, a "five" (*piatiorka*) being the highest grade obtainable in school. But in the end, the five Milgrom children—called "The Five," as in the collective of the title, *Piatero*—were not dealt "fives" in their lives, whatever their parents' hopes and dreams. But the narrator is hardly indicting them for their pathetic and tragic demise, however semi-suicidal. This novel is not so much a literary indictment of Jewish "assimilation" as a brutally pained and painful meditation on the cost of the murder of that "sweet and naïve style of the fin de siècle" by the rusty knives of ideologies (Zionism included), convinced of the truth of their ways and the erroneous—indeed "scientifically incorrect"—hopes and dreams of 1902-style Odessan optimistic pluralism. At least here, in this remarkable fictional work, which would turn out to be his last, Vladimir Jabotinsky refrained from answering this question—like the dilemma of Job his alter-ego encountered for the first time—with the oft-repeated certitudes of his polemical prose.

Piatero ends, then, not with a grotesque image of destruction, but with a complex admixture of decay and hope: over the Milgroms' destroyed home

> a half-moon hangs in the sky, one can inhale the scent of rotting flowers and hear the faint, dying sounds of music never to be played again. Marusya and I will communicate again—just as on that unconsummated night—not in words but in thoughts. I will think about what a strange word is "caress." Everything worthwhile in this world is like a caress: moonlight, the lapping of waves, the rustle of leaves, the scent of flowers, music—all of these are like a caress. And God—if you could ever reach Him, rouse Him from His slumber, tell him the real truth about the world He created, and then make peace with Him and rest your head on His lap—He too is probably a caress. And the best and most shining caress is called a woman.
>
> The city was funny—but fun is also a caress. However, no trace of that Odessa has existed for a long time, and there's no use hoping that I can ever return to it. And so, this tale comes to an end.[63]

Conclusion

Little love was lost between Max Nordau and Vladimir Jabotinsky, despite their parallel roads to Zionism and their fundamental ideological similarities. In the years immediately before the First World War, Nordau became increasingly displeased with the direction of the Zionist movement, which he felt was abandoning Herzl's political Zionism in favor of Ahad Ha'am and cultural Zionism, centered around issues such as the revival of the Hebrew language and the establishment of a Hebrew University in Jerusalem. At the Tenth Zionist Congress in 1911, he therefore proposed creating a new party that would return to the true, Herzlian principles of the movement, and for the next several years he campaigned intensively, if ultimately unsuccessfully, for the establishment of such a breakaway party.[1] At this point, Jabotinsky was one of the strongest supporters of the university idea and the cultural politics of what had earlier been called the Democratic Faction of the Zionist movement, headed by Chaim Weizmann. He therefore was by no means an advocate of Nordau's call for a return to "authentic Herzlian" Zionism.

Soon, another issue further split the two men: Jabotinsky's intense and controversial campaign for a Jewish armed unit within the Allied fighting forces. Despite his firm conviction in the necessity of creating a "Muskeljudentum," Nordau was opposed to Jabotinsky's plan—on tactical and strategic, rather than ideational, grounds. At the start of the First World War, Nordau was in an exceedingly awkward and

potentially dangerous situation, as an Austro-Hungarian citizen living
in an enemy country, France. He therefore removed himself to the neutral ground of Spain, where, as his biographer Christoph Schulte notes,

> he fared rather well. He was no immigrant like all the others—he had con-
> nections and good friends, most importantly the Salmerón family: Nicolas
> Salmerón, the son of the similarly-named first president of the Spanish Re-
> public, had translated several of Nordau's books into Spanish, and had
> known him since 1893.[2]

Though Nordau regarded the outbreak of the war as the definitive
end to the nineteenth-century world he so loved (and so hysterically
railed against!), he was by no means convinced that Zionism should
hitch its wagon to the Allied cause, particularly since that meant support
not only of England and France but the hated Russia as well, whose
nefarious treatment of its Jews he had protested vigorously. And so,
when Jabotinsky called on the grand old man of Zionism in Madrid in
November 1914 to garner his support for the idea of the Jewish Legion,
he was disappointed, if not shocked, by Nordau's adamant opposition
to the plan. Typically, in his autobiography, written two decades later,
Jabotinsky retold the story of this encounter with a heavy admixture of
retroactive creative dissimulation:

> In Madrid I met Max Nordau, who had to leave France after living in Paris
> almost his entire life. He told me how he was called to the office of the police
> and was subjected to questions meant to enrage him—he was asked not only
> about his age and family and the like, but also about his financial situation,
> his sources of income, etc., until he lost patience and said to the officer:
> "Don't bother me, sir, look in the encyclopedia!"
>
> But he related the story of his exile with humor, since he saw in it ("I am
> a doctor, am I not?") only a small indication of the insanity of the entire
> world. "In the first weeks after the outbreak of war," he told me, "I lived in
> a summer colony on the Atlantic coast, where everyone was crazy with fear
> of spies—they suspected everyone swimming in the sea as a spy—why did
> this one swim out so far this morning? Who knows if he wasn't meeting up
> with a German ship? . . .
>
> The Spaniards accorded Nordau much honor. I remember the evening
> held in his honor in the main club: a large and dazzling crowd, Dr. Jahuda
> (then a professor at Madrid University) whispered to me the names of about
> twenty important politicians who were there, and certainly there were many
> more members of the Madrid intelligentsia who remembered his electric in-
> fluence on the generation of their youth. I had never before been to Spain,
> but I knew that its Latin development was similar to that of Italy; and I
> remembered that in Rome, at the end of the century, I found youths who

were still followers of Nordau. They still learned from his writings that profound insolence in the face of any veil, any mask, the essential abomination
that lies behind any altar, the now all-but-forgotten refusal to forgive, rejection of compromise, rage and hatred of ugliness and untruth—in short, they
learned from him the secret of revolution. I remember that while I was in
Rome I met a young man who had come from Latin America to study sculpture, and he told me that in Latin America, too, Nordau was the ruler of the
rebellious spirits.

I asked Nordau's opinion about the idea of the Jewish Legion, and he gave
me a skeptical reply. Why should we ally ourselves with one camp before we
have received any promise regarding the future of the Land of Israel? And
where would we find the soldiers? In the neutral lands of Europe there is but
a tiny number of Jews, and America is too far away; and most importantly,
the emotional and absurd position of the Zionists towards "our brother Ish-
mael." There is no one in the world expert enough to tell us when and how
the Turanian Ottomans will claim family solidarity with the Semitic Arabs.
And indeed Nordau himself had suffered the consequence of this connection
after he spoke out at the Hamburg Zionist Congress in 1910 against the
Young Turks.

"I well remember that speech," I said. You said: "They recommend that
we assimilate in Turkey? Das haben wir neher, billiger und besser"—this we
can do closer, cheaper, and better! I then came to Hamburg from Constantinople and cheered you wildly.

"And how many problems I later had with the idiots around me!" he
answered.

"Doctor," I said, "we cannot run our ship according to the directions of
idiots. No, the Turks are not our 'brothers' and even with the real Ishmaelites
we have no spiritual connection. We are, thank God, Europeans, and the
builders of Europe for a millennium. I remember one of your speeches in
which you said: 'We are going to Palestine to extend the boundaries of Europe
to the Euphrates. And the obstacle is: Turkey.' Now its end is nigh—shall
we just sit back and do nothing?"

The veteran sage answered me profoundly, and it took me many years to
understand its depth: "Those are logical words, my young friend; but logic
is a Greek wisdom that is hated by our people. A Jew does not learn from
logic but from catastrophes—he won't buy an umbrella 'only' because there
are clouds in the sky, he will wait until he gets soaked and catches pneu-
monia."

Many years passed before I figured out the truth in his words, and incidentally, that there is another nation in the world with the same attitude to
logic, clouds, and umbrellas: the English. But there is also a difference between us and them: their lungs are stronger, and they have money to pay the
doctor.[3]

This was a typically brilliant Jabotinskian feuilleton, humorously re-
trojecting his own later views on the British, the Jews, the Arabs, the

Turks into the discussion with Nordau two decades earlier. Even Joseph Schechtman in his hagiography of Jabotinsky recognized that this account was entirely misleading, in that it hid from the reader Nordau's strident opposition not only to the idea of the legion, but to the overarching pro-Allied position of the Zionist movement under Weizmann. Two days after the meeting with Nordau, Jabotinsky wrote an angry letter to a friend back in Russia expressing outrage at Nordau's opposition to the idea of the legion and demand for neutrality in the war, a position the fiery Russian derided.[4] Indeed, a month after their meeting, Nordau wrote Jabotinsky a rather stiff letter in which he repeated his firm insistence that the Zionist movement take no official position on the war: "Il ne peut rien faire de bon, mais il peut faire beaucoup de mal" (It can do no good, but a lot of harm).[5]

Even angrier and more dismissive of Nordau was an article Jabotinsky published in Palestine on January 30, 1920, reacting to yet another diatribe against the policies of the Zionist leadership that Nordau, who had now returned to Paris, issued. What gall the old man has, Jabotinsky wrote, hardly masking his fury: Nordau advocated passivity when we needed intense action during the war, and now he charges us with weakness? Where was he at the beginning of the war, Jabotinsky goes on,

> when we had the chance to organize our youth [in military action] and there was only one man in the Zionist movement who understood this—Weizmann is his name—but his hands were tied by all the blind, the lame, the weak-spirited, who joined together in an effort to castrate Zionism, and Nordau contributed to this emasculation! That was the time for this great teacher to roar like a lion and sweep out all these weaklings from the Zionist movement—but this Dr. Nordau did not do; rather, in private and in public he joined in the ban against the Legion. . . . And now, he, the great prosecutor, stands and rails against the movement, calling it to account for its weakness. Alas, our weakness is substantial at present, but who is Nordau to rail against it?[6]

Before the end of 1920, another issue surfaced to intensify the rift between the two men: between September 14 and November 20, Max Nordau wrote ten articles in the Parisian Le Peuple Juif, calling for the immediate transfer of six hundred thousand Jews to Palestine. This so-called Nordau Plan aroused great animosity within the Zionist movement, with the leadership from Weizmann down attacking it as unrealistic, provocative, and hence entirely counterproductive. Jabotinsky had already spoken out against this plan when Nordau had first broached it a year earlier[7] and now joined in the all but universal condemnation of the idea and its creator.[8]

This condemnation of Nordau only intensified in the next two years, when a group of veteran western European Zionist activists, headed by Nordau, increasingly spoke out against Weizmann's moderate politics from the vantage point of a maximalist political Zionism; Nordau's group once more floated the idea of breaking away from the Zionist movement and founding a rival party to return to the original, Herzlian, core of the ideology. Jabotinsky again rejected this idea vociferously, allied as he was with Weizmann as one of his closest associates and advisors.[9]

Max Nordau died in Paris on January 22, 1923. There is no extant postmortem on his life and work by Jabotinsky for another ten years— the decade in which Jabotinsky himself broke with Weizmann and turned into his most vociferous critic, in the process not only repeating Nordau's criticisms but realizing the latter's goal of abandoning the mainstream Zionist movement to found a party calling for a return to maximalist political Zionism—the Revisionist Party and Betar youth movement. Only slowly did Jabotinsky begin publicly to espouse Nordau's most radical ideas, which he had previously rejected with intense venom and scorn. Indeed, even in 1933, when he wrote a piece on the tenth anniversary of Nordau's death, Jabotinsky was respectful and admiring but less than entirely enthusiastic about the older Zionist, who, Jabotinsky implied, had essentially outlived his fame:

> a publicist, no matter how influential, steps off the stage when the period in which he was influential ends. Who now reads Boerne? Who in France today reads the writings of Paul Louie Courie . . . or the Russian Mikhailovsky, who, still in my youth, was called the Master of Thoughts by an entire generation? Nordau is saved from oblivion and survives in the spiritual memory of our people because to us he was not a publicist but a reformer of our national life, one of the children of the Prophets.[10]

One wonders how Max Nordau might have reacted to being called a child of the Hebrew prophets whom he detested and decried, to the end of his life, as superstition-besotted degenerates. But only three years after this obituary, Jabotinsky came all but full circle in his attitude to Nordau—evidenced not only by his fictionalized retelling of the Madrid meeting between the two men cited above, but far more importantly in his dramatic acceptance of the previously rejected "Nordau Plan" for the mass evacuation of Jews from Europe to Palestine. At first, as articulated in a press conference in Warsaw in September 1936 and endorsed by the Revisionist movement in early 1938, Jabotinsky still shied away from the full force of Nordau's radical scheme, arguing instead for a ten-year plan in which a total of one and a half million Jews would be transferred to Palestine in annual installments. It was only late in 1938 that he endorsed the "Nordau Plan" in its entirety, and indeed raised the number of projected evacuees to one and a half million. This is the cause Jabotinsky would campaign for, unsuccessfully and with enormous controversy, until his death at Camp Betar in the Catskill Mountains of New York on August 3, 1940.[11]

Almost immediately thereafter, a mythology of a seamless Nordau-Jabotinsky alliance came into being, or, rather, a claim was made for a direct, uncomplicated, and seamless line of transmission (what in Hebrew is called a *shalshelet ha-kabbalah*) of "true Zionism" from Herzl to Nordau and then to Jabotinsky. Joseph Schechtman, one of Jabotinsky's deputies as well as his most influential biographer, put it most clearly: "There is a direct line leading from Herzl through Nordau to Jabotinsky. They all belong to that great dynasty of political Zionists, which ended with Jabotinsky. They form an organic and exclusive Trinity."[12]

There was no intended irony in this Trinitarian metaphor. On the contrary, Schechtman continued: "Two widely divergent lines of succession to Herzl's leadership are easily discernible: the spiritually straight and legitimate one—through Nordau and Jabotinsky; and a collateral, essentially deviating one, as represented by Weizmann and the others."[13] Moreover, Schechtman realized that this had something to do with the essential un-Jewishness of Jabotinsky's Zionism:

> Jabotinsky used to say of himself that he had a "goyishe Kop." Referring to this expression, his old comrade-in-arms, Colonel Patterson, who knew and loved him as very few did, interpreted it as meaning that Jabotinsky's mentality was fundamentally that of a Gentile, "void of the peculiar inhibitions of a Jewish mind influenced and twisted by the abnormalities of centuries of life in dispersion," and added with amazing insight: "That was probably the main reason why his political philosophy was so healthy and simple, and why with all his tremendous popularity he never became the recognized leader of the Jewish people." A similar comment this writer heard from another Gentile admirer of Jabotinsky, Count Michael Lubiensky: "You know that I hold Jabotinsky in highest regard and that my opinion of Weizmann is trimmed accordingly. But as I see it, Dr. Weizmann has all the chances to retain the allegiance of the majority of the Jewish people. Because his entire mentality is identical with that of the average ghetto Jew, while the mentality of Jabotinsky is spiritually nearer to me, a Gentile. I understand him better;

he evokes in me a kindred response. For a ghetto Jew, he is, on the contrary, too simple, too direct. He will be listened to and applauded, but he will be followed only by those who have overcome the ghetto complex."[14]

This is not the place to unpack the essentialism and indeed the hardly muted antisemitism of these testimonials, endorsed as unproblematic by the loyal Schechtman, who failed to note, moreover, that the Yiddish expression "goyishe kop" means someone who is stupid, not just un-Jewish. Indeed, Schechtman endorsed Patterson's and Lubiensky's accounts, adding with only slightly less tendentiousness:

> As so many of the great master builders in Jewry in the tradition stretching from Moses to Herzl [one wonders whom he had in mind?], Jabotinsky was not part of the main stream of Jewish life; like them, he came to his people as a stranger when he reached manhood. He was cast in their great mold. His underlying contribution to the national redemption of Jewry was not extracted from the mines of the Jewish mode of life: its roots must be sought in the outside world. His Zionism was not nourished by the messianic emotional and mystical longings of the ghetto Jew. Herzl, Nordau and Jabotinsky were all products of assimilation, so far removed from actual Jewish life, and yet, because of it, so much more able than their predecessors to forge into a nation their dispersed and desperate people. Deeply steeped in the Western way of life, they had to discover their people in order to possess it, and find themselves. Like Herzl and Nordau, Jabotinsky had little in common with that brand of Jewishness which Arthur Koestler describes as "tradition-bound, jargon-bred," and which is largely typical of Weizmann's mentality. Weizmann was born in Motele, a hamlet deep in the Jewish Pale of Settlement, and reared in the spiritual climate of Jewish small-town society. Jabotinsky was born in Odessa. . . . Similarly, Herzl and Nordau grew up in cosmopolitan Budapest, Vienna, and Paris. Their upbringing was secular, their outlook worldly, their sense of values European. Their Zionism was built on modern ideas of national normalcy, on a virile, instinctive self-assertion in the face of a fundamentally hostile and often provocative non-Jewish world.[15]

This view of the relationship between Weizmann and the Jewish masses of eastern Europe is, of course, preposterously antihistorical; I would urge any reader not familiar with Isaiah Berlin's astonishingly acute essay on Weizmann to refer to that piece as an antidote to Schechtman's strident caricature.[16] In fact, there was a paradoxical relationship in their attitude to the masses of Jews and their Judaism on the part of the political versus the cultural (and, later, the socialist) Zionists. Political Zionists, especially those among the leadership who came to Zionism from outside the Jewish world, like populists everywhere, claimed an inherent fealty with the Jewish masses, even as they in fact created a form of nationalism entirely committed to the destruction of the way of life of the "folk" they lionized (and often, in fact, despised), attacking their opponents as less nationalistic, more "assimilated." The cultural and socialist Zionists saw in Zionism not a road back to the ghetto but precisely the opposite—an escape route from traditional Jewish insularity to the world at large. As the eminent Israeli historian Zeev Sternhill has recently argued in a highly tendentious and problematic but nonetheless astute book on the socialist Zionists—and the same can be said for the Weizmannians and other latter-day Ahad Ha'amians—their universalist pretensions and radical political commitments ultimately (if often unconsciously) gave way to their nationalism. As one of their most forthright leaders, Golda Meir, would later famously quip, to her socialism meant bringing Jews to Israel.[17]

I hope this book has demonstrated not only the terrible errors of fact and interpretation in the traditional historiographic representations of Herzl, Nordau, and Jabotinsky, but, more important, the profundity of the truth it all but conceals: the extent to which these three men, along with Ephraim Moses Lilien, came to Zionism not so much from outside the Jewish world—East, West, or in between—but, rather, in sharp and conscious opposition to that Jewish world (or rather those Jewish worlds, which they detested and rejected). They came to Zionism on the basis of their parallel engagements not with "Europe" or with a "virile instinctive" notion of nationalism but from a particular and fascinating moment in European history, culture, and thought—the fin de siècle. Despite the nearly universal repetition of the claim that they were liberals, either before and after they became Zionists, I hope I have demonstrated that this was not the case, and that Nordau and Jabotinsky can only be understood against the backdrop of Social Darwinism in the West and the peculiar variation on positivism embraced by Russian radicals as well as the fundamental aesthetic and philosophical stances of Symbolism, Decadence, and art nouveau in the fin de siècle, which also defined the development of the Zionist art of Ephraim Moses Lilien. Even as Nordau, Lilien, and Jabotinsky, like Herzl before them, turned to Zionism, they did not abandon the cosmopolitan aesthetic and ideational preconceptions of the pan-European fin de siècle. On the contrary, they molded and reconceived Zionism in line with that cosmopolitanism, that aesthetic, those intellectual and philosophical underpinnings that defined and determined their lives and their times.

To parody these experiences (or anyone else's) as those of "assimilation" or their pre- or post-Zionist conceptions (or anyone else's) as those of an ideology of "Jewish assimilation" is, I argue, conceptually empty, ideologically overdetermined, and hence analytically useless.

In the end, moreover, there is a curious parallel between the fate of Lilien's art and the Zionist ideologies of Max Nordau and Vladimir Jabotinsky. While serving as a army photographer in Palestine for the Austrian Army during the First World War, Ephraim Lilien discovered a new style and a new obsession with the topography, flora, and fauna of his Middle Eastern posting, which he rendered with virtually photographic accuracy and a heavy dose of sentimentalism and kitsch. This radical switch in style and subject matter was connected with the overarching death of Jugendstil and art nouveau, which had begun to be regarded as hopelessly retrograde and old-fashioned. Lilien found a much bigger and more lucrative market for his simple, sweet, and all too realistic renderings of the streets of Jerusalem, the Western Wall, and Galician market scenes than he ever had for his earlier liquid nymphets, androgynous angels, or bemuscled Hebraic lovers. In a parallel manner, in the past half century, the Zionism of Vladimir Jabotinsky (and to some extent that of Max Nordau, if and when it is remembered at all) has been ineluctably transformed, cleansed of its embeddedness in cosmopolitan European culture, and—as it were—re-Judaized, denuded (both Jabotinsky and Nordau would say emasculated) of its intriguing complexity, its fundamental cultural and intellectual values, its rejection of both sentimentality and religion, not to speak of the self-doubts Jabotinsky himself revealed in his novels and plays. Schechtman's embrace of the Trinity metaphor in his evaluation of Herzl, Nordau, and Jabotinsky would seem not only heretical to the vast majority of current followers of Nordau and Jabotinsky, but, even more profoundly, incomprehensible—both literally and symbolically.

This is true not only in the real world of politics, but in the realm of history writing as well. In the past few years, the history of the State of Israel since 1948 has been subjected to a wrenching process of reinterpretation and debate as the so-called New Historians have attacked every premise of traditional Israeli historiography and collective memory. It is fascinating to note, from the sidelines, that both these historical revisionists as well as the traditionalists often invoke the name and memory of Vladimir Jabotinsky as a combatant in their debates; but the Jabotinsky they invoke, either as friend or most often as foe, is the mythologized Jabotinsky of post-1948 internecine Zionist polemics, not the multifaceted translator of Poe and Verlaine, the author of "Edmée," *Alien Land,* and *Piatero.* The goal of this book has been to restore to history the far more complex, far less kitschy, and, I think, far more interesting life stories of Vladimir Jabotinsky, Max Nordau, and Ephraim Lilien.

Notes

INTRODUCTION

1. Joseph B. Schechtman, *Rebel and Statesman: the Vladimir Jabotinsky Story* (New York: Yoseloff, 1956), and *Fighter and Prophet: the Last Years* (New York: Yoseloff, 1961), and Shmuel Katz, *Lone Wolf: A Biography of Vladimir Jabotinsky*, 2 vols. (New York: Barricade Books, 1996).

2. See, for example, those written or available in English: Amos Elon, *Herzl* (New York: Holt, Rinehart and Winston, 1975); Steven Beller, *Herzl* (London: Halban, 1991); Andrew Handler, *Dori, the Life and Times of Theodor Herzl in Budapest (1860–1878)* (University, Ala.: University of Alabama Press, 1983); Ernst Pawel, *The Labyrinth of Exile: A Life of Theodor Herzl* (New York: Farrar, Straus & Giroux, 1989); Avner Herzl, *King of the Jews: A Psychoanalytic Biography of Theodor Herzl* (Lanham, Md.: University Press of America, 1993).

3. Delphine Bechtel, Dominique Bourel, and Jacques Le Rider, *Max Nordau (1849–1923): critique de la dégénérescence, médiateur franco-allemand, père fondateur du sionisme* (Paris: Cerf, 1996). The new biography by Christoph Schulte, *Psychopathologie des Fin de siècle: Der Kulturkritiker, Arzt und Zionist Max Nordau* (Frankfurt am Main: Fischer Taschenbuch Verlag, 1997), is an excellent narrative summary of Nordau's life and works but does not attempt analyses of his works. The only previous biography was by Nordau's wife and daughter, Ana and Maxa Nordau; see their *Max Nordau: A Biography* (New York: The Nordau Committee, 1943).

4. See Anthony Smith, *National Identity* (London: Penguin, 1991), and his most recent *Nationalism and Modernism: A Critical Survey of Recent Theories of Nations and Nationalism* (New York: Routledge, 1998).

5. Benedict Anderson, *Imagined Communities: Reflections on the Origin and Spread of Nationalism* (London: Verso, 1991); Ernest Gellner, *Nations and*

Nationalism (Ithaca, N.Y.: Cornell University Press, 1983); Eric Hobsbawm, *Nations and Nationalism Since 1780: Programme, Myth, Reality* (New York: Cambridge University Press, 1990).

6. Steven J. Zipperstein, *Elusive Prophet: Ahad Ha'am and the Origins of Zionism* (Berkeley: University of California Press, 1993); Jehuda Reinharz, *Chaim Weizmann: The Making of a Zionist Leader* (New York: Oxford University Press, 1985), and *Chaim Weizmann: The Making of a Statesman* (New York: Oxford University Press, 1993); Anita Shapira, *Berl: The Biography of a Socialist Zionist, Berl Katznelson 1887–1944* (New York: Cambridge University Press, 1984).

7. Benjamin Harshav, *Language in Time of Revolution* (Berkeley: University of California Press, 1993), 53–54.

CHAPTER ONE. COSMOPOLITANISM, ZIONISM, AND ASSIMILATION

1. Theodor Herzl, "Der Sohn," in his *Philosophische Erzählungen* (Berlin: B. Harz, 1919), 121–33.

2. Ibid., 127.

3. Ibid., 131–32.

4. Alex Bein, *Theodore Herzl, a Biography* (Philadelphia: Jewish Publication Society of America, 1940), 67.

5. See Bein's autobiography, *Hier kannst Du nicht jeden grussen: Erinnerungen und Betrachtungen* (Hildesheim: Olms, 1996).

6. "Der Sohn," 125.

7. Bein, *Theodor Herzl,* 75.

8. John Munder Ross, *What Men Want: Mothers, Fathers, and Manhood* (Cambridge: Harvard University Press, 1994).

9. Carl E. Schorske, *Fin-de-Siècle Vienna: Politics and Culture* (New York: Knopf, 1979), 9.

10. Gerson D. Cohen, "The Blessing of Assimilation in Jewish History," reprinted in Steve Israel and Seth Forman, *Great Jewish Speeches Throughout History* (Northvale, N.J.: Jason Aronson, 1994).

11. Chaim Weizmann, *Trial and Error* (New York: Harper, 1949), 31.

12. Milton M. Gordon, *Assimilation in American Life: The Role of Race, Religion, and National Origins* (New York: Oxford University Press, 1964).

13. See Ezra Mendelsohn, *On Modern Jewish Politics* (New York: Oxford University Press, 1993), 16.

14. Schorske, *Fin-de-Siècle Vienna,* 147.

15. Robert A. Kann, *Theodor Gomperz: ein Gelehrtenleben im Bürgertum d. Franz-Josefs-Zeit: Ausw. seiner Briefe u. Aufzeichnungen, 1869–1912* (Vienna: Verlag der Osterreichische Akademie der Wissenschaften, 1974), 93–94.

16. Ibid., 101–102.

17. Ibid., 173.

18. Ibid., 351.

19. Ernst Pawel, *The Labyrinth of Exile: A Life of Theodor Herzl* (New York: Farrar, Straus & Giroux, 1989), 534.

20. Cynthia Ozick, *Art and Ardor* (New York: Knopf, 1983), 153.

21. Jacques Kornberg, *Theodor Herzl: From Assimilation to Zionism* (Bloomington: Indiana University Press, 1993), esp. 190–200.

22. Reproduced in Paul R. Mendes-Flohr and Jehuda Reinharz, *The Jew in the Modern World: A Documentary History* (New York: Oxford University Press, 1980), 423.

23. Theodor Herzl, *Altneuland* (Leipzig: Hermann Seemann Nachfolger, [1902]).

24. Ahad Ha'am's review is reprinted in his *Al parashat derakhim* (Berlin: Yudisher Farlag, 1921), vol. 3, 143–59; Nordau's response was published in *Die Welt* 7 (March 13, 1903): 1–5. See also Steven Zipperstein, *Elusive Prophet: Ahad Haam and the Origins of Zionism* (Berkeley: University of California Press, 1993), 195–99.

25. *Die Welt* 7 (March 13, 1903): 1–5.

CHAPTER TWO. MAX NORDAU, THE IMPROBABLE BOURGEOIS

1. Max Nordau, *Der ligen fun der religyon* (London: Frayhayt, 1901). The translation here generally follows that in note 2 below, with my own emendations.

2. Max Nordau, *Die conventionellen Lügen der Kulturmenschheit* (Leipzig: B. Elischer Nachfolger, [1883?]); translated as *The Conventional Lies of Our Civilization* (New York: Arno Press, 1975).

3. The best study of this problem is Moshe Halevi, "Darko shel Maks Nordau el ha-zionut," *Ha-Zionut* 16 (1991): 63–92, which, however, takes a substantially different position from the one argued here.

4. P. M. Baldwin, "Liberalism, Nationalism and Degeneration: The Case of Max Nordau," *Central European History* 13 (1980): 99–120.

5. George Mosse, "Max Nordau, Liberalism and the New Jew," *Journal of Contemporary History* 27 (1992): 565–81, reprinted in French in Delphine Bechtel, Dominique Bourel, and Jacques Le Rider, *Max Nordau (1849–1923): critique de la dégénérescence, médiateur franco-allemand, père fondateur du sionisme* (Paris: Cerf, 1996), 11–29; the same claim about both Nordau's liberalism and the "novel" *The Right to Love* is made in Mosse's introduction to Nordau's *Degeneration* (New York: Howard Fertig, 1968), reprinted in the 1993 English edition of that work published by University of Nebraska Press.

6. *Das Recht, zu lieben: ein Schauspiel in vier Aufzugen* (Berlin, 1893).

7. Richard Hofstadter, *Social Darwinism in American Thought,* with a new introduction by Eric Foner (Boston: Beacon Press, 1992), 7–8.

8. Michael W. Taylor, *Men Versus the State: Herbert Spencer and Late Victorian Individualism* (Oxford: Clarendon Press, 1992), 49–50.

9. Peter Gay, *The Cultivation of Hatred* (New York: Norton, 1993), 53.

10. Nordau, *Conventional Lies,* 25–26; emphasis added.

11. Ibid., 57.

12. Ibid., 58–59.

13. Ibid., 63–64.

14. Ibid., 269–74.

15. Max Nordau, *De la castration de la femme* (Paris: Lejay, 1882).
16. *Conventional Lies*, 277.
17. Ibid., 278.
18. Ibid., 322.
19. Ibid., 323.
20. Ibid., 58.
21. Ibid., 58–59.
22. Max Nordau, *Der Sinn der Geschichte* (Berlin: C. Duncker, 1909); translated as *The Interpretation of History* (London: Rebman, 1910).
23. Ibid., 130.
24. Ibid., 126–27.
25. Ibid., 195–96.
26. Ibid., 197–98.
27. Ibid., 202–203.
28. Ibid., 390.

CHAPTER THREE. NORDAU AND NOVIKOVA

1. Max Nordau, *The Right to Love* (New York: F. T. Neely, 1895).
2. There is no scholarly biography of Novikova. I have reconstructed her life story from the very problematic and partisan two-volume work on her edited by one of her admirers, William Thomas Stead, *The M.P. for Russia; Reminiscences & Correspondence of Madame Olga Novikoff* (London: A. Melrose, 1909).
3. See A. A. Kireev, *Slavianofil'stvo i natsionalizm* (St. Petersburg: Izdanie russko-slavianskago knighnago sklada, 1890). He also had interesting discussions with Theodor Herzl over Zionism; see Herzl's *Briefe und Tagebücher* (Berlin: Propylaen, 1983–1996), vols. 2–3, passim.
4. These include *Is Russia Wrong? A Series of Letters, by a Russian Lady, with a Preface by J. A. Froude* (London: Hodder and Stoughton, 1877), *Russia and England from 1876 to 1880: A Protest and an Appeal with a Preface by James Anthony Froude* (London: Longmans, Green, 1880); *Skobeleff and the Slavonic Cause* (London: Longmans, Green, 1883); and an introduction to Harry De Windt, *Siberia As It Is* (London: Chapman & Hall, 1892).
5. See her *Russia and England*, 375–76, which reproduces the preface from the 1877 edition.
6. The collection is entitled "Novikova correspondence, MS 30." The letters to Nordau are in Section N and are indexed as N:1, N:2, etc. I refer below to specific letters by this system, along with their original dates.
7. N:1, August 22, 1886.
8. Ibid.
9. Ibid.
10. N:2, September 9, 1886.
11. Ibid.
12. Ibid.
13. N:3, October 6, 1886.
14. Ibid.

15. N:8, December 19, 1886.
16. N:11, May 18, 1887.
17. Ibid.
18. N:12, June 8, 1887.
19. N:13, June 16, 1887.
20. N:16, August 22, 1887.
21. Ibid.
22. MS 30, Ad:1, July 29, 1887.
23. N:23, December 19, 1887.
24. Ibid.
25. N:24, December 25, 1887.
26. N:30, February 29, 1888.
27. N:32, April 20, 1888.
28. The prescription is N:33, April 22, 1888. The letter that followed is N:34, also on the same date.
29. N:40, July 24, 1888; N:41, July 29, 1888; N:44, August 7, 1888.
30. N:47, September 4, 1888.
31. Ibid.
32. N:55, October 9, 1888.
33. N:54, October 5, 1888.
34. N:59, October 24, 1888.
35. N:114, December 18, 1889.
36. N:115, January 15, 1890.
37. N:116, February 13, 1890.
38. See her introduction to De Windt, *Siberia As It Is*.
39. Cited in Simon Dubnow, *History of the Jews in Russia and Poland* (Philadelphia: The Jewish Publication Society of America, 1916), vol. 2, 387.
40. *The Times,* November 22, 1890.
41. Letter to the editor from Oswald John Simon, *The Times,* November 22, 1890.
42. *The Times,* December 3, 1890.
43. *The Times,* December 10, 1890.
44. Ibid.
45. Ibid., December 11, 1890.
46. N:133, December 16, 1890.
47. N:134, December 31, 1890.
48. N:135, February 3, 1891.
49. N:148, February 26, 1892.
50. N:146, February 21, 1892.
51. N:162, October 12, 1892; N:163, October 17, 1892; N:164, October 21, 1892.
52. N:172, December 4, 1892.
53. See Christoph Schulte, *Psychopathologie des Fin de siècle: Der Kulturkritiker, Arzt und Zionist Max Nordau* (Frankfurt am Main: Fischer Taschenbuch Verlag, 1997), 30–35.
54. N:186, May 7, 1893.
55. N:192, September 3, 1893.

56. N:194, September 25, 1893.
57. N:240, March 16, 1895.
58. Theodor Herzl, *Briefe und tagebücher* (Berlin: Propylaen, 1983–1996), vol. 2, 210–11.
59. Ibid., 277.
60. Shalom Schwartz, *Max Nordau be-igrotav* (Jerusalem: Ha-po'el ha-mizrahi, 1944), 55.
61. N:245, July 29, 1895.
62. N:252, October 11, 1895.
63. N:253, November 4, 1895.
64. N:256, December 30, 1895.
65. Schwartz, *Max Nordau*, 295.
66. N:262, June 15, 1896. The end of the sentence, unfortunately, has been excised—it reads either "et il est fort" or "il est fou."
67. N:275, September 13, 1897.
68. N:280, January 3, 1898.
69. Anna and Maxa Nordau, *Max Nordau: A Biography* (New York, 1943), 98–99, 137–38. It is fascinating to note that the date of Nordau's marriage is never given and in fact is elliptically antedated by two years. Whether this was a deliberate error to make it appear that the Nordaus were married *before* he joined the Zionist movement is unclear (97–98).
70. N:288, September 20, 1899.
71. N:285, February 5, 1899.
72. N:301, May 12, 1901.
73. N:285, February 5, 1899.
74. N:286, April 11, 1899.
75. N:291, December 25, 1899.
76. N:293, February 27, 1900.
77. See Schulte, *Max Nordau*, 265–70.
78. N:287, September 4, 1899.
79. N:288, September 20, 1899.
80. N:289, October 11, 1899.
81. Ibid.
82. N:290, November 4, 1899.
83. N:295, September 5, 1900.
84. N:296, September 9, 1900.
85. N:302, February 2, 1902.

CHAPTER FOUR. NORDAU'S ZIONISM: FROM HEINE TO BAR KOCHBA

1. *Ost und West* 1 (1901): 907. See Mark H. Gelber, "Heine, Herzl, and Nordau: Aspects of the Early Zionist Reception," in Mark H. Gelber, ed., *The Jewish Reception of Heinrich Heine* (Tübingen: Max Niemeyer Verlag, 1992), 139–51.
2. Ibid., 912.
3. Max Nordau, *Zionistische Schriften* (Cologne: Jüdischer Verlag, 1909),

399–402. On this poem see Hubert Cancik and Hildegard Cancik-Lindemaier, "Philhellenisme et Sionisme," in Delphine Bechtel, Dominique Bourel, and Jacques Le Rider, *Max Nordau (1849–1923): critique de la dégénérescence, médiateur franco-allemand, père fondateur du sionisme* (Paris: Cerf, 1996), 177–220.

4. "Nachtrag," in Nordau, *Zionistische Schriften,* 401–402.

5. Brigitte Hamann, *The Reluctant Empress* (New York: Knopf, 1986), 302.

6. See ibid., 287–305 and 338–39; and Klaus Gallas, *Korfu: Das antike Kerkyra im Ionischen Meer-Geschichte, Kultur, Landschaft* (Cologne: DuMont Buchverlag, 1989), 250–54.

7. Marie Louise, Countess Klarisch von Wallersee-Wittelsbach, *Her Majesty Elizabeth of Austria-Hungary* (Garden City, N.Y.: Doubleday, Doran, 1934), 211–12.

8. Ibid., 212–14.

9. "Trauerrede auf Herzl," in Nordau, *Zionistische Schriften,* 159. See also Gelber, 147.

10. Max Nordau, *Doktor Kohn: Bürgliches Trauerspiel aus der Gegenwart* (Berlin: Ernst Hoffman, 1902).

11. Ludwig Robert, *Die Macht der Verhältnisse: Ein Trauerspiel in fünf Aufzugen* (Stuttgart & Tübingen: Cotta, 1819).

12. See Charlene A. Lea, *Emancipation, Assimilation and Stereotype: The Image of the Jew in German and Austrian Drama (1800–1850)* (Bonn: Bouvier Verlag Herbert Grundmann, 1978), 20–23.

13. See S. S. Prawer, *Heine's Jewish Comedy: A Study of His Portraits of Jews and Judaism* (Oxford: Clarendon Press; and New York: Oxford University Press, 1983).

14. *Doktor Kohn,* 83.

15. Ibid., 95.

16. Ibid., 96.

17. Ibid., 98.

18. *Doktor Kohn,* 26. Sander Gilman refers to this comment in his interesting article on this play but quotes only the poor English translation, "Good Lord, command," which hardly captures the complex nuances of this gesture and declamation. See Sander L. Gilman, "Max Nordau, Sigmund Freud, and the Question of Conversion," *Southern Humanities Review* 27, no. 1 (1993): 5.

19. *Doktor Kohn,* 166.

20. Ibid., 167.

21. Ibid., 200.

22. Ahad Ha'am, "Ha-musar ha-leumi," *Al parashat derakhim,* vol. 1 (Berlin: Yudisher Farlag, 1921), 87–88.

23. Ibid., 88.

24. *Doktor Kohn,* 76.

25. "I. Kongressrede," in Nordau, *Zionistische Schriften,* 39–57.

26. Amos Elon, *Herzl* (New York: Holt, Rinehart and Winston, [1975]), 241.

27. "I. Kongressrede," in Nordau, *Zionistische Schriften,* 48–49.

28. See Prawer, *Heine's Jewish Comedy,* 61–62.

29. Ibid.

30. See, for example, Arthur Hertzberg, *The Zionist Idea* (New York: Atheneum, 1979), 235–41.

31. "Muskeljudentum," in Nordau, *Zionistische Schriften,* 379–81.

32. See Michael Berkowitz, *Zionist Culture and West European Jewry Before the First World War* (New York: Cambridge University Press, 1993), which to my mind totally misunderstands and hence misrepresents this phenomenon. Even more problematic, if far more provocative and passionately argued, is Daniel Boyarin, *Unheroic Conduct: The Rise of Heterosexuality and the Invention of the Jewish Man* (Berkeley: University of California Press, 1997), which hardly addresses with any depth Nordau's crucial role in the development of Zionist concepts of masculinity. See the important review of this work by Allan Arkush, "Antiheroic Mock Heroics: Daniel Boyarin Versus Theodor Herzl and His Legacy," *Jewish Social Studies* 4 (1998): 65–92, and Boyarin's revealing, anti-Wissenschaft "Response to Allen Arkush," 93–95.

33. See especially Mosse's *Nationalism and Sexuality: Respectability and Abnormal Sexuality in Modern Europe* (New York: H. Fertig, 1985).

34. Anita Shapira, *Land and Power: The Zionist Resort to Force, 1881–1948* (Stanford, Calif.: Stanford University Press, 1999), 13.

35. Max Nordau, *Ketavim zioniyim,* vol. 1 (Jerusalem: Ha-Sifriah ha-Zionit, 1954), 171.

36. Heinrich Graetz, *Geschichte der Juden,* vol. 4 (Leipzig: O. Leiner, 1893), 149–53.

37. *Midrash Lamentations* 2.5.

38. See Richard G. Marks, *The Image of Bar Kokhba in Traditional Jewish Literature: False Messiah and National Hero* (University Park: Pennsylvania State University Press, 1994), 26–28.

CHAPTER FIVE. FROM JUGENDSTIL TO "JUDENSTIL": COSMOPOLITANISM AND NATIONALISM IN THE WORK OF EPHRAIM MOSES LILIEN

1. Börries von Münchhausen, *Juda* (Goslar: F. A. Lattmann, 1900).

2. *E. M. Lilien: Sein Werk, mit einer Einleitung von Stefan Zweig* (Berlin and Leipzig, 1903), 21.

3. Münchhausen, *Juda,* unpaginated.

4. For the most extensive, if still incomplete, bibliography, see Ekkehard Hieronimus, "E. M. Lilien, Leben und Werk," in E. M. Lilien, *Briefe an seine Frau* (Königstein/Ts.: Jüdischer Verlag, 1985), 30–32.

5. Ibid.

6. *Epistle to Titus* 1:14–15.

7. Carl E. Schorske, *Fin-de-Siècle Vienna: Politics and Culture* (New York: Knopf, 1981), 226.

8. See Hieronimus, "E. M. Lilien, Leben und Werk," 10.

9. Schorske, *Fin-de-Siècle Vienna,* 212.

10. Hieronimus, "E. M. Lilien, Leben und Werk," 11.

11. Lothar Brieger, *E. M. Lilien* (Berlin and Vienna: Benjamin-Harz, 1922), 35.

12. Ibid., 42–47.

13. Ibid., 48–61.

14. Robert Goldwater, *Symbolism* (New York: Harper & Row, 1979), 60–70.

15. Eduard Fuchs, *Geschichte der erotischen Kunst* (Munich: A. Langen, 1908).

16. See the late prints in Otto M. Lilien, *E. M. Lilien: Bookplates, 1897–1907* (London and Jerusalem: Lilien Offsetprint, 1973).

17. Schorske, *Fin-de-Siècle Vienna*, 215.

18. Debora Silverman, *Art Nouveau in Fin-de-Siècle France* (Berkeley: University of California Press, 1989), see esp. 7–13.

19. Similarly, a recent study of the Polish painter Jacek Malczewski—another Galician—demonstrated how Malczewski expressed his newfound Polish nationalism through the regnant avant-garde style, heavy with allegorical symbolism of Poland's glorious past and current enslavement. Finally, though the vast bulk of the literature on the Russian avant-garde has stressed its leftist orientation and contribution to the Revolution, there was as well an aggressively nationalistic strand in this avant-garde, represented by figures such as David Burliuk, Mikhail Larianov, and Natalia Goncharova who seized on the traditions of Russian folk art and especially the *lubki* for their hardly traditional, but increasingly nationalistic, paintings, drawings, ceramics, and sculpture. See Agnieszka Lawniczakowa, *Jacek Malczewski* (Warsaw: Krajowa Agencja Wydawnicza, 1976).

20. See *Stenographisches Protokoll der Verhandlungen des V. Zionisten-Congresses in Basel* (Vienna, 1901), Beilage D, for a list of the art work exhibited at the Fifth Zionist Congress.

21. Ibid., 161–62.

22. See for example, ibid., 305–306, 318.

23. *Stenographisches Protokoll der Verhandlungen des V. Zionisten-Congresses in Basel*, 395.

24. Ibid., 395–96.

25. Berthold Feiwel, *Lieder des Ghetto von Morris Rosenfeld* (Berlin: Marquard, 1903).

26. See Millie Heyd, "Lilien and Beardsley," *Journal of Jewish Art* (1980): 58–69. This oft-cited article presents a radically different view of Lilien from that argued here.

27. Natan Zach, "Hanefesh ha-hazuya o sippuro shel tavlit," in *Igra* 1 (1984): 14–17. I am indebted to Marcus Moseley for bringing this article to my attention.

28. See Lilien's *Biblisches Lesebuch* (Braunschweig/Hamburg: Georg Westermann, 1914).

29. Gideon Efrat-Friedlander, in *Ha-Arez,* supplement, December 25, 1981, 21–25.

30. See George Mosse, *Nationalism and Sexuality: Respectability and Abnormal Sexuality in Modern Europe* (New York: H. Fertig, 1985), 31–57.

31. Ibid.
32. See his *Briefe*, 184–99.
33. Schorske, *Fin-de-Siècle Vienna*, 264.

CHAPTER SIX. VLADIMIR JABOTINSKY, FROM ODESSA TO ROME AND BACK

1. The original letter, dated Odessa, April 26, 1898, has recently been published in V. Zhabotinskii, "Pis'ma russkikh pisateliam," *Vestnik evreiskogo universiteta v Moskve*, ed. Kh. Firin and A. Kolganova, no.1 (Moscow, 1992), 203; a Hebrew translation is available in Ze'ev Z'abotinski, *Iggerot 1898–1904*, ed. Daniel Carpi and Moshe Halevi, vol. 1 (Jerusalem: Jabotinsky Institute, 1992), 3. Henceforth, to avoid ambiguity, I will transcribe the Hebrew version of his surname as "Jabotinsky," since this is the way it was done in all the Latin-alphabet title pages of these works, while in Russian titles I will retain the correct "Zhabotinskii."

2. See *Iggerot*.
3. V. G. Korolenko, *Izbrannye pis'ma v trekh tomakh*, ed. N. V. Korolenko and A. L. Krivinska (Moscow, 1936), vol. 3, 122–23.
4. "Sippur yammai," in the volume entitled *Autobiographical Writings* in his *Ketavim* (Jerusalem: Eri Zhabotinski, 1947), vol. 1, 23.
5. *Pis'ma*, 123.
6. Ibid.
7. See, for example, Menachem Begin's foreword to Joseph B. Schechtman's *Rebel and Statesman*: "A versatile brain, applying itself to various fields of creation and excelling in all of them, is but a rare phenomenon in human history. Aristotle, Maimonides, Da Vinci—and above all, the greatest of leaders and lawgivers—Moses; these are the names of the very few who prove the existence of this phenomenon and its extreme rarity. *Ze'ev Jabotinsky* was such a versatile brain"; also see Schechtman's own comments in his *Rebel and Statesman: The Vladimir Jabotinsky Story* (New York: Yoseloff, 1956), 15.
8. See Gideon Shimoni, *The Zionist Ideology* (Hanover, N.H.: University Press of New England, 1995), 236–49.
9. For all bibliographic references, see the generally reliable Yisrael Yevarovitch, *Kitvei Ze'ev Jabotinsky, 1897–1940* (Tel Aviv: Mekhon Jabotinsky, 1977); for the *Story of the Jewish Legion*, see #5, p. 3.
10. Ibid., #13, pp. 52–53, 190–91.
11. Ibid., #13, pp. 8–9.
12. Schechtman, *Rebel and Statesman*, 18.
13. "Odessa sheli," in *Ketavim*, vol. 1, 27.
14. "Sippur yammai," in *Ketavim*, vol. 1, 11.
15. See David Sorkin, *The Transformation of German Jewry, 1780–1840* (New York: Oxford University Press, 1987).
16. See my article "Russian Jewry, the Russian State, and the Dynamics of Jewish Emancipation," in *Paths of Emancipation: Jews, States, and Citizenship*, ed. Pierre Birnbaum and Ira Katznelson (Princeton: Princeton University Press, 1995), 262–83.

17. See Patricia Herlihy, *Odessa: A History, 1794–1914* (Cambridge: Harvard University Press for the Harvard Ukrainian Research Institute, 1986).

18. See Stephen Zipperstein, *The Jews of Odessa: A Cultural History, 1794–1881* (Stanford, Calif.: Stanford University Press, 1985).

19. "Iz detskago mira: pedagogicheskaia zametka," *Iuzhnoe obozrenie*, September 11, 1897, 2.

20. He writes: "I hereby give to the generations that follow the date [of this article]: the twelfth of August 1897" ("Sippur yammai," in *Ketavim*, vol. 1, 23). Actually, the article appeared on September 11, 1897, according to the Russian calendar, which corresponds to September 23.

21. "Gorod mira," *Voskhod*, November 1898, 142–44.

22. Ibid.

23. "Sippur yammai," in *Ketavim*, vol. 1, 26–27.

24. Nahum (as opposed to the more famous Nachman) Syrkin was a Zionist publicist and activist who worked with Jabotinsky on many projects; see *Evreiskaia entsiklopediia*, vol. 14, 658.

25. Schechtman, *Rebel and Statesman*, 47.

26. "Sippur yammai," in *Ketavim*, vol. 1, 27–28.

27. Ibid., 38.

28. See esp. Raphaela Bilski Ben-Hur, *Every Individual, A King: The Social and Political Thought of Ze'ev Vladimir Jabotinsky* (Washington, D.C.: B'nai B'rith Books, 1993).

29. See my "Jabotinsky as Playwright: New Texts, New Subtexts," in *Studies in Contemporary Jewry* (12) 1996, 48–54.

30. See the valuable introduction by Bernice Glatzer Rosenthal and Martha Bohachevsky-Chomiak to their *A Revolution of Spirit: Crisis of Value in Russia, 1890–1924* (New York: Fordham University Press, 1990), esp. 32–33.

31. Ibid., 29.

32. "Sippur yammai," in *Ketavim*, vol. 1, 35.

33. See Denis Mack Smith, *Italy and Its Monarchy* (New Haven: Yale University Press, 1989), 132–39.

34. "Rim," *Odesskii Listok*, March 13, 1899, 2.

35. "Rim," *Odesskie Novosti*, February 13, 1901, 1.

36. *Krov' (Ministr Gamm), na siuzhet "Sangue," dramma soziali di R. Lombardo* (Odessa, 1901).

37. "Sippur yammai," in *Ketavim*, vol. 1, 37.

38. Letter to Modest Pisarev, *Iggerot*, vol. 2, 263.

39. See, for example, Elizabeth Kandyba-Foxcroft, *Russia and the Anglo-Boer War, 1899–1902* (Roodepoort: Cum Books, 1981), and Thomas Packenham, *The Boer War* (New York: Knopf, 1979). It is also possible that Jabotinsky was influenced by the Italian Abyssinian War, in which Crispi played a part reminiscent of the fictional Minister Gamm in this play. See Smith, *Italy and Its Monarchy*, 113ff.

40. *Krov'*, 11.

41. Ibid., 28.

42. "Rim," *Odesskie Novosti*, March 7, 1901, 1.

43. "Rim," *Odesskie Novosti*, January 3, 1901, 3.

44. *Ladno* is extant only in a typescript submitted to the St. Petersburg theater censor in 1902 and recently discovered in the St. Petersburg Theatrical Library. It is signed "Altalena" and bears the catalog number 23929.

45. "Sippur yammai," in *Ketavim*, vol. 1, 37.

46. *Ladno*, 18–20.

47. In Russian, "Noella," in his *Stikhi* (Paris: Imp. d'art Voltaire, 1930), 103–11; in Hebrew translation in the volume "Shirah" in his *Ketavim*, 261–64.

48. *Ladno*, 23.

49. "Piazza di Spagna," in *Stikhi*, 99–100.

50. "Shaflokh," in *Stikhi*, 83–89.

51. Heinrich Heine, "Berg-Idylle," in *Harzreise*, trans. Charles G. Leland (New York: Marsilio, 1995), 61, 63.

52. "Shaflokh," in *Stikhi*, 83–89.

53. Simon Karlinsky, *Letters of Anton Chekhov* (New York: Harper & Row, 1973), p. 109; emphasis added.

54. Ibid., 110, n1.

55. "Anton Cekhof i Massimo Gorki," *Nuova Antologia*, Quarta Serie, vol. 96 (November–December 1901): 722–33.

56. Ibid., 732.

CHAPTER SEVEN. JABOTINSKY'S ROAD TO ZIONISM

1. See Nathalie Babel, ed., *Isaac Babel, the Lonely Years, 1925–1939* (New York: Farrar, Straus, 1964), 26.

2. "Studentesca: iz zhizni rimskikh studentov," *Odesskie Novosti*, April 14, 1902, 3.

3. "Studentesca: mi-hayei ha-studentim be-Roma," in *Ketavim*, vol. 15, 235–40.

4. David Lowenthal, *The Past Is a Foreign Country* (New York: Cambridge University Press, 1985), 3–34.

5. See, for example, "Mirra Lokhvitskaia," *Odesskie Novosti*, November 8, 1902, 1.

6. "O sionizme i po povodu sionizme," *Russkoe Bogatsvo*, no. 7 (1902): 27–69.

7. "O sionizme," *Odesskie Novosti*, September 8, 1902, 3.

8. Ibid.

9. "Vskol'z'," *Odesskie Novosti*, January 30, 1903, 3.

10. Ibid.

11. See Richard Pipes, *Struve, Liberal on the Left, 1870–1905* (Cambridge: Harvard University Press, 1970), 234–70, and Hans Rogger and Eugen Weber, eds., *The European Right* (Berkeley: University of California Press, 1966), 475.

12. Shlomo Salzman, *Min he-avar: zikhronot u-reshumot* (Tel Aviv: Hotsaat ha-mehaber, 1943), 240–45.

13. "Sippur yammai," in *Ketavim*, vol. 1, 46–47.

14. *Iggerot*, vol. 1, 13–14.

15. "Sippur yammai," in *Ketavim*, vol. 1, 48–49.

16. Schechtman, *Rebel and Statesman*, 85–86, 441.

17. *Stenographisches Protokoll der Verhandlungen des VI. Zionisten-Congresses in Basel* (Vienna, 1903), 94.

18. See Michael Heymann, ed., *The Minutes of the Zionist General Council; the Uganda Controversy* (Jerusalem: Israel Universities Press for the Institute for Zionist Research at Tel-Aviv University, 1970), vol. 2, 11.

19. The four articles published in *Odesskie Novosti* are "Nakanune kongressa," August 15, 1903, 2–3; "Bazel'skie vpechatleniia," August 19, 1903, 2; "Bazel'skie vpechatleniia: Mizrakhi," August 20, 1903, 1; and "Bazel'skie vpechatleniia: Gertsl' I Neinsagery," August 23, 1903, 1.

20. Last will and testament, in *Ketavim*, vol. 17, 18.

21. See Jehuda Reinharz, *Chaim Weizmann: The Making of a Zionist Leader* (New York: Oxford University Press, 1985), 65–89.

22. See "Bazel'skie vpechatleniia: Mizrakhi," August 20, 1903.

23. Ibid.

24. "Bazel'skie vpechatleniia: Gertsl' I Neinsagery," August 23, 1903.

25. "Sippur yammai," in *Ketavim*, vol. 1, 49–50.

26. "Bazel'skie vpechatleniia: Gertsl' I Neinsagery," August 23, 1903, 1.

27. Ibid.

28. Ibid.

29. "Vskol'z': Getto," *Odesskie Novosti*, October 12, 1903, 5; October 18, 1903, 3; and October 29, 1903, 4.

30. "Vskol'z': Getto," October 12, 1903, 5.

31. Schechtman, *Rebel and Statesman*, 57.

32. See G. Romano, "Zionism in Italy," *New Encyclopedia of Zionism and Israel* (Madison, N.J.: Herzl Press, 1994), 733–35.

33. "Vskol'z': Getto," October 12, 1903, 5.

34. Ibid.

35. Ibid.

36. "Vskol'z': Getto," October 18, 1903, 3.

CHAPTER EIGHT. JABOTINSKY'S EARLY ZIONISM

1. Joseph B. Schechtman, *Rebel and Statesman: The Vladimir Jabotinsky Story* (New York: Yoseloff, 1956), and *Fighter and Prophet: The Last Years* (New York: Yoseloff, 1961); Jacob Shavit, *Jabotinsky and the Revisionist Movement, 1925–1948* (London: F. Cass, 1988).

2. "Sionizm i Palestina," *Evreiskaia zhizn'*, no. 2 (February 1904): 203–21.

3. Ibid., 205.

4. "Zionut ve-erez yisrael," in *Ketavim*, vol. 8, 111.

5. "Sionizm i Palestina," 205.

6. Ibid., 209.

7. Ibid., 221.

8. Richard Pipes, *Struve, Liberal on the Left, 1870–1905* (Cambridge: Harvard University Press, 1970), 30–31.

9. Ibid., 295–96.

10. Schechtman, *Rebel and Statesman*, 78.

11. Ibid., 171.

12. See, for example, Ben-Zion Katz, "Al masa nemirov," *Moznayim* 4 (1932): 33.

13. Edward Judge, *Easter in Kishinev: Anatomy of a Pogrom* (New York: New York University Press, 1992).

14. Shmuel Werses, "Bein tokhekha le-apologetikah: 'Be-ir ha-harega' shel Bialik umisaviv lah," *Mehkarei yerushalayim be-sifrut ivrit* 9 (1986): 23–54.

15. See Dan Miron et al., eds., *Hayyim Nahman Byalik: Shirim 659–694* (Tel Aviv: 1990), 161–67.

16. Ibid.

17. Yaakov Goren, ed., *Eduyot nifgiei Kishinov, 1903: ke-fi she-nigbu al yede H. N. Byalik va-haverav* (Tel Aviv: Ha-Kibuts ha-meuhad, 1991).

18. Uzi Shavit, "Model ha-intertekstualiyut ha-parodit kemafteah le-'Be'ir ha-harega'," in Uzi Shavit and Ziva Shamir, *Be-mevoei ir ha-harega* (Tel Aviv: Ha-Kibuts ha-meuhad, 1994), 160.

19. See Uzi Shavit's collection of essays for the most recent critical scholarship on this poem and an up-to-date bibliography.

20. The dean of Israeli Jewish historians, Shmuel Ettinger, wrote the following in his textbook on modern Jewish history, widely used both in Israel and the United States: "It was not by chance that the ineffectiveness of the great Russian Jewish community after the Kishinev pogroms aroused [Bialik] to harsh condemnations of his people. As against this spiritual enslavement he raised the banner of renaissance, of the profound revolution in the life of the people that was eventually to lead them to full redemption in their ancient homeland." H. H. Ben-Sasson et al., *A History of the Jewish People* (Cambridge: Harvard University Press, 1976), 933. And the most authoritative students of early Zionism, David Vital and Walter Lacquer, made similar comments in their histories of the movement. Vital says: "55 percent [*sic*] of the population of [Kishinev] was Jewish and it was intolerable that they, as Bialik wrote of the Jews of Kishinev in his great and terrible poem *Be-ir ha-harega* ('In the City of Slaughter'), 'flee like mice and hide like beetles and die like dogs wherever they be found.'" David Vital, *Zionism, the Formative Years* (Oxford: Clarendon Press, 1982), 312. Laqueur says: "The feeling in the Jewish community was one of horror, but also of shame that Jews had been beaten and killed like sheep without offering resistance. 'Great is the sorrow and great is the shame,' Bialik wrote soon after the massacre; 'and which of the two is greater, answer thou, o son of Man.' 'The grandsons of the Maccabeans—they ran like mice, they hid themselves like bedbugs and died the death of dogs wherever found.'" Walter Laqueur, *A History of Zionism* (New York: Schocken Books, 1976), 123.

21. See Katz, "Al masa nemirov."

22. "Kh. N. Bialik: Mart 1904. Pered Paskhoi," *Evreiskaia zhizn'* 11 (1904): 160–62.

23. Ibid.

24. "Hakedamah la-targum ha-rusi shel Masa Nemirov," in *Ketavim,* vol. 2, 231–34.

25. See *Iggerot,* vol. 1, 14–16.

26. Kh. N. Bialik, *Skazanie o pogrome, perevod s evreiskago i predislovie Vl. Zhabotinskago* (Odessa: Kadimah, 1906).

27. Kh. N. Bialik, *Pesni i poemy: avtorizovanyi perevod s evreiskago iazyka i vvedenie Vl. Zhabotinskago* (St. Petersburg: Zal'tsman, 1911).

28. See the recent translation in Yevgeny Yevtushenko, *Twentieth Century Russian Poetry: Silver and Steel* (New York: Doubleday, 1993), 51–54.

29. The complex issue of Bialik's intertextual manipulation of biblical verses, locutions, and fragments has itself engendered a substantial scholarship; for an attempt to decode the biblicisms in "Be-ir ha-harega," see A. Avital, *Shirat Byalik veha-Tanakh* (Tel Aviv: Dvir, 1952), 265–77.

30. Bialik's Yiddish version was published at the same time and in the same format as Jabotinsky's first Russian translation, as "In shkhite-shtot," *Fun tsar un tsorn* (Odessa: Kadimah, 1906); on Peretz, see Chone Shmeruk, *Peretses yiesh-vizie* (New York: YIVO, 1971), 113–16, and the article by Werses, "Bein tokhekha le-apologetikah."

31. "City of Slaughter," Israel Efros, ed., *The Complete Works of Hayyim Nahman Bialik* (New York: Histadruth Ivrith of America, 1948), 129–34.

32. Alan Mintz, *Hurban: Responses to Catastrophe in Hebrew Literature* (New York: Columbia University Press, 1984), 147–48.

33. Introduction to Bialik, *Pesni i poemy*, 30.

34. *Chaim Nachman Bialik, Poems from the Hebrew*, ed. L. N. Snowman with an introduction by Vladimir Jabotinsky (London: Hasefer, 1924), xiii–xiv.

35. See Katz, "Al masa nemirov," and Werses, "Bein tokhekha le-apologetikah."

36. "Ot izdatelei," in *Skazanie o pogrome*, ii–iv.

37. Ibid.

38. *Chuzhbina; komediia v piati dieistviiakh* (Berlin: Zal'tsman, 1922.) The Hebrew translation, *Nekhar,* was published as a separate (unnumbered) volume in *Ketavim*. There is no difficulty in ascribing Jabotinsky's views as expressed in the printed version of the play to the time of its composition, since a summary of the play with extensive quotations was published by S. Gepshtein in *Rassvet*, no. 13 (March 28, 1910): 14–17, revealing no differences between the original and the later published version. I have published part of this analysis in my "Jabotinsky as Playwright: New Texts, New Subtexts," in *Studies in Contemporary Jewry* 12 (1996): 48–54.

39. Schechtman, *Rebel and Statesman,* 139–41.

40. *Chuzhbina,* 35.

41. Ibid., 43–44. The "citation" of Christ is an imprecise allusion to Jesus' Parable of the Marriage Feast, Matthew 22:1–14.

42. Ibid., 225–26.

43. Ibid., 21.

44. Ibid., 50–52.

CHAPTER NINE. VLADIMIR JABOTINSKY, COSMOPOLITAN ULTRA-NATIONALIST

1. T. J. Reed, *Death in Venice: Making and Unmaking a Master* (New York: Twayne Publishers, 1994), xii.

2. "Edmée," *Odesskie Novosti,* June 17, 1912, 3.

3. Ibid. I have mostly followed here the English translation of Jabotinsky's *A Pocket Edition of Several Stories, Mostly Reactionary* (Paris, 1925; reissued Tel Aviv: Jabotinsky Institute, 1984), 134-35; the 1984 edition contains emendations and corrections.

4. See Korolenko's response in chapter 6, in which he appears to disparage Jabotinsky's admiration for Verlaine.

5. Ibid., 127.

6. Ibid., 128.

7. Ibid., 137-38.

8. Ibid., 138-39. The line about the "sacrosanct hedges cutting humanity into sections" does not appear in the Russian original, but since the English translation was prepared by Jabotinsky himself, I have no problems including it here.

9. See Yisrael Yevarovitch, *Kitvei Ze'ev Jabotinsky, 1897-1940* (Tel Aviv: Mekhon Jabotinksy, 1977), 107.

10. *The Political and Social Philosophy of Ze'ev Jabotinsky, Selected Writings*, ed. Mordechai Sarig, trans. Shimshon Feder, foreword by Daniel Carpi (Portland, Ore.: Vallentine Mitchell, 1999).

11. Schechtman, *Rebel and Statesman*, 160-65.

12. Ibid., 160.

13. "Kopiia zapiski Nachal'nika vilenskago gubernskago zhandarmaskago upraveleniia po raionu ot 3 fevralia 1912 goda za No.414, na imia Nachal'nika varshavskago okhrannago otedeleniia," file no. 13746/ 1911g; "Spravka iz del' zhandarmskago upravleniia gor. Odessy, 27 fevralia 1915 goda," K No. 761/ 18. I am grateful to the late Professor Mattityhau Minc of Tel Aviv University for providing me with copies of these materials.

14. See Yael Zerubavel, *Recovered Roots: Collective Memory and the Making of Israeli National Tradition* (Chicago: University of Chicago Press, 1995).

15. See Schechtman, *Rebel and Statesman*, 201-368.

16. See Walter Laqueur, *A History of Zionism* (New York: Schocken Books, 1976), 368.

17. See ibid., 346-83; Jacob Shavit, *Jabotinsky and the Revisionist Movement, 1925-1948* (London: F. Cass, 1988).

18. Raphaela Bilski Ben-Hur, *Every Individual, a King: The Social and Political Thought of Ze'ev Vladimir Jabotinsky* (Washington, D.C.: B'nai B'rith Books, 1993).

19. "Sippur yammai," in *Ketavim*, vol. 1, 38.

20. See Efrayim Volf, *Yosef Poper-Linkeus: ha-humanist ha-gadol ve-hogeh ha-deot ha-ravgoni* (Jerusalem: E. Vulf, Dalyah Maarekhet, 1996); Henry I. Wachtel, *Security for All and Free Enterprise; A Summary of the Social Philosophy of Josef Popper-Lynkeus* [pseud.], with an introduction by Albert Einstein (New York: Philosophical Library, 1955); Jacques Le Rider, "La signification de Josef Popper-Lynkeus pour Sigmund Freud," *Austriaca* 21 (1985): 27-33.

21. Josef Popper-Lynkeus, *Das Recht zu leben und die Pflicht zu sterben* (New York: Johnson Reprint, 1972).

22. Josef Popper-Lynkeus, *Die allgemeine Nährpflicht als Lösung der sozialen Frage* (Dresden: C. Reissner, 1912).

23. Ibid., 321–22.

24. "Vegn militarizm," in *Zamelbukh far beytarisher yugend* (Warsaw, 1933), 68–71.

25. "Perokim vegn sotsialer filosofye fun tanakh," in *Zamelbukh far beytarisher yugend* (Warsaw, 1933), 128–30.

26. *Ra'ayon ha-yovel* (reprint, Jerusalem: Hevrah le-hotsaot ha-Tanakh bi-Yerushalayim, 1964).

27. Friedrich Stadler, *Vom Positivismus zur "wissenschaftlichen Weltauffassung"* (Vienna: Locker, 1982).

28. "Vegn militarizm," 68–69.

29. Ibid., 69–70.

30. Ibid.

31. Ibid., 70–71.

32. "Ra'ayon Betar," *Ketavim—Be-derekh la-medinah,* 319–20.

33. Ibid., 321–22.

34. Ibid., 321–23.

35. See my *For Whom Do I Toil? Judah Leib Gordon and the Crisis of Russian Jewry* (New York: Oxford University Press, 1988).

36. "Samson Nazorei," *Rassvet,* January 31, 1926–July 17, 1927; also published as a separate volume (Berlin: Slovo, 1927).

37. Alice Nakhimovsky, *Russian-Jewish Literature and Identity: Jabotinsky, Babel, Grossman, Galich, Roziner, Markish* (Baltimore: Johns Hopkins University Press, 1992), 45–69.

38. *Samson the Nazarite* (London: Seeker, 1930), 37–38; beginning with this excerpt, I shall follow the 1930 English translation except when I emend the text to follow the Russian original more closely.

39. Ibid., 131.

40. Ibid.

41. Ibid., 203.

42. Ibid., 273.

43. Ibid., 274–75.

44. Ibid., 276.

45. Ibid., 313.

46. *Piatero* (Paris: ARS, 1930; reprint, New York: Jabotinsky Foundation, 1947).

47. *Hamishtam,* in *Ketavim,* separate volume.

48. See Nakhimovsky, *Russian-Jewish Literature and Identity,* 62.

49. *Piatero,* 18.

50. Ibid., 18–19.

51. Ibid., 84.

52. Ibid.

53. Ibid., 85.

54. Ibid., 86.

55. Ibid., 108.

56. Ibid., 159–60.

57. Ibid., 163–64.

58. Ibid., 179–80.

59. Ibid., 183–84.
60. Ibid., 186.
61. Ibid., 187–88.
62. Ibid., 189–90.
63. Ibid., 190.

CONCLUSION

1. See Evyatar Freisel, "Les dernières activités sionistes de Nordau," in Delphine Bechtel, Dominique Bourel, and Jacques Le Rider, *Max Nordau (1849–1923): critique de la dégénérescence, médiateur franco-allemand, père fondateur du sionisme* (Paris: Cerf, 1996), 313–15.

2. Christoph Schulte, *Psychopathologie des Fin de siècle: Der kulturkritiker, Arzt und Zionist Max Nordau* (Frankfurt am Main: Fischer Taschenbuch Verlag, 1997), 349.

3. "Sippur yammai," in *Ketavim*, vol. 1, 111–13. This episode is also included, in a shorter and slightly different version, in Jabotinsky's history of the Jewish Legion, first published in Yiddish and Hebrew in 1929, and translated into English as *The Story of the Jewish Legion* (New York: Ackerman, 1945), 31–32.

4. See Schechtman, *Rebel and Statesman*, 208–209; letter to Israel Rozov written two days after his meeting with Nordau, in *Iggerot*, vol. 2, 6–7.

5. Letter from Max Nordau to Vladimir Jabotinsky, December 24, 1914. Jabotinsky Institute, file A1/3/2.

6. "Zara'at ve-kazeret," *Ha-Arez*, January 30, 1920, 1.

7. See his "Aliyah," *Ha-Arez*, November 14, 1919, 1–2.

8. See Schechtman, *Rebel and Statesman*, 350–51.

9. See Jehuda Reinharz, *Chaim Weizmann: The Making of a Statesman* (New York: Oxford University Press, 1993), 368–69.

10. "Max Nordau ha-hu," in *Ketavim*, vol. 17, 228.

11. See Schechtman, *Fighter and Prophet*, 350–52.

12. Ibid., 553.

13. Ibid., 554.

14. Ibid.

15. Ibid., 553.

16. Isaiah Berlin, *Personal Impressions* (New York: Viking Press, 1981), 32–62.

17. Zeev Sternhell, *The Founding Myths of Israel: Nationalism, Socialism, and the Making of the Jewish State* (Princeton: Princeton University Press, 1997).

Bibliography

ARCHIVAL SOURCES

Archive of Russian Police Files on Zionism, Prof. Mattityahu Minc, Tel Aviv: "Kopiia zapiski Nachal'nika vilenskago gubernskago zhandarmskago upravleniia po raionu ot 3 fevralia 1912 goda za No. 414, na imia Nachal'nika varshavskago okhrannago otedeleniia," File No. 13746/1911g; "Spravka iz del' zhandarmskago upravleniia gor. Odessy, 27 fevralia 1915 goda," K No. 761/18.

Jabotinsky Institute, Tel Aviv: Letter from Max Nordau to Vladimir Jabotinsky, December 24, 1914, File A1/3/2.

Kenneth Spencer Library, Kansas University: "Novikova correspondence," MS 30. Section N. Letters from and to Max Nordau.

St. Petersburg Theatrical Library: Vladimir Jabotinsky, *Ladno* typescript, 1902.

PRIMARY SOURCES

WORKS BY THEODOR HERZL

Altneuland. Leipzig: Hermann Seemann Nachfolger [1902].
Briefe und Tagebücher. Berlin: Propylaen, 1983–1996.
Judenstaat. Leipzig, 1896.
Letter to *Jewish Chronicle,* January 17, 1896, 12–13.
Philosophische Erzählungen. Berlin: B. Harz, 1919.

WORKS BY MAX NORDAU

Das Recht, zu lieben: Ein Schauspiel in vier Aufzugen. Berlin, 1893. Translated as *The Right to Love.* New York: F. T. Neely, 1895.
De la castration de la femme. Paris: Lejay, 1882.

Degeneration. New York: Howard Fertig, 1968; reprint, Lincoln: University of Nebraska Press, 1993.

Der ligen fun der religyon. London: Frayhayt, 1901.

Der Sinn der Geschichte. Berlin, C. Duncker, 1909. Translated as *The Interpretation of History*. London: Rebman, 1910.

Die conventionellen Lügen der Kulturmenschheit. Leipzig: B. Elischer Nachfolger, [1883?]. Translated as *The Conventional Lies of Our Civilization*. New York: Arno Press, 1975.

Doktor Kohn: Bürgliches Trauerspiel aus der Gegenwart. Berlin: Ernst Hoffman, 1902.

Ketavim zioniyim. 4 vols. Jerusalem: Ha-sifriah ha-zionit, 1954–1962.

Response to Ahad Ha'am. *Die Welt* 7 (March 13, 1903).

Speech at Heine Monument. *Ost und West* 1 (1901): 907.

Zionistische Schriften. Cologne: Jüdischer Verlag, 1909.

WORKS BY VLADIMIR JABOTINSKY

"Aliyah." *Ha-Arez*, November 14, 1919, 1–2.

"Anton Cekhof i Massimo Gorki." *Nuova Antologia*, Quarta Serie, vol. 96 (November–December 1901): 722–33.

"Bazel'skie vpechatleniia." *Odesskie Novosti*, August 19, 1903, 2.

"Bazel'skie vpechatleniia: Gertsl' I Neinsagery." *Odesskie Novosti*, August 23, 1903, 1.

"Bazel'skie vpechatleniia: Mizrakhi." *Odesskie Novosti*, August 20, 1903, 1.

Chaim Nachman Bialik, Poems from the Hebrew, ed. L. N. Snowman with an introduction by Vladimir Jabotinsky. London: Hasefer, 1924.

Chuzhbina; komediia v piati dieistviiakh. Berlin: Zal'tsman, 1922. Translated in Hebrew as *Nekhar* and published as a separate, unnumbered volume in *Ketavim*.

"Edmée." *Odesskie Novosti*, June 17, 1912, 3.

"Gorod mira." *Voskhod*, November 1898, 142–44.

"Hakdamah la-targum ha-rusi shel Masa Nemirov." In *Ketavim*, vol. 2.

Iggerot 1898–1904, ed. Daniel Carpi and Moshe Halevi. 2 vols. Jerusalem: Jabotinsky Institute, 1992–1998.

"Iz detskago mira: pedagogicheskaia zametka." *Iuzhnoe obozrenie*, September 11, 1897, 2.

Ketavim, 18 vols. Jerusalem: Eri Zhabotinski, 1947–1959.

"Kh. N. Bialik: Mart 1904. Pered Paskhoi." *Evreiskaia zhizn'* 11 (1904): 160–62.

Kh. N. Bialik. *Pesni i poemy: avtorizovanyi perevod s evreiskago iazyka i vvedenie VL. Zhabotinskago*. St. Petersburg: Zal'tsman, 1911.

Kh. N. Bialik. *Skazanie o pogrome, perevod s evreiskago i predislovie Vl. Zhabotinskago*. Odessa: Kadimah, 1906.

Krov' (Ministr Gamm), na siuzhet "Sangue," dramma soziali di R. Lombardo (p'esa v 3x kartinakh). Odessa, 1901.

"Max Nordau ha-hu." In *Ketavim*, vol. 17.

"Nakanune kongressa." *Odesskie Novosti*, August 15, 1903, 2–3.

"O natsionalizme." *Odesskie Novosti,* January 30, 1903.

"O sionizme." *Odesskie Novosti,* September 8, 1902, 3.

"Odessa sheli." In *Ketavim,* vol. 1.

"Perokim vegn sotsialer filosofye fun tanakh." In *Zamelbukh far beytarisher yugend.* Warsaw, 1933.

Piatero. Paris: ARS, 1930; reprint, New York: Jabotinsky Foundation, 1947. Translated in Hebrew as *Hamishtam,* in *Ketavim,* separate volume.

"Pis'ma russkikh pisateliam," ed. Kh. Firin and A. Kolganova, *Vestnik evreiskogo universiteta v Moskve,* no. 1 (Moscow, 1992).

A Pocket Edition of Several Stories, Mostly Reactionary. Paris, 1925; reissued Tel Aviv: Jabotinsky Institute, 1984.

The Political and Social Philosophy of Ze'ev Jabotinsky, Selected Writings, ed. Mordechai Sarig; trans. Shimshon Feder, forward by Daniel Carpi. Portland, Ore.: Vallentine Mitchell, 1999.

"Ra'ayon Betar." In *Ketavim—Be-derekh le-medinah.*

Ra'ayon ha-yovel. Jerusalem: Hevrah le-hotsaot ha-Tanakh bi-Yerushalayim, 1964.

"Rim." *Odesskii Listok,* March 13, 1899.

"Rim." *Odesskie Novosti,* January 3, 1901, 3; February 13, 1901, 1; and March 7, 1901, 1.

"Samson Nazorie." *Rassvet,* January 31, 1926–July 17, 1927. Published separately as *Samson Nazorei.* Berlin: Slovo, 1927. Translated as *Samson the Nazarite.* London: Seeker, 1930.

"Sionizm i Palestina." *Evreiskaia zhizn',* no. 2 (February 1904): 203–21. Translated in Hebrew as "Zionut ve-erez yisrael." In *Ketavim,* vol. 8.

"Sippur yammai." In *Ketavim,* vol. 1.

Stikhi: Perevody—Plagiaty—Svoe. Paris: Imp. d'art Voltaire, 1931.

The Story of the Jewish Legion. New York: Ackerman, 1945.

"Studentesca: iz zhizni rimskikh studentov." *Odesskie Novosti,* April 14, 1902, 3. Translated in Hebrew as "Studentesca: mi-hayei ha-studentim be-Roma." In *Ketavim,* vol. 15.

"Vegn militarizm." In *Zamelbukh far beytarisher yugend.* Warsaw, 1933.

"Vskol'z'." *Odesskie Novosti,* January 30, 1903, 3.

"Vskol'z': Getto." *Odesskie Novosti,* October 12, 1903, 5; October 18, 1903, 3; October 29, 1903, 4.

"Zara'at ve-kazeret." *Ha-Arez,* January 30, 1920, 1.

OTHER WORKS

Ahad Ha'am. *Al parashat derakhim.* 4 vols. Berlin: Yudisher Farlag, 1921.

Anderson, Benedict. *Imagined Communities: Reflections on the Origin and Spread of Nationalism.* London: Verso, 1991.

Arkush, Allan. "Antiheroic Mock Heroics: Daniel Boyarin Versus Theodor Herzl and His Legacy." *Jewish Social Studies* 4 (1998): 65–92.

Avital, A. *Shirat Byalik veha-Tanakh.* Tel Aviv: Dvir, 1952.

Babel, Nathalie, ed. *Isaac Babel, the Lonely Years, 1925–1939.* New York: Farrar, Straus, 1964.

Baldwin, Peter. "Liberalism, Nationalism and Degeneration: The Case of Max Nordau." *Central European History* 13 (1980), 99–120.

Bechtel, Delphine, Dominique Bourel, and Jacques Le Rider. *Max Nordau (1849–1923): critique de la dégénérescence, médiateur franco-allemand, père fondateur du sionisme.* Paris: Cerf, 1996.

Bein, Alex. *Hier kannst du nicht jeden grussen: Erinnerungen und Betrachtungen.* Hildesheim: Olms, 1996.

———. *Theodore Herzl, a Biography.* Philadelphia: Jewish Publication Society of America, 1940.

Beller, Steven. *Herzl.* London: Halban, 1991.

Ben-Sasson, H. H., et al. *A History of the Jewish People.* Cambridge: Harvard University Press, 1976.

Berkowitz, Michael. *Zionist Culture and West European Jewry Before the First World War.* New York: Cambridge University Press, 1993.

Berlin, Isaiah. *Personal Impressions.* New York: Viking Press, 1981.

Bialik, H. N. "City of Slaughter." In *The Complete Works of Hayyim Nahman Bialik,* ed. Israel Efros, 129–34. New York: Histadruth Ivrith of America, 1948.

———. "In shkhite-shtot." In *Fun tsar un tsorn.* Odessa: Kadimah, 1906.

———. *Shirim 659–694,* ed. Dan Miron et al. Tel Aviv: Devir, 1990.

Bikerman, Iosif. *Russkoe Bogatsvo,* no. 7 (1902): 27–69.

Bilski Ben-Hur, Raphaela. *Every Individual, a King: The Social and Political Thought of Ze'ev Vladimir Jabotinsky.* Washington, D.C.: B'nai B'rith Books, 1993.

Boyarin, Daniel. "Response to Allan Arkush." *Jewish Social Studies* 4 (1998): 93–95.

———. *Unheroic Conduct: The Rise of Heterosexuality and the Invention of the Jewish Man.* Berkeley and Los Angeles: University of California Press, 1997.

Brieger, Lothar. *E. M. Lilien, eine künstlerische Entwicklung um die Jahrhundertwende.* Berlin and Vienna: Benjamin-Harz, 1922.

Cohen, Gerson D. "The Blessing of Assimilation in Jewish History." Reprinted in Steve Israel and Seth Forman, *Great Jewish Speeches Throughout History.* Northvale, N.J.: Jason Aronson, 1994.

Dubnow, Simon. *History of the Jews in Russia and Poland.* 3 vols. Philadelphia: The Jewish Publication Society of America, 1916.

Efrat-Friedlander, Gideon. *Ha-Arez,* Friday supplement, December 25, 1981, 21–25.

Elon, Amos. *Herzl.* New York: Holt, Rinehart and Winston, [1975].

Falk, Avner. *Herzl, King of the Jews: A Psychoanalytic Biography of Theodor Herzl.* Lanham, Md.: University Press of America, 1993.

Feiwel, Berthold. *Lieder des Ghetto von Morris Rosenfeld.* Berlin: Marquard, 1903.

Fuchs, Eduard. *Geschichte der erotischen Kunst.* Munich: A. Langen, 1908.

Gallas, Klaus. *Korfu: Das antike Kerkyra im Ionischen Meer-Gechichte, Kultur, Landschaft.* Cologne: DuMont Buchverlag, 1989.

Gay, Peter. *The Cultivation of Hatred.* New York: Norton, 1993.

Gelber, Mark H. "Heine, Herzl, and Nordau: Aspects of the Early Zionist Reception." In *The Jewish Reception of Heinrich Heine,* ed. Mark H. Gelber. Tübingen: Max Niemeyer Verlag, 1992.

Gellner, Ernest. *Nations and Nationalism.* Ithaca: Cornell University Press, 1983.

Gepshtein, S. *Rassvet,* no. 13 (March 28, 1910): 14–17.

Gilman, Sander L. "Max Nordau, Sigmund Freud, and the Question of Conversion." *Southern Humanities Review* 27, no. 1 (1993): 5.

Goldwater, Robert. *Symbolism.* New York: Harper & Row, 1979.

Gordon, Milton M. *Assimilation in American Life: The Role of Race, Religion, and National Origins.* New York: Oxford University Press, 1964.

Goren, Yaakov, ed. *Eduyot nifgiei Kishinov, 1903: ke-fi she-nigbu al yede H. N. Byalik va-haverav.* Tel Aviv: Ha-Kibuts ha-meuhad, 1991.

Graetz, Heinrich. *Geschichte der Juden.* 11 vols. Leipzig: O. Leiner, 1897–1911.

Halevi, Moshe. "Darko shel Maks Nordau el ha-zionut." *Ha-Zionut* 16 (1991): 63–92.

Hamann, Brigitte. *The Reluctant Empress.* New York: Knopf, 1986.

Handler, Andrew. *Dori, the Life and Times of Theodor Herzl in Budapest (1860–1878).* University, Ala.: University of Alabama Press, 1983.

Harshav, Benjamin. *Language in Time of Revolution.* Berkeley and Los Angeles: University of California Press, 1993.

Herlihy, Patricia. *Odessa: A History, 1794–1914.* Cambridge: Harvard University Press for the Harvard Ukrainian Research Institute, 1986.

Hertzberg, Arthur. *The Zionist Idea.* New York: Atheneum, 1979.

Heyd, Millie. "Lilien and Beardsley." *Journal of Jewish Art* (1980): 58–69.

Heymann, Michael, ed. *The Minutes of the Zionist General Council; the Uganda Controversy.* 2 vols. Jerusalem: Israel Universities Press for the Institute for Zionist Research at Tel-Aviv University, 1970.

Hobsbawm, Eric. *Nations and Nationalism Since 1780: Programme, Myth, Reality.* New York: Cambridge University Press, 1990.

Hofstadter, Richard. *Social Darwinism in American Thought,* with a new introduction by Eric Foner. Boston: Beacon Press, 1992.

Judge, Edward. *Easter in Kishinev: Anatomy of a Pogrom.* New York: New York University Press, 1992.

Kandyba-Foxcroft, Elizabeth. *Russia and the Anglo-Boer War, 1899–1902.* Roodepoort: Cum Books, 1981.

Kann, Robert A. *Theodor Gomperz: Ein Gelehrtenleben im Burgertum d. Franz-Josefs-Zeit: Ausw. seiner Briefe u. Aufzeichnungen, 1869–1912.* Vienna: Verlag der Osterreichische Akademie der Wissenschaften, 1974.

Karlinsky, Simon. *Anton Chekhov's Life and Thought: Selected Letters and Commentary.* Berkeley and Los Angeles: University of California Press, 1975.

Karlinksy, Simon, ed. *Letters of Anton Chekhov.* New York: Harper & Row, 1973.

Katz, Ben-Zion. "Al masa nemirov." *Moznayim* 4 (1932): 33.

Katz, Shmuel. *Z'abo: biyografyah shel Zeev Z'abotinski.* Tel Aviv: Devir, 1993.

Translated as *Lone Wolf: A Biography of Vladimir Jabotinsky*. 2 vols. New York: Barricade Books, 1996.

Kireev, A. A. *Slavianofil'stvo i natsionalizm*. St. Petersburg: Izdanie russko-slavianskago knighnago sklada, 1890.

Kornberg, Jacques. *Theodor Herzl: From Assimilation to Zionism*. Bloomington: Indiana University Press, 1993.

Korolenko, Vladimir. *Izbrannye pis'ma v trekh tomakh*, ed. N. V. Korolenko and A. L. Krivinska, vol. 3. Moscow, 1936.

Laqueur, Walter. *A History of Zionism*. New York: Schocken Books, 1976.

Lawniczàkowa, Agnieszka. *Jacek Malczewski*. Warsaw: Krajowa Agencja Wydawnicza, 1976.

Le Rider, Jacques. "La signification de Josef Popper-Lynkeus pour Sigmund Freud." *Austriaca* 21 (1985): 27–33.

Lea, Charlene A. *Emancipation, Assimilation and Stereotype: The Image of the Jew in German and Austrian Drama (1800–1850)*. Bonn: Bouvier Verlag Herbert Grundmann, 1978.

Lilien, Ephraim Moses. *Biblisches Lesebuch*. Braunschweig/Hamburg: Georg Westermann, 1914.

———. *Briefe an Seine Frau*. Königstein/Ts.: Jüdischer Verlag, 1985.

———. *Sein Werk, mit einer Einleitung von Stefan Zweig*. Berlin and Leipzig, 1903.

Lilien, Otto. *E. M. Lilien: Bookplates, 1897–1907*. London and Jerusalem: Lilien Offsetprint, 1973.

Lowenthal, David. *The Past Is a Foreign Country*. New York: Cambridge University Press, 1985.

Marie Louise, Countess Klarisch von Wallersee-Wittelsbach. *Her Majesty Elizabeth of Austria-Hungary*. Garden City, N.Y.: Doubleday, Doran, 1934.

Marks, Richard. *The Image of Bar Kokhba in Traditional Jewish Literature: False Messiah and National Hero*. University Park, Pa.: Pennsylvania State University Press, 1994.

Mendelsohn, Ezra. *On Modern Jewish Politics*. New York: Oxford University Press, 1993.

Mendes-Flohr, Paul R., and Jehuda Reinharz. *The Jew in the Modern World: A Documentary History*. New York: Oxford University Press, 1980.

Mintz, Alan. *Hurban: Responses to Catastrophe in Hebrew Literature*. New York: Columbia University Press, 1984.

Miron, Dan, et al. *Hayyim Nahman Bialik: Shirim 659–694*. Tel Aviv: Divir, 1990.

Mosse, George. "Max Nordau, Liberalism and the New Jew." *Journal of Contemporary History* 27 (1992): 565–81.

———. *Nationalism and Sexuality: Respectability and Abnormal Sexuality in Modern Europe*. New York: H. Fertig, 1985.

Münchhausen, Börries von. *Juda*. Goslar: F. A. Lattmann, 1900.

Nakhimovsky, Alice. *Russian-Jewish Literature and Identity: Jabotinsky, Babel, Grossman, Galich, Roziner, Markish*. Baltimore: Johns Hopkins University Press, 1992.

Nordau, Anna, and Maxa Nordau. *Max Nordau: A Biography.* New York: The Nordau Committee, 1943.

Novikova, Olga. Introduction to Harry De Windt, *Siberia As It Is.* London, Chapman & Hall, 1892.

———. *Is Russia Wrong? A Series of Letters, by a Russian Lady, with a Preface by J. A. Froude.* London: Hodder and Stoughton, 1877.

———. Letters to *The Times,* November 22, December 3, December 10, and December 11, 1890.

———. *Russia and England from 1876 to 1880: A Protest and an Appeal with a Preface by James Anthony Froude.* London: Longmans, Green, 1880.

———. *Skobeleff and the Slavonic Cause.* London: Longmans, Green, 1883.

Ozick, Cynthia. *Art and Ardor.* New York: Knopf, 1983.

Pakenham, Thomas. *The Boer War.* New York: Random House, 1979.

Pawel, Ernst. *The Labyrinth of Exile: A Life of Theodor Herzl.* New York: Farrar, Straus & Giroux, 1989.

Pipes, Richard. *Struve, Liberal on the Left, 1870–1905.* Cambridge: Harvard University Press, 1970.

Popper-Lynkeus, Josef. *Das Recht zu leben und die Pflicht zu sterben.* New York: Johnson Reprint, 1972.

———. *Die allgemeine Nährpflicht als Lösung der sozialen Frage.* Dresden: C. Reissner, 1912.

Prawer, S. S. *Heine's Jewish Comedy: A Study of His Portraits of Jews and Judaism.* Oxford: Clarendon Press; New York: Oxford University Press, 1983.

Reed, T. J. *Death in Venice: Making and Unmaking a Master.* New York: Twayne Publishers, 1994.

Reinharz, Jehuda. *Chaim Weizmann: The Making of a Statesman.* New York: Oxford University Press, 1993.

———. *Chaim Weizmann: The Making of a Zionist Leader.* New York: Oxford University Press, 1985.

Robert, Ludwig. *Die Macht der Varhältnisse: Ein Trauerspiel in fünf Aufzugen.* Stuttgart and Tübingen: Cotta, 1819.

Rogger, Hans, and Eugen Weber, eds. *The European Right.* Berkeley and Los Angeles: University of California Press, 1965.

Romano, G. "Zionism in Italy." In *New Encyclopedia of Zionism and Israel,* 733–35. Madison, N.J.: Herzl Press, 1994.

Rosenthal, Bernice Glatzer, and Martha Bohachevsky-Chomiak. *A Revolution of Spirit: Crisis of Value in Russia, 1890–1924.* New York: Fordham University Press, 1990.

Ross, John Munder. *What Men Want: Mothers, Fathers, and Manhood.* Cambridge: Harvard University Press, 1994.

Salzman, Shlomo. *Min he-avar: zikhronot u-reshumot.* Tel Aviv: Hotsaat ha-mehaber, 1943.

Schechtman, Joseph B. *Rebel and Statesman: The Vladimir Jabotinsky Story.* New York: T. Yoseloff, 1956.

———. *Fighter and Prophet: The Last Years.* New York: T. Yoseloff, 1961.

Schorske, Carl E. *Fin-de-Siècle Vienna: Politics and Culture*. New York: Knopf, 1979; ppb. ed., 1981.

Schulte, Christoph. *Psychopathologie des Fin de siècle: Der Kulturkritiker, Arzt und Zionist Max Nordau*. Frankfurt am Main: Fischer Taschenbuch Verlag, 1997.

Schwartz, Shalom. *Max Nordau be-igrotav*. Jerusalem: Ha-po'el ha-mizrahi, 1944.

Shapira, Anita. *Berl: The Biography of a Socialist Zionist, Berl Katznelson, 1887–1944*. New York: Cambridge University, 1984.

———. *Land and Power: The Zionist Resort to Force, 1881–1948*. Stanford, Calif.: Stanford University Press, 1999.

Shavit, Jacob. *Jabotinsky and the Revisionist Movement, 1925–1948*. London: F. Cass, 1988.

Shavit, Uzi. "Model ha-intertekstualiyut ha-parodit kemafteah le-'Be'ir ha-harega'." In Uzi Shavit and Ziva Shamir, *Be-mevoei ir ha-harega*. Tel Aviv: Ha-Kibuts ha-meuhad, 1994.

Shimoni, Gideon. *The Zionist Ideology*. Hanover, N.H.: University Press of New England, 1995.

Shmeruk, Chone. *Peretses yiesh-vizye*. New York: YIVO, 1971.

Silverman, Debora. *Art Nouveau in Fin-de-Siècle France*. Berkeley and Los Angeles: University of California Press, 1989.

Simon, Oswald John. Letter to the editor, *The Times*, November 22, 1890.

Smith, Anthony. *National Identity*. London: Penguin, 1991.

———. *Nationalism and Modernism: A Critical Survey of Recent Theories of Nations and Nationalism*. London: Routledge, 1998.

Smith, Denis Mack. *Italy and Its Monarchy*. New Haven: Yale University Press, 1989.

Sorkin, David. *The Transformation of German Jewry, 1780–1840*. New York: Oxford University Press, 1987.

Stadler, Friedrich. *Vom Positivismus zur "wissenschaftlichen Weltauffassung."* Vienna: Locker, 1982.

Stanislawski, Michael. *For Whom Do I Toil?: Judah Leib Gordon and the Crisis of Russian Jewry*. New York: Oxford University Press, 1988.

———. "Jabotinsky as Playwright: New Texts, New Subtexts." *Studies in Contemporary Jewry* 12 (1996): 48–54.

———. "Russian Jewry, the Russian State, and the Dynamics of Jewish Emancipation." In *Jews, States, and Citizenship*, ed. Pierre Birnbaum and Ira Katznelson, 262–83. Princeton: Princeton University Press, 1995.

———. "Von Jugendstil zum 'Judenstil': Universalismus und Nationalismus in Werk Ephraim Moses Liliens." In *Zionistische Utopie-israelitische Realität*, ed. Michael Brenner and Yafaat Weiss, 68–101. Munich: Beck, 1999.

Stead, W. T. *The M.P. for Russia; Reminiscences & Correspondence of Madame Olga Novikoff*. London: A. Melrose, 1909.

Stenographisches Protokoll der Verhandlungen des V. Zionisten-Congresses in Basel. Vienna, 1902.

Stenographisches Protokoll der Verhandlungen des VI. Zionisten-Congresses in Basel. Vienna, 1903.

Sternhell, Zeev. *The Founding Myths of Israel: Nationalism, Socialism, and the Making of the Jewish State*. Princeton, N.J.: Princeton University Press, 1997.

Taylor, Michael W. *Men Versus the State: Herbert Spencer and Late Victorian Individualism* Oxford: Clarendon Press, 1992.

Vital, David. *Zionism, the Formative Years*. Oxford: Clarendon Press, 1982.

Volf, Efrayim. *Yosef Poper-Linkeus: ha-humanist ha-gadol ve-hogeh ha-deot ha-ravgoni*. Jerusalem: E. Vulf, Dalyah Maarekhet, 1996.

Wachtel, Henry I. *Security for All and Free Enterprise; A Summary of the Social Philosophy of Josef Popper-Lynkeus* [pseud]. Introduction by Albert Einstein. New York: Philosophical Library, 1955.

Werses, Shmuel. "Bein tokhekha le-apologetikah: 'Be-ir ha-harega' shel Bialik umisaviv lah." *Mehkarei yerushalayim be-sifrut ivrit* 9 (1986): 23–54.

Yevarovitch, Yisrael. *Kitvei Ze'ev Jabotinsky, 1897–1940*. Tel Aviv: Mekhon Jabotinsky, 1977.

Yevtushenko, Yevgeny. *Twentieth Century Russian Poetry: Silver and Steel*. New York: Doubleday, 1993.

Zach, Natan. "Hanefesh ha-hazuya o sippuro shel tavlit." *Igra* 1 (1984): 14–17.

Zerubavel, Yael. *Recovered Roots: Collective Memory and the Making of Israeli National Tradition*. Chicago: University of Chicago Press, 1995.

Zipperstein, Steven J. *Elusive Prophet: Ahad Haam and the Origins of Zionism*. Berkeley and Los Angeles: University of California Press, 1993.

———. *The Jews of Odessa: A Cultural History, 1794–1881*. Stanford, Calif.: Stanford University Press, 1985.

Index

Text: 10/13 Sabon
Display: Sabon
Composition: Binghamton Valley Composition
Printing and binding: Maple-Vail Book Manufacturing Group